65
60
ARIBBEAN SEA
W9-CAG-566
Margarita
Trinidad
Guanipa R.
Tigre R.
Ipiri R.
Luata R.
Orinoco R.
Caroni R.
Coura R.
VENEZUELA
Barima R.
Baramo R.
Cuyuni R.
GEORGETOWN
Asito R.
Tencua Falls
Oso Falls
Mono Falls
Erebato R.
Paragua R.
Angel Falls
Mazuruni R.
Essequibo R.
Demeravi R.
Candracuni R.
RORAIMA
KALOMERA'S VILLAGE
Abandoned Hut
Guaharibos
VILLAGE OF THE COUSINS
OKOMATADI
SIERRA PACARAIMA
Berbice R.
Yemecuni R.
Ueyelo R.
Cuaro R.
MARUTANI
Uania R.
Santa Rosa R.
PORVENIR
Rupununi R.
FRENARIO'S VILLAGE
Auari R.
Uraricuera R.
GUADEMA
Maraca Rapids
BOA VISTA
ESMERELDA
SIERRA PARIMA
Parima R.
KASERAPI PATH
Mucajahy R.
FERDINAND DE LESSEPS
Branco R.
Demini R.
BRAZIL
UPPER AMAZON VALLEY
MANÁOS
BELÉM
Equator

JOURNEY TO THE FAR AMAZON

AN EXPEDITION INTO UNKNOWN TERRITORY BY *Alain Gheerbrant*

TRANSLATED BY EDWARD FITZGERALD

19 54

SIMON AND SCHUSTER · NEW YORK

PUBLISHED BY SIMON AND SCHUSTER, INC.
ROCKEFELLER CENTER, 630 FIFTH AVENUE
NEW YORK 20, N. Y.

First Printing

Library of Congress Catalog Card Number: 54–5814
Dewey Decimal Classification Number: 918

MANUFACTURED IN THE UNITED STATES OF AMERICA
BY KINGSPORT PRESS, INC., KINGSPORT, TENN.

CONTENTS

EVEN before setting out on the principal expedition, we discovered these ancient, mysterious, and dramatic paintings on the white face of a rock overlooking the Guayabero River. *Page 34*

Our first Indians in primitive canoes and wearing white men's clothing on the Orinoco River. *Page 65*

This handsome, Spanish-speaking Peruvian called himself an Incan.

Page 41

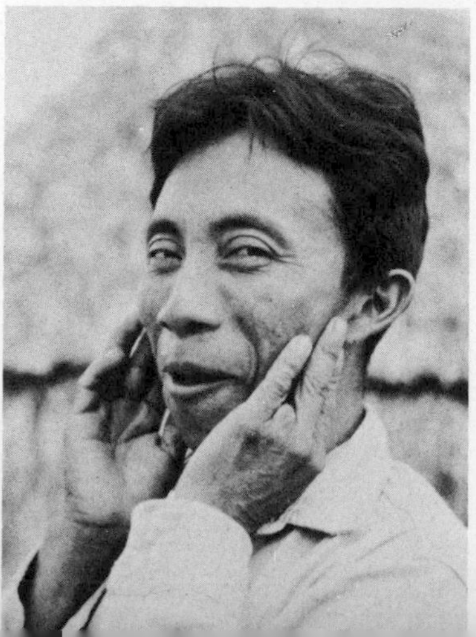

Mario, self-styled Captain-General of the Piaroa Indians, turned out to be an elusive but useful politician.

Page 81

The Piaroan dwellings were built in strange proportions; their women engaged in normal housewifely habits of dressmaking, cooking, raising children.

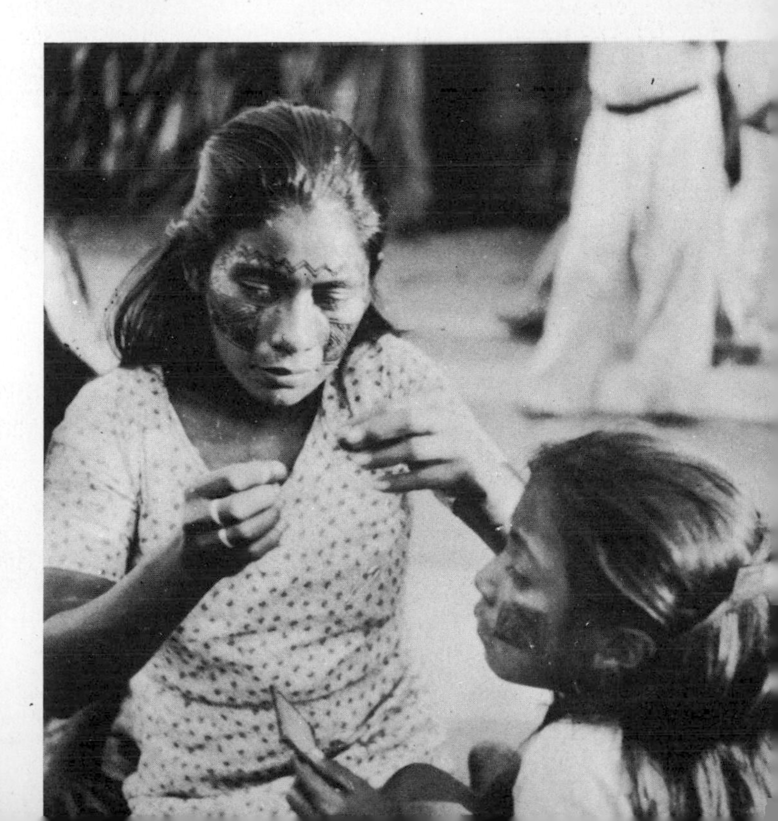

We made ourselves quite at home among the Indians. José Catire, a Spanish-speaking jungle chief, proved a skillful, albeit reluctant, guide on the part of the trip that landed us unexpectedly in Guaharibo territory. *Page 150*

Piaroan boys are often good-looking and the young women handsomely painted.

Page 97

Four young Piaroan boys chosen to undergo the painful initiation rites. *Page 116*

Before the initiation rites, the whole village, including the boys, drank quarts of fermented cassava juice, dutifully vomiting after each calabashful, and then taking more. This lasted hours. *Pages 123-124*

The celebrations lasted a whole month. Each night, while the women hid in the huts, the men danced and made music with flutes played through the nose and conical, trumpet-like instruments of bark.

Page 94

Masks and costumes are carefully prepared for the priests. These priests are five in number, completely hidden by their strange costumes, which include scarlet macaw feathers as a badge of their office. They are known as "tiger-panthers."

Page 93

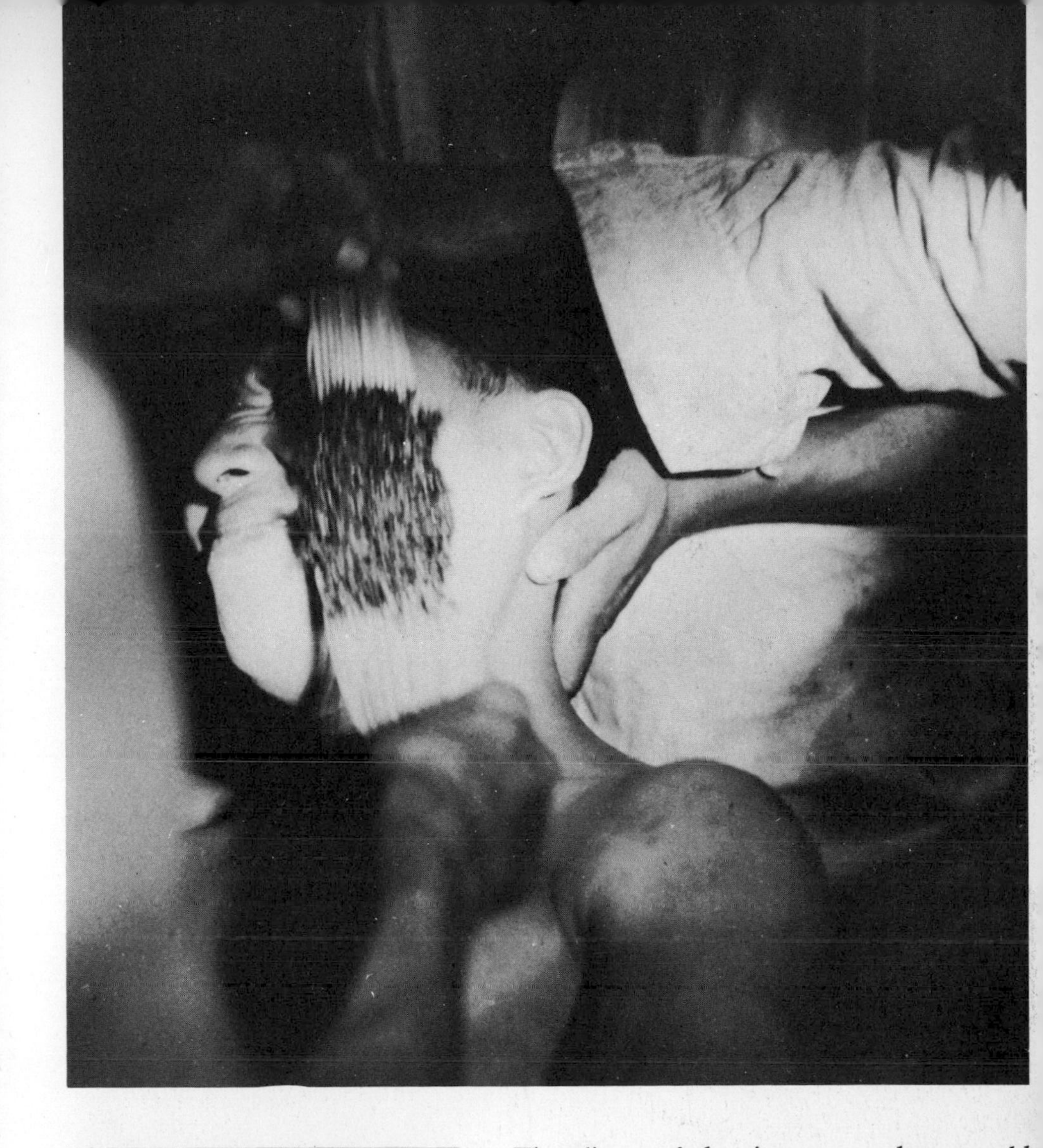

The climax of the rites came when an old priest passed 200 dangerous ants over the body and face of the initiates. *Page 128*

Days before, the huge ants had been skilfully woven into wickerwork so that the stings protruded on one side. *Page 115*

ON the next portion of the trip, two distinctive types of Indians were encountered—the Maquiritares and the Guaharibos. The former were tall, often handsome, and proud of their traditions. The latter were the most primitive men encountered. Felipe was a Maquiritare. *Page 139*

Ideas were exchanged with the Maquiritares, especially with old Cejoyuma, the greatest of their singers, who improvised a long, fascinating epic. *Page 272*

Like the Piaroans before them, the Maquiritares were deeply impressed with Western classical music. Louis Armstrong did not move them at all; but we were considered great men when we played a symphony by Mozart. *Page 278*

A snapshot of a handsome Maquiritare listening to a Mozart *allegro*. *Page 279*

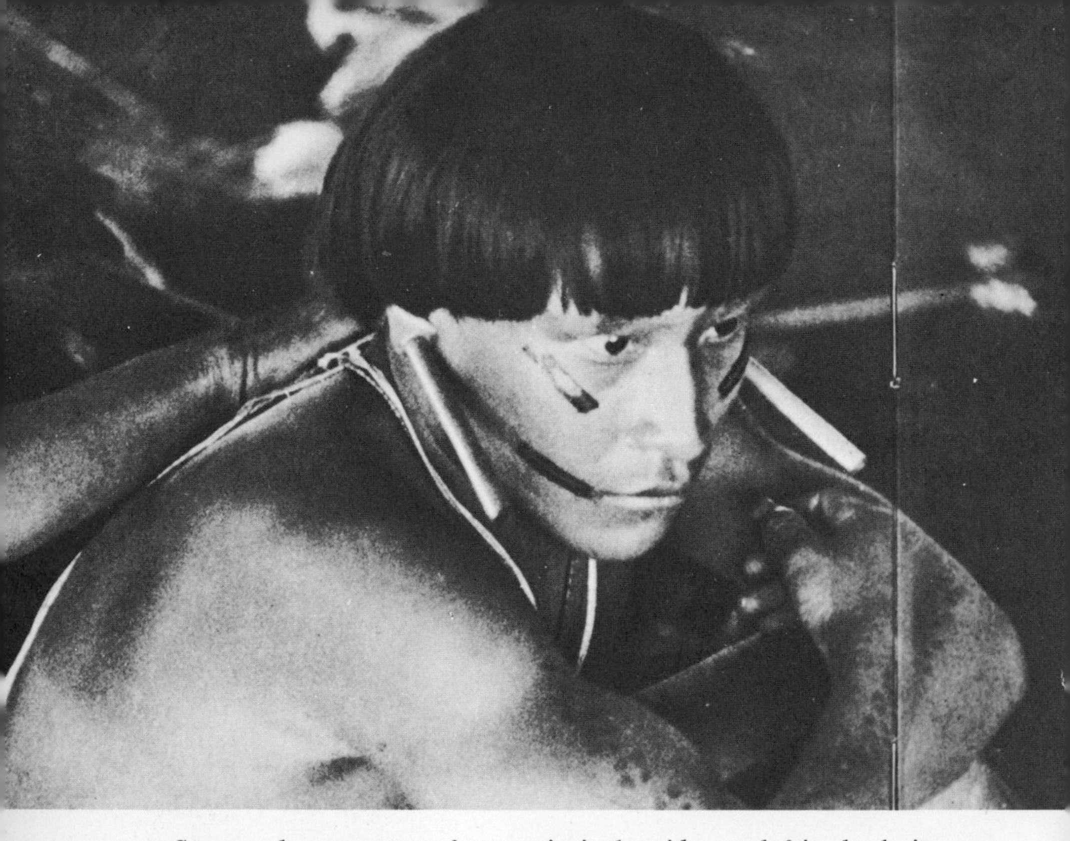

Sanoma became one of our principal guides and friends during our dangerous visit to the Guaharibos. *Page 196*

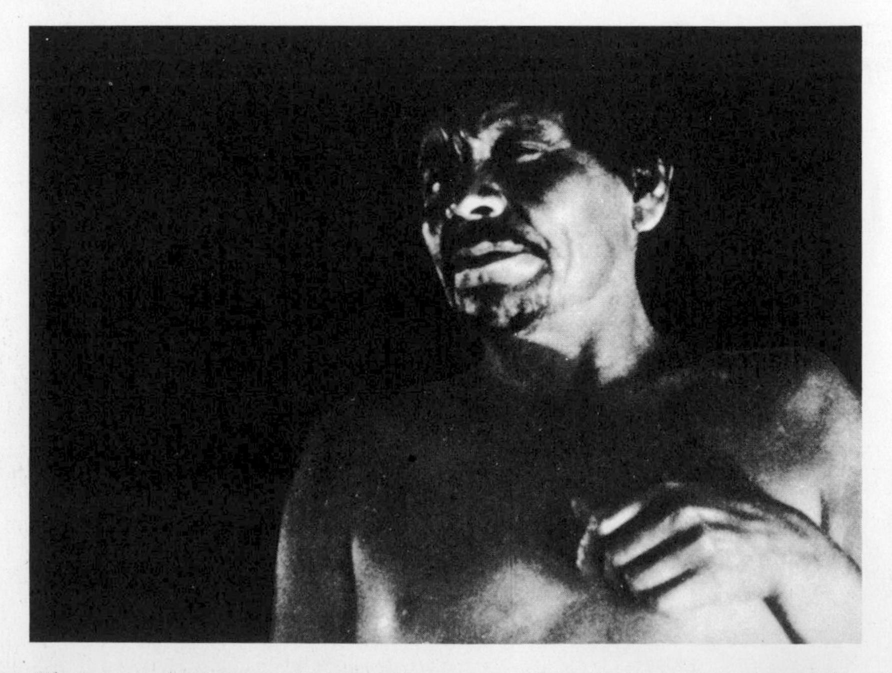

The great chief Frenario turned out to be a great singer too, though he tried, in the dark, to hide his performance. *Page 299*

An old Guaharibo sorcerer, whom it was very difficult to photograph. *Page 178*

We won over the child-like Guaharibos partly by feeling their beards and letting them feel ours. *Pages 177-178*

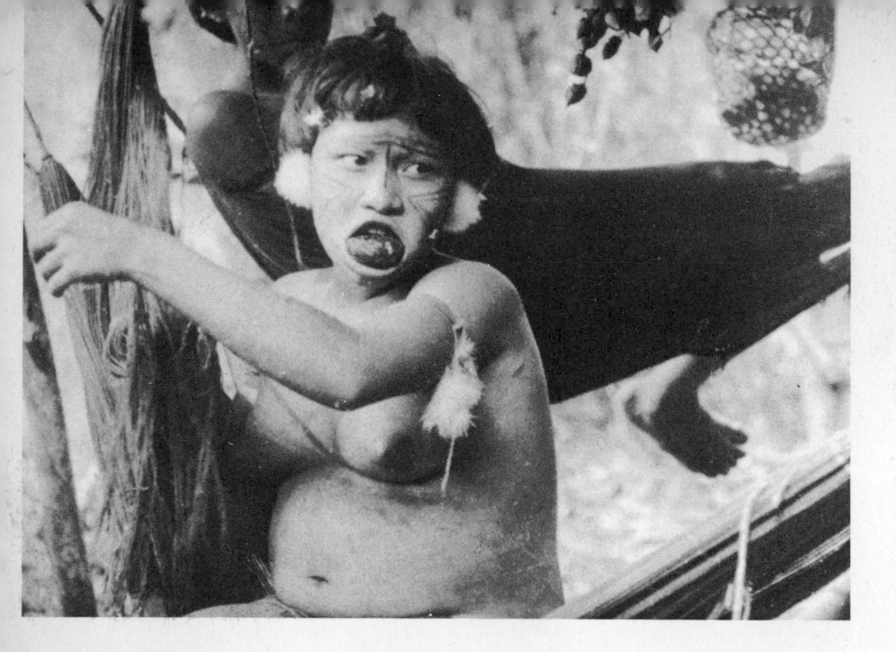

Guaharibos constantly chew a mixture of green tobacco and ashes. Their women were especially suspicious, even hiding their children's faces from the sight of white men. *Pages 308-309*

So primitive are the Guaharibos that they believe they are descended from monkeys, and they worship the animal. The women suckle dogs and their own children indiscriminately, and they have reached the level of sophistication of playing cat's cradles. *Page 314*

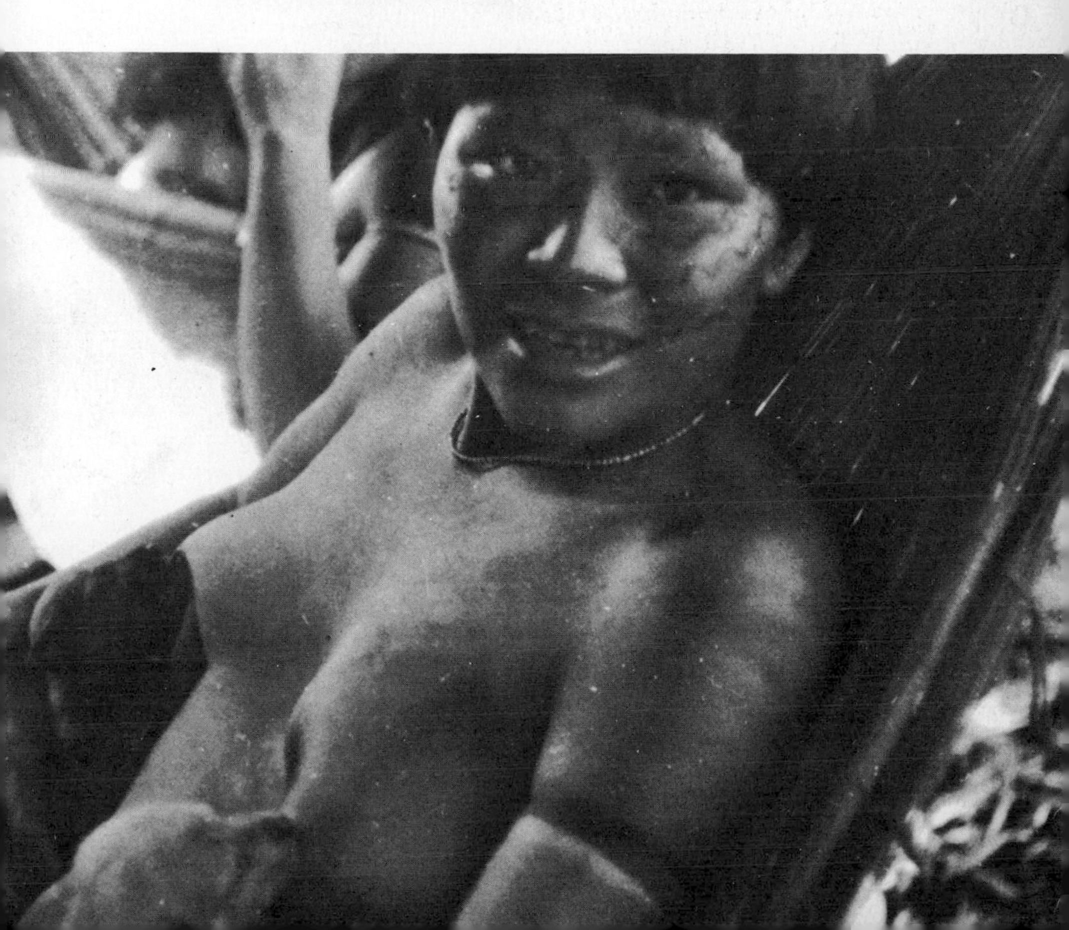

THE final part of the adventure—from the Sierra Parima and down the Amazon—proved the most dangerous, and large portions of our pictures and other valuables had to be sacrificed. On July 3, 1950, utterly exhausted, we were at last greeted by Brazilian farmers. *Page 329*

JOURNEY TO THE FAR AMAZON

AUTHOR'S PREFACE

WHEN I descended from the plane I was disappointed.

It was cold and raw, and it was raining. A nasty autumn drizzle carried on a nasty autumn wind under a nasty ten-o'clock-in-the-morning sky in the middle of the afternoon.

All color had gone out of the world. It was like night in the middle of the day. My fingers seemed to grope blindly for that thread of adventure which had sustained me so many years, through school, through war and my country's occupation, through my ethnographic studies, through years of wishing and planning.

Reporters and the curious met me at the airport. What was this madcap adventure I and three of my friends had planned, they wanted to know.

It was our plan to travel out from Bogotá along the Ariari, Guayabero and Guaviare rivers to the great Orinoco, to follow the Orinoco to its very source and then to traverse the unexplored Sierra Parima, where monkeys climbed and chattered, fierce tribes of naked Indians roamed and Incan treasures waited to be found. Beyond this virgin forest the great Amazon River would carry us eventually to the first white settlement on the other side of this vast continent.

"And you will take no weapons?" they asked.

"We will take weapons, but only for hunting game."

"And a camera?"

"Several cameras to film in still and motion pictures the people and the animals that inhabit that unexplored part of the world."

"If you aren't eaten alive by alligators or armies of ants or torn to bits by the sharp-toothed piranha fish of the rivers, you'll be sautéed by the cannibals," they said nodding their heads wisely.

"We will succeed," I said.

In Bogotá's airport hall I saw the first sign of the jungle toward which I had been moving so long and so circuitously. There was a mountain of orchids, fresh-cut and wrapped in a sarcophagus of cellophane.

Every morning these forest flowers were flown off to New York for, presumably, platinum blonds covered with furs and dripping diamonds.

Later in the Museo del Oro at the Banco de la República I found other sarcophagi. They were arranged along walls hung with blood-red velvet that served as a background for statuettes and Chibchan pendants as still as fixed suns.

The thread of my adventure then led to the Museo Colonial, where the Virgin in a peacock's cloak spread out her arms amidst carved and gilded woodwork. And from there to the Museo Nacional de Arqueología y Ethnografía, a star-shaped building of long white galleries. Feathers, cudgels and necklaces were there, and grains, smells, bows and bone-tipped arrows, maps of the forest dotted with names, calabashes for curare, calabashes for eating, and calabashes for drinking.

Finally, in the street, I saw a cacique smoking a cigarette—"Red Indian" brand—and crouching down like a blind man behind a little tray of buttons and laces; another sitting on a sack disguised as a poor man, drinking beer; then a sorcerer selling melons and papaws; and a warrior carrying the baggage of civilized people.

My friend the Colombian coffee plantation owner Luis Saenz was with me. We had first met in France in 1926 when he had sat next to me on a school bench, sticking out his tongue laboriously and getting his fingers grubby and ink-stained. Chance had brought us together again some eleven years later when, seated on somewhat more elevated benches, we attended the lectures on philosophy delivered by a young don named Jean-Paul Sartre.

But for my friendship with Luis I might never have realized

this dream of traveling to South America and exploring its dark mysteries. His studies in Paris completed, he had said to me, "I am leaving France soon." There was an ill-concealed sadness in his voice. "Why don't you come with me? Take a notebook and we'll buy a camera. In three months we shall both learn something: you because you know nothing whatever about the beauty and the poetry of my country, and I because I shall never really know it as long as I see it alone."

I had waited a full day before giving him my answer.

"Not for three months but for six. Not a small camera but two big ones. Not me alone, but at least two others as well. We will make a film and perhaps there will be a book too."

Now in Bogotá we continued to prepare for our journey. There were arrangements to be made, letters of introduction to local officials to be secured from the Colombian and Venezuelan governments, financial assistance and some equipment which was to be supplied by the Ethnographic Institute of Bogotá. The route we would travel had to be carefully planned with an eye to the weather (great rains would make the passage of the Orinoco impossible in certain seasons), and a running correspondence with the Musée de l'Homme in Paris and the Explorer's Club of France had to be kept up.

As Luis and I worked and planned in Bogotá, that dark, foreboding day of our arrival receded into the twilight of the past. Ahead of us was the excitement of the great adventure we were about to undertake. We waited impatiently for the arrival of the other two members of our party, Jean Fichter and Pierre Gaisseau. They had stayed behind in Paris to supervise the preparation of our technical equipment: the cameras and the sound-recording apparatus.

I had come to know Pierre Gaisseau at the French Explorer's Club. He was twenty-five years old, three years younger than Luis and I. What he didn't know about radio and phonographic equipment wasn't worth knowing (he had picked up this knowledge as a parachutist and saboteur during the war) and, too, he was an experienced explorer, having recently won his spurs searching through unknown parts of Equatorial Africa. Pierre's thirst for adventure had been communicated to his young brother-in-law, Jean Fichter; and when Pierre decided to throw in his lot with Luis and me, Jean was included as cameraman. Jean was the baby of the expedition. He celebrated his twentieth birthday in a little-known country, and he attained his majority one memorable day in the heart of a forest that no white man had ever penetrated before.

At times rapidly, at times interminably, eight months passed by. One by one our preparations were made, and slowly the wisp of a thread which had led me to this far-off country became tangible. Pierre and Jean arrived laden with equipment and bursting with excited anticipation. Luis put his affairs at home in order. I rushed around seeing to last-minute details, occasionally returning to the museums to take one more look at the artifacts from the strange world toward which we were going. Still invisible, the forest was approaching. After so many years of waiting, it was now coming nearer each second, with each completed plan, with each beat of my heart.

Finally, on May 6, 1949, the four of us clambered onto a truck and settled ourselves as comfortably as possible between the cases and barrels and crates which contained our equipment —a five-horsepower outboard motor we called "Archimedes," our cameras and film, the small electric generator, the recording equipment, our medicines and clothes and cooking utensils, the rifles and ammunition which would be turned upon no man, and the myriad of other "bare necessities" essential to such a trip as ours.

The truck's motor roared, we waved our arms and shouted, and with a jolt and a creaking of wooden crates our journey began. Soon the last house disappeared behind us. Ahead was the Orinoco, that great blue serpent that writhes its way across the map of South America. Beyond that, the unknown land we sought . . .

MAY 6TH TO AUGUST 6TH 1949

PART I

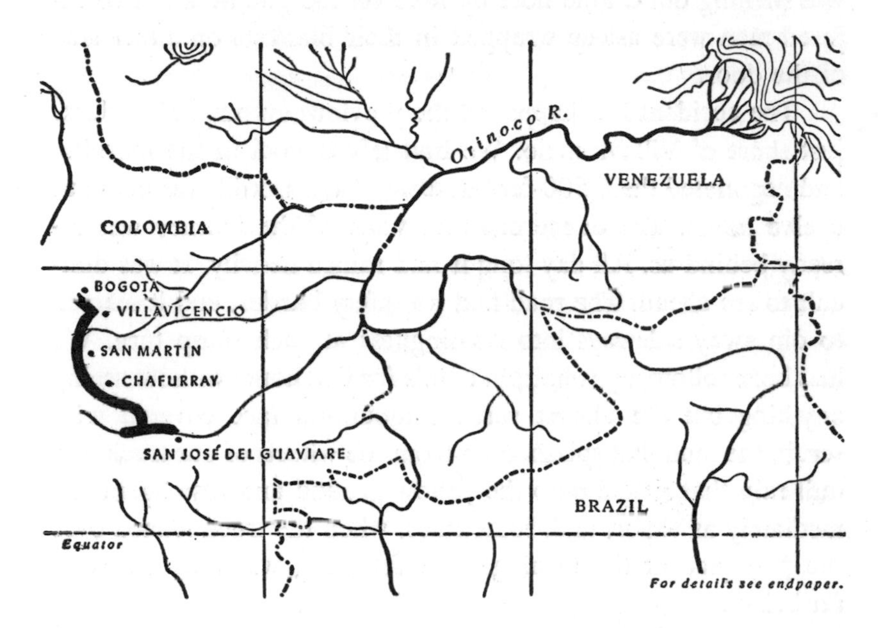

Llano and Forest—The Rock Paintings of Guayabero

The Impasse of San José del Guaviare

Villavicencio, May 7th at 11 P.M.

I SAT WITHIN FOUR WHITE WALLS under a tin roof writing up the first notes of our expedition. From my camp bed I could see out through French windows with neither fastening nor panes into the deep blue of the night, darkened here and there by the shadow of a clump of trees. From behind the house came the noise of a torrent falling down the mountainside. The sound seemed to rise and spread over the dark sky. Beyond the last thatched huts began the llano, that sea of giant vegetation that extends over six hundred miles from the Amazon to the Orinoco. Above it the twinkling of the stars seemed brighter, and all sounds more distinct. In the next room a peon I had never seen was picking out a tune note by note on the guitar. The two injured men were asleep wrapped in their blankets on either side of the door.

The accident had happened the previous evening, after dark, just short of Villavicencio. We had left Bogotá in the morning and negotiated the 6,500-foot descent of the Cordilleras in about twelve hours. The dangerous first stage of the journey was already behind us. All day long it had rained heavily. It was difficult to see ahead. The road had no safety barrier, and it seemed to dip away sideways into nothingness at each sharp turn. We had been following its hairpin bends for five hours without seeing anything but the almost vertical mountain face covered with scrub, the mud that splashed up from the wheels of our truck, the dull rain that pelted onto the yellow ground and rose again immediately as vapor, and, sometimes, when the truck leaned over the precipice at the turnings, the tumbling water of the river far below.

Suddenly the brakes were jammed on. We stopped between two hairpin bends as though adrift in a hollow made of solid rock. About three feet above the ground we could see an uncertain double glimmer of light. Our driver appeared with a battered tin in his hand.

"Una limosna por favor, señores!"

He was asking for a thanksgiving offering. We gave him some money and he went off toward the lights. We got down from the truck and followed him. The lights were two votive lamps burning before a chipped plaster cast of the Virgin Mary in garish blue and gold holding the infant Jesus in her arms. She smiled out at us from her niche in the rock. On a plaque cemented to the rock face were the words: "Thanksgiving to the Blessed Virgin from the Autobus Company XX limitada."

The driver placed the battered tin with our offering—it had once contained peas—at the foot of the statue, and went back to the truck. We clambered onto our cases again; the engine spluttered and we were off. The road was broken and full of potholes, and it grew more and more slushy as we went along. At one bend after the other we watched the wheels of our truck skirt the edge of the precipice. The road fell away more and more steeply, and at each dip the old carcass of the truck shuddered as our driver accelerated fiercely to take the dangerous curve at speed. At last the road improved a bit, and we went forward fairly smoothly for a few hundred yards. Darkness had already fallen and ahead of us we saw the yellow rectangle of an open door. The driver pulled up in front of it.

In the smoky little bodega, lighted by an oil lamp suspended from the ceiling, several men in *ruanas* were drinking beer and munching maize cakes out of packets made of banana leaves. It seemed strange to see men in such a wilderness. We drank a glass or two of the Colombian firewater known as *aguardiente*. Leaning on the plank counter, our driver talked earnestly to the serving girl, who finally went into another room and returned with a small bunch of flowers wrapped in tissue paper. Our driver took the flowers back to his truck. Above the steering wheel, near the driving mirror, was a colored picture postcard representing the Blessed Virgin with the *niño* Jesus. This too was illuminated—by a green light attached to the instrument panel. He arranged the flowers around it, and then we went on again.

We lay stretched out on the cases, each busy with his own thoughts. Although we had left Paris eight months previously, it was only now that our expedition was really to begin. In a few days there would be no more roads, no more trucks and no more bodegas where we could stop and drink *aguardiente*. There would be only the sun-drenched llano and the brown rivers running toward the forests.

Suddenly something happened. The truck seemed to hesitate, the chassis shook violently, the engine accelerated wildly, and we were thrown into a heap among the cases. With one hand I grabbed a rail and with the other I seized Luis by the jacket. Then the roof of the truck fell in and I was buried under its steel hoops. All noise and movement ceased.

"Let go!" Luis shouted.

I heard him scramble down from the truck, and with some difficulty I wormed my way out of the swaddling hoops and followed him.

In breaking loose, the top of the truck had dragged away half our cases and the rear of the truck itself. They had disappeared into the night. We found ourselves at the side of the road and the front of our truck piled up on a rock. I managed to discover a torch and ran back along the road with Luis. As far as the beams of the torch reached, the road was strewn with our possessions—tins of food, rolls of film, and other debris.

Then I saw a pair of long legs sticking out of a ditch, as though someone had thrown away a doll. The legs belonged to Jean. I ran up and found him with his hands in front of his face. Blood was running between his fingers down onto his clothes. The top of his head had been cut in several places as though with a razor.

"Are you badly hurt, Jean?" I inquired anxiously.

"I don't think so," he replied. "I'm all right. Find out what's happened to Pierre."

It took us a good five minutes to do that. He was also in the ditch, but a couple of hundred yards away. Blood was spurting from the back of his head onto the sticky earth.

"That's done it," he said. "I think I've fractured my skull."

I found his raincoat a little distance away and used it as a pillow for his head.

"We'll see about that when we get you to a hospital," I said. "Don't worry now."

I called Elie, our Boy, to help me collect the contents of the broken cases.

"Pile up what you can find on the spare wheel," I said.

"Sí, señor," he replied as nonchalantly as though I had told him to do the dishes, and he whistled between his teeth as he began to collect the debris.

Another truck approached out of the darkness, and Luis stood in the roadway waving his torch. The pitch of the engine remained unchanged as it drove on. I began to shout with Luis, and at last the truck consented to pull up. A surly head poked out of the driver's cab.

"What's up?"

"We've had an accident, and we want to get a couple of injured men to a hospital as quickly as possible."

We got Pierre out of the ditch and carried him to the truck. As we were making him as comfortable as possible on a bench, we heard Jean call out in the darkness:

"Take me too," he said in a weak voice.

We helped him to the truck. His face had gone very white and he looked as though he were going to faint. The moment we got him to the bench he went limp and collapsed in our hands. The engine was already revving, and Luis had just time to jump back onto the truck again as it moved off. Jean's head had fallen alongside Pierre's. He had managed to stay conscious until we got him safely into the truck.

They disappeared into the darkness and I was left behind in the rain. A steady drizzle was still falling. Elie was conscientiously piling broken packets of chocolate in a pyramid onto the spare wheel. A little way off our driver was trying to straighten a bent piece of iron with a stone about the size of his fist. I felt depressed.

About two hours later a jeep arrived for us, and I went to the hospital to see how our two injured friends were getting on. They had just been examined when I arrived.

"I don't think any bones are broken," the surgeon said. "Come along again tomorrow. With a bit of luck they ought to be fit for the road again in a few days."

The modest hospital in Villavicencio has two nursing Sisters. They came toward us with serene faces, and to our great surprise, began to speak in a soft French that immediately betrayed their origin. We discovered that one of them came from Picardy and the other from Burgundy. One fine day they had arrived at Le Bourget—with their wicker hampers, their big black umbrellas, and their rosy cheeks—to be winged away from France and set down in the capital of a different sort of Wild West, for that is more or less what Villavicencio is. Since then almost the only patients they had received in their little white hospital with its tin roof were poor peons with sun-tanned skins and patent-leather hair. These men were brought in to them every Monday as regularly as clockwork: rolled up in their hammocks, their eyes shining feverishly, and their clothes stiff with congealed blood.

MEN OF THE LLANO

On two occasions when I made trips into the llano in connection with our expedition I saw these men close up. I had been imprudent enough to take the bus back into Villavicencio from Puerto Lopez and San Martín, two villages out in the llano which are connected with the town by a bus service. On each occasion the bus had its full complement of passengers, but three of them were wounded peons, and they lay stretched out on the benches, occupying about eighteen seats between them. Each time I had to stand for about eight hours in a temperature of between 85 and 95 degrees Fahrenheit, jolting up and down in the narrow space between the two rows of seats, and trying to avoid banging my head on the low roof by bending over one of the blood-caked bodies.

Sunday is a day of rest in the llano as elsewhere, and on that day all the local peons and cowboys converge on these two villages, where they park themselves for the day in the local café, whose chief civilized amenity is an American juke box decorated with gilt flourishes. For a few cents it grinds out a tune for their amusement from worn and scratched records. Four men sit at each table playing dice, their sombreros pushed into their necks, their matchets swinging to hand under the table top. For hours bottles of lukewarm beer follow black coffee, and when they have drunk as much beer as they can hold they go on to shorts, *aguardiente* and anise. Toward the middle of the afternoon discussions begin to grow heated, and before long matchets are whipped out of their leather scabbards. When the fracas is over, two or three men will be sprawling on the floor with slashed ears, noses, or thighs. Then peace descends again.

The police arrive to take charge of the wounded, who are slung up in their hammocks at the station until the following morning. Then they are carried to the bus in their hammocks; slung on poles like some sort of big game being brought back from the chase.

Apart from such Sundays, and the annual cattle fair at Villavicencio, which is a sort of super-Sunday, the cowboy lives an austere and monotonous existence in the llano, rather like any other hermit. He rises with the sun at about six o'clock in the morning, swallows a cup of bitter coffee—which is all he will put inside himself until he dismounts from his horse perhaps twelve hours later—and sets off into the llano. He spends practically half his life in the saddle, and when he is mounted he is almost one with his horse. His matchet dangling from the saddlebow and the long lasso of untanned hide looped around the pommel, he is soon dwarfed in the immensity of the llano, and his figure disappears over the horizon.

Under the sombrero of felt or straw, which he wears well pulled down for protection from the glare of the sun, his eyes are fixed ahead, and for hours on end, as his horse breasts the undergrowth, he sees nothing but an endless waving plain and a remote skyline. Then he sights a group of cattle, perhaps a tawny bull and a half-dozen cows standing together silently. When they are still far away he will know whether they belong to his herd or not, and he will count them at a glance, looking keenly, almost tenderly, to see if they have met with some mishap. If he is reassured he will go on his way, and the whole day will pass in this fashion. The horse beneath him will hardly change its pace, and he will sit motionless in the saddle, whilst all around him the great silence, trembling in the heat, will be broken only by the growling of some beast on the prowl or by the high winging of a flock of migratory birds as it crosses the sky.

By six o'clock in the evening, when the sun is dipping down toward the horizon, he will be back at his rancho. Dismounting, he will take off his *zamarros,* the great leather trousers of the cowboy, and sit down at a bench under the rectangular porch of the rancho not far from where his hammock is suspended. His wife will bring him a cup of coffee, a glass of water, a pan of cooked rice seasoned with pimento, and a small piece of meat. Perhaps ten minutes later he will clamber into his hammock, close his mosquito net, and go to sleep. Mosquitoes whine steadily around him and bullfrogs croak in the brown and flattened grass.

That is how his life unfolds from day to day, monotonously, with an economy of energy, gesture, food, and words—except on Sundays. And then, struck off by drink, music, and dice, a spark will ignite within him, and the dry but passionate little man will flare up like a resin torch for a while, fighting fiercely as though for a woman, urged on by some sudden desire to assert himself. The violence of his reaction then will be all the greater because of the days, and even months together, in which such desires lie dormant.

When I call these *llaneros* to mind I can always see the fire smoldering in the fixed and steady gaze that looks out from under the shade of a large, colorless, ageless sombrero.

One day a giant of a man with large-calibre Colts dangling from his belt came to live in Puerto Lopez. He was not a *llanero,* but his size, his Colts and his money were all impressive. The real *llaneros* didn't like him: for one thing he talked too much, and even his violence was theatrical. The only friends he made were among those who thought they might get something out of him.

Like him, they were hard drinkers. One Sunday they all appeared in the local café. Striding up to the bar, the big man loudly ordered whiskies. Whisky in Puerto Lopez? The landlord served him without comment. No one moved. The *llaneros* ignored him. The man was obviously rattled by their silence. He drank; he spat; he swore; and he became insulting. He ordered more drinks, and all the time his eyes were roving round the company. No one took the slightest notice of him.

Near the middle of the room a little old man sat blowing at his coffee. Casually his glance met that of the big man. It was enough. The bully flushed and began to bluster. The little man continued to blow at his coffee. He might have been deaf and dumb. It was too much. The swashbuckler drew one of his Colts and fired point blank. As though by a miracle the little man was unharmed. Whipping out his matchet, he sprang up and with a backhanded blow slashed open his assailant's throat.

True story or invention? It could be true, and it was told to me in Puerto Lopez. A day or so later, perhaps by the side of some crystal stream under the shade of palm trees, that same little man would just as adroitly cut off the tail of a sick heifer with his matchet, cauterizing the stump with a red-hot iron. But above all he would ride *de paso* on his old horse, a creature as dry and leathery as himself, and go on doing the same thing for days and months and years, crossing and re-crossing the sea of llano, perhaps dreaming now and again of the sacks of gold pieces buried by some dead and gone *llanero*—you find their hiding place because will-o'-the-wisps dance over it on nights when the moon is full. Until one day, without ever having found that hidden gold—or any other—he will die as an old tree dies, and his black matchet with its razor-sharp edges will be laid beside him in the earth all ready for the last great journey.

Unless, of course, he is destined to meet his fate one Sunday in the café. And then, in a little hospital with whitewashed walls and a tin roof, attended by two good Sisters from Picardy and Burgundy, he will learn for the first time in his life what it is to lie in a bed between white sheets. And how much will they learn about him? How much will they even suspect of the months and years of dreams and silence that preceded that one outburst in the café?

"What a pleasure it is to be able to speak French again!" exclaimed both the good Sisters, softly rolling their *r*'s.

They first discovered the nationality of Pierre and Jean when they were assisting the surgeon at the operating table. Up to then, it appeared, neither of the injured men had said a word, but when the surgeon's examination proved painful they both began to swear horribly in very plain French. The joy of the good Sisters dated from that moment.

The next morning we went back to the hospital for our two casualties. In the night the Sisters had brought them tasty little dishes they had prepared—having waited for hours and not dared to wake them. Jean strode across the patio of the little hospital toward a waiting taxi. One of the two Sisters was standing at my side. She looked for a moment or two at Jean's loose-limbed figure. His long, striped pajamas were in folds over his boots, and a khaki jacket was flung round his shoulders. Blushing with sudden enthusiasm, she exclaimed:

"Poor fellow! He reminds me so of my German lads back in France during the war. Now they had really bad wounds!"

CROSSING OF THE RIO GUAMAL, AND A FAREWELL

The telephone line from Villavicencio to San Martín is in operation every day between twelve and two, and I used it to call up D., whose truck was to take us through the llano. I didn't know whether the route—mere wheel tracks through the savanna—was still practicable after the rain or not. The few people, like D., who are prepared to let their trucks venture beyond the roads, usually do so only during the dry season, and our mishap had so delayed our departure that we were now at the beginning of the rains. Clouds pile up against the face of the Andes, and from one day to the next roads can become impassable. D. had obviously read the interviews we had given to the press in Bogotá, and he was very amiable on the telephone. He assured me that his truck was still at our disposal and that he would take us as arranged to Rancho de Chafurray, the last rancho of San Martín, on the bank of the Rio Ariari. From there we were to go on by canoe to the Orinoco. However, it appeared that owing to the rains the Rio Guamal had swollen into a torrent and carried away the bridge by which the road from Villavicencio to San Martín crosses it. D.'s truck could therefore meet us only on the other side of the Rio Guamal. We arranged to be at the river on the following Thursday, which was May 12th.

A closer examination of our baggage had shown that only the cases of foodstuffs, munitions, and heavier gear had really been damaged. Our irreplaceable photographic and sound-recording apparatus was intact. When I remembered that I had rescued the recording apparatus from between the wheels of the wrecked truck, and that Jean had said that our drum of oil, weighing perhaps four hundred and fifty pounds, had crashed to the ground within an inch of his head, I realized that we had only just escaped irreparable disaster. Our luck made us optimistic again and gave us the necessary confidence to tackle the next stage of our journey.

On the morning of May 12th our patched-up cases were loaded onto a truck, and we set off. Two or three hours later we were at the banks of the swollen Rio Guamal. Normally it is about a hundred and fifty feet across, but now it was more than twice that width, and the buttresses of the large stone bridge that had been swept away by the torrent were not easy to see. An emergency bridge had been built. It was spatchcocked together out of a variety of planks and held together about three feet above the water by two steel cables. It was difficult for two people to cross at a time because the weight of one was quite sufficient to make the whole flimsy structure swing erratically from side to side. However, that did not prevent the porters waiting at the bridge from getting our baggage over in record time, and they sprang from plank to plank carrying cases weighing not far short of a hundredweight on their backs.

When all our things were safely stowed away in D.'s truck, the doctor of Villavicencio, who had been good enough to accompany us that far, produced a bottle of *aguardiente* from his pocket, and it went from mouth to mouth amongst the whole company. There were cheerful shouts of "Long live the French expedition!" from the porters.

It was amid this impressive scene of nature's primeval violence that we received perhaps the warmest good wishes for our success. And those who encouraged us so enthusiastically were simple fellows we had not known a quarter of an hour before and probably never would see again. But they were as excited about our adventure as though they were taking part in it themselves. For a long time after we had left them we could see the doctor and the porters still throwing their hats into the air and cheering us on our way. We waved our own hats in acknowledgement until the little group was out of sight. To our secret shame, our hats were still very new and not washed out by the rain and bleached by the sun.

OF ALLIGATORS, MOSQUITOES, SNAKES, AND BARNABY

In San Martín we slung our hammocks in a large room which gave directly onto the village square, and all the inhabitants assembled there to let us know what we might expect on the other side of Chafurray.

"The rivers are full of alligators," one man declared, gesticulating excitedly. "You won't be able to get along for them. And you know what you must do? Cut yourself thick cudgels and hit them over the snouts. Then they'll go away."

"Oh, no!" exclaimed another man. "You mustn't hit them over the snouts whatever you do or they'll smash up your canoe with one flick of their tails, just like that. And then they'll gobble you up in the water."

"Alligators," said still another contemptuously. "What chance do you think the alligators will get? The cannibals will do the job first. The forests of Guaviare are full of them. They'll attack in the middle of the night and before you know where you are they'll be digesting you."

Someone else said that the Indians were very handsome fellows all dressed in feathers, but another man pooh-poohed the idea altogether and declared that they wore shirts and trousers just like ordinary folk. In fact, there just weren't any savages in Colombia any more. The Indians were a poor lot: they drank so much they were unable to work, and we shouldn't find them in the least interesting.

Twenty-four hours later it was still pouring, and D. said that for the time it was impossible to go on.

"We shall have to wait till it stops and the ground dries up a bit."

And his arm made a sweeping gesture to embrace the whole llano.

We waited for another couple of days, but then we did start off again. At the last moment D. decided to go ahead with us in a jeep and to let the heavier truck follow. We drove for eight hours between bare hills that extended right to the horizon. Nothing interrupted the monotony of the journey but the occasional appearance of a spindle-shanked wader, with white, black, or bright red plumage, standing motionless on the edge of a stagnant pool. But at last the square roof of a rancho appeared on the brow of a hill. Beyond it the Rio Ariari flowed yellowish from the rains, and on the far bank the forest began, low, somber and dense.

Our jeep drove down to a quay on which a man was working amid a number of enormous fish hanging from poles. The stench took us by the throats as we approached.

"That's Barnaby," said D.

The man greeted us.

"It's not bad here," he said, indicating the llano, the river, and the fish, "but you get a bit bored."

The next morning we were up at dawn. Barnaby was already busy at the fire, and he handed us bowls of steaming coffee. It was like a gift from the gods, after the exasperating night we had spent. We had slept aboard D.'s boat—on deck and without mosquito netting, having forgotten to bring our bedding along. All night the anopheles mosquitoes had indulged in an orgy of blood at our expense, and our bodies were swollen in great lumps as though we had been thoroughly drubbed.

At dawn the anopheles retires to its own quarters, but that brings no relief—merely a change of guard in the mosquito world, and its duties are taken over by a newcomer called the "jejen." It is smaller than the anopheles, but ten times more numerous and even more bloodthirsty. We drank our coffee to a rattle of slaps, as we sought to defend ourselves against this new pest.

Barnaby found our sufferings very funny and laughed heartily. Apart from his fishing he was also the caretaker, and once a year he would become the pilot of D.'s boat when it went down river to San José del Guaviare to bring back the catch of the great annual fishing festival, which is the one industry of the little village. San José del Guaviare is situated about ninety-three miles away from Chafurray. It lies just beyond the confluence of the rivers Ariari and Guayabero where the two combine to form the great Rio Guaviare. It represented the end of the next stage of our journey.

At about eight o'clock we heard the sound of our truck coming across the llano. It arrived bespattered with mud. Elie sprang down. He was covered with mud from head to foot, and he explained eagerly that the truck had got stuck in the mud three times, and that each time they had had to unload it before they could dig the wheels out and free it.

"And yesterday evening," he went on excitedly, "we saw a snake about twice as long as this truck. If you had only left me a rifle we could all have had snake belts for the forest."

He had obviously seen a *traga-vendao,* or antelope crusher. Along the Amazon some specimens of this South American anaconda grow up to twenty-four feet in length and eighteen inches in thickness. Fastening their tails round the trunk of a tree for support, they are capable of crushing a three-year-old bull in their coils, and, in fact, the *llaneros* fear their depredations more even than those of the jaguar or the puma.

We unloaded our baggage and found our hammocks and our mosquito nets again. Once our things were safely deposited on deck, we discussed the next stage of our journey with D. and Barnaby. It was out of the question to use D.'s boat—a United States army-surplus craft—because our entire stock of gasoline would hardly have been enough to take it to the mouth of the Rio Ariari.

After thinking the matter over carefully, Barnaby informed us that an Indian canoe was on its way down the Ariari and would soon arrive at Chafurray. Two of us could go down to San José del Guaviare in it, and, once we were there, the authorities would probably let us have the *canoa del gobierno,* or official boat. With our economical little five horsepower outboard engine, we should then be able to navigate it up to

Chafurray. It had a capacity of more than five tons and could easily carry all our load.

This plan would allow us to get to the Rio Guaviare without making any very deep inroads into our fuel reserves. We had about fifty-five gallons of gasoline with us, and there would be no chance of replenishing our store before we reached the Orinoco, which was over six hundred miles away from San José del Guaviare.

The wait began. We spent a good deal of our time looking up the river for the first sight of the Indian canoe. At the hottest hours of the day it was almost as though a desolate emptiness had descended on everything and robbed it of reality. The river was like a great expanse of lacquer, and its reflections in the sunlight dazzled the eyes intolerably. Two or three sandbanks, whose yellow was hardly distinguishable from that of the river itself, rose above the surface, and motionless waders, ibis, and egrets stood there in a ceaseless vigil, long-legged and as though turned to stone. We never saw them settled, and we rarely saw them fly away; and when they uttered their harsh cries the sound seemed to come from anywhere but where they stood, so uniformly did it echo over the still waters. We lay half naked and dripping with sweat under our mosquito nets, and all around the jejens kept up a faint whine. We had been talking for hours, but without looking at each other, and gradually our words grew fewer and fewer and finally ceased altogether in the middle of a phrase.

The silence weighed heavily on us for a long time, and then, unexpectedly, the sun covered its face and the wind rose. The waders on their sandbanks spread their wings and shook their feathers. The sky, which had clouded over almost unnoticeably, now burst suddenly, and rain as cold as glass fell, pitting and slashing the water fiercely. It broke not only the unruffled surface of the river but also the great silence all around. For ten minutes the rain pelted down heavily. And then it stopped as suddenly as it had started. Great clouds of steam rose above the forest skyline like phantoms, the trees dripped, and the river again looked like frozen fire under the ardent rays of the unclouded sun.

Only five hundred yards of still water separated me from the forest. Above it there was a blue haze in the sky. Only at dusk did it come alive, in that ten minutes when the day and the night change places as though by legerdemain. Then all the reddish-brown monkeys in the branches begin to howl in chorus, a vast, eerie, moaning sound. I lay and stared at that forest almost all day. Now that it was so close, I found my patience wearing thin under the long wait. Since I had left Paris I had been on my travels for a year, and at last I had arrived before the walls of that new world I had come so far to seek. But now, somewhere, some gate must open for me to enter.

Barnaby's hammock was slung at the other end of the boat. It was two o'clock and no one spoke. The jejens swirled around us, flying into my mosquito netting and away again. My mosquito net was carefully closed. Barnaby's was open. One foot and a dark, tanned leg stuck out. The knee disappeared in the folds of gauze. Barnaby had an empty tin which he was turning round and round in his hand. With surprise I realized that he was talking to himself, or rather to the tin. He seemed to be telling some story and his voice was low.

"Barnaby was born in the forest," D. had told me a day or so before. "The biggest place he has ever seen is San José del Guaviare with its ten houses and its population of fifty souls. For years he was the fisherman and hunter of the village, quartering the forest on foot and going up and down the river in his canoe. For a few sous he would sell tapir or peccary meat to the villagers, and dry pieces of the 'Valenton,' the great fish of the Guaviare which can weigh up to four hundred and fifty pounds. He still does. No one has ever known him to have either a woman or a friend. He's a lonely fellow, something like the old boars he tracks down in the forest. One day when he was managing my boat I suggested that he should look after it for me, so he slung his hammock where you can see it now."

Our table was laid on two large planks on stakes, something like a bar four feet or so from the ground. On it was an oil lamp made out of a bottle with a piece of string for wick. Swarms of mosquitoes and a few moths did a saraband round its swaying flame. Two dark-skinned men came out of the night and helped themselves to rice on fragments of banana leaf. The few words they exchanged with each other and with Barnaby were spoken in a rapid, guttural language we did not understand. One of them was wearing a kidskin cap with blue and white stripes, and the other wore a straw hat without color or shape. D. explained that they were the two Indians Barnaby had been expecting. Their canoe must be in, and we should no doubt soon be able to start our journey down river to San José del Guaviare.

But more days passed, and D. went back to San Martín.

"I'll be back in a few days," he said. "Then I'll go down with you to San José, but first of all I've got one or two things to settle at home."

But one morning the canoe of the two Indians disappeared round the river bend on its way to San José del Guaviare, taking Luis and Pierre along and leaving me behind with Jean, Barnaby and our Boy Elie. We passed the time in fishing, but our lines seemed to be maliciously in league with the monotony of our days and we never caught anything but the same type of fish. One day there were signs of life at the Rancho de Chafurray, which up to then had been closed up and silent. Two peons on horseback appeared. They had been in the llano for a good week. They dismounted and shook us all by the hand as though we were lifelong friends. Then the elder of the two asked me if I could let him have a little powder. He was carrying an ancient double-barrelled shotgun. About six or seven inches had been sawed off the barrels. When I asked him what sort of game he had sawed it off for, he told me that he had bought a case for it:

"But when I got back I found the case wasn't long enough, so I sawed off the barrel to make the gun fit just the same."

Two days later a small plane landed in the llano and soon afterward the man with the sawed-off shotgun arrived to inquire whether "the French scientists" would care to dine with his master.

When we went up the hill, we found the rancho no longer deserted. A large trestle table had been set up in the open. Our host, the owner of Chafurray, a wrinkled old man, courteously bade us welcome to "his desert." With him was a corpulent fellow in khaki with red hair. In a mixture of French and Spanish spoken with a strong German accent, he introduced himself as the pilot of the Piper Cub which belonged to our host. We sat down with them at the table and rum, coffee and cigarettes were passed round. After having asked us curiously what strange idea had impelled us to travel in the llano in anything but a plane, the German glanced at his wrist-watch and rose hurriedly.

"You must excuse me for leaving you so abruptly," he said, "but my wife will be waiting for me to go to the movies."

During the two hours he had spent in the llano he had found time to throw a stick of dynamite into the river, and he now made his way to the plane with a basket of fresh fish.

The next day the master of the rancho went off on horseback to make a tour of inspection around his herds, and once again the rancho with its tin roof was nothing but an abandoned shell amid the silence and the mosquitoes.

At last D. reappeared in his jeep and a second canoe put in at the quay.

"Are you ready right away?" he inquired.

I hadn't the courage to refuse and so we went off with Barnaby and two Indians, leaving poor Jean behind with Elie and a peon to look after our baggage.

FIRST NIGHT IN THE FOREST

May 22nd at 10 A.M.: The air was clear and tenuous and the water around us shone with bubbles. A changing, shot-grey sky was mirrored in it and made it look as though it had been polished. Around and ahead of us there was nothing but the river, apparently immobile but gliding imperceptibly between the walls of forest. Stretched out in the middle of the canoe, D. was asleep behind me. Barnaby sat in the stern slowly moving his paddle. He looked as though he were carved in wood. Before me two silent Indians moved rhythmically backward and forward as they paddled, and every now and again their paddles grated on the gunwales. Chafurray was four hours behind us already, together with the llano and the waiting hours. We were on our way.

Here and there a sandbank rose above the surface in the middle of the river. Cayman alligators and turtles the color of mud slept fraternally side by side half out of the water, opened one eye at our approach, and slid off the sandbanks into the water with hardly a ripple. A green network of liana hung down from the trees on either side of the river, trailing in the water like tresses. There was a grey mist in the air. Knock-kneed waders passed in couples and sometimes a flight of chattering parakeets. The forest swallowed them up without trace. Brown trunks of trees with black branches outstretched like arms floated down stream. The sun climbed steadily into the sky over cloud after cloud. Gradually the sky turned leaden and then everyone came to life, quickly stripping off his clothes and putting them under a canvas to keep dry. Soon the rain was pelting down again, running off our backs in rivulets and rising in steam into the air. The paddles continued to move steadily and soon the storm passed over. As we turned a bend in the river, the sun came out again, the alligators and the turtles reappeared on their sandbanks, and Barnaby put on his shirt without letting go of his paddle.

We were due at San José del Guaviare the following evening, and now it was time for lunch. The canoe was beached on a strip of sand. There was a zigzag spoor of velvety prints leading from the forest down to the water's edge.

"A tiger," said Barnaby. (Jaguars, ocelots, and panthers are all indifferently referred to as "tigers" along the Amazon, just as the pumas of the savanna are called "lions.")

We ate rice and dried fish, and drank beer. Afterward I handed around cigarettes and then we paddled on. The sky was clear now. The afternoon wore on and the sun began to sink. My first night in the forest was at hand. Along the bank there were so many mosquitoes that I found it difficult to keep my eyes open. Our Indians plunged into the liana and wielding their matchets vigorously cleared a few square yards of ground which was so deeply covered with black humus that we sank ankle deep into it. Hammocks were quickly slung and mosquito nets arranged, and the Indians then lit a large fire. Barnaby made coffee and strained it through the bottom of a straw hat. The night was full of humming, crackling sounds. I fell asleep while I was smoking a cigarette and woke up suddenly when it began to burn my fingers. Above my head the foliage of the trees made patterns against the sky and the stars.

When I next woke up the sky was becoming grey. Barnaby had replenished the fire and he was crouching there making coffee. We began to fold our hammocks. It was not yet day and the forest was still asleep when once more our paddles began their steady movement. Then the first birds appeared, streaking across the light sky. Once again it was ten o'clock on the Ariari, then eleven o'clock with parakeets chattering, and then midday with the hot sun beating down on the forest and the silent air.

In the heat and the silence we turned into a small creek where the water lapped softly beneath the undergrowth. Murmuring noises now filled the forest around us. Barnaby spoke over my head to the paddlers.

"Gently does it. Peccaries!"

He was standing behind me, naked to the waist, with a satisfied smile on his face. I gave him a rifle and he climbed up the bank. Five minutes passed and then there was a shot. We heard his voice rather muffled by the trees. The two Indians took their matchets and plunged into the undergrowth. Barnaby reappeared grinning happily and climbed back into the stern of the canoe. I could hear the Indians laughing and shouting and then they burst through the foliage and came down to the river's edge bent under the weight of a big peccary which they had already gutted. They were carrying it on a thick branch from shoulder to shoulder.

They put the beast down at my feet and went back to clean their matchets and to cut leaves of the false banana to cover it up with. Then we went on. The foliage parted before us and we slid out into the broad river again. High up in the trees groups of little reddish-brown monkeys chattered noisily.

The forest has its varying moods. Along the banks of the river it presents a kaleidoscope of changing scenery. Perhaps for three or four hundred yards or so there will be terraces massed in wonderful perspective and great curved avenues of trees. Then further on one could imagine oneself on the edge of some great park with an enchanted river meandering beneath the walls of a great palace. After that the tangled mass, the overflowing luxuriance and ripeness, the unfinished and the unattainable will begin again joyously, pitching the rotted colonnades helter-skelter into the water in a jungle of branches and liana. And again the scene will suddenly change and one might be between the flowery mills of the Marne, so real that one could easily imagine a bottle of white wine awaiting the thirsty traveler on the bank. And then comes a somber island dividing the river into two, and one could imagine the beribboned boats of an elegant marquis. But at that moment the sky jumbles everything together again and chooses to deck itself out à la Corot.

We were now approaching the confluence of the Guayabero. Through an open space in the forest on our left the savanna appeared, encroaching brown and yellow on the perpetual green. Under a palm tree stood an abandoned hut. That single hut boasts a name, "Concordia," and it is marked so prominently on the map that the traveler would expect to find at least a village there. It was once the beginning of a road that led to Villavicencio, but that was in the days when an American rubber company exploited the forest rubber of Guaviare. Once the war was over the Americans went away, and within a very few years the savanna had covered everything again.

Our shadows lengthened over the water, and then on our right the river suddenly doubled in size and the forest skyline was pushed far away. At the same time our canoe seemed to have got very much smaller, and although the paddles were still working away steadily they no longer seemed to be driving us forward. The wind rose and carried the song of the cicadas to our ears. The Guayabero had just united with the Rio Ariari and we were now floating on the Rio Guaviare. Five hundred miles ahead of us, having burst its way through land and forest, it would pour its yellow waters into the mighty Orinoco.

Barnaby used his paddle as a rudder and our canoe now crossed the river at an angle and slowly approached the right bank. The river bends grew shallower and shallower and the forest seemed to grow taller and taller. The surroundings became romantic, a primeval, untouched forest and river landscape. The wind grew stronger and the scene trembled. The wind began to howl and the dream scene disappeared altogether. Then again the river was a sheet of lacquer, and as we rounded a last shallow curve we saw a group of about twenty houses with thatched roofs. They were huddled together on a yellow tongue of land between the green forest and its mirrored counterpart in the river like a frightened herd of cattle. We had arrived at San José, the only village on the Rio Guaviare.

WE GO IN SEARCH OF INCAN GOLD

In the darkness burned a yellow star of light. It was suspended by a length of wire from a broad roof of palm leaves. The hut had walls of dried and whitewashed clay, and around them were four benches on which men were sitting. From a neighboring room sounded a rather discordant wireless. An English tenor was singing an aria from "Tosca." Two of the walls went right up to the roof, but the other two were only about three feet high. Above one of them was nothing but the dark night in which a still darker avenue of mango trees could be seen running down to the river. Above the other was an *anjeo,* a screen of fine gauze wire intended to keep out the mosquitoes. But in fact all the mosquitoes had to do was to skirt the house and soar in from the side where the mango trees were visible, and they circled round the electric light in clouds. Behind the metallic gauze and outside the hut was a row of motionless heads belonging to a group of Indians. Whenever there was a light in the house of Don Jesus they would arrive silently, warned by the humming of the generating plant, which carried over a long distance, and gather behind the screen to look at the light and listen to the voices of the white sorcerers.

They were Guayabero Indians, the only natives for miles around. Since the founding of San José del Guaviare they had stopped daubing their faces and their bodies with bright red *achiote* sap and *caranna* resin, and they no longer went through the forest naked singing the hymns and performing the dances of the Sun God. The coming of the white man had interrupted the life they and their ancestors had lived for thousands of years.

But they were far from civilized. They continued to live in straw shelters hidden in the forest and they did not altogether appreciate the white man's progress. They worked for the white man, but only long enough to buy themselves a new pair of cotton trousers when the pair they wore had fallen to rags, or perhaps a new matchet. The collective spirit of their tribe had gone and nothing had come to take its place, and so the groups of Guayaberos around San José del Guaviare were gradually dying out one after the other. They no longer accepted what they were, or what they were doing, or what they should do, and the spiritual malady to which this loss of confidence gave rise shriveled them up as plants shrivel when for some reason they no longer have the strength to draw nourishment from the soil in which they are rooted. Today there are only about a couple of hundred Guayaberos in the whole forest and soon there will be none at all. But every night when Don Jesus, the white sorcerer, turns on his radio and sets his generating station going, a few score of them appear silently out of the night and press their faces against the wire gauze, staring through it unblinking at the electric light. Unlike the mosquitoes, they have not confidence enough to skirt the house.

Don Jesus was our host, and we sat on the benches under the electric light and listened to his talk. All the village notables were there too, encouraging his remarks with approving nods of their heads. There was A., the old Venezuelan hunter of alligators. Twenty years earlier he had been compelled to seek safety in Colombia, because his attempt to storm a village whose inhabitants held political views which differed from his own had failed. And there was also Corporal Nepo. For fifteen years he had lived among the Indians, and he was quite prepared to undertake a thousand-mile journey through the forest with nothing but his hands and teeth to help him. Then there was X., a rich man who owned two hundred head of cattle in the llano on the other side of the river, and Garcia, who was sergeant of police, as his khaki hat with its great tin star indicated, but who was by natural aptitude and inclination a player of billiards.

"Yes, gentlemen," Don Jesus was going on in a nervous voice, "it wasn't three months ago. You are scientists, you will be acquainted with the secrets of Indian paintings. You should go into the forest and search for that stone. It was first seen by an old Indian woman, a poor Guayabero, the mother of a lad I employ once a year in February when we do our fishing. For years we have camped in the same place, at the foot of the rapids, about a day's journey from here. We never suspected a thing, and yet that stone can't have been more than an hour or two's journey away from our camp.

"Listen to how it happened: the old woman used to go into the hills to look for resin, or grain, or whatever it was she looked for. That day when she wanted to return she found herself cut off by a forest fire, so she had to make a big detour through strange country where neither she nor the others had ever been, clambering over rocks near where the river narrows. And then suddenly, as she told me the same evening when I saw her, still trembling with fear, she came face to face with an enormous white stone at the edge of the forest. And on that stone, she said, people, animals, and red devils were looking out at her, some of them no bigger than your hand, and others as big as the side of a house. The devil himself must have put all that there, she thought. And of course it was bad luck to look at it, so she turned round and fled, arriving back in the camp very late in the evening. That was all I could get out of her, but it sounds true. If you care to make the expedition, taking along a couple of Guayaberos, I'm sure you'd find the place."

"Perhaps there's a treasure hidden under the stone," someone ventured.

"It's full moon now," added another. "If there's really Inca gold hidden there you'll see will-o'-the-wisps dancing over the spot. The place where gold is hidden can always be seen when there's a full moon, and that's a fact everybody knows."

"You ought to go and have a look at it," said D., passing

around the bottled beer we had brought with us from Chafurray. "It would make an interesting film even if you don't find any gold."

With a great deal of mush and spluttering the radio ground out a rumba from the Antilles. It sounded as though the orchestra was exhausted by the task of reaching our ears over all that distance. Don Jesus had built the set himself and it wasn't altogether up to the mark. For some years he had been taking a correspondence course in radio engineering from a school in Massachusetts. The lessons arrived in San José del Guaviare by fortnightly plane. He now intended to build himself a bigger and better set—provided the government didn't cancel the plane to San José, which he feared it might. After his long story about the stone he fell silent, apparently deep in thought. The only sound, apart from the radio, was the slapping of his hand as he automatically crushed the mosquitoes that settled on his bare arms. We sat there quietly enjoying our beer.

"Well," inquired D. after a while, "are you going to look for the stone, or aren't you? If you are, then go tomorrow. I'm going back to Chafurray with the government canoe, and as you'd probably be away three or four days, your friend and your baggage would be here when you got back. So you'd really lose no time."

The next day we went off up the Guaviare making for the Guayabero and the rapids near which the famous stone was allegedly to be seen. Two Indians accompanied us, nameless, gloomy fellows who stopped paddling only to swallow a few handfuls of cassava flour from time to time. Pierre, Luis, and I looked at each, while one by one the enchanted forest scenes slid away behind us. We were all engrossed with the same thought: we had suddenly changed a carefully thought out itinerary merely on the strength of some local chatter at San José del Guaviare. We ought to have been using the time to fetch Jean and our baggage. We had a five-hundred-mile journey down the Guaviare ahead of us, and if we lost too much time the rainy season would bar our passage of the Mapiripán Rapids. Mapiripán had become legendary. It was reputed to be the home of Indian cannibals. No one had ever seen them but everyone knew all about them. Mapiripán was the center of the unknown Guaviare. And instead of pressing on toward our objective, here we were, practically without baggage, in a ramshackle canoe without a motor, manned by two surly Indians we had seen for the first time only the day before, chasing after mythical treasure. . . .

I remembered something I had read in a book while we were in Bogotá:

"From San Martín to Guaviare there is a good deal of talk about the existence of remains identifying a great highway which is thought to have stretched from Peru across the Upper Ariari and the Eastern Cordilleras to the plateau of Bogotá. It is supposed that Indians came from Peru with their llamas as far as the Ariari, where they loaded them with gold, returning with the precious metal to decorate the palace of the Inca."

For all *llaneros* this mythical gold is like the proverbial carrot to the donkey. They live their comfortless lives day after day and year after year in their windswept wilderness, and all the time they are sustained and encouraged by the secret hope that one day they will stumble on the *guaca,* the Inca treasure of gold pieces, statues and bars that lies hidden somewhere under their feet. The treasure of the Incas consisted mainly of gold. It was the venom and at the same time the stimulus of the Spanish conquest. Today, four centuries after Columbus, it is a fantasy which lives on in the minds of those South Americans who venture beyond the main roads and the towns. Incidentally, *guaca* is a word as old as the Spanish conquest. Originally it did not mean treasure at all, but grave, or tomb, and the confusion arose from the search for buried treasure. *Guaquero,* someone who searches tombs for treasure, an excavator of treasure, is derived from *guaca.* Everyone in the Cordilleras of the Andes from Peru to the Caribbean Sea, everyone in the llano and in the forest, is something of a *guaquero.*

As we traveled up stream in our canoe, making for the Guayabero rapids, Luis, Pierre, and I were busy with such thoughts. We looked at each other doubtfully from time to time, and although we said nothing we knew exactly what was exercising the others.

Is this *guaca* business contagious? Do you succumb to its fatal influence without even noticing it? Was it possible that during the few days we had spent in the llano we had been bitten by some invisible bug as a man is stung by the anopheles mosquito and contracts malaria? Had we contracted guaquerism, so to speak—the pathological urge to search for buried treasure? After eight months of careful planning and scheming, and after only eight days of practical operations, here we were: going up river when we ought to be going down.

Up to the mouth of the Ariari we had been taken in tow by the *canoa del gobierno,* an enormous vessel by our present standards. It measured at least forty-five feet from stem to stern and over five feet across its central beam. It could easily hold five tons of cargo. The wretched little Indian canoe, hollowed out of a tree trunk by fire, in which we were now going off on our wild-goose chase, had cast loose from the bigger vessel at the confluence of the Ariari and the Guayabero to turn to the left and make its way up the latter river by paddling. The *canoa del gobierno,* in charge of Corporal Nepo and powered by our outboard motor, had disappeared to the right in the direction of Chafurray. In the bottom of our canoe between us and the Indians was our equipment: sticks of dynamite, shovels, picks, and ropes.

CORPORAL NEPO

While in San José we slept in the house of Don Jesus, the man of science, but we ate in the house of the next in importance in the village, the same Corporal Nepo who was now on his way to Chafurray. During dinner the previous day he had given us a brief sketch of his life. He had first come to the forest at the age of twenty as a soldier in the war between Colombia and Peru. The campaign was tough; only a fearless and robust man could have hoped to survive. Nepo was sent to the Rio Putumayo, the bone of contention between the two countries. Now the maps show it as the boundary line between the two countries. Then it was a disputed river running through the thickest and most pestilential forest in the whole Amazon area. Most of the soldiers who perished there did not die of bullets, but of starvation, mosquitoes, exhaustion, and the forest itself. But while Nepo was there his weight increased from 150 to 190 pounds. He became the man who blazed the trail, carried despatches through the forest, obtained information about the enemy's movements from the Indians, and, finally, the man who remained on the Putumayo when the war was over. He was made a corporal and put in charge of a frontier post somewhere on the imaginary line separating Colombia from Brazil.

After a while he abandoned his public functions, and, gliding from river to river in his canoe, he ended up in San José, where he built himself a house. While continuing to hunt the jaguar, the tapir, and the antelope, he decided to search for the famous blue stone of legend. He had never seen such a thing, but an old Indian had told him about it. He knew neither what it was nor where it could be found, but he did know that it was as blue as a bluebird. He also knew that when the Americans were still looking for rubber in the forest, one of their drivers flung up his job and returned to town because he had been fortunate enough to buy such a blue stone another old Indian had just found.

So without saying a word to a soul he laid his plans and gaily tolerated the boredom of his waiting life until they should materialize. We were the first to whom he had even mentioned the matter, but, there, we were "scientists," and that was different. In the meantime he had acquired various treasures which made his life sweeter. There was a phonograph with records, a big matchet, a blunderbuss for which he had made himself a new butt, and a powder horn. And over his bed hung his corporal's saber with its Solingen blade and its bronze handle. It gleamed there like a fixed star to remind the world of his adventures. And, above all, there was his little Brazilian wife, and she sang and laughed all day long much as a bird sings and cheeps. Negro blood sparkled in her eyes and put rhythm in her walk. In her flowered cotton dress she looked like some strange flower herself, and when she passed she left a warm and strangely attractive odor in her wake. She was a rare vision of gaiety in a country which is either sad or impressive as solitude is impressive. Her name was Lilia and she had been born and bred in Rio, so she knew the sea, the casinos, the big moving picture houses, and the department stores. She chattered away in the liveliest fashion and she danced the samba.

"Ah, monsieur!" Nepo said to me. "I just must find the blue stone because this really isn't the life for Lilia."

And in his house, seated at his table, made from the trees he had cut down and worked himself, Nepo would affectionately call her his little lady, and she would potter around in her kitchen, poking gentle fun at her big husband who liked to talk so much and who had once been a soldier.

It was four hours since we had left Nepo and the big canoe at the confluence of the Ariari and the Guayabero. Despite the steady paddling of our two Indians we were making only very slow progress. The force of the current against which we were advancing was growing stronger every minute. We were approaching the rapids. And then as we turned a bend we saw the river hemmed in between two walls of high rock with the forest on either side. It rushed toward us violently, boiling and roaring. The two Indians quickly turned the canoe into a little creek which offered shelter from the swirling waters and there we climbed out onto the bank at a spot where a path disappeared into the forest. We had arrived.

But it was nearly nightfall and there was no question of starting our exploration until the following day, so we quickly slung our hammocks and adjusted our mosquito nets while the Indians lighted a fire. Its smoke protected us a little from the attentions of the mosquitoes which were already dancing around our heads. Night fell, and after we had each eaten a calabash of cassava flour made into a porridge with river water—all the provision we had with us because our equipment and stores had not yet arrived—we retired one by one into the shelter of our mosquito nets and went to sleep, our minds full of long lines of llamas bearing gold, piles of blue stones, and dancing will-o'-the-wisps.

THE ROCK PAINTINGS OF GUAYABERO

It took us ten hours of difficult going through the spongy forest and over rocks covered with moss and mold, where each step was a hazard. But at about five in the evening we were rewarded, and all our tiredness disappeared as though by magic. For hours the forest had been steadily rising toward the sky, which we could see from time to time in blue or white rents above us through the interlaced branches of the trees. Then suddenly the forest opened out to a great, flat, rocky plateau split all around like an iceberg with cracks which we had to jump one after the other as we went forward. To the north the plateau ceased suddenly at a canyon from whose somber depths rose the tremendous thunder of the boiling river. To the west it swept up to a hill perhaps six hundred feet high, where the forest began again, separated from the sky by a narrow white line along its ridge. Once we had climbed up the last hill through the undergrowth, the thin white line above our heads developed into a cliff of startling whiteness more than a hundred yards long and perhaps ninety feet high. Its whole surface was covered with drawings of animals and human beings and red symbols in one vast petrified saraband. This was it.

How long had this great book of pictures been there open to the silent sky and seen only by the birds of the heavens and the beasts of the forest? For hundreds of years certainly, and perhaps thousands.

As I sit and write this book I can see again the exact moment when we arrived at the scene. We were wet with sweat from our exertions, and our faces and hands were scratched and our clothing torn from our struggle through the thick forest. We looked at the rock face and we just sat down, and for about an hour no one spoke. We studied the drawings one after the other. The red pigment of some of them looked as fresh and brilliant as though they had been made only yesterday. Others again were partly

effaced so that they were now little more than rose-colored shadows running over the rock face.

Who? When? How? The questions went round and round in our heads. Some of the drawings were at a convenient height for a man standing at the foot of the great rock, but others—six or eight feet across—were high up, perhaps seventy-five feet above our heads, drawn on a vertical rock face too difficult for even an experienced Alpinist to climb.

We camped at the foot of the rock and for twenty-four hours we eagerly discussed our find, mentally comparing the drawings with the prehistoric inscriptions at Altamira and Lascaux, with the rock drawings in the Hoggar Mountains and in South Africa, with Indian paintings, and with the drawings in the Cordilleras of the Andes, along the Rio Negro, the Casiquiare Canal, and the Orinoco as described by travelers through the Amazon from Humboldt to Spruce, and from Spruce to Koch-Grünberg. Beyond all doubt there was a relationship between them. From time to time one of us would draw a comparison between this or that detail of the drawings before our eyes and those we knew about from the reports of others. But as the hours passed we were persuaded more and more to the conclusion that we had come upon something quite new and completely original in the history of primitive man's art.

Some of the drawings which appeared of more recent origin were purely abstract and geometrical in design. Perhaps they originated in a historically transitional epoch from ultra-stylized design to the dawn of writing. Most of the others above which these were painted represented a tangled mass of animal and human forms more or less freely interpreted. The attention of all three of us was caught by a representation of two big animals in the center of a large expanse of rock face. Our Indian guides, who had immediately recognized the drawings of turtles, cayman alligators, and peccaries which ran along the rock face in a frieze, were silent before these two and quite unable to offer any suggestion as to what they might represent, because they were so different from any of the usual fauna of the lowlands of equatorial America. Because of the characteristic shape of the heads,

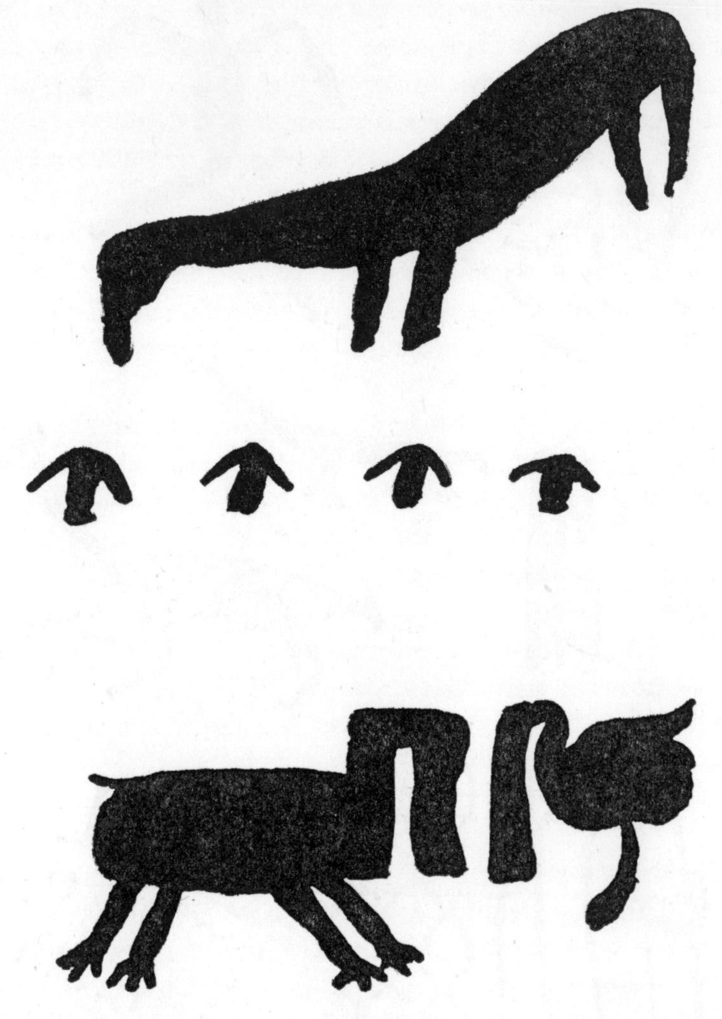

the tails, and the lower part of the legs, we guessed that they might be llamas. But the only llamas had been on the Andean plateaus of Peru a thousand miles and more away. And then we suddenly thought of the famous golden road along which the Incas were supposed to have carried their treasures of gold and precious stones in caravans of llamas from the Chibchas and Quimbayas of Colombia.

Perhaps we were in the presence of the first tangible proof of the existence of such a road? Therc was no reason to doubt that it passed along the upper reaches of the Guayabero, since, according to legend, it went to the source of the Ariari. The lowland tribes, who had made these drawings long before the days of Christopher Columbus, might well have seen the llamas of the rulers of Peru and then incorporated such fabulous creatures in their rock drawings together with other more or less mythological images.

We were all in agreement that we should pitch our camp at the base of the rock face and stay there long enough to make a detailed study of our marvelous find, so that we could take back the fullest possible documentation and a color film of the rock face itself.

A week later, after Jean and our baggage had arrived safely from Chafurray, the complete Orinoco-Amazon expedition set off for the white rock face of Guayabero to study and film the drawings. Close examination reinforced our original impression that we had really come across a discovery quite valuable enough to justify all the delay it was going to involve for us, though the *llaneros* did not share our enthusiasm. No will-o'-the-wisp ever danced above our rock, and we saw no trace of gold apart from the reflection of the sun in this or that detail of the paintings.

THE FILM, AND AN INCAN REMEDY

The rainy season advanced, and the work on the rock paintings of Guayabero became more and more difficult. At first it rained only for perhaps an hour a day, but nevertheless the day on which we had an hour of sunshine in which we could take films was rare. The atmosphere of the forest was now saturated with moisture, and if we happened to leave any leather object uncovered during the night, we found it green with mildew the next morning. It was not long before we noticed that the climate was attacking our health as well as our equipment. The forest became more hostile and dangerous to us every day, but gradually we served our apprenticeship to its rigors. We could not stay more than five or six days at a time at the foot of the rock, and every week we had to return to San José to rest, sleeping in the house of Don Jesus and taking our meals with Nepo and his wife. A plate of soup and a glass of lemonade sweetened with thick muscovado seemed more and more wonderful to us each time we returned, and in the evenings we listened with serenity to the chatter of Nepo and the grinding radio of Don Jesus. And then one morning early Jean, who was not only the cameraman but also the mechanic of the expedition, would rip the cord of our little outboard motor vigorously and we would start off in the canoe with our two Indians for the third, the fourth, and the fifth time to go up the Guaviare and the Guayabero.

At the beginning of July our troubles really started. We had almost completed the film. We were at San José again, and we reckoned that a last journey to the rock face and a few more days there would provide us with all we needed to complete our record. After that we could make arrangements to continue our expedition, to obtain the canoes and hire the men we should require to take us over the five hundred miles which separated us from the Orinoco. We began to make our inquiries, and although at first no one said definitely no, no one said yes. Gradually as the days passed it became more and more clear that we were to be left to our own resources; no one was willing to accompany us on the adventure we had in mind. The thought of Mapiripán intimidated everyone. No one was willing to take the risk, and certainly not during the rainy season. At the same time it was also quite clear that we could not undertake the hazardous voyage alone. We had too much fragile equipment, essential for the expedition, to risk it on our own. After all, we had had very little experience in forest and river navigation.

And then Pierre fell ill. One morning he woke up with a fever and found that he could hardly walk. His right leg was stiff and there was a swelling in the groin. We decided to ask the authorities in Bogotá to let us have a plane in which we could fly over the Mapiripán zone. The following Sunday, Luis, who was the Colombian member of our expedition, flew to the capital in the plane which maintained a fortnightly service between San José and Bogotá. There was a military radio station at San José and every day we anxiously awaited a reply. In the meantime Pierre's condition grew worse. There was no obvious local center of infection, but now he was confined to his hammock. The fever grew more and more severe and he was already half delirious. In the night we would hear him groaning aloud in pain.

At last Luis's message arrived: "Impossible obtain hydroplane. Hope get DC3 for Carimagua in llano. From there could descend Vichada to Orinoco. Hope give you definite rendezvous within week."

That was disappointing. It would mean that we should have to travel two hundred and fifty miles or so to the north again before being able to turn east to reach the Orinoco. The Rio Vichada was much better known than the Guaviare, and it had the great advantage of being navigable throughout its entire length. At least that meant that we could be sure of reaching the Orinoco under our own steam in the end. But it also meant that we should have to abandon in part our intention of penetrating into the mysterious unknown. However, as against that, we should arrive sooner at our real jumping-off ground for the most important stage of our expedition, which was the crossing of the Sierra Parima from Venezuela to Brazil. I therefore sent off a message to Luis agreeing to his proposal, and then we waited again for days. Poor Pierre's right groin was now swollen up like an apple, but there was still no clearly defined abscess.

When the next regular plane touched down on the little airfield, a mere clearing in the forest, three strange figures descended from it. At first it was not easy to discover whether they were men or women, for they wore their glossy black hair long, and round their necks was a vast number of assorted necklaces of blue glass. Each man—as it turned out, they were men—wore a voluminous overcoat of dark blue linen with white stripes. They were barefoot and they moved with great dignity. The noble features of their beardless and bronzed faces were reminiscent of the anthropomorphic pictures on certain Peruvian vases. They wore soft felt hats which had been much used, and each man carried a small painted metal case in his left hand.

"We are Incas," they informed us serenely, and the astonished villagers parted respectfully to let them through.

They established themselves in a deserted hut a little way

outside the village on the edge of the airfield, and when they heard of our presence they came to pay us their respects as from one group of travelers to another.

We offered them cigarettes, and the handsomest of them, who also appeared to be their chief, began to speak in impeccable Spanish.

"We are traveling to improve our minds," he said. "Every year our chief sends out young men to travel through the world. We have just come from Villavicencio and we propose to go on to Brazil, since these parts do not seem to be of any very great interest. Next year we shall go home for the Feast of the Nativity. We come from Sibundoy in the Cordilleras of the Andes near the frontier of Ecuador. We have already visited that little republic, which, of course, once belonged to our ancestors, as also, incidentally, did a great part of Colombia. We have also been to Central America, which we found very beautiful."

I was wondering what these noble travelers lived on, when their leader turned his head and noticed Pierre in his hammock.

"Your friend is unwell?" he inquired, and he rose and went over to Pierre, who groaned.

My affirmative reply immediately aroused the interest of the other two strangers, who also rose and followed their chief over to Pierre's hammock.

"He has fever," they said at once. "He needs attention."

And as Jean and I nodded, their leader went on:

"He is very ill. Would you care for me to treat him with our Indian remedies?" and he nodded toward the little painted metal case he had put down at his feet. Pierre was in agreement. He raised himself on his elbow.

"Let him try," he said. "I don't suppose he'll do any harm, and you never know."

"Are you sure you can cure him?" I asked.

The Inca bent down and opened his case, taking out a little round jar full of a brownish ointment which smelt strongly of resin.

"This is the remedy," he said. "It draws out the evil. By suction, you understand?"

"All right," I agreed. "Get on with it."

"First of all I should like to know what you are prepared to pay," he said politely but firmly.

"How much do you want?"

"To cure him of that fever is worth ten pesos."

His tariff was the same as that of Bogotá doctors, and I began to understand what the travelers from Sibundoy lived on.

"Very well," I said. "Treat him, but I won't pay you until after the cure."

"Monsieur, this ointment is made from a very rare herb which grows only in the Putumayo. We get it from our cacique, that is to say, our chief," he explained amiably. "We have only this one pot. Other remedies might bring about a partial improvement, but the trouble would subsequently return. This ointment is the only thing which will get rid of the trouble once and for all. If you are not fully confident, then give me five pesos now and the other five when he is cured."

This I agreed to do. Tearing a piece out of a newspaper which was lying on the table he went over and sat by Pierre. He spread a little of the ointment on the paper and heated it up for a moment or two with a lighted match. When he was satisfied with the temperature, he applied the strange plaster to Pierre's right groin with great dexterity.

"So far so good," he declared, rising. "That will draw out the evil. I will return tomorrow."

Picking up his case, he took leave with great dignity, followed by his two companions.

Pierre called out to me in the night. I found him dripping with sweat, and the fever had definitely subsided.

"It's working," he said with relief.

I examined his groin in the light of my electric torch. The abscess had burst and the plaster of our Incan doctor was soaked in pus. A great deal more was oozing out. Pierre was already much better, and after that he slept soundly until daylight. Our Sibundoy doctor appeared at eight o'clock in the morning, his little case in his hand. Having politely wished us good morning, he sat down at the side of his patient.

He removed the bandage I had put on in the night and examined the abscess.

"Now we must get out all the evil that still remains," he said. "For that I need tobacco poison."

At first I didn't understand what he meant, but he looked round the room, spotted my pipe lying on the table, and pounced on it delightedly. Unscrewing the mouthpiece, he carefully smeared the tobacco juice on to another piece of newspaper. My pipe was very dirty and the dottle was soaked with tobacco juice, but to judge from the expression of our Indian doctor, the dirtier the better.

"Why didn't *you* think of that?" asked Pierre sardonically.

Another little pot was produced from the case. This time it contained green powder, and our doctor mixed a pinch of it with the tobacco juice, warmed up the piece of newspaper as he had done before, and once again placed it expertly on what remained of the abscess. That concluded the treatment for the time being and off he went. The curious mixture seemed to act as a very efficient cupping glass and a few hours later the abscess again discharged pus in large quantities. At the same time the inflammation disappeared and the fever declined still further.

Two days later a plane landed at San José and we thought that a little penicillin might complete the cure, so Pierre, who could already get about again, was flown off to Bogotá and I handed over the second five pesos to the doctor from Sibundoy to complete his honorarium.

We reckoned that we should have to wait another fortnight at San José before the promised plane and our two companions arrived to pick us up, so we had time to go once more to the rock face to take the last shots we needed to complete our picture. Just before we were ready to go I went to the hut of the two Indians who had accompanied us on all our previous trips. They were lying in their hammocks and made no attempt to get up when I came in. A muttered growl was all the reply I got to my greeting.

"Come on, boys," I said. "Get up. We're off to the rock drawings again."

To this there was no reply at all. I said it again, but with no more success. Then I went up to the nearest hammock and shook it.

"What's the matter? Didn't you hear me?"

There was a renewed muttering.

"Well, are you coming or not?"

More muttering.

"Don't you want to come?"

This time the muttering was distinguishable as a refusal.

"Why don't you want to come along?" I asked.

"Because we've done enough work," a dolorous voice replied, and then, apparently worn out by the effort, the fellow rolled over and went off to sleep.

I realized that I was going to get nowhere with them, so I gave up. No doubt the two had decided that they had now earned enough money for a while from their work with us, and there was nothing further to be got out of them. Jean and I then scoured the village hastily to see if we could mobilize replacements. However, for some days it had been raining steadily and the river had risen by about three feet. In such weather no one was willing to "go into the hills," and it soon became clear to us that if we wanted to go we should have to go alone.

We went alone. We got there all right, but the weather was so bad that it took us a week to get the few shots we still needed. The rain thrashed down and robbed everything of shape and form. There were hours, and even days, when we were able to do nothing at all. All the birds and the animals of the forest had fled to some invisible retreat away from the rain and so there was nothing to hunt. The only living things left with us were mosquitoes, flies, and a great variety of other insects, and they were all anxious to shelter under the roof of our tent so that we had to take refuge in our mosquito nets. Even our state of mind seemed to have gone soggy and the rain washed away the urgency we had originally felt. The world was now nothing but an enormous cloud of vapor, and we sat in the middle of it and dozed apathetically while the rain pelted down on our tent like the incessant rolling of a drum.

But the moment it stopped we would jump up, seize our camera, and rush off to take advantage of the short truce, never knowing how long it would last. In this way we would shoot a few more feet of film at a time. Sometimes we had an hour or two in which there was no rain, sometimes only ten minutes or a quarter of an hour.

It was impossible to hunt anything to supplement our food, and we got used to living with a disagreeable feeling of emptiness in our stomachs, which, from time to time, we tried to deceive with a little cassava porridge, and, once a day only, because we had to economize, a bowl of chocolate with condensed milk. Apart from us there seemed to be not a living human being left in the world—except a palm-bear, quite a big one to judge by the size of the prints he left behind.

We never caught sight of the beast, but every day he prowled around our camp. He seemed to be playing hide and seek with us. He would follow our tracks from the camp to the rock face and back again, strewing fragments of chewed nuts along his path as though to invite us to take part in a sort of paper-chase. I accepted the invitation and for hours I stalked him with beating heart and a loaded rifle in my hands, but to no purpose. He was more cunning than I was.

WE HUNT THE TAPIR AND THE ARMADILLO

When we got back to San José there was still no news of our two companions. The weather chose just this time to improve out of all knowledge and for a few days there was a sky every bit as clear and blue as during the dry season. When we told Nepo of our misadventures at our last camp, and the story of the bear, he suggested that we should go on a trip with him to a rocky savanna about a day's journey to the south of San José where he grazed the few head of cattle he possessed. Some people said there were drawings on the rocks in those parts too. Perhaps we could supplement our Guayabero discoveries there, but even if we proved unlucky at least he could promise us some good hunting as a consolation. Within twenty-four hours he had organized this new trip, and we set off with him and far more equipment than we were used to. There were three Indians and Nepo had an old and feeble horse that had to be led but which served at least as a pack animal. This saved us the trouble of carrying about a couple of hundred pounds of equipment on our backs, as we usually did.

At the last moment another inhabitant of San José decided to join us. It was the police sergeant Garcia with his impressive peaked khaki hat. Garcia owned two horses and we proposed to take the second, but the poor beast turned out to be in such a state of emaciation that we much preferred to walk. In the end we arranged to move off in two groups, the one consisting of Nepo, Jean, and the Indians, and the other, the "mounted" group, of Garcia and me. We were to meet that evening at a grotto both Garcia and Nepo knew and pitch our camp there.

A few hours later I was making my way on horseback at Garcia's side, sometimes at a walking pace and sometimes at a painful little trot, and as we went Garcia, who was feeling very pleased with himself, treated me to a running fire of commentary on the beauties of the countryside through which we were passing. At first it was sparse savanna with bushes here and there, and then there was a wood with a bridle path wide enough for our two horses. Garcia had brought four dogs along, and they were going forward ahead of us. Suddenly they raised their heads and sniffed. Obviously they had got wind of something, for they all dashed off into the forest.

"We'll pull up and wait for them," Garcia said, and we did.

For a minute or two there was silence, and then in the distance we heard them giving tongue hysterically. Garcia listened carefully, then he shook up his nag and moved on.

"They've raised a band of monkeys," he said. "It's not worth the trouble of getting your clothes torn in the forest. We'll go on."

As we jogged along I asked him how he had guessed that it was monkeys. He smiled.

"I didn't guess," he replied. "The dogs told me so themselves. When they give tongue so shrilly and with short pauses in between you can be fairly sure it's nothing very dangerous. Something in the tone tells you they're after game beyond their reach, probably jumping through the trees. They get hysterical because they can't follow. So you know it's probably monkeys. If it is a tiger their baying is very different, no longer so high pitched for instance. They lower their heads and go forward almost on their bellies. And they growl rather than bark. They've whiffed blood and they're afraid and so they sound savage."

Apparently the dogs understood that we were not interested in monkeys, and after a while their barking ceased altogether. For half an hour after that we ambled on our way in silence, each of us occupied with his own thoughts. I was thinking of the wretched forest dogs. They were so emaciated that their ribs stuck out like those of an umbrella. They looked so miserable that at home you would have taken them for masterless, half-starving curs, but here they were prepared to raise and hunt jaguars, though to see monkeys springing from branch to branch made them behave like hysterical women.

After a while they began to give tongue again. Then they crossed the path ahead of us at full pelt, baying in sustained chorus.

"Oho! They've probably got a peccary there," said Garcia, and when we came up he sprang down from his horse and went into the thicket while I tethered our nags at the side of the path. He called me and I ran after him and found him planting a fence of twigs across the entrance to a large burrow. The four dogs were standing a little distance away, their tails stiff in the air, their heads to one side. Then suddenly, barking loudly, they plunged toward another entrance to the earth.

"It's a cerillo," said Garcia, "a smaller kind of peccary. It lives in burrows like a rabbit. It's better eating than a peccary. Stand near the bolt hole and I'll go to the other hole and drive it out to you. You've only got to fire point blank when it makes a dash toward you."

He went over to where his dogs were besieging the other entrance to the earth, and cutting a big branch thick with foliage, he inserted it into the entrance and shook it violently. I heard dull sounds from inside the burrow, and then suddenly the trelliswork of twigs across the hole began to shake violently. As the animal bolted I caught sight of an open red mouth and enormous canines. I fired point blank as instructed without even raising the gun to my shoulder. The beast fell back into the hole, dropped in its tracks. The dogs had rushed round to my side, and after my shot their barking rose shrilly, the four voices mingling into one long drawn out high-pitched howl as though they were about to go into hysterics. When the smoke of the explosion had cleared away, the most courageous of the four plunged into the earth. With its four legs set firmly wide apart and its spine arched, the dog sunk its teeth into the dead peccary and began laboriously to drag it out of the earth, inch by inch. The other dogs joined in and before long had pulled the whole body out into the open. It was covered with black earth. The dogs were beside themselves with delight and began to ravage the dead body, sinking their teeth into the throat, the ears, and the belly until Garcia drove them off with vigorous kicks.

We cleaned the dead beast at a stream and laid its body by the side of the path while we attended to our horses. I happened to notice the most excitable of the dogs, the one which had first plunged into the earth after the peccary: it was now lying down quite calmly by the side of the carcass. It was no longer barking, but with long movements of its head was licking the carcass and smoothing the hairs much as a cat licks its kitten.

We started off and before long were once again in the savanna. Straight ahead of us it ended in a dark blue line which grew larger and larger as we approached. It was the edge of the forest, and here and there the blue was interrupted by masses of white and grey. These were the rocks where we were to meet the others. The sun was already low in the sky, and as we went forward we began to distinguish a column of smoke which rose from the foot of one of the rocks. It was the camp fire of our companions, who had arrived ahead of us. The place was known as the Lindosa, which means, more or less, the beautiful, and it was well named. As far as the eye could see it was a collection of grey rocks lying between the blue forest on one side and the savanna, rising like a gold-flecked carpet to the sky, on the other.

For hundreds of years the force of erosion had patiently

worked on this wilderness to turn it even in its details into a gigantic mirage of stone. It was a triumph of the theatrical, a scenic illusion, like magic dust strewn in the eyes. The first thing I thought to see rearing up against the forest was a fantastic barbaric palace, its façade broken by a thousand windows and gateways, and decorated with gangways, sculptured balconies, and fretted galleries. It was crowned by a forest of towers, turrets, and belfries, some pointed, others rounded, while still others spiralled in a great upward proliferation like the dancing flames of a fire suddenly stilled. Great avenues of green foliage converged toward its base, enchased between perpendicular walls, straight as sword strokes and ornamented here and there with sculptured groups, vases of stone, and petrified spinneys that might have been shaped by the gardener of the Great Khan himself.

But a few steps further the whole scene faded like a dream, the lines dissolved and broke up, and all that was left was a collection of worn rocks, a chaos of natural ruins pitted with holes and broken with fissures. Under my horse's feet the beautiful sward of the avenues had given way to a grey expanse dotted here and there with small tufts of green herbage.

Our companions had pitched their camp at the end of one of these avenues in a large fissure sweating with moisture, which penetrated deep into the castle of stone. The Indians had made a great fire of brushwood at the entrance, and the smoke and flames prevented the mosquitoes from getting into the rocky retreat. We slept on the ground on dried grass which had already been strewn along the rock face for us. Despite the fire at the entrance we had to set up our mosquito nets because above our heads hung hundreds of motionless little vampire bats all clustered together. At night they awoke and, but for the mosquito netting, they would certainly have taken advantage of our slumber to tap our veins.

Above our improvised beds the rock face was pierced with the openings of other galleries running in all directions around the fissure in which we camped. While our Indians flayed and prepared the peccary for supper we were unable to resist the temptation to explore the place. Each of us took a torch and we made our way into the first of the many natural corridors. Apart from the monotonous splash of dripping water as it fell to the ground, the silence was complete. Disturbed by the light of our torches the vampire bats awoke, one by one, and retreated further into the darkness as we advanced. Sand and gravel crunched under our feet and our voices sounded strangely hollow. Nepo was a little ahead of us, ferreting around, when he called us. We found him shining his torch into a niche in the wall which was full of sand and dried foliage. It was like a large nest and the imprint of some heavy body was clearly visible.

"The lair of a jaguar," he said.

A little farther on the corridor suddenly debouched into the open. It was a clearing entirely surrounded by rocks, and there on the ground was another hollow in the ground, larger and deeper than the jaguar's lair. Nepo, who was still ahead of us, was examining it on all fours.

"It's a tapir's hole," he shouted enthusiastically.

I was advancing more slowly, carefully examining the walls foot by foot in the hope of coming across some sign of human origin, but I could find nothing. And yet this wonderful site seemed admirably suited as an inspiration to the natives who had decorated the great rock face of Guayabero, thirty miles or so away. It was only later when we were almost back to our camp again that I discovered what I was seeking. On the face of a natural chimney in the rock, at the back of a sort of crypt into which we had crept on hands and knees, there were two red silhouettes, one behind the other, raising their arms in adoration to a blurred and half effaced representation of the sun.

Seated in a semicircle around the fire we made a good meal of the peccary stew the Indians had prepared for us. Jean and I were discussing plans for our exploration the next day when Nepo, whose mind was full of tigers and tapirs, discarded a bone which he had been chewing. Tossing it to the wretched yellow, four-legged beast which had been growling behind him in the shadows, he exclaimed enthusiastically:

"We'll go out hunting straight away. Hurry up. I'm going to

show you how to kill a tapir by torchlight, and you'll see what a formidable brute it is."

A quarter of an hour later we were on our way, walking Indian file. I was just behind Nepo, a torch in one hand and my rifle in the other. Behind me came Jean armed with cameras and flashlights. We were excited at the thought of making a sensational coup. The dogs trotted around us, their noses sniffing the air or lowered to the grass, trying to distinguish the mixture of scents floating in the night. Nepo led us confidently along a winding path which went sometimes over the savanna and sometimes through the forest. He rounded his lips and whistled to attract the tapirs. But no tapirs were attracted. It was very wet and the ground was soaking. They had probably gone to higher ground where it was dryer. Every time we tramped through undergrowth we felt as though we were treading on piles of sponges. The mosquitoes were ever present, swarming around us insistently from the beginning to the end of the expedition. There were so many of them and they were so famished that they stung me not only through hair and beard, but also through shirt and trousers. We went on for two hours without a single incident to encourage us and break the monotony.

"It looks as though we're not going to find any tapirs," conceded Nepo. "They must have gone somewhere else."

But at last, while we were making our way along the edge of a thicket, the dogs disappeared. We heard a chorus of baying which gradually mounted to a shrill pitch of excitement. I remembered what Garcia had said to me earlier. It seemed a good occasion for me to demonstrate my new-found knowledge.

"Cerillo," I said to Nepo.

"No," he replied confidently. "Armadillo."

With that he lumbered off into the forest, insinuating his large body through the thicket with surprising agility. I had difficulty in following him, while Jean tried to keep up with us and at the same time to protect his apparatus with his arms. He swore as the branches tore his flesh. The tatu or armadillo lives in a burrow like the cerillo, so I had not been very far wrong. We came up with the dogs. There were six of them and they had their heads and forequarters buried in the earth. As their tails wagged furiously among the leaves, their forelegs worked away vigorously, throwing out a great rain of soft earth. Nepo immediately joined them and began to work away with his matchet to assist in the digging. He thrust his arm into the earth, withdrew it, and put his ear to the hole. Then he dug in again with his matchet to enlarge the hole. He thrust his arm in again, and withdrew it. This went on for about a quarter of an hour, during which the furious barking of the dogs and Nepo's own impatience grew steadily. The rest of us stood around and watched. Jean was calm but alert, the model press photographer, camera ready in one hand and flash bulb in the other. It was no easy thing to stand there motionless, because the mosquitoes seemed to have called out their last reserves to deal with us while we were so conveniently still. I puffed away furiously at a cigarette in the hope that the smoke would drive them away. At last we could hear scraping and scuffling from the burrow, then Nepo's voice shouting.

"Look out now!" and as he rose to his knees he dragged something black and kicking out of the hole by its tail. The flash of Jean's bulb surprised it at the entrance to its hole, like a minister emerging from a parliamentary assembly, just at the moment when Nepo killed it with a blow of his matchet.

The fauna of the American equatorial forest is strange and peculiar, and the armadillo is certainly one of the strangest of all animals. It is a rodent, a sort of black rat about the size of a rabbit, but the whole of its body from head to tail is covered with a light greyish armor of small scales. It looks as though it were wearing chain mail. This carapace is rigid over the shoulders and the hindquarters and articulated in the middle like the joint of two railway coaches. This armor accounts for its Spanish name *el armadillo,* which can be freely translated as "the armored little fellow."

After that hunting expedition, which was not as exciting as we had hoped, but quite useful all the same, because, as Nepo said, the armadillo eats as good as any pullet, we returned to our camp and I stretched myself out under my mosquito net. A natural gutter, like a gargoyle on the imaginary palace, discharged its monotonous drips near me. I had lost the habit of sleeping flat on the ground and it was some time before I could drop off. Fabulous images passed before my mind's eye, and I saw the rocks of Lindosa reawaken and form themselves once again into that barbaric palace, while tame jaguars and panthers padded through its courtyards. I thought of the vampire bats zigzagging to and fro above the heads of sleeping men, and I imagined one coming to a halt abruptly against the wall above the head of its chosen victim. Waiting until the man's breath became regular, it would drop in silence to his feet, waving its wings to the rhythm of his breathing. Perched there for a while, at last the bat would lower its head and bury its beak in the tender flesh and begin to suck the blood, its wings still beating rhythmically. It is said that this rhythmic movement keeps the sleeper motionless until the vampire's thirst is quenched.

The vampire bat has given rise to many legends among the Indians. One of them concerns a man, half-god, with a dark blue skin, who descends noiselessly on the woman he wishes to possess and, by waving the two wings which render him invisible, wafts her away into sweet dreams while he has his will with her. When she awakes she remembers nothing of what has happened to her, but in her womb a child with a dark-blue leathery skin is growing.

Then all these pictures vanished, giving place to the captured armadillo, flung on its back by Nepo's powerful hands, its head split with his matchet in the light of my torch. It contracted in a final spasm as I watched it, and dung dropped to the ground. Immediately a dog rushed forward, spread the dung out with its paw, and rubbed it first over shoulders and neck and then over its whole body.

Pierre had once been a member of another expedition, in Africa, and he had seen how the pygmies hunt elephants. He had been describing it to me only a little while before.

"They follow the spoor of elephants until they find fresh droppings. Then they carefully rub the dung over their whole bodies. They hunt stark naked, of course. Now an elephant is very shortsighted, but as against that its sense of smell is extraordinarily keen. However, thanks to this ruse, when the pygmies come up with the herd they can get under an elephant without its scenting them, and then they thrust their spears up into its soft belly."

There was a clear parallel between the ruse of the pygmies in the African forest and the behavior of my dream dog. Both savages and animals are moved by instincts we civilized beings have lost. We do not belong, rather we no longer belong, to the primeval world, the twilight world of the dense forest.

At last ideas and pictures grew confused in my head and I fell off to sleep. For a long time it seemed to me that the silence all around was absolute, apart from the noise of the water falling from the stone roof. Half asleep I heard a different sound, a sort of muffled nibbling not far away. It awoke me with a shock and I started up. Now the sound filled the whole grotto. It was a sort of steady scraping noise and it was coming slowly nearer. Someone sprang to his feet and at the same time a light went on. The voice of Nepo sounded:

"Ants!" he shouted.

I too sprang up and got out of my mosquito net, torch in hand. I directed it over the ground. An army of red ants was approaching from the depths of the gallery in a column about sixteen inches across, and as it advanced it made a noise like the humming of a factory. The ants had already eaten my handkerchief, my belt and half my trousers, which I had left on the ground beside my mosquito net. They had also attacked the leather case of our camera. There was nothing to do but collect our things and retreat. Nepo and the Indians had already folded up their mosquito nets, and we followed their example.

We were quite helpless against the advance of the ants. All we could do was find another grotto without ants. Fortunately the day was just breaking and the growing light assisted us.

LUIS AND PIERRE REJOIN US

We stayed five days at Lindosa. Every morning Jean and I went off to explore the rocks in the neighborhood and to film anything of interest we discovered. We found one or two other rock paintings, but unfortunately they were very much effaced. In the evening when the sun went down we returned to our camp through the savanna and over the rocks. Nepo and the Indians spent their time in hunting, and when we got back we always found them busy around the stewpot, preparing a tasty ragout of antelope or peccary.

On August 5th we were back again in San José, where we found good news awaiting us: the very next day our companions were due to arrive with the DC3 which the Colombian government had placed at our disposal. The first part of our expedition was now at an end, and that evening all our friends and acquaintances in the village turned up to discuss every possibility that might await us on the second lap. We had already explained our intentions to them at some length, and they knew that above all we wanted to share the life of those they called the *Pelados,* the hairy men of the forest; that is to say, those last of the original Indians who continued to lead the life of their ancestors in the depths of the forest untouched by the white man's civilization, refusing all part of it, even to the wearing of shirts and trousers. Antonio, the hunter of cayman alligators, knew the reputation of the Guaharibos of the Sierra Parima:

"Don't be in too much of a hurry to make their acquaintance in the forest," he said, "or they'll make you into *pot-au-feu* and play the flute on your bones."

Nepo's wife, the pleasant little Lilia, was sitting down beside him. Half laughing, half seriously she grimaced horribly, moving her brown legs. She was wearing white cotton socks embroidered with flowers.

"Get on with you, Antonio," she said. "Not all the forest Indians are like that. We Brazilians know more about them than you do. I was once with them on a steamboat traveling from Rio to Pará. That's right. There were three of them: the head of the tribe, his wife, and his second in command. They had come to see the president of the republic to get tools for their people. They had long hair down to their shoulders like the Sibundoys, and it was difficult to tell which were the men and which was the woman. Our president gave them what they asked for and then I was instructed to take them as far as Pará. They traveled third class and they were afraid to come out of their cabin. They were bored to death so they asked for firewater. Then they danced, to keep off sea sickness, so they said. One day they came up on deck stark naked. And do you think they were embarrassed when they were told to dress themselves? Not a bit. They just got dressed as naturally as they had got undressed. They weren't in the least embarrassed. At Pará they asked me to take them to a movie. They had heard of such things. However, we never got there because we were practically mobbed on the streets by rubbernecks. But if anyone was too inquisitive and came too close, the chief's wife just drew her nails down his face. That was the only sign of hostility I ever saw in them, and even then it was in self defense. An American wanted to take a photograph of them, but the chief wouldn't let him and told him he must go to the president of the republic and get permission first. When we parted they went back quite happily to their forest."

Our plane landed at ten o'clock in the morning. It was a quite new machine and by the cabin door was a row of painted flags. Luis and Pierre explained that they were the flags of all the Central American states where the plane landed on its flight to Bogotá. On its fuselage was the registration number 686 in large black figures.

It was August 6th. Our expedition had left Paris on August 6th the previous year and Bogotá on May 6th, three months ago.

Where shall we be on September 6th, I wondered, as the last of our baggage was hoisted in and the doors closed.

AUGUST TO SEPTEMBER 1949

PART 2

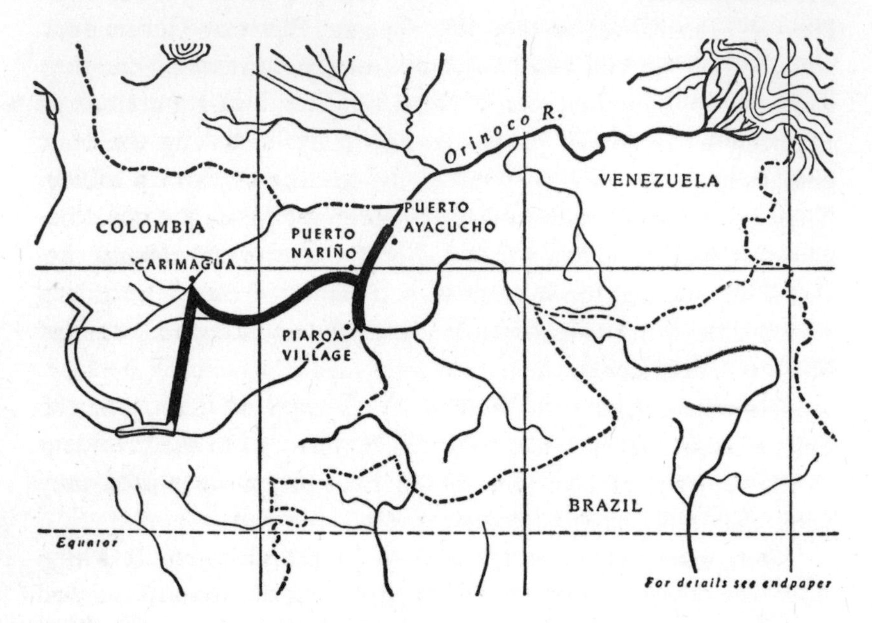

The Orinoco—The Last Whites and the First Indians

The Secret Life of the Piaroa Indians

WE BEGIN THE SECOND LAP OF OUR TRIP

FOR TWO HOURS the plane flew northward, its engines roaring steadily. Sitting on our cases we watched the llano below us, an endless yellow carpet unrolling slowly and with nothing to break the monotony. Occasionally we could just make out the thatched roof of some Indian hut, close to the ground and seemingly part of it. Then a great river came in sight, stretching across the horizon from west to east. It was the Meta. Map in hand we studied the land on its south bank, looking for the indent of a lagoon. It appeared below us at the same time as a black rectangle which delimited part of the llano. A number of tracks—they were nothing but the muddy imprints of truck wheels—crossed a barbed-wire enclosure and converged toward a roof of palm-tree crowns bordering the lagoon. This was Carimagua. Our plane described a great arc and turned toward the landing field. Its white guiding signals were in a line facing the houses.

At one end of the airfield we saw a truck driving out of a hangar, its whole carcass shaking. Our plane was already rolling along the ground. The noise of its engines ceased. It came to a halt and the doors were opened. The truck reversed toward the plane to take our cases on board. Standing up in it were the brothers Solano, the founders of Carimagua, smiling and waving their hats in welcome.

Half an hour later the plane took off again, in a hurry to get back to its base before nightfall, winging away toward the west, its engines going at full speed to carry it over the forty thousand square miles of savanna between Carimagua and Bogotá.

Once again we were on our own, but about six miles away there was the river Muco which flows for about a hundred miles to join the Vichada, which flows another couple of hundred miles to join the Orinoco. It was these two rivers we now had to negotiate in order to reach the foot of the Sierra Parima.

Many different tribes inhabit the intervening countryside, scattered in little groups along the riparian territory. The Salivas and the Piapicos live along the Muco. They are warriors and vendors of talismans famous throughout the llano. The Guahibos dwell along the Vichada. They live a peaceable and sedentary existence, spending their time cultivating cassava and making hammocks of fiber. Their trade in these hammocks with the more civilized peoples along the Orinoco provides them with iron instruments and clothing. Their cousins the Cuivas, a sub-group of the Guahibo tribe, are very different in character and have remained in a state of barbarism. They live in an oblong area of bushland to the east of Carimagua between the Vichada, the Orinoco and the Meta. The neighborhood is practically unknown and there, daubed with paint and naked apart from feathered ornaments, they live the same life their ancestors lived before them. The only tradition the Cuivas have added to their inherited store is that of emerging from time to time from the hinterland to discharge volleys of arrows against the boats going down the Meta. Sometimes they even organize systematic attacks on the nearest settlements, burning and pillaging whatever lies in their path.

The brothers Solano had had more than one bone to pick with them in the past, and quite recently the Cuivas had destroyed in a single night a whole banana plantation established along one of the tributaries of the Meta a few days journey away. To make the matter worse, only a few days before the raid a herd of about two hundred pigs—brought down at considerable expense from Villavicencio—had been settled in the plantation. It was on their next visit that the brothers Solano had found all the banana trees felled and all the pigs slaughtered.

On a number of occasions these Cuivas had even attacked Carimagua itself, though such attacks had been neither very serious nor very costly, having entailed no more than the loss of a cow or two and their calves. The Solano brothers had borne their losses patiently. They had armed their peons and they had never gone abroad themselves without loaded revolvers at their belts. But now their patience was exhausted. It was the principle of the thing, and they had decided that, as soon as the dry season arrived and allowed freer movement, they would organize a punitive expedition into the haunts of the Cuivas. Meaning to be friendly, they invited us to join them, but, apart from the fact that for us to do so would have meant spending another three months in the llano, the terms of reference of our expedition quite clearly forbade us taking part in theirs. Non-violence was our principle.

From September onward the rains become less frequent and the volume of water flowing through the Orinoco greatly diminishes. In October the level of the waters subsides sufficiently to permit the negotiation of the headwaters, while the mountain torrents and rapids of the rainy season also begin to diminish. It was desirable for us to reach the upper Orinoco without loss of time if we wanted to penetrate into the Sierra Parima. Once we were on our chosen site, then, if the season were not too far advanced, and if anything particularly interesting turned up, we might be able to consider spending time on the study of this or that particular group of natives.

The day after our arrival the Solanos sent off a peon to find one of the Muco Indians, a man with whom they were on particularly good terms. This Indian was brought in and the eldest Solano spoke to him at some length, explaining that the Indians need not fear us because we were scientists and had come to help them, not to do them harm:

"Go back to your kinsman straight away and get a big canoe with a crew. If these gentlemen like the canoe they will buy it. Otherwise they will hire it to the Orinoco, and they will pay the crew every day. You can rely on this. I am saying it to you. And now go, and don't waste time on the way. We shall expect you back again here within four days."

As an earnest of our good will we gave the man some money as an advance payment and he went off.

During the four days we occupied our time by making a detailed examination of our equipment and stores. Everything seemed to be in order. Our film was enclosed in metal cases kept tight by an ingenious system of soldering, and this and our paraffin and sticking plaster had resisted the all-pervading dampness of San José del Guaviare. Our cartridges were all wrapped in waxed paper and were as dry as on the day they had been taken out of the stores. Our matches struck efficiently without spluttering as good matches should, and there were no more ants in our sugar than was usually the case in Carimagua. In short, everything was satisfactory, though I did come across a large packet covered with green mildew at the bottom of one case. It was my reserve of pipe tobacco. However, I had just broken my last pipe, so the matter was of no very great importance.

Pierre, who was in charge of our recording instruments, had set up his equipment in the main room of the Solano menage which was serving as our all-in-one dormitory, refectory, and workshop. That evening the inhabitants of the settlement gathered around the open door to listen to the concert we put on for our hosts. We had no radio with us, but our sound apparatus had an amplifier for playing back our recordings, and, in addition, it was possible to use it for ordinary records. We had brought along a large assortment with which to test the musical appreciation of the native tribes we came in contact with. Thus it was possible to make the concert we gave more varied than any radio program.

First of all we played a French military march, then some American boogie-woogie, an Armstrong blues, a Wagnerian chorus, a piano piece by Stravinsky, and finally a Mozart symphony. Apart from our hosts, our audience consisted of old bandy-legged peons of the llano who seemed only half there without their horses, muchacho Indians and the almond-eyed girls of the settlement. They all sat there in perfect silence and listened without even blinking.

On one side or the other of our records everyone found something to set him dreaming, and not a word was spoken. One of our six-foot hosts seemed to be thinking and when the concert was over he spoke his thoughts.

"You know," he said, "I'm very fond of music, and I've often thought of getting a radio set, but on second thought I don't think I will. It doesn't really suit our style of life and it might even be a danger to the settlement."

The four days of waiting passed, but our Indian messenger did not reappear. Two more days passed, and we began to grow anxious.

"Do you think the fellow will really come back?" I asked one of the brothers. "Mightn't he just clear off with the money?"

"Not a chance. He'll come back all right. You can rely on that. Oh, I don't mean he's honest. No Indian is ever honest where white men are concerned. But he'll come back because he'll be afraid not to. Sooner or later we'd catch up with him. He knows that. He's half-civilized and too much attached to his own dunghill to go very far away."

"What would he be afraid of in particular?"

"What would he be afraid of? The same that happened not so long ago to that fellow over there," and with a jerk of his thumb he indicated a peon who happened to be passing at that moment.

"He stole a packet of cigarettes—not much perhaps, but it's the principle of the thing. First of all I beat him up pretty thoroughly. Then I took him out into the llano and fastened about three hundred pounds of chain to his feet and left him there for three days to think the matter over carefully. He won't do any more stealing. I've no doubt you think that was very inhuman of me, and I quite understand you, but you don't know the Indians. When my brothers and I founded Carimagua five years ago I should have been every bit as indignant at such a thing, but since then we've had plenty of time to realize that our civilized humanitarianism doesn't mean a damn thing out here in the llano amongst the Indians—and we've paid for the knowledge too. This part of the world is hard: the land and the people that live on it, the sun and the rain as well. There's just no room for civilized kindness in the llano. Make a present to an Indian who has served you well, and you'll find it's the surest way to corrupt him. He'll immediately think you owe him something you're not prepared to acknowledge, something worth far more than the present you've been fool enough to give him. And after that he'll distrust you and have a grudge against you. Or perhaps he'll think you're afraid of him and come to the conclusion that you're really a weakling he can easily dispose of. And if one man thinks that of you, before long they all will, and then the only thing to do will be to pack your grip and clear out of the llano to seek your fortune elsewhere. Believe me, the Cuivas I was talking about to you the other day, barbarians as they are, are often preferable to the Indians we regard as more or less civilized because they wear shirts and trousers and speak a bit of Spanish. With the Cuiva accounts will be settled openly and above board one day, either with an arrow or with a bullet, but with the Indians here you've got to be on your guard the whole time. Their contact with the white man's civilization has made them lose their own, but all they've taken in its place is the worst side of ours. We've got to use them here, but in order to use them we've got to knock a bit of respect into them first, and the only way to do that is by fear.

All the rest is fine theory. Apart from my fists and the chains hanging up in the store-room, I base my policy on another very practical thing: food. We need the Indians to develop the tens of thousands of acres of virgin soil we've settled on and which one day will feed millions of people. We need Indian labor-power, and in exchange we provide them with food they could never obtain on their own. Everyone knows just how things stand here and the result is we get the job done. And that's why that man will come back all right."

We were sitting on a bench in front of the main building of Carimagua. Under a low ceiling of grey sky a diffused light spread over the llano before us, making the fronds of herbage look almost luminous. The long, yellow llano swept away toward the horizon without a single tree or a single rock to break its monotony.

A child with a smeary face was playing with a green parakeet quite near us. The bird's wings were clipped to prevent its flying away, and it perched on the child's left wrist, squawking and trying to get at a piece of maize cake held in the other hand. A little further away two large ducks were paddling around in a pool of water. One was called Dorian and the other Gray, Solano told me with a smile.

The shadows drew in and a voice called out from the kitchen to tell us that supper was ready. We went into the main room of the house. The walls were decorated with hardwood spears, bows and steel-tipped arrows, and on the floor were the skins of jaguars and panthers. They were all trophies taken from the various enemies of the settlement the brothers Solano had founded in Carimagua.

THE "ORAM I"

Thirty-six hours later, at seven o'clock in the morning on August 13th, the Indian returned as Solano had said he would. He trotted up to the table where we were just finishing a very substantial breakfast of salted meat and maize pancakes. He carried his bow and arrows and an old felt hat was pulled down over his eyes.

"The canoes are at the quay," he informed us. "I couldn't get a big one so I brought two smaller ones. But I haven't been able to get crews. There were no men. They were all away. The man who owns the boats is waiting with them, and there are paddles for everyone. The gentlemen can go down and see for themselves. The man will take them to San José de Ocuné. The gentlemen can buy the canoes or hire them as far as that, just as they like."

A quarter of an hour later the truck of the settlement took our cases down to the quay and we went down after it. The two canoes were certainly not very big, and once they were loaded with our baggage they were burdened almost down to the surface. At the advice of the brothers Solano we fastened them together with poles and ropes. Fixed firmly side by side they were much more stable.

We shook hands heartily with the brothers Solano. Then each of us took a paddle and we started on our journey. We made our way rapidly down the long river corridor between the trees and the little tongue of savanna along the quay was soon lost to sight. The figures of the Solano brothers stood out among the crowd of Indian men, women, and children who had gathered to see us off and then vanished forever.

The Vichada has its one village just like the Guaviare. This was San José de Ocuné, about a score of huts lying between two bends of the river below the confluence of the Muco, rather more than a hundred and sixty miles from our point of departure. Our canoes were so heavily laden that it took us five days to cover this distance. It was clearly quite impossible to go on to the Orinoco with such makeshift craft. Somehow or other we had to get hold of a larger canoe on which we could use our outboard motor. But the Vichada is not so wooded as the Guaviare, with the result that big canoes made out of a single tree trunk are very rare, and no one in San José de Ocuné had a canoe any bigger or better than the ones we had come in. A different solution was suggested.

Maestro Sinforino, our host in the village, was a ship's carpenter by trade, and he assured us that it would be quite simple for him to enlarge the larger of our canoes and raise its sides with planks to make it into a strong little boat of two or three tons burden, called a *falca,* big enough to take us and our baggage to the Orinoco. We agreed, and so we bought the boat from its owner, and the day after our arrival our shipbuilder set to work. His shipwright's yard was set up on the quay itself, in the shade of a clump of big mango trees at the foot of the one little street of the village. For six days Maestro Sinforino and his helpers sawed, nailed and planed. They removed the stern and the bows and they hollowed out the hulk still further by fire. When this part of the job was done our canoe looked like a big black leaf slightly curved inward at the edges. But as soon as the large ribs of fresh timber were fixed athwart the dead leaf it was transformed into a proper sea bottom, and all it required then was planking to become the launch that would take us to the basin of the Orinoco. We immediately named it "Oram I" in honor of our Orinoco-Amazon Expedition.

What we needed now before we could set off for the Orinoco were more provisions. All we had were a few pounds of condensed milk and chocolate, and those we intended to preserve carefully for use in the forest. Maestro Sinforino, the man with many ideas, once again came to the rescue and obtained a sack of maize and a little mill to grind it, so that our Boy could make maize pancakes. Then he proposed that the village slaughter a heifer and share the meat with us. This was agreed to, and by August 23rd our vessel, Oram I, was launched, provided with a canvas cover from our tent, and loaded with our baggage. We were ready for the next stage of our journey. On the morning of August 24th we started up our outboard motor and sailed out into the great silver river amidst the acclamations of the population of San José de Ocuné.

According to our information, there were only three civilized settlements on the Vichada along the whole of its hundred and sixty miles below San José de Ocuné. In other words, we had to make our way through a vast no man's land in which there were only a few groups of nomad Indians, and about them and their ways the white man knew very little. The era of settlements of the Carimagua type is not yet at an end in this kind of remote Colombian territory. We were curious to make the acquaintance of the three small groups of white men who had come from the Cordilleras of the Andes to seek their fortune in these wild and isolated parts of their country.

For hours on end our boat chugged through stretch after stretch of absolutely deserted savanna. There was not the slightest sign of human existence on either side of the river, nor even any trace of life at all. And then finally we came in sight of a small quay at the edge of a lagoon. Two canoes were fastened there, and a small path climbed up a hill toward two palm-leaf roofs. About five hundred yards from the river, they dominated the countryside. This was Awini, the first of the three outposts of civilization on our long journey. We decided to make a halt there, and the Oram I nosed its way into the lagoon.

As it approached the quay a tall, thin, leathery-looking man came down the path and saluted us with a rather florid sweep of his straw sombrero. He seemed to be expecting us, and he led us with long strides to his house, assuring us that he was enchanted at the opportunity of doing us the honors of his humble home. A few minutes later we were seated on four benches around a square of beaten earth which had been very carefully swept, and two servants set up a table on which there was a mountainous dish of roast antelope, fried eggs, and bananas.

We were very hungry and we waded into that meal with a lack of ceremony which still makes me blush to think of it. Our stomachs seemed to be almost endlessly capacious, and before long all that was left of that huge mountain of victuals was a little pile which dwindled as we looked at it. But our host seemed delighted. He saw to it that there was no need to ask for anything and so we were able to devote our whole attention to the meal. He moved around the table constantly seeing that we had everything we wanted, leaving a great wake of *eau de cologne* floating behind him and keeping up an endless flow of conversation, punctuating his remarks with swift darts here and there as he noticed an opportunity to serve us. He had started off by bidding us most welcome, and that had led him to discuss the region and the rarity of visitors. When his hands were disengaged he fiddled nervously with his fingers. His nails, I noticed, were long and very well cared for.

"You'll probably wonder why I am here and not at Bogotá or Medellín," he said. "But the explanation is really very simple. Five years ago I worked for a transport firm in Bogotá. On the day I had saved up a thousand pesos (over two hundred dollars), I went down to Villavicencio to get to know the famous gateway of the llano, where I had always intended to settle down. But, God forgive me, I quickly turned my pesos into good strong drink. And what was I to do then? I couldn't go back to Bogotá, and so off I went to the Meta, with that drink as my sole baggage —and it was inside me. And what a tongue I had! Dreadful! I shall never forget it. I landed at San Pedro de Arimena with nothing but three centavos in my pocket. I hadn't a mosquito net. I hadn't even a packet of cigarettes. It was possible to buy cigarettes, of course, but what with? When I said I wanted to go to the Vichada everyone thought I was mad. Very well, I said: so there are tigers and mosquitoes and Indians? But I don't care what's there: I'm going. And go I did."

And at that he executed a triumphant pirouette.

"And I've seen tigers. I've seen mosquitoes. And I've seen Indians. But I muddled through somehow and here I am."

A tall woman in a flowered cotton dress had appeared at his side, and she looked at us silently. In her very dark hair was a large comb incrusted with imitation stones of the type we had in our trading bundle. There were three small and grubby children with her and their skin was as dark as hers, but in their eyes was the same keen restlessness that shone from the eyes of our host. He looked at all four members of his family for a moment, flicking off the ash of his cigarette with his index finger. Then he made a new pirouette and went off into another story. Two peons came up and removed the table. We talked for a little while with our host and then we took our leave. The sun was already sinking, and we had to hurry if we wanted to go a little farther before nightfall.

Our motor started up and soon we were out in the river on our way again. Night fell over the savanna and we drew into the bank and slept on the boat, stretched out on our cases. As day broke we started up the motor again and went on. We sighted the two last outposts of civilization along the river but went past them without stopping: we were drawn toward the Orinoco now as a horse is drawn toward its stable. We wanted to get there as quickly as possible and began to feel that even minutes counted. For four months we had been waiting to get there, and it represented the first of the really big stages of our expedition.

A GUAHIBO VILLAGE

At midday the sky clouded over and there were signs of a storm. A long way ahead of us where the sky was blackest the clouds burst and the falling rain looked like a grey sheet hanging from the sky. We were quite certain that within a few minutes we should get it too, but hours passed and nothing happened: sometimes it was raining on our right, and sometimes on our left, but we chugged along in a rainless patch between. We were passing through a long corridor of swamped forest and it was impossible to put into the bank. The sun was sinking, but just before it reached the horizon we came to a stretch of savanna.

About three-quarters of a mile from the river we saw two huts silhouetted sharply on top of a small hill. We put into the bank but the ground was soaking and to camp there was impossible. We decided to see if we could get a shelter for the night in the huts. By this time it was quite dark and, as the batteries of our torches were exhausted, we took our boat lamp, an enormous watertight contraption whose strength was in inverse proportion to its weight, and started off. I was in the lead and the others followed in single file.

The journey took us about an hour. Our trousers were rolled up to our thighs and we splashed along barefooted, sometimes sinking into the mud right up to our knees. And to make things more difficult sharp edges of tough grass wrapped themselves round our toes and cut into the flesh painfully. I wondered what we must look like, staggering along through that morass, carrying our hammocks and our mosquito nets round our necks like enormous scarves. Just in case, I had taken a matchet along. At last we approached the first of the two huts. Two silhouettes appeared in the doorway, barefooted, in old washed-out trousers and shirts, and with old soft hats on—the classic silhouette of the llano.

"Buenas noches, señores."

They greeted us in a nasal voice and looked up, presenting their two faces glistening with red paint as though they had been freshly slashed. They were Guahibo Indians, the intermediate type, half civilized, half savage, that had caused our hosts at Carimagua the greatest misgivings. Perhaps they had been naked before they saw us and had slipped into shirts and trousers in order to receive us. Or perhaps they were peones of Awini, or San José de Ocuné, or some other settlement, who had returned to their own huts and freshly painted their faces in order not to cut too strange a figure among their like. Who could tell?

To start a conversation we asked them if they could sell us a chicken and some eggs. After discussing the matter together, they informed us that it would be possible but that we should have to give them a piece of material in exchange, and they quoted a length which would be about ten times the value of a chicken. All bartering with the Indians must be done patiently, taking one's time, and so before we made any reply we entered the hut. The interior consisted of one large rectangular space. From the palm-leaf roof hung bows and arrows, matchets, and an axe. Two hammocks had been slung at the end of the room, which was otherwise bare. In a corner near the doorway there was the red glow of a small fire. We sat down on the floor, warmed our cold hands at the fire and lit cigarettes. Silently, first two or three, and then a dozen men with painted faces and soft felt hats began to gather around us along the walls. We could no longer tell which of them were the two we had spoken to.

"How many eggs can you give us?"

It was the voice of Luis, and a hand rose indicating three.

"How much do you want for the eggs alone?"

"Ten cigarettes," the man replied.

"Right!" said Luis. "And how much for the chicken alone?"

The man scratched his head.

"I don't know," he replied dolefully. "It isn't mine."

Luis took the three eggs and made preparations for boiling them on the fire in a little earthenware pot he had found on the floor beside him. In the meantime we were wondering what to do. Would it be altogether prudent to sleep here? The hut was still filling up with silent men coming in out of the night. They kept at a distance, occasionally exchanging a furtive remark in their own tongue, but their eyes were fixed on us all the time. Should we go on trying to buy the chicken? The situation dragged out in silence.

"You can do what you like," said Jean finally, "but I'm not going to sleep here. We've always got the boat, and I'd sooner sleep on board."

With that he took the lamp and went out. Some time passed. I was squatting on the ground beside Luis, who was steadily blowing up the fire in order to boil his eggs. Pierre was standing up leaning against a post. A few yards away the Indians stood together along the wall, talking together in low tones and keeping their eyes fixed on us. Gradually an enormous chasm seemed to open up in the few yards which separated our two groups. It was the chasm that separated our two languages and the two worlds they represented, the very chasm we had come so hopefully to bridge. But now it was becoming wider and deeper every moment, like a ditch that widens as one walks along its edge. Someone put down a thick slab of badly cooked *cazabe,* the cassava pancake which is the bread of the Indians.

We munched it in silence, chewing steadily, mixing it thoroughly with our saliva. It was doughy and very hard to swallow. In order to drink we had to go over almost surreptitiously to a jar in one corner and take a dip with a calabash spoon about the size of the palm of a man's hand. The mouth of the jar was so narrow that in withdrawing the calabash and the hand holding it half the water splashed back again. We felt ourselves blushing at our clumsiness. It was unpardonable not even to know how to take a calabash of water decently. But from the other side of the chasm came a chuckle or two. Our very clumsiness was the first thing to bring us a little closer to these Indians. But the mild chuckles disappeared quickly in the silence and it seemed almost as though somewhere something was sliding toward an inevitable catastrophe. Luis went on looking at his eggs dancing about in the water.

Suddenly we heard shouts outside the hut, and the sound of rapid steps. High and pressing voices cracked like whips. Two men ran in.

"The other gentleman has missed his way," they said. "Instead of going down to the river he went straight toward the hills."

We knew you could go on all night in that direction and find yourself utterly lost in the morning. We were outside very quickly, and Luis began to shout between his cupped hands:

"Jean! Jean!"

His voice traveled down the hill and across the grass and was lost in the immensity of the savanna. We strained our ears into the wind, but it brought us nothing apart from the dry clicking of the fireflies which were beginning to glow over the plain. Luis shouted again. At last we saw a lamp waving among the thousands of glowing points in the grass. The savanna at night is like a sky studded with little stars, and Jean's lamp was for some time nothing but a larger star among all the others. He had heard us and was making his way back. Then we heard his voice, and his shadow loomed up in the darkness.

"Didn't you hear the Indians shouting that you were going the wrong way?" I asked.

"Would you have trusted them in my place?" he countered.

The incident made up our minds for us and we decided to spend the night on board.

"Come along with us to the boat," Luis said to the owner of the eggs, "and we'll give you your cigarettes."

The Indian nodded and began to roll his trousers up over his knees. To our surprise about a dozen of his companions began to follow his example. We were to have a strong escort, it appeared.

Before leaving one of them took down a long wooden lance from the ceiling, and another armed himself with a bow and three arrows.

We set off. The owner of the eggs went at the head of the column and I followed him, holding the lamp above my head. Was the whole thing some sort of trap? We put a good face on it, but we were not altogether reassured. We had been told too many things about these Indians not to be anxious.

But after only a quarter of an hour's trudge, during which we splashed little more than ankle deep in the watery mud, we saw the dark mirror of the Vichada ahead of us, and on it the shadowy bulk of the Oram I. In the bows, sprawled amongst the pots and the cordage as though he had been put to sleep instantly at the touch of a wand, was Elie. He awoke with a start as we came aboard.

"You gave me a fright," he said. "Those fellows with the paint all over their faces look horrible."

But the Indians burst out laughing at the sight of his alarm and that reassured him. Once on board we lighted the pressure lamp and gave the owner of the eggs his cigarettes. All the Indians gathered round the Oram I to look at our treasures. Seen from the boat they formed a strange collection of grubby shirts and dark skins in the uncertain light of our lamp. When the cigarettes had been handed over another Indian stretched out his hand with three eggs in it.

"Here," said a voice. "Me cigarettes too."

In a moment or two everyone was smoking and we lit our pressure cooker to prepare a few slivers of our beef. The Indians watched our every movement and discussed our actions first in undertones and then louder and louder, until finally there was a good deal of laughter at this or that, to them, strange antic on our part. Their eyes were wide open in the shadows as they studied the new world we had brought to their doors. They were much amused and they grew bolder and came closer. Confidence was obviously growing. It was as though the chasm which divided us, and which only a little while before had been growing wider and deeper, was now narrowing. We felt a pressing desire to hurry on the process, to bridge the gap once and for all. I noticed one of the men in particular, and I felt that he was just as anxious to be friendly as I was. He was strikingly painted in long vertical lines which gave his face somewhat the appearance of a noble animal. He was the man who had taken down the lance from the roof of the hut. He still held it upright in his hand. I went to our case of trading goods and took out a little mirror. I pointed to the lance and showed him the mirror.

"Will you exchange that for this?" I asked.

He nodded his head eagerly and handed me the lance at once in exchange for the mirror. All the others smiled approvingly and I smiled too because I felt a pleasure I had not experienced since my early school days, when I had fixed my eyes covetously on a bag of marbles or perhaps a bone penholder with a view of the Eiffel Tower in it.

The chasm now diminished rapidly. The man with the tiger-like mask was at my side. He knew a few words of Spanish and I explained to him that we had come from a very far-off country in order to get to know the Indians.

"And to trade with them," added Luis, giving me a dig with his elbow. "You'll make them think we're daft," he whispered.

I had read one or two ethnographical studies about the Guahibo Indians, and so I was able to ask sensible questions about their festivals and their music, and this quite impressed them.

"You seem to know as much about it as I do," one Indian said with a smile.

The session ended with a jug of chocolate we made for them and it passed from mouth to mouth like a pipe of peace.

It had got rather late and we asked them jocularly whether they intended to spend the night leaning on the edge of our canoe: *we* intended to go to sleep. With that their visit ended and, after shaking hands all round, they went back, splashing one after the other in single file. We prepared our blankets, made ourselves comfortable on top of the cases, blew out the lamp and settled down for the night.

I dropped off to sleep with the comforting thought that despite all the brothers Solano had said, it might still be possible to get to know the Indians properly one day without first kicking their teeth in.

STORM ON THE RIVER

The next day we realized from the freshening of the wind, the steady widening of the river, and the increasing strength of its current that the Orinoco was not so very far ahead. A strong wind sprang up as it does when approaching the sea. We got out the 35mm film camera to shoot some of the scenes as we passed through the flat llano landscape we were soon to leave behind us for good, but the mechanism jammed. Jean took it to pieces and adjusted it. It worked for a short while and then it jammed again. Sitting under the canvas awning he worked on it for hours, but he was unable to get it to go. The damp had affected the cogs and it proved impossible to repair. That was a blow. We had no other camera of a professional type with us. The only thing to do was to send it back to Bogotá in the hope that someone there would be able to repair it, and if that didn't work then we should have to order another one from the United States. The bad luck which had already dogged the expedition and made us lose so much time seemed closing in on us again.

The wind strengthened from hour to hour. Flights of waders, ducks, and parakeets crossed the sky above us. Around us floated what looked at first like the trunks of trees, black against the silver surface of the water: they were cayman alligators, fine, big fellows of the best species, the black cayman, from twelve to fifteen feet long. On the horizon we saw a fringe of forest and above it the sky grew darker. The Orinoco must be somewhere ahead there. All day long we did not set eyes on a single human being, and in the evening we moored the boat by a tree on the bank. Before going to sleep we discussed at some length what we could do about the mishap to our camera. Luis proposed to go back to Bogotá from the Orinoco, leaving us there to explore the neighborhood. As soon as the camera was repaired he would return and join us to undertake the crossing of the Sierra Parima. It was quite clear that there was nothing else we could do, and when we arrived at the Orinoco we should see. So we went off to sleep.

A few hours later we were awakened with a start by the breaking of the storm. It was pouring in torrents and the rain thrashed down onto the canvas awning and onto the surface of the water with such violence that the whole boat shuddered. At each gust of wind sheets of rain swept into the boat and lashed our faces. Hurriedly we lighted our pressure lamp and with our rainproof ponchos and anything else that came to hand we closed up each end of the awning as well as we could. Then we went to sleep again until the first sign of dawn. We were on our way before the sun had appeared above the horizon.

The river was as flat as a pool of oil. All around the savanna was utterly still in the silence. All we could hear was the whispering of the blue forest along the distant horizon. It was cold and there was no sun. The sky remained a dirty grey and soon a chill rain began to fall steadily. It was the sort of rain that can go on for hours and even days at a time.

I had been at the tiller since dawn and I tried to make out the bank and the bends of the river ahead. All around us was a grey, vaporous mist in which confused forms took shape and then dissolved. At each bend of the river I observed that the banks were wider and wider apart. The river was steadily broadening. Through the rain I could hear the muffled sound of monkeys screaming in the forest as they awoke. We sailed past a number of islands with dark green vegetation. First one, then two, then four, and more and more as we went along. After rounding each bend we looked carefully at the surface of the river to check the current, but we could neither feel nor see it. The rain beat steadily down on the surface of the water, destroying its eddies and concealing its movement.

Perhaps we had been going up stream for hours now without noticing it? We might almost have been at sea. Pierre got out our compass. The needle wavered between N.E. and S. After that we began to ship water. Elie bailed away with a large bowl and Pierre came to take his turn at the tiller. I was numb from head to foot with the cold. Under the awning Luis had got the spirit stove going and he handed me a mug of hot sugar water. Pierre stood up to see over the awning ahead of us, keeping the tiller firm with one bare foot. It made an unexpected pink smudge in the symphony of black and grey that surrounded us. The river widened steadily and we began to wonder whether we had already sailed into the Orinoco without having noticed it.

The rain kept on monotonously, neither growing stronger nor diminishing. It seemed to us that such rain was out of season. After a while we heard the sound of an engine approaching and then a vessel appeared making its way up stream with some difficulty. It was a so-called *falca* of much the same type as the Oram but of bigger tonnage. It might almost have been out of the same shipyard. It was loaded up with bales of brownish-red fiber piled on the deck six feet high. It moved slowly up stream keeping to the bank and we were able to see its crew distinctly. It seemed to have been chosen, man for man, with a pirate film in view. However, it was not carrying specie, precious stones, Spanish doubloons or pieces of eight—the brown bales on the deck were "chique-chique" fiber, a much sought after raw material for the manufacture of brushes and brooms in South America. The boat was moving so slowly that by reducing our own speed we were able to talk to them from deck to deck. They shouted a greeting and we asked what time it was.

"A quarter to one," they replied.

"How much farther is it to the Orinoco?"

"Four hours perhaps. Could be five or six; depends on what speed you make."

It was beginning to rain harder now and the noise as it splashed into the river greatly increased. What with the rain and the increasing distance between us we had to shout so much that we strained our throats. Four hours, five hours, six hours—should we get to the Orinoco before nightfall? The pirates with their cargo of broom fiber disappeared into the midst of rain. Hours passed. Our motor, half flooded, spluttered and choked. Then it went on all right for a while, only to splutter and choke again. Should we arrive in time? We knew that a little distance beyond the mouth of the Vichada the Orinoco plunged into the worst series of rapids throughout its course, ending about thirty-five miles down stream in the famous Maipures-Atures Narrows, a name constantly repeated in the chronicles of the Spanish conquest owing to the great number of ships which were lost there.

We also knew that Colombia maintained a small establishment at the mouth of the Vichada, half warehouse, half military and customs control point, because the Orinoco was the frontier between Colombia and Venezuela there. This was Puerto Nariño, and it represented our only possible landing place. If we missed it we should be in danger of being swept away toward the rapids in the darkness.

THE ORINOCO

And then the grey covering of clouds which had been across the sky since dawn broke up and the sun came out, red and enormous as though bloodshot. It was right ahead of us practically touching the water. The rain stopped and the purple glow of evening became visible in the west, revealing a vast sweep of water where the Vichada widened enormously until finally it seemed to lose its banks altogether. We had all come out from under the awning. Standing upright on the Oram we gazed at the horizon where the forest disappeared in a thin sliver of blue. Both to the right and to the left of us there was nothing but blue and white water sparkling and hissing in the sun. Pierre put the tiller over and the Oram veered to the left. The sound of our outboard motor was almost lost in that immensity and even our shouts of joy were carried away like the cries of birds in the air. At last we were on the Orinoco. To the west the sun dipped below the skyline as though it had been waiting for that moment and darkness fell all around us over the waters. We were neither in Colombia nor Venezuela, but on the Orinoco, a river as international as the Amazon, as international as the sea itself. But we certainly could not stay there. We must return as quickly as possible to the Colombian bank.

"Hug the shore," we cried out to Pierre, who was still standing upright at the tiller.

A confused mass of land appeared again on our left. The closer we came in the higher it seemed to rise, rising, falling, and rising again. The llano was behind us. Now there were hills and mountains in the night. We went on for almost an hour in this way, and gradually we became anxious again. One of us stood upright in the bows directing the white beam of our most powerful torch over the surface of the waters ahead, and we discovered the beginning of the rapids at the same time as we saw the first light on the bank, followed quickly by a second. It could only be Puerto Nariño. The current grew more powerful every minute and the water began to boil more and more dangerously around us. By now we were slipping down stream at an increasing speed. Pierre unceremoniously flung over the tiller so hard that we almost fell over and with our little motor in high we gradually got closer to the bank across the current.

Gallant little outboard motor! With only five horsepower it valiantly drove our heavy boat through the whirlpools and eddies and across the current that tried to sweep us away out of control! We made it, but it was a bit difficult getting alongside and we drove hard onto a mud bank. Reinforced by its strong ribs, the Oram I proved itself capable of withstanding even more later on.

When we finally stuck in the mud we found ourselves about five hundred yards below the hill on which we had seen the lights showing. We got out and floundered through the mud dragging a rope behind us, making for firm ground. Someone carrying a lamp came out of one of the houses and made his way down the hill toward us. Before we could see who it was we shouted:

"Is this Puerto Nariño?"

And a rather surprised voice shouted back:

"Of course it is. Where else could it be?"

We did not sleep much that night. The hospitable Colombian in charge raided his reserve of rare bottles in our honor, and our enthusiasm at having reached the Orinoco at last burned brightly through the night until the sky began to grow light again. A few hours later Luis got into a canoe with a man from Puerto Nariño and set off down the Orinoco to Puerto Ayacucho, the chief Venezuelan town in the district. From there he could fly to Bogotá. The minimum time he would need to get there and back to Puerto Nariño was three weeks.

And what were we to do with those three weeks while we waited for his return? There were two suggestions for our consideration: to visit a little known tribe of Guahibos or to visit the Piaroa Indians. On the whole we were in favor of the latter, for the Piaroa Indians had never been studied *in situ*. But we had only three gallons of gasoline left, and that would greatly hamper our movements unless Luis managed to arrange to send us some from Puerto Ayacucho on a boat going up the Orinoco. It would therefore be some days before we could leave Puerto Nariño at all.

"That doesn't matter," said our host easily. "Whether you go to the Guahibos or to the Piaroas you'll need someone you can trust, someone who can speak Spanish and who knows the Indians well enough to be useful as a guide. As far as the Piaroas are concerned you couldn't have anyone better than Mario. He's actually their chief. But he's very proud of being civilized, and he wouldn't ask anything better than to take you to people who aren't so civilized as he is. I know him very well: he comes here occasionally to sell me chicle or cassava. He lives a day's journey by canoe from here and I'll send my Boy to fetch him. On the way back he can call at the Guahibo village of Toninas. There are one or two Indians there who speak Spanish quite well and have their wits about them. They can also be brought in. In two or three days from now you'll be able to make your choice, and you won't have lost any time because it will take at least that long before you can get any gasoline here from Puerto Ayacucho, and you must have a guide anyway."

It sounded quite the best thing for us to do and so we agreed. The Boy, a young fellow who had himself left the Piaroa tribe to serve the white man, received his instructions and went off to put on his best white shirt for the journey. Then with a paddle over his shoulder he stalked proudly down to the quay and put off in his canoe. We watched him make his way up stream, hugging the bank and making skilful progress against the current. The tail of his white shirt floated out on the breeze above the stern of his small black canoe.

The next day he was back again and we learned that the Guahibos would come in to see us in a few days. Unfortunately he had been unable to meet Mario, who had gone off on a journey and would not be back for a month.

"Where's he gone to?" our host asked.

"Quien sabe?" the Indian replied with a smile, and he went back to his kitchen, taking off his white shirt; it was the only shirt he possessed.

Another three days passed. Unless the elusive Mario got the idea of dropping into Puerto Nariño it looked as though we ought to give up the idea of visiting his tribe. In that case we should have to fall back on the Guahibos, and we now awaited the arrival of the men from Toninas with some impatience. In the meantime we carried all our equipment up from the boat and prepared what we thought we should need for a trip that would take about a fortnight. The remainder of our baggage could then remain safely in our host's house until we returned.

September came and the rains grew less frequent. A water line was already visible on the rocky banks of the Orinoco. The level of the water was clearly falling. The period of subsidence which comes annually between the rains and the dry season was now beginning. The rain, what there was of it, was no longer persistent: just sudden, short, sharp storms which broke once or twice a day. It certainly rained heavily, but it was all over in perhaps half an hour.

The two huts at Puerto Nariño overlooked the river from a height of about forty feet or so, and we spent hours outside looking over the immense, shining surface of the water, unbroken above the rapids even by a breeze. Occasionally we saw boats coming up river from Puerto Ayacucho. They were chiefly big Brazilian or Venezuelan *falcas* maintaining a shuttle service on the upper Orinoco, the Casiquiare Canal, and the Rio Negro between Manaos and Puerto Ayacucho, carrying rubber, chicle, *sarapia,* balata and other local raw materials, which was all there was to trade with other millions of square miles of virgin forest traversed by the great rivers—the only trade routes known to equatorial America. As they came nearer we always expected that one or the other of these boats would swing over from the right bank to Puerto Nariño to unload our gasoline, but no, the "pouki-pouki," as the Indians call them because of the characteristic throb of their oil-fuel engines, disappeared up river one by one without changing course.

But we got up early one morning to find a group of swarthy Colombians, very much like the gatherers of chique-chique we had met on the Vichada, unloading three large metal drums onto the quay. In addition to this precious cargo they had also brought a letter from "Don Luis" in which he informed us that he was leaving for Bogotá in a military plane—as it was dated two days previously he was obviously there by now—and urged us to get in touch under all circumstances with a certain Doctor Baumgartner, the head of a medical unit at Puerto Ayacucho, who was also a keen and knowledgeable ethnographer and had interested himself closely in the Piaroa Indians since he had been stationed in Venezuela.

On seeing Dr. Baumgartner's name for the first time we had no idea that we should have a great deal to do with him in our subsequent adventures, that he would become our best friend on the Orinoco, and that one day he would extricate us from a very nasty hole. That's all very well and good, we thought, but how do we get to the Piaroas?

On September 9th some more visitors turned up: three brown-skinned little men in drab clothing but with their faces painted a brilliant red arrived. They might have been the blood brothers of "the man with the lance" and "the man with the eggs" we had met higher up the Vichada. They were the Guahibos of Toninas. One of them carried a little reddish-brown monkey on his shoulder. The beast was about the size of a cat, and at the sight of us it opened two great eyes wide with astonishment and scratched its head so comically that we decided that it must certainly become the fifth member of the expedition. The owner agreed with us as soon as we had shown him a little tube of glass beads from our stock in trade. And thus Oscar—as we christened him in honor of the movies—joined us. But when the Guahibos learned that we wanted them to take us to see their "naked cousins" they protested indignantly.

"You can't really want to go and visit people like that! It's impossible. Why we never even see them. They're a disgrace to our tribe. They can't even speak Spanish. No! Anything you like, but not that."

We asked them if they knew Mario, the chief of the Piaroas.

"Yes, of course, we do," they replied. "But he's away at the moment. He's gone to the celebrations on the Mataveni."

Our host's Boy, who up to then had been listening with a smile to our talk, now went out of the room looking furious.

"What's the Mataveni? And what sort of celebrations?"

They looked at us with pity for our ignorance.

"The Mataveni is a river higher up. It flows into the Orinoco above the Vichada. The river divides into two. On one side is the real Mataveni, which isn't Piaroa but Puinave, and on the other side is the Fruta Canyon which is pure Piaroa. That's where they're having their celebrations. They believe that when the river falls it's a New Year, and you have to drink and eat and make music to celebrate it. So that's where they all are now, and they'll eat and drink and make music for a whole moon. It's the same as when you say it's New Year. It lasts a bit longer that's all."

They seemed a little puzzled that it should be necessary to explain to us about things everybody knew already. We didn't care about that, and what they had told us made us very keen to go there and see it all for ourselves.

"Could you take us there?" asked Pierre.

They frowned.

"It wouldn't be easy to take you there. The Piaroas don't like strangers coming to them, and certainly not during their celebrations."

Our host intervened at this point and explained to them that we were scientists and likely to prove very useful to the Indians, both Piaroas and Guahibos. They had therefore good reason to take us there, particularly as we were prepared to give them shirts and trousers in exchange for their services.

That last argument settled the question and it was arranged that we should leave for Fruta Canyon the very next day, which was September 10th. According to them, with our outboard motor it would not take more than about twelve hours to get there—a very short journey by their reckoning.

PIAROAN NEW YEAR CELEBRATIONS

We started off at dawn the following morning. Until midday we went up the Orinoco and then, under the instructions of our guide, we turned to the right into a smaller river almost hidden in a tangled mass of vegetation. This was the Mataveni. We made our way up it for several hours through a network of grass, vegetation, and liana, and we came across nothing to indicate that any human being had ever been that way before. At last our guide told us to turn to the left and there, once again hidden behind vegetation, we found a small tributary of the Mataveni, the Fruta Canyon. We should certainly have passed by without noticing it had we been alone. The branches and the growth ahead of us now became denser and denser, and we had to shut off the outboard motor and go forward by paddling. Several more hours passed in this way and the course of the Fruta became almost lost to sight under the reeds and rushes of an immense marshland with here and there a few trees jutting out. But at last we got through this terrain and found ourselves in a big lagoon skirted by forest. A column of smoke rose straight up into the sky ahead of us, hanging there almost motionless above the trees.

"That's where it is," said our guide.

As we came closer we heard the sound of strange music, long drawn out and monotonous. A new mass of vegetation rose up in front of us and for the time being we lost sight of the column of smoke we were making for. The two Guahibo Indians now put down their paddles, stood up in the canoe, and using their hands as megaphones gave out a long call. The far-away music stopped at once.

"They'll be here before long," they said.

A quarter of an hour passed and then from between the trees

on the edge of the lagoon a canoe manned by a crew of three emerged and paddled toward us. When they came up they spoke to our Indians without taking any notice of us, and then they jumped into our canoe with their paddles and guided us through the tangled vegetation which concealed the landing place of their village. We landed at a sort of terrace. Tied up there were perhaps a dozen little canoes of the type that had come out to meet us. A well-kept path rose from the quay between three or four huts made of straw. There was not a soul about. In the background and apparently raised over the path, the roof of a large rectangular hut towered above the others.

Apart from this there was nothing around us or ahead but muddy ground disappearing into a jungle of branches and undergrowth—the advance guard of the forest at whose verge the little village had been founded.

While we were making fast our canoe, timid faces began to appear between the palm leaves which closed the entrances to the huts, and after a while men, women, and children came out and walked down toward us, until in the end the entire population was assembled on the quay, all huddled together and looking at us with a mute question:

"Why have you come here to us?"

I ran my eye over the crowd in search of a pith helmet.

"You'll easily recognize Mario," our Colombian host at Puerto Nariño had told us. "He always wears a pith helmet painted blue. He's so proud of it he'd never be seen without it."

I spotted my man almost at once. He was rather simian looking and seemed ill at ease. His high social position was easily recognizable not only from his wonderful headgear but also from the fact that he wore a white shirt and white trousers infinitely cleaner than anything worn around him. The wrinkled little eyes he fixed on us looked malicious.

I made no sign that I recognized him. Since we had landed, our two Guahibos had been standing to one side apparently a little uncertain of their welcome. Perhaps they feared the Piaroas would be angry with them for having introduced strangers into their midst during tribal celebrations. I now called one of them over and told him to tell the Piaroan chief, Mario, that I should like to shake hands with him and that I had brought a letter for him. While saying this I rather ostentatiously flourished the letter I had held in my hand since we landed. It was a letter from the Colombian authorities in the person of our friendly host at Puerto Nariño to Mario, Chief of the Piaroan Indians.

Mario now came toward us as though casually, but with a broad smile on his face. He was clearly flattered to think that I knew about him already, and he listened with a complacent air to the speech I delivered concerning the letter. It was written on letterhead notepaper and it had many paragraphs and a number of official-looking violet stamps. He read it, carefully put it away in his pocket, and then proceeded to give a free translation of its contents—no doubt with suitable embellishments—to his fellow tribesmen. It was a long discourse in the Piaroan tongue, and, of course, we did not understand a word of it.

The scene remains in my memory as an excruciating parody of almost any official small-town reception anywhere—complete with unrehearsed mishap. During my own discourse there was a sudden startling splash behind me, followed by a general burst of laughter. Jean, who was the photographer of our expedition and wished to record the occasion for posterity, had stepped back a couple of paces to obtain a better view, and having forgotten how close he was to the water, had fallen in, the whole six feet of him.

The following is the letter I had brought with me:

Puerto Nariño,
September 9th, 1949.

To Don Mario, Chief of the Piaroa tribe on the Rio Orinoco, or the Rio Mataveni, or the Rio Fruta:

My most esteemed Mario,

Receive with this letter my special greetings and good wishes for your health and that of your wife Mariano and your children.

The gentlemen whom I introduce to you herewith are on a special mission from my government with a view to making your acquaintance and that of your people, taking photographs of all interesting matters, and finding out what your problems and difficulties are in order that they may be remedied.

The government of Venezuela is equally interested in their expedition. Please do us the pleasure of receiving them as well as you are able, providing them with all possible facilities and accompanying them on their investigations. If you are unable to accompany them in person, please provide them with one of your tribesmen who can speak Spanish and who knows the neighborhood well.

I should have very much liked to come with them myself and greet you in person, but I have so much to do at the present time that I am unable to leave.

Please God we shall see you again soon at the mouth of the Vichada. You know already that this house is yours.

While awaiting the pleasure of seeing you again, allow me to remind you that I am,

Your servant and your friend,

Alvaro B. de C.

Representative of the Government of the Republic.

When Mario's discourse was at an end I made a sign to Elie, who brought me a small packet we had prepared before landing. I undid it under the eyes of the assembled Piaroa Indians to reveal three lengths of striped cotton cloth which I handed to Mario, saying:

"Here is a little present for you and your children."

I waited in vain for Mario to thank me, but the cloth disappeared at once together with a group of women, of whom one was Mario's wife. I remembered what one of the brothers Solano had said: A present isn't a present to an Indian, but a payment for some service previously forgotten. In that case, where is the need for thanks?

While Elie and our two Guahibos were taking the things out of our canoe, we held a long conversation with Mario.

All this is very flattering, he said to us in effect, but what do you really want here?

We explained to him that we had heard about the celebrations of the Piaroa tribe. We were very much interested in them and would like to be present at them if that were possible.

"Celebrations?" he exclaimed. "What celebrations?"

"Oh come, Mario," I said. "You are having celebrations here, making music, and singing and dancing."

He continued to deny it, and his face expressed the greatest possible surprise, but I was not deceived.

"We heard your music only a little while back," I insisted. "It stopped only when we came into the lagoon and our Guahibos called out to attract your attention."

I told him that in any case we wanted to stay in the village for a few days at least. It was difficult for him to refuse us hospitality and a hut was placed at our disposal. We carried our things into it and slung our hammocks. Mario stayed with us, looking curiously at our heavy cases, which were painted with the French and Colombian colors. A number of other tribesmen joined him and soon there was quite a gathering in the little hut. We continued to question Mario about the Piaroa celebrations and about the strange music we had heard when we came into the lagoon. He smiled, equivocated and evaded our questions as far as possible. From time to time he rapidly translated what we said to the other tribesmen, who all laughed with him in chorus, and watched us with growing curiosity.

We opened our cases and unpacked our recording apparatus, assembling the instrument and its loud speaker. Pierre produced our albums of records. We said nothing further until everything was ready.

"You don't want to talk to us about your music," I said finally. "Very well, we'll let you hear ours."

And at full strength Pierre started up a Mozart symphony. All the Indians immediately fell silent. It was quite obvious that they were flabbergasted. Then we heard the sound of quick footsteps outside and the mat which covered the entrance to the hut was lifted as more and more Indians came in. They stood there in silence and listened without moving a muscle, their eyes glued on the strange apparatus from which the glorious sounds came. Before long the entire male population of the village must have been assembled in and around our hut. It was not so much the strange thing itself that impressed them as the music. Quite a number of them, Mario for example, had been to Puerto Ayacucho, and there they had heard the noises made by the local juke box, the American mechanical player to be found in all the cafés of South America. A nickel in the slot produces atrocious Tin-Pan Alley music from scratched records. But that was the full extent of their acquaintance with the white man's music.

When the symphony was over we began to talk again. Our audience was very attentive now. I explained to Mario that the world was very large and that there were many different kinds of white men in it, some of whom he had never met, and that these white men had all sorts of music that he had not yet heard. Then I began to talk about other kinds of music—music, for example, played on bone and wooden instruments carved by men who lived in forests in various parts of the world. When I began to approach the question I was anxious to broach again with him he pretended to be listening with only half an ear, and he took refuge in embarrassed smiles. But neither he nor any other of those present lost a word of what I was saying.

An old man had followed the scene wordlessly, crouched in a corner of the hut. Mario now went up to him and took him outside. After a moment or two all the others followed them and we were left alone. The last man had left the mat at the entrance open, and the darkness, for night had already fallen, made a rectangle of blackness. The village might have been deserted, for the only sound was the whine of mosquitoes and the rattling of wing cases as the elytrons crawled around in the grass at the edge of the lagoon. We made our hammocks ready for the night, a little disturbed at the sudden and unexplained departure of the Indians.

MUSIC NO WHITE MAN HAD HEARD BEFORE

Some time passed and then suddenly we heard again the same deep trumpet-like sound we had heard from the distance when we came into the lagoon, but this time it was quite close and extraordinarily loud. Above the deep and throbbing bass notes which stirred our vitals like the rolling of a great organ, there was a clear high-pitched melody, soft and harmonious.

A dozen or so Indians came forward out of the darkness and entered our hut. They were hardly recognizable as our visitors of a little while before. They had taken off their shirts, and their brown backs shone with beads of sweat and their dark eyes gleamed with joy. They were playing a variety of trumpets and flute-like instruments, blowing away with all their might and keeping on the move the whole time. They did not stop when they came in but went on marching round the interior walls one behind the other. Mario brought up the rear, and when he saw the mixture of surprise and pleasure on our faces he looked even happier than his men. It was our turn to remain silent and listen, our turn to hear and admire strange music we had never heard before.

The last man in carefully closed the door of the hut and the musicians went on marching round and round still playing at the top of their bent. It seemed almost as though the sounds of their music were accumulating in the confined space of the hut as smoke gradually thickens and makes the air almost unbreathable after a while. And we were almost breathless now, but with emotion and delight.

We were witnessing something unique, living, unforgettable and unknown. The first miracle had happened. Before our eyes was a collection of primitive instruments which, in all probability, no white man had ever had an opportunity of examining. The music produced from them in the hands of these Indians was astonishingly harmonious and impressive. Jean and I rushed to set up the microphones while Pierre started up the sound recorder.

Thanks to the music of Mozart—which, incidentally, was to render us many valuable services throughout the course of our expedition—we were able to begin recording Piaroan tribal music from the very first day of our arrival in the village on the Fruta Canyon.

When the music was finally at an end, which was some two

hours later, we played back our discs and let the Indians hear what we had recorded permanently of their music. When the players had departed Mario remained with us for a while. He was very proud and quite moved, and his emotion had the effect of making him more talkative. He was now prepared to admit that his tribe were celebrating. In addition to the music there were, it appeared, special masks worn for the celebrations—"tigers," he called them. The celebrations took place on the village square between the large tribal hut and the small hut facing it across the square. When he finally left us we tried to sleep.

However, we did not sleep very much that night, for we were excited, partly by our arrival in this Piaroan village and partly by all the strange and unknown things we felt around us, hidden behind the walls of palm leaves, behind the great black trunks of the trees which formed the horizon around the village and the lagoon, behind the faces of these Indians, behind their expressions, their laughter, their fears and their enthusiasms, and, finally, in the very air itself, a strange humid atmosphere which seeped into our hut and around our hammocks, charged with a ripe-rotten odor both sour and sweet. It seemed to be the characteristic atmosphere of the Piaroan world.

And another reason why our night was far from restful was that Pierre had an attack of neuralgia which rapidly grew more and more insupportable. The dank atmosphere of the forest not only affects wood and iron, it also attacks stones and the living bone itself. Ordinary toothache was nothing to what poor Pierre had to endure. Aspirin, barbiturates—nothing was any good. His whole jaw was affected and he twisted and turned in his hammock all night in an agony, trying to suppress his groans.

We knew that the capital of the "Federal Amazonas Territory," Puerto Ayacucho, had a hospital, and we just had to get Pierre there as quickly as possible. We arranged that Jean should go with him in the canoe and that while they were away I would make preparations for the 16mm film we proposed to shoot of the Piaroan New Year celebrations. When we told Mario what had happened he immediately offered two of his men to go along as well. Hurriedly we packed them off and a few minutes later I was alone with Elie and the strange bitter-sweet odor of the Piaroan village.

Just before Jean and Pierre left we drank a bowl of hot coffee. On his own initiative Elie handed Mario a steaming bowl.

"Would the chief care for some coffee?" he asked politely.

Mario drank the coffee straight off and then turned to me.

"Come along with me," he said.

We walked up the village street toward the square. The big hut on one side was the collective gathering place, the tribal hut, a sort of village hall. The small hut on the other side of the square was really hardly a hut at all. It had no window and no visible door: just a few palm leaves stacked loosely against the side to cover a dark hole. It was a sacred place, a sort of shrine. Mario pushed the loose palm leaves aside and we crawled through the hole one after the other on all fours.

My eyes gradually accustomed themselves to the semidarkness inside, and the first thing I saw was several men squatting silently around, their heads lowered to some mysterious task. A number of objects were on the floor around them and against the walls. The interior of the little hut was hardly more than ten feet across. We were in the sacristy, the holy of holies. It contained all the sacred objects of the traditional religious cult of the Piaroas. Religion is part of the warp and woof of their lives, and they are more profoundly imbued with religion than any other people I have met, either Indian or White. This hut was the material heart of their collective religious life, as this month of celebrations, with all its traditional observances, was the spiritual heart. The hut was the stronghold of the tradition that God had confided to men. And here the use of the term men is exclusive: women are not allowed to enter the holy of holies under pain of death.

Quite close to me a small bunch of herbs hung from the roof by a strip of liana and burned slowly away as incense does. As the spikes were consumed, a long white ash formed like a fine stalactite, and now and again the ash fell onto a small, flat stone on the floor beneath. This was niopo, the basis of the narcotic taken by the religious head, or chamane, of the tribe, to enable him to shake off the restraining bonds of his physical body and soar away into the spiritual world.

A man crouched motionless beside the stone, waiting to collect the ash as soon as it fell. Treated by fire and water and mixed with many other substances, it forms a deep brown mixture which is pounded in a special mortar by the sorcerer. The resulting powder is sniffed up into the nostrils.

Before the entrance, suspended about three feet above the ground, hung five strange objects made of palm, feathers, and wickerwork and covered with painted clay. These were the ritual masks, the conic headgear of the *uani-mesa* or *ye-uiuini-kusa,* the "palm men" or "tiger-panthers." These were the five anonymous priests who would officiate in the tribal hut, their features hidden behind the palm fringe depending from this headgear, their bodies completely covered by long robes reaching to the ground and made of strips of vegetation. In this way no part of them would be seen apart from the hand which shook the maraca. At the top of the masks was a sort of ring protruding like the collar of a vase. A large bunch of scarlet macaw feathers about twenty inches long was fastened by a strip of liana to this ring. These feathers are the special sign of their office. The priests never wear them outside, but as soon as they enter the tribal hut to begin their sacred office they adjust it before their faces.

Mario crouched beside me and explained all these details one by one, talking fluently in a monotonous voice as though he were reciting a litany, the corners of his mouth and his eyes wrinkling in his constant little smile. Five pairs of eyes shone behind him in the darkness, staring at me, for I had taken out my notebook and was carefully sketching the details of the masks and spelling out their names as I wrote them down. The men began to smile broadly.

"The 'tiger-panthers' go out twice a day," Mario went on. "Each time they go out they dance and sing for two or three hours in the center of the tribal hut."

By my side willing hands were feeling amid a heap of green palm leaves. Apparently the Indians intended to show me something else. A number of wooden objects of tubular and conical shapes were produced. Some of them were made of large spirals of bark and the others seemed to be just plain pieces of bamboo wood tubes from which the pith had been scraped. They were the instruments on which the sacred music had been played the night before in our hut. Every evening during the month of celebrations the women all gather in the tribal hut. Through the walls they can hear the blowing of these instruments as the musicians march round and round the hut, as they had marched round and round us. While the instruments are being played the women are forbidden to leave the hut under pain of death. They do not know that the music they can hear is being played on instruments of bark and bamboo invented and manufactured by the men of the tribe from time immemorial. They are taught to believe that what they can hear through the palm-leaf walls of the tribal hut is the voice of the protective spirits of the tribe who have come down to earth to talk with the menfolk.

This is not fraud in the sense that we understand the word, and although the men know the truth this does not prevent them from establishing an intimate relationship between this and that instrument and this and that personage of their mythology, and for them too the voice of the instruments is the voice of the spirits. There is a pair of each type of instrument, and the two are of unequal length.

"The male and the female of each voice," Mario said.

But there is one exception to this rule, and they showed it to me. It was perhaps the strangest instrument of all. It consisted of a clay vase painted with esoteric designs, and in the bottom was a fragment of rock crystal. It was played, Mario explained, by alternately inserting two flutes, the one of dark wood and the other of light wood, and then playing them. The vase served as a sounding box and modified the tone of the flutes. I asked Mario what this instrument was called but he only laughed.

"All right," he said when I insisted. "It's called the devil's wife."

"Why?"

"Well, you know what the devil is, don't you? It's the evil

spirit which is always on the lookout to do men harm. Now this spirit has a wife just like everyone else, and it's the voice of the wife that comes out of the vase."

For me this instrument was the most astonishing of all the treasures of the Piaroan tabernacle. No ethnographer had previously recorded anything of the sort throughout South America. I observed with keen interest that the strange designs on this vase were similar to those which had been found on the necks of certain Aztec vases discovered during excavations in Mexico. Here on the Upper Orinoco, we had come across the only known evidence of the survival of a pre-Colombian Mexican instrument. By what devious ways had the tradition arrived in these parts?

When I had finished sketching and taking down the details of the masks I did the same for the musical instruments. Mario told me their names and the names of the various woods out of which they were made. When I picked up the vase instrument which was known as "the devil's wife" in order to examine it more closely, the Indians looked at me rather anxiously. When I had finished and put it down carefully, they audibly sighed in relief.

THE STORY OF A MURDER

"I'll tell you a story," said Mario. "One day, when there was a Piaroan village farther down, on the river Mataveni, quite close to the Orinoco, a white man came to us at the same time as you have come, at the beginning of the New Year celebrations. It was in the evening, the masks had just danced in the tribal hut, and the musicians were preparing to go out.

"This white man needed paddlers. He wanted to go into the forest to look for resin. He had a big *falca* something like yours. 'Give me men for my boat,' he said to the Piaroan chief. The chief said nothing, but he turned to two muchachos and told them to take down their hammocks and go on board the *falca*. But the muchachos didn't want to go off and work for the white man; they wanted to stay in the village for the celebrations. So after a while they deserted the white man, returned to the tribal hut and slung up their hammocks again. The white man was very angry. He ran through the village searching for the men. He looked everywhere, but he couldn't find them, because as soon as they saw him coming they ran away and hid themselves in the forest. The white man broke into the sacred hut where the musical instruments and the masks were kept, and he flung everything out. He was so angry that he trampled on everything, smashing the instruments and the masks and tearing off the palm leaves and the feathers—all the things that women must never see. Apart from the two muchachos who had made good their escape, the whole village was assembled, men, women and children.

" 'Kill that man,' said our chief. So all our men took their lances, their bows and arrows and their blow pipes, and they fell upon the white man. He fled and fell into the water. Some pierced him with their spears and others fired their arrows at him.

"He managed to crawl out of the water, and he talked very differently now. 'Don't kill me,' he cried. 'Don't kill me.'

" 'Kill him,' our chief repeated, and this time they killed him.

"His *falca* was full of merchandise. It was worth thousands and thousands of pesos. There were cooking pots, bales of cloth for making dresses, trousers, and shirts, knives, matchets, and glass pearls for making necklaces. There was everything there the Whites sell us. But our Indians didn't want the things. The white man was a bad man and his goods were bad, so the Indians sank his boat in the river and gave everything to the fishes.

"Now you know why I didn't want to tell you anything about our celebrations, neither about the music nor the *uani-mesa*. We didn't know what you wanted here. You didn't want resin, and you didn't want rubber, and you didn't want cassava. So what did you want? We didn't understand. We were afraid you might have come to destroy our masks and our instruments, or buy them and take them away from us. Do you know what would have happened if you had taken away our music? The spirits would have killed us all because the music is their voice and it mustn't be heard anywhere else but here. So we should have had to kill you to save our own lives, but that would have been very dangerous. One mustn't kill white men; there are too many of them and they come back too quickly. That is why we were very worried yesterday evening."

Mario looked at me and smiled. Then he rose and, going to the entrance, drew back the palm leaves which hid the interior of the sacred place. Standing back, he indicated that his explanation marked the end of my visit. I went out into the village square and the palm leaves closed over the entrance behind me. The square was deserted. After the semi-darkness of the little hut the full sunlight dazzled me, and after the talk in the confined space the silence outside was enormous. As I walked down the little path toward the waterside two girls went by. They had been to fetch water, and they carried earthenware pitchers on their heads. They smiled at me in a friendly fashion but with a certain timid reserve. Their long hair shone with the vegetable oil which had been used to dress it. It was done up in a quite complicated fashion and fastened with red and green strips of liana. Their cheeks were freshly painted in brilliant colors.

I entered our hut and made myself comfortable in my hammock to note down the details of what I had heard and seen. I realized that the confidence of the Indians must be won by their own methods of patience and passivity, that no attempt must ever be made to override their misgivings and their fears, and that one must never go too far at once if one hopes to penetrate into their spiritual world, which is not dead, but merely hidden. But it hides itself more and more with the passing of time in order to escape the prying eyes of the white man who, since the days of Christopher Columbus, has sought to establish nothing but his own world over the whole universe. The Indians have sought refuge from him in the night, and yet they love the sun as all other men do.

A small bedaubed child came up to watch me writing. He stood for some time at the head of my hammock and watched with fascination as my pencil ran over the paper making its strange marks. When he grew tired of that at last, he began to study the label on a tin of powdered milk Elie had left on one of the cases that morning. It represented a woman with flaming hair drinking—presumably the powdered milk—with marked satisfaction. On the label was the word "Chicago," the town of origin of the delectable beverage, followed by many other letters and figures. The boy went to the case and picked up the tin. It occupied him for perhaps half an hour, during which time he was completely indifferent to the mosquitoes which were sucking his blood. (They were also sucking mine.) The lad was naked, bronzed, and obviously healthy. He was also unvaccinated.

Then a round head appeared in the entrance to the hut. It belonged to a tall and affable Indian who was unable to converse with me except by signs, as he spoke no Spanish. He appeared to be inquiring whether I had spent a good night. I indicated by further signs that I had indeed. He was the regular occupant of our hut, and it had taken him only five minutes to move out the previous evening. Hammock over his shoulder and matchet in hand, he had gone off to the tribal hut followed by his wife and children, carrying his three bows and about a dozen arrows, a large knife and a small one, two little calabashes of curare, a blow pipe and an aluminium cooking pot, representing the sum total of his personal property.

He now came closer and carefully examined the knots of the cord which held my hammock in position. He seemed to find them complicated. The Indians sling their hammocks in a much simpler fashion. All they have to do is to pull a string and their whole fastening comes undone at once. But you have to know how to do it. And if you don't, you must find out for yourself. You mustn't ask for information. That would diminish your prestige.

MARIO

It was past midday and the whole village appeared to be asleep, exhausted by the broiling sun. Mario appeared again. His blue headgear shone in the sun like a mirror. I invited him to stretch himself out in a neighboring hammock and I offered him "a real cigarette." The Piaroas have made the acquaintance of real cigarettes properly rolled in thin paper from the white men, and they are very fond of them. The Indians cultivate the tobacco plant, but they roll its leaves green and smoke them in a covering of banana leaf. They are not the only ones to do this, for "real cigarettes" are very rare along the upper Orinoco.

For some time we lay and smoked in silence, our eyes fixed idly on the regular pattern of the palm leaves which formed the roof of the hut. Mario was enjoying his cigarette voluptuously. I began to question him about his birthplace, about his family, and how he had come into contact with the white man. He answered me readily and talked for an hour while I remained silent, listening to him. He told me that he had first come into contact with the white man's civilization as a child. His mother and father had lived in the forest quite naked apart from many beads round their necks, their wrists, and their ankles. One day a white man had come to the village and taken him, Mario, away, giving his father two knives in exchange. For a year this white man had taught Mario to tend the rubber trees in the forest and to collect the liquid rubber in pots, which were then loaded into a boat. The white man had taught him Spanish and given him several pairs of trousers and a number of shirts. This white man smoked a pipe, it appeared, just as I did.

"So you were living *en guayuco* then?"

He laughed a little shamefacedly and nodded. (In the Orinoco Basin the public girdle of the Indians, which is made of a strip of material passed between the legs and held up by a cord round the waist, is called "guayuco.")

"And do you ever go back to it now?"

He laughed at the question, shaking in his hammock. Then he answered simply:

"No, I don't. Trousers are much better, particularly on account of the mosquitoes."

I wanted to know something about the traditional texts of the Piaroas, and to learn from Mario the significance of the ceremonies carried out during the month of celebrations. He had already shown me the objects of the cult. I wanted to know in particular why the sacred music was played every evening during the month, why there were five masks, why they were called "tigers," and why their wearers officiated twice daily in the tribal hut. I wanted to penetrate into their world beyond the mere outward forms. I explained to Mario what an oral tradition was, though no doubt he knew what it was even better than I did. I told him that all over the world men knew where they had come from and how they had become what they were. I knew that the affair would take a long time and I didn't want to go too fast. After having given him to understand that I was anxious to learn about the origin of the Piaroas according to their own tradition and to understand the significance of their religious ceremonies, I went on further.

I thought to take advantage of his pride, the double pride that animated him, the pride of the Indian toward the white men because he was aware of secrets that they did not even suspect, and his pride toward his own people as the man who was recognized as "the Chief of the Piaroa Indians," Don Mario of the blue helmet. But that privilege had its obverse side. For to the white men Mario was only a barefooted illiterate who would never be a full citizen either of Colombia or Venezuela, the two abstract entities across which his natal Orinoco sprawled. And perhaps to the Piaroa Indians, who did not even speak Spanish, he was not such a great chief after all. Perhaps he was only a sort of "collaborator," a suspect to whom they would not dream of confiding the fundamental things which were really essential for the tribe. But Mario's own ambition was simple enough: he wanted to be a man. He had the pride of race and his own pride. He was unwilling to sacrifice anything, and he wanted to advance himself. The problem was as simple to formulate as it was difficult to elucidate. He had to be made to forget when he was talking to me that I was a civilized human being. Unless he could be brought to forget that he would always be on his guard against me, and he would not tell me what I wanted to know. He must be persuaded to tell me out of pride what his cunning would suggest he should conceal.

"It is very important for people to know where they come from and who they are," I said. "Everywhere in the world, long after everyone has apparently forgotten, there is always some old man here and there who still knows. If no one knew what we were and where we came from, there would no longer be men in the world at all. The rains and the tigers would have finished us off. And it is very important that before the old man dies he should pass on to others what he knows. The white men have told me that you are the chief of all the Piaroas."

He reacted promptly to this.

"Oh, yes!" he exclaimed. "I am the chief of the Piaroas, their great leader."

"Very well then, Mario, if you should happen not to know the things I ask you, then it is absolutely necessary that you should find an old man who does know, and get him to tell you all he knows. Because unless you do that you will never really be the chief of the Piaroas. You have only to go to the old man who knows, the old man who cures, the old man who breathes on the sick and shakes the maraca. There is sure to be such an old man here and he will know all about these things. And you can tell him that I know the things as they are known in my country, that I care for the sick, that I know where I come from and what I am, and that I should like to know what he knows, and that in exchange I would tell him what I know, and that I would care for the sick that he cannot care for if they suffer from sicknesses that I know about."

Mario remained silent. One might have thought that he had not heard what I said. I changed the subject and began to talk about animals. I told him that in the colder parts of the world where we came from there were no peccaries, no tapirs, and no tigers. This seemed to astonish him vastly.

"What!" he exclaimed. "You have killed them? Killed all of them so that none are left?"

Another hour passed. He got up and made as though to go. At the threshold he turned.

"You remember the old man I went out with when we were here yesterday evening, before we showed you our music? The old man who was sitting beside the niopo in the little hut this morning? Well, he's like you say. He knows. He breathes on the sick to drive away the sickness and he shakes the maraca. He's the one who gives orders here, not me. But we don't let the white men know, that's all, because the white men don't believe in such things. They laugh at them. They say: Indian foolishness. But you know it's true although it's different. I'll go and tell him."

And then Mario added: "This morning after you had left the little hut where we had shown you the masks and our instruments, and you had put it all down in your little book, they asked me: 'Well, what does he say? Does he want to buy them? Has he said he wants to take them away with him?' They were very worried. They thought they might have to kill you. When I told them that you didn't want to take anything away, only look at them, and put them down in your little book and photograph them, and that you wanted to hear the music again and see the *uani-mesa* dancing in the big hut, they were very relieved.

"You know we don't like showing such things to the white men. They don't understand. It's like when the white man came to my parents. When they see us going around almost naked and with feather headdresses they either get angry and tear up everything, or they like it and want to take it all away. The whites we know always want to smash up everything or take it away from us."

And having said that Mario departed.

Night fell, a wonderful night with a full moon. I had invited Mario and the real chief of the village to come to our hut and share the kind of forest pheasant brought in by one of the Indians I had sent out with a rifle in the morning. I was sitting in my hammock when he came up with rapid steps and put down his bag at my feet: an armadillo and a pheasant. Then he went over to the wall, leaned the rifle against it, and put down three empty cartridge cases. I gave the armadillo to the village chief for his people and invited him and Mario to share the pheasant with me.

Mario and I sat astride the bench which formed the chief item of furniture in the hut, the mess tins and the cooked bird between us, and a pot of rice on the floor at our side. The chief ate standing up, using his hands, not knowing what to do with the metal fork and spoon I had given him, though Mario demonstrated with considerable aplomb how they should be managed. Our meal must have been a very interesting spectacle to judge from the crowd of people who came along to watch us. First of all there were all the men of the village, including the hunter himself, and then, one by one, the women, who squatted down around us with their backs to the wall and their babies in their arms. Before long they were giving their babies the breast to keep them quiet, while the mothers whispered their comments to each other between smiles and little furtive glances toward the bench where their chiefs, both spiritual and temporal, were breaking bread with the white man. It was not easy to make dinner-table conversation, because only one of my guests spoke a language that I could speak. Doing my best to be as natural as possible in these difficult circumstances, I talked to Mario about the wild animals of Europe, Africa, and so on, about which no one else present knew anything at all. The most complicated task I had set myself was trying to explain to a South American Indian what an elephant was and what it looked like.

Despite my best efforts and the evident good will of my partners, a gap gradually opened up over the bench between Mario and me. It was the same gap that I had first encountered on the Vichada in the big hut of the Guahibo Indians. Strangely enough it materialized out of *my* pannikins and *my* metal cutlery with which we were engaged in devouring *their* pheasant. There seemed something incongruous and irreconcilable between my possessions and that bird, a sort of antipathy, and the awareness of it steadily developed between Mario and me, between the world of those Indians and my world. I began to feel discouraged and the dinner came to an end almost in silence.

The women stowed their breasts away and lifted up their babies. All those present got up and went off one by one except Mario, who stretched himself out in a hammock. We smoked in silence.

Elie took the dishes and the cutlery away to do the washing up.

"Time to go to bed," said Mario, throwing the butt of his cigarette out the doorway.

With that he rose and left the hut.

I blew out the lamp and the moonlight came flooding through the open doorway. Elie came back and tucked himself away in his hammock without a word. Somewhere a dog began yapping. When it stopped, the milky light of the moon seemed fraught with an enormous silence, extending all the way up to the stars. I lay in my hammock and went on smoking, and gradually my discouragement was dissipated. I lay there thinking with my eyes open. I recalled the previous evening in this hut, so very different from now:

Outside the hut the noise of trumpets and flutes had sounded, and inside my heart had beaten rapidly with excitement. There had been warmth and noise and pleasurable excitement. The musicians had marched around the walls, and I had gone from one to another with the microphone in my hand. A cold sweat had broken out of all my pores and run down my body. The hairs on my skin had stood upright. The blast of the trumpets had shaken the walls, the roof of the hut, and the very ground itself. The sounds had seemed full of sweat and smoke, and they had moaned and howled as though they really were the voices of spirits, simple animal spirits of the heavens and the earth. They rose from the ground and echoed from the walls and the roof; they went through and through my vitals like beasts roaring in the forests. The high-pitched melodies of the flutes wove in and out above them, while below the devil's wife rumbled and grunted. It was a sonorous temptation of Saint Anthony.

A cloud now slid over the moon like a hand over a mouth and the silence became blackness. My eyes were still open and I was thinking anxiously. There must still be many things the Indians were concealing from me. I felt exhausted, and I was unable to sleep. I noticed that Elie was still awake. He began to whistle a rumba softly. I lit another cigarette and interrupted his whistling to deliver a long speech. I explained to him that the Indians were men just as we were; that they thought many things that we thought, and that they were highly sensitive. I told him that one must be extremely careful about what one asked of them, and that whatever they did one must never laugh, unless they were laughing themselves. One must, above all, never laugh at them.

"Sí, señor," he said laconically, and went to sleep.

"MONSIEUR GHEERBRANT, THE PLACE IS FULL OF PEOPLE!"

I was half dreaming in the silence when I heard a noise. It seemed to come from the direction of the village square, from the sacred hut into which only men might penetrate. It was a regular throbbing sound which stopped and went on again, as a lighthouse lamp disappears every few seconds. I tried to persuade myself that what I could hear was the buzzing of blowflies, or perhaps bumblebees or hornets, circling round the walls, but it went on for hours and the noise rose like the sea. Elie woke up and went to the lagoon to get me a glass of water. He was scared when he returned.

"Monsieur Gheerbrant," he whispered, "the place is full of people. There are people on the square, people in the little hut and people in the big one. They're all crouching on the ground as though they were grinding something. They're all talking at once as though they were saying their prayers."

"That's all right," I said soothingly. "Keep quiet and go to sleep."

He climbed into his hammock and went off to sleep.

I remained motionless in the darkness listening to the noise. I tried to open my ears to it as widely as possible, to open my spirit and my body so that the throbbing that filled the air and penetrated the walls would penetrate me too, surmounting the obstacles of my white skin and my white understanding, and recording the message it was undoubtedly carrying through the night. I could now clearly distinguish the choir of men's voices taking up one verse of a litany after the other as they were spoken by a solo bass voice, sorrowful and broken, accompanied by a high-pitched maraca. The litany went on for hours and spread out in the night as though under the cold vault of some immense church. It could have been the grey litany of a choir of monks lying prostrate with their arms spread out in the form of a cross, their faces to the ground, a litany of soil and sweat, the litany of the night seeking the day endlessly, since the world began. . . .

I did not move. I did not go out into the night to witness the scene. I made no attempt to encroach on the ceremony. Mario had said: "Time to go to bed." And the hint was enough.

I decided to wait patiently, to wait until they invited me of their own accord to witness the most secret ceremony of their religion.

I felt myself back in the Middle Ages. All around me, present and almost palpable, were those things which have retreated into the darkness away from the white man's world since words became empty husks and speech was made disincarnate.

I lay there and relaxed, and I seemed to be borne away on the music into the night.

At last I slept.

THE CEREMONY OF THE MASKS

In the morning when I awoke, Mario was already there, smiling and shaking my hammock.

"Get up," he said. "You sleep far too much. It's broad daylight already. Hurry. The *uani-mesa* are just coming out."

We arrived at the tribal hut just as the five masks were about to enter. We went in before them, walking down the center of the hut where a group of women were crouching low, steadily and rhythmically grinding cassava roots. Behind this group Mario indicated a hammock slung next to his own and I sat down in it. On my right in another hammock was the enigmatic "old man who knew," the one Mario had spoken of and whom I now took to be the spiritual head of the tribe.

The five masks entered behind us and lined up in a free space in the center of the hut, in front of the women who were grinding the cassava roots. Other men gathered round them eagerly, attaching the plumes of macaw feathers to the top of their headdress, and then, like dressers at a theatre, they carefully checked the costumes of the five priests, adjusting the arrangement of their capes and their cloaks of palm leaves. When all was ready the priests began to shake their maracas rhythmically and to sway from one foot to the other in unison, while uttering the first verses of their chant. The great tribal hut, which was perhaps fifty feet long and half as high to the summit of its pointed roof, had no windows of any kind, but in four or five places the covering palm leaves were pushed aside by the ends of long poles, so that narrow rays of sunlight penetrated, cutting through the smoky air and throwing brilliant stripes over the costumes of the officiating priests. The rest of the hut was in semi-darkness. The women steadily went on with their work, and the grating sound as the silex stones ground the cassava roots followed the rhythm of the maracas and the chant of the priests. Their faces invisible behind the fringe of palm leaves hanging down from their headdress, the priests droned the same verse nine times, and the tenth time they ceased rattling their maracas and bowed deeply before them. An old woman stood upright and motionless in front of them, squeezing her nose with one hand and intoning a sort of long amen in a high-pitched whine. At a sign from her a younger woman got up from her work and came forward, a child perched astride one hip. Facing the old woman she extended one arm and put her hand on the old woman's shoulder. Then she pinched her nose with her free hand. This was done rapidly and in silence, without interrupting the litany of the five masked priests, to which the two women now replied in unison.

It was probably about eight o'clock in the morning and the sun was already high. However, the thick roof of palm leaves kept off the heat very effectively and the temperature in the hut was barely warm. The cool air was sharply scented with the rather pungent odor of the freshly-ground cassava roots.

All around in the half light I could see other hammocks with dim forms swinging gently in them. Lying near me with his eyes staring up indifferently at the weave of palm in the roof was the old man. He lay there silently and he seemed unconcerned at my presence. He took not the slightest notice of Mario, or the women who were still grinding the cassava roots, or even of the five priests and their chanting. His spirit seemed elsewhere, and it came back to earth only when one of the many children, naked and bedaubed, climbed into his hammock and squatted down on him. Instantly the enigmatic old man with the sorcerer's face was transformed into the incarnation of an indulgent old grandfather. He unbent completely toward the laughing child, tickling it happily and playing with it tenderly. In the meantime the five masked priests went on chanting their litany with the monotonous regularity of a praying wheel. I turned to Mario and asked what it was they were chanting.

"It's rather difficult to explain," he replied, "but it's more or less what you were talking about the other day. You know, about the mountains from which the first men came down, and about the animals which were also men then."

A woman rose and went over to a great pitcher from which she filled a large calabash with a syrupy liquid the color of *café au lait*. It was fermented cassava juice, the wine of the Indians. She placed the calabash on the ground behind the masked priests. The acolytes who had previously guided the priests into the hut came forward again. The priests stopped chanting and were guided back a few steps by the acolytes to form a circle round the calabash. Then, one after the other, they bent right down and drank deep, but in such a manner that their faces remained invisible. Then they straightened themselves, went back to the middle of the hut, and began their chanting again. A woman now brought us the fermented cassava juice. Mario drank first and then passed the calabash to me. It was the first time I had tasted the drink, and hardly had I bent my head over the calabash than I recognized the odor I knew so well already, the tepid, bittersweet smell which had been present everywhere around the village on the day we had arrived in the lagoon of the Piaroas.

The old man next to me stretched out an arm and without even looking to see what he was doing, felt around in a wickerwork basket on the ground beside him and produced his supply of niopo. He crushed up the brown mixture on a small board with raised edges and then, taking a bone tube with two branches which fitted into his nostrils, he passed the end over the powder and sniffed it up. Putting his niopo outfit back into the basket, he once again began feeling around in the darkness below his hammock and picked up a small bazaar ukulele. Heaven knows by what devious routes the instrument had arrived in such a place! Leaning back in his hammock and dreaming again, his eyes on the ceiling of palm leaves, he casually plucked at the strings, producing terribly discordant sounds. But that didn't seem to trouble him in the least, nor did it arouse any attention around us. The hammocks continued to rock gently, the women went on grinding their cassava roots, while the five priests swayed from one foot to the other and reeled off the verses of their interminable litany. Mario said nothing. He too seemed to be plunged into the strange dream which arose in the hut from the odor, the semi-darkness, the chanting, and the noise interrupted by monotonous silences. Then in his turn he took a pinch of niopo, as though he wished to arrive more speedily in the unreal world toward which I could feel us all slowly but surely moving.

At last the acolytes appeared again in the luminous center of the hut. The priests were standing still now, but the shaking of their maracas grew swifter. The litany stopped suddenly and they panted three times in succession like wild beasts in the forest. This sound was followed by a clucking, gobbling bird-like noise, also repeated three times, and, finally, three times repeated, a cooing sound. After that the file of priests turned and moved toward the door with short steps, guided by the acolytes. Then they disappeared. The office was over.

It was nearly midday, and I got out of my hammock and went out too. The sun in the village square dazzled me for a moment or two. Making my way back to our hut I took off my shirt, trousers, and boots and ran down to the lagoon and plunged in. Even after I climbed out of the water I noticed that my whole body still gave off the same tepid, bittersweet odor.

A few hours later Mario's head appeared in the doorway of our hut.

"Come," he said. "The masks are just coming out again."

WE RECORD THE STRANGE NIGHT LITANY

Days passed. Mario spent more and more time in our hut. The little smile was always at the corner of his mouth and his eyes sparkled. He laughed and joked, looked keenly at me when he thought I wasn't looking, and all the time he gradually opened the book in which the traditions of the Piaroas were recorded. With the point of his foot he drew a map of the upper Orinoco in the dust, showing its tributaries and the foothills of the Sierra Parima. I learned that the name Piaroa signified "men of the mountain," and that they had originated in a mountainous area, now deserted, where their great river, the Sipapo, rose. The Sun, the father of all the gods, sent two of his sons down to the earth, two brothers, one named Guahari and the other named Muhoka. They could be heard moving and singing within the stone which formed the summit of the mountains, and they opened up this stone to release shapeless animals out of which they made the first Piaroas, who then went down to the Orinoco. With the point of his foot Mario drew a small line among the numerous rivers which formed the upper Sipapo:

"That's where we come from," he said. "The mountain remained opened at the spot where Guahari released the first men in the world, and Guahari left *proofs* behind. There are two huge stone men there, one lying down without a head, and the other standing up, ready to be transformed into a living man. Guahari did not forget them; he left them there as *proofs.*"

I also learned that this same Guahari created the five tigers represented by the five masks, and that one of the instruments of the sacred music represented his voice, and that another represented the voice of his brother Muhoka.

After the second appearance of the masks there was a break in the religious life of the village from four o'clock in the afternoon until six. The women left their work, came to the village square, and sat around in little groups. Some of them gossiped, others searched for vermin or touched up the paint and rouge on their faces, while still others daubed the cheeks and the foreheads of their children to protect them from evil spirits.

The hunters and the fishermen, who had gone out at dawn, returned toward dusk, coming up from the river carrying in addition to their bows and arrows and their blowpipes a mixed booty of gold and silver fishes, reddish brown monkeys brought down by their curare tipped darts and still with an expression of astonishment like surprised children, turtles, agoutis, and—if they had been lucky—even antelopes. The bag was laid at the feet of the headman of the village, who then divided it equitably between the various households. But when one hunter returned empty-handed except for a big toad transfixed on one of his arrows he had to be content with it as his share.

The night came nearer and just before the sun reached the horizon a long and plaintive flute-like melody came from between the trees which bordered the lagoon. The women hastily seized their babies and disappeared into the big hut and the orchestra of sacred music made its appearance. The flutists came up the path from the quay as though they had emerged from the lagoon and on the village square they met the trumpeters holding their enormous instruments. One by one the other musicians came out of the sacred hut. There was "the devil's wife," and the *Guahari u'ufte'u,* the nasal-toned flute which represented the voice of Guahari, the *Me'otsa,* a small, shrill instrument which represented the voice of his brother Muhoka, and a thin vibrating blade which an adolescent flourished vigorously at the end of a strip of liana.

At a little distance a group of children about twelve years old formed into a line and drummed on the ground with their bare heels while a man shook the branches of a tree with all his might. In this way the wind was made to whistle and the ground to tremble while the flutes sang and the trumpets blew as the sacred musicians trotted round the tribal hut. For the women who had taken refuge in the hut all this represented the sonorous background against which the spirits came down to earth to take council with the men.

In the meantime my companions returned from Puerto Ayacucho, and day after day we made new recordings of the strange sounds we were privileged to hear.

When night had fallen and the moon sailed along high in the sky through the myriads of milky stars covering the heavens, the mysterious nocturnal chant began again in the tribal hut and went on till dawn. It was the hour at which all the men took pinches of the brown powder niopo to combat sleep and to help them slough off their physical husks and rise to the upper regions where both good and bad spirits reside, the spirits whose mercy and benevolence is essential to the fortunate conclusion of the liturgical month. As yet we were still not privileged to know its real aim.

Every day we questioned Mario anew, and he always proved evasive.

"Mario, why do you all chant like that at night, and what is it you sing? That's the moment when you all take niopo, isn't it?"

My impatience and my curiosity amused him. His eyes wrinkled and he smiled. He made jokes and avoided answering my questions. One day I decided on a more direct assault.

"Tonight if you chant we will come to the big hut. We would like you to translate for us what you are singing, so that we can record it on our instruments as we have already recorded the music and the chanting of the masks. Unless we can do that our journey here will hardly have been worth while. All we shall be able to tell our people about the Indians will be incomplete."

We had just had lunch and it was the hottest hour of the day. We were swinging gently in our hammocks smoking. Mario listened quietly to what I had to say and then without a word he got up and went out. Soon after that the masked priests began their second office. I went to the big hut and settled myself in my usual hammock between Mario and the old man. After quite a while Mario leaned toward me and plucked at my sleeve.

"I have told the old man about what you said a little while ago, and he's not willing. He says you have no right to be in the big hut in the night, and if you did it would displease the gods. You don't know enough for that. You aren't an Indian, you see. And even if we were willing to let you come in the men wouldn't like it. They all take niopo in the night. They might be angry. During the day you can come into the big hut as often as you like, but not at night. There are men the niopo drives mad, you see. It isn't serious. They are mad only for a moment, but they mustn't see you at that moment. The old man is the one who sings, and he shakes his special maraca. It is the one he uses when he heals people. Everyone then repeats what he says. I can't tell you what it is he sings. I have forgotten. It's a story about all the animals and all the plants, and all there is in the forest. At first he says: 'The first Indians came down to the earth, and they were everything there was on earth, and everything there is in the forest was created for the Indians. And after that—I don't know any more. He says a lot of things, about all the animals and all the plants in the world. And then he talks about the gods and he says the gods themselves are speaking. But I don't know any more. No one does. In the morning as soon as the sun rises and we go to bathe, no one knows anything any more. But he said that if you want to take the chants down on your machines like you did with the music, all you need do is to come in the evening with your things and set up the microphones in the big hut and lead the wires outside, and when the chanting begins you can do your work that way."

At five o'clock that evening the old chief condescended to give us a rehearsal of his nocturnal chanting. He climbed into his hammock and chanted a verse which he invented for the purpose while we set up the microphones around him, clambering into the roof to lay our wires and lead them outside. Then we set up our apparatus in the square against the wall of the hut, and Mario immediately constructed a little awning to protect them. At last we were ready and all we had to do was to wait. At two o'clock in the morning we plugged in, and the booming chant of the choir of drugged Indians was registered in the wax of our recording discs. All night long the old sorcerer chanted his words directly into the microphone which we had set up at the head of his hammock, and our recordings turned out excellent. But when we played them back there was a new surprise for us: at night the Piaroas chanted in a different tongue from that they used during the day, and we were unable to understand a single word. Apparently the Indians had their own Latin for religious purposes.

PREPARATIONS FOR THE CELEBRATION'S CLIMAX

It was a strange situation. We had filmed the life of the village in all its aspects; we had succeeded in setting up our camera in the big hut while the masked priests were chanting, and we had set it up in the village square when the musicians were playing. We had over thirty discs of recordings of the sacred music and the chanting, but we still did not know the point of the whole group of celebrations. During the time we had passed with the Piaroas we had been present only during the prologue of the main office. We were like Christians who had been able to follow all the liturgy of Lent, but who remained in ignorance of what was to follow in Easter Week. The moon entered into its final quarter, and there was only a week left. Then the month of celebrations would be over. The activity of the women redoubled, and it was through them that light at last fell on the real significance of the ceremonies.

They became as active as any busy ants, and their work went on from morning to night and far into the night. At dawn they went off en masse to where the cassava was grown, and a few hours later they returned to the tribal hut bent under the weight of enormous baskets of cassava roots. It looked as though they were preparing to provision an army. Every time we went into the hut we found them busily engaged in peeling, scraping, drying, and cooking the roots. A sort of mania for the work seemed to have seized them. Two canoes were drawn up from the lagoon and carried into the hut. The women then washed and scrubbed them thoroughly, filled them with water and put in hundreds of the cassava loaves they had just baked, breaking them up with swift fingers until the water was like a yellow soup, or a gigantic mixture of *café au lait*.

"They are preparing our drink," Mario informed me with gusto. "That's for later. The canoes will be covered up and left standing until the liquid begins to ferment and bubble. When it's ready we shall drink it all, and we shall all be as drunk as though it were rum. You too, or you won't see anything."

The two canoes cannot have contained much less than a

couple of hundred gallons of liquor, and there were not more than perhaps fifty people in the village all told, including the children.

Rather later we were sitting on a tree-trunk at one side of the village square. It was late afternoon and the musicians were soon due to appear. Three children stood and looked at us. After a while they went off toward the quay just before the music of the flutes made itself heard from the edge of the forest sending the women hurrying into the tribal hut. Mario gave them a sidelong glance while he was engaged with the palm leaves which covered the entrance to the sacred hut.

"It's for them," he said with a wink.

Two men emerged from the sacred hut and came toward us. One was the sorcerer, the spiritual chief of the tribe, and the other was an old man of about the same age and much the same appearance, whom we had never seen before.

"He has just come from the Sipapo to help," Mario explained.

The two old men crouched on the ground beside us, bending over an aluminum cooking pot such as all the stores in the Orinoco area sell to the Indians. Mario and the other men who now surrounded us looked alternately at the two old men and at the three children who stood there close together, their eyes fixed on the hands of the old chief.

Lukewarm water steamed gently in the pot and big black insects were swimming around in it.

"Twenty-fours," I murmured.

They were not the usual ants to be met with along the banks of the Orinoco, but an exceptional variety, black ants about an inch and a half in length, the biggest and most dangerous species to be found anywhere in the Amazonian forests. They have developed an enormous pair of hard, powerful pincers like surgical clamps, and in the tail there is a sting like that of a bee. This sting is used to paralyze their victims before they are devoured. The mestizos of the Orinoco declared that to be stung by such an ant meant a twenty-four-hour bout of fever, hence the name: "twenty-fours."

With the precision of a watchmaker using his tweezers, the

sorcerer and his assistant picked the ants out of the water one by one, holding them in the middle between finger and thumb. Now and again they were bitten, however, and the pincers bit into the flesh, closing tightly like a clasp. Without turning a hair the men would then seize the insect with the other hand and quickly remove it. The pincers were embedded so firmly in the flesh that when an ant was removed in this fashion its head came away and was left adhering to the finger. One by one the ants were fixed by the thorax in the interstices of a square piece of wickerwork about the size of a man's palm. The strips were then drawn together round the ants in such a fashion that their heads with their waving pincers protruded on one side of the wickerwork and their tails with the stings protruded on the other. Fastened in rows like this the ants gradually formed a living, wriggling square in the center of the wickerwork mat.

Mario raised his voice and began to talk in Piaroa to the three children, who were fascinated by the strange operation the sorcerer and his assistant were carrying out. Two of the children were Mario's sons, neither of them much older than perhaps twelve. The third boy might have been thirteen or even fourteen years old. Mario delivered a long lecture to them in a bantering tone. All the other men listened to what he said, nodding their heads and laughing heartily with him at the important passages, while all the time they kept their eyes fixed on the three boys.

"What are you saying to them?" I asked Mario.

"I'm telling them that the ants are for them and that it hurts. They say they are men now and there's no longer any need for them to live with the women. They can go into the little hut and see who it is that puts on the masks. They will play the trumpets and the flutes and get to know all the musical instruments. Then don't you think that they ought also to get hurt badly, just once, very badly, in front of everyone else? They must bear it like men. Without that they will never really grow up to be men, and there will be nothing to prove that they won't go off and tell the women what they've seen. So they are going to be stung by the ants, and in that way we can be quite sure that they will say nothing of what they see."

"When is the ceremony going to take place?"

"When the moon is dead. The day after tomorrow, the day of the great feast, the day we drink all the juice prepared by the women. You will see it. It will take place in the great hut when the sun is there."

He pointed to the center of the sky.

"After the drinking," he added.

Night approached. The sorcerer and his assistant went off toward the tribal hut, and the men around us dispersed. A moment or so later the first notes of the flutes sounded from the edge of the lagoon and their melody rose softly to the village. One star after the other began to appear in the sky. The moon came out, touching the silhouette of a tall and bosky tree. It was now no more than a small horizontal crescent, a brilliant milky yellow, somewhat the color of the cassava brew which was already fermenting in the canoes and awaiting the hour of the final ceremony. The trumpets began to sound from the other side of the village, something like swine grunting in the night, responding to the sound of the flutes and blindly punctuating their melody.

We had gone back to our hut and we lay in our hammocks discussing the work to be done tomorrow and the day after if we were to miss nothing of what was going on. At last we had grasped the significance of the celebrations. The harvest festival was in reality an initiatory rite for the induction of the adolescents of the tribe into man's estate. All that we had seen during the greater part of a month, and everything that we had filmed and recorded, represented the propitiatory ceremonies carried out before the great day itself. To film the initiation of the children, which was to take place in the tribal hut, would not be easy. We should not be able to take repeat shots as we had done with the ceremony of the masks. In this case we should have to work throughout a ceremony whose various phases were unknown to us, reacting speedily according to the circumstances as they arose, quickly moving our camera, the battery of accumulators, and our portable arc-light. We should also have to persuade the sorcerer to let us place our apparatus as close to the scene as possible.

That was as far as we had got with our discussions when a messenger arrived to tell us that Mario and the old man were waiting for us in the tribal hut. We went along at once, a little surprised at the unexpected invitation. We found Mario, the old sorcerer, and the new arrival from Sipapo crouching together in the center of the hut at the spot where we had installed our microphones in order to record the nocturnal chanting. In the light of a small oil lamp they were completing the preparation of their wickerwork screens of ants.

"The old man has called you so that you may make pictures of these ant screens," Mario informed us. "In that way you can show them on the other side of the Great Lagoon that the Indians are men."

Mario always referred to the ocean, which, I had explained to him, separated our continent from his, as the Great Lagoon. The two old men who were crouching there looked up at me and smiled encouragingly. We went back to our hut and prepared the camera, the battery, and the arc-light. We were a little astonished at the turn things were taking: it was the Indians who now proposed to dictate the scenario of our film.

When we got back to the tribal hut we found a number of other Indians watching the final preparations of the sorcerer and his assistant. When we began to set up our apparatus they turned their attention to us. We directed the arc-light on the two old men and then began to take. But the spectators, who up till then had only watched, now indicated that we should wait and they hurried off, returning after a short while with various things, including the sacred maracas of the nocturnal chant, the hanging talismans and the feathered ornaments. These they then scattered on the ground in calculated disorder and with a keen eye to effect.

The whir of our camera began again. All the time the two old men went on with their task imperturbably, assembling many hundreds of the "twenty-fours," one after the other in their wickerwork screens. As they worked steadily on, our imitation sunlight flung their silhouettes over the floor and onto the walls of the hut fantastically as though to complete the strange scene.

From outside we heard the harsh blowing of the trumpets as the musicians began to march round and round.

We returned to our hut, but we were unable to sleep. The sacred chanting sounded again and filled the whole night until the dawn, growing stronger and stronger and more and more insistent. This was the last time but one that the Indians would invoke the good offices of both benevolent and malignant spirits before the initiatory rites were consummated, and their prayers now had an urgency and ardor more vehement and supplicating than before. It was two or three o'clock in the morning before we finally fell asleep, and at half-past five Mario was there again.

"You're sleeping far too long," he said. It was becoming a permanent reproach. "Go quickly and bathe. The masks will be out again soon and you must be there with your machines to get everything."

I went down to the lagoon and plunged in. The bittersweet smell of fermented cassava had grown very much stronger. I seemed almost to be swimming in a sea of it. Striking out lazily toward the middle of the lagoon, I suddenly heard a violent snorting close at hand. The sun was not yet up and it was not easy to see anything, but at a little distance I made out two or three dark shapes disporting themselves in the water. They were lamentins, the whale-like creatures of the Amazonian rivers. They were gamboling around me, turning over and over and snorting happily. I counted at least a dozen of them.

By the time I got back to the bank, the sun had risen and it was daylight. It was then that I noticed that the bottom of the lake was covered with cassava parings. There must have been hundredweights of it. Mario was waiting for me in front of the hut and I mentioned the sportive mammals to him.

"Oh yes," he said smiling. "The grandmothers."

"What do you mean, grandmothers?" I asked.

"Why, our grandmothers, of course. Don't you know that? You know so many things and you don't know that the lamentins are our grandmothers! That's why our people never kill them. I don't take any notice of that. I've lived with the whites. A fat lot they care about killing their grandmothers. At home on the Orinoco I've killed them and eaten them. They're full of fat, you know. But I wouldn't do that here. The old man would be angry if I touched the grandmothers. Of course they're in the lagoon this morning. They've come in for the feast. That's why the women flung the cassava peelings into the water. We're all going to get drunk tomorrow. The grandmothers must get drunk too."

"Listen, Mario," I said. "You must keep with us tomorrow and explain everything as it happens, and let us know in good time exactly what's going to happen and where it's going to happen so that we shall have time to move our apparatus around."

He went off without saying a word. I was getting quite used to this and I knew what it meant: he was going to see the old man and tell him what I had said. Then they decided together what he should come back and say to me.

Two or three hours later he came back as I expected and climbed into the hammock next to me. At first he said nothing and waited until I offered him a cigarette. Then he began to talk about one thing and the other, but at last he came to the point.

"It's all right," he said. "The old man is quite willing for me to explain everything to you and for you to set up your machines in the big hut when the boys are stung with the ants. But there are two conditions. First of all you mustn't use your machine to make lightning."

He meant the flash bulbs for instantaneous photography.

"That would be too dangerous. It would drive away the good spirits and attract the bad ones. And then you must give us fifteen pesos, or if you like, instead, shirts and trousers for the old man and the headman of the village. When you show the things you have got here you're bound to earn money with them, enough to buy lots of shirts and trousers, and therefore the old man thinks it's only right that the village should benefit too."

I agreed to the conditions. Fifteen pesos was about five dollars. Mario went off happily to let the old man know that everything was in order.

The masked priests had emerged again and we went up to the

big hut with our camera. They no longer danced in line. That part of the proceedings was over. During the last day of the preparations for the great feast it was their business to occupy themselves exclusively with the two canoes full of drink. Once the cassava juice had fermented, it no longer belonged to the women and passed under the protection of the priests. In the sacred hut the men had woven two large mats. The masked priests took first one and then the other and went to cover up the canoes with them.

"Tomorrow when they take off the covers the drinking will start," said Mario.

A little later the masks came out again. Instead of their usual maracas each man carried a small piece of matting about the size of a handkerchief and held it in such a fashion that it made a sort of carrier. Inside were the wickerwork screens with the imprisoned ants, which were now quite ready. Once again the masks went off to the tribal hut and, executing a dance around the two canoes containing the cassava juice, they placed their little packets on the mats which covered the canoes. There were hundreds of ants and they were all wriggling madly. They were to guard the cassava juice until the next day.

The time passed quickly for us in the filming of all these strange comings and goings. Then night fell. It was the last night of the celebrations. The sacred chanting rose again. We listened, conscious that this was the last time we should ever hear it. We were very tired but toward one o'clock we went out of our hut to make one or two more recordings. Pierre and I waited for an hour or two sitting on the ground in the village square in silence. We heard the rattling of the sacred maracas and the men's voices rising and falling, breaking, and sobbing, as their spirits took the nebulous path opened up by the drug niopo. We waited until they had gone farther along this path than ever before and then we used our first disc, followed by a second, and a third. Everything seemed to be growing confused around us, as though we too were being caught up in the religious intoxication of the chanting Indians.

When we could do no more we went back to our hut, but

before we turned in we were anxious to hear what we had recorded. Pierre plugged in the loudspeaker, switched on the apparatus, put the tone-arm onto the record, and then let it blare out at full volume. The hut around us seemed to disappear. We had heard the chanting only through the palm leaf walls which had deadened the sound, but now we heard it just as it was heard inside the tribal hut. It thundered out into the night. Dogs came and rolled over and over in front of our apparatus, gnawing at the electric wires and howling. We had to drive them off vigorously.

Since we had turned on our record there was silence in the tribal hut. The door opened and Mario appeared, stripped to the waist and, for once, without his famous hat. Other Indians came in after him. They gathered in front of the loudspeaker, listening to the sound of their own chanting. They recognized one man as he coughed, the particular tone of voice of another, and the rattling of the maracas in the hands of the sorcerers. Suddenly they burst out laughing, but became grave and attentive again at once. I could see that they were trembling. One or two men returned to the tribal hut to fetch their niopo. They took a sniff or two and the excitement of the possessed showed in their dilated eyes and in the trembling of their hands, though outwardly they were very calm. When the record was at an end they turned away without a word and went back to the tribal hut with rapid steps.

A little later the rattle of the maracas began again and the voice of the old sorcerer chanted a verse which was like a jumble of vowels without end. The choir joined in with redoubled enthusiasm.

We dismantled our apparatus. The night air was beginning to tremble. Little gusts of fresh air passed over like birds in the sky. The dawn was near. A few mosquitoes were already about and their whine could be heard along the banks of the lake. They were awaiting the first glimmer of light before setting off on their quest for blood. We went to our hammocks almost overcome with weariness and fell into a deep sleep. It was not to last long: before the sun was fully above the horizon we were up again.

THE DAY OF THE GREAT RITUAL

At seven o'clock in the morning the masked priests uncovered the two canoes of fermented cassava juice and the old sorcerer gave the order for the drinking to begin. A large space had been cleared around the two canoes. In the center of the tribal hut a small stool had been set up. It was carved out of one piece of some dark wood and it represented the ritual seat from which the spiritual leader of the tribe officiated at the ceremony. The old man sat down on the stool. An old woman came forward and took the first calabash of liquid from the larger of the two canoes and brought it to him. A man was crouching on the ground before him. The old man slowly raised the calabash and made three circles with it round his head and across his chest and then three circles over the head of the man before him, to whom he then handed the calabash. The man drank the contents straight off and rose. A woman took the empty calabash from him and handed him a full one. In the meantime a second man had advanced toward the old sorcerer to receive his first calabash. Then came a third and a fourth, and so on and on until all the men had come forward. They were followed by all the women and their children.

The old sorcerer sat there stripped to the waist, performing his office impassively, repeating the same ritual gestures to each member of the tribe who came forward. When the last calabash of liquid had been handed over he still did not move from his seat. Lighting one of his large cigarettes rolled in banana leaf, he began to smoke quietly. All around him and out in the square, which could be seen through the wide open door, the cassava-juice orgy began.

He was the only one who did not drink. He was the one who watched, the one who knew, the one who led his people through the ceremonies of the sacred day as he led them every night with his prayers and his invocation of the spirits.

The orgy gradually increased in vehemence, as though in accordance with the slow movement of the sun as it rose higher and higher in the sky. Most of the tribe had now moved out into the square. Some of them drank standing up, others sitting or even lying down. Attentive women handed round brimming calabashes of cassava juice and saw to their replenishment as soon as they were empty, going swiftly backward and forward from the square to the two big canoes in the tribal hut. Each calabash held about a quart of liquid, and before long the stomachs of the drinkers could hold no more, and after each calabash they had to vomit before they could drink the succeeding one. They simply bent their heads forward to vomit, and then they bent them back to drink. Gradually the ground all around them turned into a shallow lake of yellowish liquid in which they stood or sat. While we were filming this scene Mario did not move from our side. Women whose hair was decorated with strips of liana and glistening from the amount of vegetable oil applied to it came up to us smiling and offered us calabashes, their fingers half in the liquid. They had stuck gaily colored feathers in their hair and their shining faces were painted with complicated patterns. We could not always refuse to drink, and before long our stomachs began to swell too. Jean began to have difficulty in managing his camera at all. In the end we vomited too, and as we did so a great shout of delight went up from the Indians. We went on with our filming.

We noticed that Mario was following our example and drinking as little as he could. However, the Piaroan drinking ritual was strict and there were no heel taps. He had to drink with the others, but our presence embarrassed him. He was unwilling to behave like a real Indian in front of us. He was afraid of what we might think of him. When we took a close up of a man who was vomiting in great streams his face became severe and he looked anxiously at us. We took care not to laugh or to show disgust at the spectacle, and we began to take the side of the Indians against him, applauding those who drank and vomited most, particularly his own brother and his wife, who were leaning against the wall of the tribal hut and drinking calabash after calabash. We explained to him that the only reason that we did not do the same was because of our work: we had to keep reasonably sober if we were to operate our apparatus right to the end of the ceremony.

The old sorcerer went by. He walked slowly and his face was grave. He looked round at the men, the women and the children, and watched to see that each one did his duty. Gradually the level of the liquid in the two canoes began to sink. Many hundreds of quarts had already been scooped out to flow into the stomachs of the Indians and then be vomited out again. Naturally, we were wondering what reason there could be for such deliberate and forced excess. Why did all these people have to swallow such enormous quantities of the cassava juice? I used the word orgy, and yet I could not help feeling that it was not an orgy in the sense in which we understood the word. Among all these men and women there was not one who was really drunk. Indeed, how could anyone get drunk on liquid which could hardly have contained more than three degrees of alcohol? No, there must be some other explanation.

All these Indians were preparing themselves for the coming test. They were preparing themselves for the one object toward which the ceremonies we had been privileged to witness since the beginning of the ritual month all converged. During the night all the men of the tribe had followed the example of the old sorcerer and taken niopo, and at dawn their spirits had not entirely returned to their bodies. Indeed, it was necessary that this should be so and that the men should not be in a normal state. The desired *other* state was attained both physically and mentally by progressive relaxation, during which the whole organism gradually approached a state of total surrender. After about two hundred gallons of liquid had passed rapidly through their bodies they would have attained the necessary freedom of soul.

No doubt there was a profounder and more complex significance to the ritual but I feel that was as much as I managed to grasp, and what I have tried to convey here approximates the truth. It is enough for me to recall the concentrated, almost ecstatic, faces of those men and women, who were, so to speak, taken possession of, ravished, by the vast quantities of liquid they took into themselves and then vomited out, to know that something of the sort was true.

They had gone beyond their ordinary, everyday world and

were feeling their way forward into the unknown spaces of their tribal destiny under the guidance of the tranquil old sorcerer who was in charge of their souls. And part of his task was to guide the boys safely through the initiatory rites to the great culmination which would make them into men.

I looked around for the young neophytes, and after a while I saw them. They were sprawled on the ground quite incapable of taking any further part in the proceedings on their own initiative. Their relatives were around them, attending to them zealously and pouring calabash after calabash of liquid into their open mouths. They had to drink more than anyone else, and soon the cassava juice was being pumped out of their mouths almost as it was poured in.

Gradually the scene grew calmer. One after the other the drinkers returned to the tribal hut as the old sorcerer gave the signal to stop drinking. It was just midday and there were no shadows on the ground. The puddles of yellowish liquid steamed in the sun. Then the sound of maracas came from the tribal hut and the five masked priests appeared again. They gathered round the three boys who were soon to be men and took them by the arms, leading them, half carrying them toward the hut. The boys dragged along the ground between the long fringes of the costumes of the tiger priests. The priests made their way across the village square, dancing backward and forward slowly, and then they went into the hut. Men crowded forward to meet them and took the boys from their arms. Across their backs the boys each carried a package done up with liana. The package contained the hammock which an Indian always takes with him on a journey. These hammocks were now unfolded and slung to the nearest posts in the hut, and the masked priests picked up the boys and laid them in them. Then they left the hut. The old sorcerer had sat down on his stool again to the right of the canoes, which were now almost empty. To his side, on the floor, were various accessories: two flat pieces of wickerwork, long cigarettes of green tobacco rolled in banana leaf, and a calabash of cassava juice. The five masked priests reappeared. On the forehead of each one, in place of the usual painted design, was a rectangular piece of wickerwork containing two hundred imprisoned and wriggling ants, black and shining. Facing the old sorcerer, they danced from one foot to the other while their acolytes detached the five pieces of wickerwork containing the ants from their head-dress and placed them at the feet of the sorcerer. Then the tiger priests retreated a couple of paces and began to pant louder and louder. This was the original chant of the tribe, the chant of the tigers who had brought the first infant Piaroas to the earth in their claws.

One of the boys got out of his hammock and went toward the old sorcerer with a firm and assured step and sat down facing the old man on a second stool which had been placed there. He looked into the old man's face, and leaning forward he placed his hands on the old man's knees. The ceremony of initiation was about to begin.

TRIAL BY PAIN

The old man picked up one of the squares of wickerwork with the ants. The masked priests no longer chanted. In the absolute silence which now prevailed one could hear the wild clicking movements of the legs and pincers of the ants. But apparently the insects were still not sufficiently excited to sting at once and all together as the ritual required, so the old sorcerer dipped the wickerwork square into the calabash of liquid at his side. Then taking a lighted cigarette he gently blew the smoke over the ants. The blue fumes filtered through the wickerwork and rose up to the roof of the hut. The wild excitement of the ants caused the sound of their struggles to increase in volume like the crackling of a fire as it flares up. Holding the square in his hands the old man described three circles with it as he had done earlier with the first calabash of liquid. Leaning forward he described another three circles round the head of the seated boy. Up to then the old man had held the square so that the heads of the ants were facing the boy. Now he turned it round. Several men stepped forward and seized the boy by the wrists and the head, and the old man then placed the square on the boy's chest. This time two hundred abdomens of the giant ants touched the boy's flesh and two hundred stings penetrated simultaneously, injecting their venom. The boy's body suddenly contracted but he forced it back. A large hand closed over his mouth firmly to prevent him from crying out.

Slowly the old man moved the wickerwork square over the most sensitive parts of the boy's body. He performed the operation with great care and a minimum of movement. It went on for two, three, four minutes, and then finally the ants were passed in a last slow, caressing movement over the cheeks and forehead of the boy. The men released their grip. The boy's body straightened. He still sat there with his hands on the old man's knees without moving. In the eyes of all he was now a man. His eyelids opened slowly and a somnambulistic look filtered between the lashes. A woman came forward and bathed his chest, his arms and his back with a little of the liquid which she scooped out of the calabash with the palm of her hand. The old man had taken up his cigarette again and now he puffed great clouds of bluish smoke over the body of the tortured boy.

Until then the lad's eyes had been half closed, now they opened wide. He looked around slowly, as though astonished. He seemed to have returned from another world, or to have entered a world which was completely new to him. He stood up, walked back to his hammock, and lay down. From all parts of the great hut now wreathed in smoke rose a long, shrill cry. It was a shout of triumph from a community which now had another man in its ranks.

The second boy came forward and took his place in front of the old sorcerer. Behind him the masked priests performed their dance and panted the chant of the tigers to the rhythm of their maracas. The lad suffered the torture of the initiation in his turn, and then the third boy took his place.

If this Indian ritual is hard for the boys, it is no less hard for the adults. It demands that those who watch must also suffer, and therefore after the last of the three boys had gone through the initiatory ritual, all the men came forward one by one, and then all the women, to sit before the old sorcerer and submit to the imposition of the wickerwork ant screens, though the squares used for the women were not so large. When Mario's turn came the old man took particular care to see that his ordeal should be greater than that of the others because he was the chief. In the middle of it Mario fainted. Four men sprang forward at once to raise him up again. Imperturbably the old sorcerer continued to pass the ants over the flesh of Mario's inert body. We knew that on our account Mario had not drunk so much as the others and now he had not the same resistance to the torture. He had to suffer his ordeal to the very end.

Then came the turn of the women. They came forward arrogantly and defiantly to sit before the sorcerer. Instead of putting their hands on his knees they put them behind their heads, their elbows raised high and spread wide to lift their naked breasts proudly and present them in the most favorable position. While the ant screens were being applied to them they affected a complete indifference to the pain. They even seemed to be very proud to be the center of attention. Not a muscle of their faces twitched and they had no need of any assistance. They did not even wink an eyelid, but continued to chat in high-pitched tones with their friends during the whole ordeal, and not once did their voices break. One would have said that they felt nothing at all. When it was over they walked back to their hammocks with a firm tread and then collapsed into a coma.

I rose, covered with sweat and dust, for I had spent the whole ceremony lying flat on the ground holding the battery of accumulators, while Pierre lit up the various phases of the torture with our lamp, and Jean took reel after reel of film. The old sorcerer had forbidden us to film the torture of the women, but we had been able to record all the details of the initiatory rites suffered by the three boys and the subsequent ordeal of the men.

When everything was over, the few men who could still stand on their feet now crowded round the old sorcerer and appeared to be urging him to do something. He sat calmly on his little stool and listened to them. From the sinister glances they cast in our direction we suddenly realized what it was they wanted: we had witnessed the ordeal, and now, they were demanding, we should suffer it as well. There was no Mario at our side now to explain matters; he was still stretched out in his hammock, lost to the world, his body twitching violently and spasmodically.

It looked as though a singularly unfortunate situation was about to develop. The prospect of being stung on the body, the chest, throat and arms, the face and the forehead by literally hundreds of giant ants was alarming. It was quite impossible for us to know whether we should prove more or less immune to the poison—as the Indians undoubtedly were. What chance should we have of recovering from such a frightful experience? But if the old sorcerer should decide that we too must suffer the ordeal of the ant stings, what could we do about it? They had played fair with us and it was up to us to play fair as far as possible with them. We were the first whites ever to be permitted to watch such a ceremony, and that privilege had been granted to us on condition that we respect all the precepts of their ritual—and if it now insisted that all who watched must suffer?

We were already gingerly unbuttoning our shirts when the old sorcerer said a few words and a man came toward us. Fortunately it was to tell us to go back to our hut. The old man had seen us unbuttoning our shirts, and with a smile he had shaken his head. Although we had witnessed, it was not necessary that we should suffer.

We made our way back to our hut. A terrible silence now weighed on the village. There was no doubt that the Indians had demanded that we should submit ourselves to the ordeal of the ant stings, and that the old sorcerer had been against it. Why?

Hours passed and night fell again. The village still seemed like a place of the dead. All the Indians were now asleep in their hammocks, exhausted by the experiences of the day. We too were exhausted, and we turned in. But it was quite another thing to find sleep. The horrible scenes we had witnessed pursued us like a nightmare. We got up again and looked round for something to do. We switched on our little generating set to recharge the batteries which the lamp had exhausted during the day. The sound of the motor helped to soothe our nerves, and to some extent it filled the great emptiness all around us, the almost terrifying silence of the village after so many hours of excited noise, shouts of joy, and cries of pain. By about nine o'clock the batteries were recharged and we switched off.

It was then that we heard a noise which the humming of our motor had concealed from us. It had probably been going on for some time, but we had failed to perceive it. Someone, not the old sorcerer, was chanting in the tribal hut and shaking a maraca. The voice was breathless, urgent and imperative, and a choir took up the sound and developed it shrilly. As we listened the voice of the soloist began a new verse, and the choir joined in again. We stood silently on the threshold of our hut. Without knowing why, we were frightened. The chant sounded like an appeal for help. It seemed to well up from some urgent necessity, but what? However, there was nothing we could do about it and so we went back to our hammocks. Half an hour later Pierre and I were at the door again. Neither of us had said anything to the other. The chanting was still going on. We both had the same idea, and together we walked up to the village square. The moon was still visible, a narrow crescent in the sky, just light enough to show the forest, the roofs of the huts and the yellowish ground sodden with the remains of the vomited liquid. A sour, cold smell rose from it. Four dogs were sitting on their haunches and they growled as we approached, but they did not move. We could see their yellow eyes as they stared at us unblinkingly. The door of the tribal hut was closed, but the sound of the chanting penetrated shrilly through the grass walls.

We still did not know what to do, but something held us there. We were unable to retrace our steps and go to our hammocks. We sat down on a tree trunk at the edge of the square and waited in silence. We did not even smoke. There was something in the air, something which originated in those closed huts and circulated around us invisibly in the air. An hour went by. Then there was a sudden shriek. It came from behind the tribal hut, from the smaller hut of the women which was situated there. It sounded again, and longer. It seemed almost endless. It was like the cry of a young girl being hacked to pieces. It was an atrocious scream and it was repeated a dozen and more times, and yet there was no kind of movement anywhere and not a glimmer of a light between the interstices of the walls or roofs of the darkened huts.

There was nothing for us to do but to return once again to our hammocks after having discussed the most fantastic suppositions. By this time fatigue had weighted our eyeballs as though they were of lead. Why were men chanting after the ceremony was over? What did that terrible shrieking mean? It pursued us into our dreams. We were unable to go into either the tribal hut or the small hut. A new mystery had arisen in the Piaroa village and we remained outside and in ignorance of it.

MARIO'S SILENCE

The next morning the life of the Piaroas went on as though nothing at all had happened. There were women bathing at the edge of the lagoon. Other women were striding up toward the tribal hut carrying pitchers of water on their heads. Children were playing on the village square with little bows of green wood and with balls made of rolled banana leaves. Men were going off in their canoes to hunt or fish. The old sorcerer had been transformed once again into an indulgent old grandfather watching the children at play. He was seated on a tree trunk at the edge of the square, the same trunk on which Pierre and I had sat during the night and wondered fearfully at the shrieking.

The day wore on, but there was no sign of Mario. The owner of our little hut, the man with the big head, came to ask by signs when we intended to vacate his home. There was nothing much more for us to do here if everything really was over. But what had happened to Mario? We had already offered him a place in our canoe on the journey back, because he had come only to take part in the celebrations and would be leaving when they were over.

At last we spotted him, but he turned away, pretending that he had not seen us. I suddenly remembered his behavior the previous evening. He had fainted in front of us and now he was probably ashamed to meet us again. He had been at our side during the day, and it was on our account that he had not drunk enough to lend him resistance to the pain of the ant stings. When the turn of his children had come to sit before the old sorcerer, he had been very anxious to have the camera there so that every detail of their initiation should be recorded in the film. When they had opened their mouths to shout he had sprung forward before anyone else, and he had seized them and held them himself, refusing to let anyone else touch them. Without excitement, but with a set yet sensitive face he had gripped their heads as though in a vice. And I shall never forget the expression on his face when his turn came to sit down before the old sorcerer and he began to feel that he would not be able to stand the dreadful stings of the ants. In the space of a few seconds he grew red and then white; his face wrinkled like an apple and then suddenly relaxed and began to swell until his powers of resistance definitely betrayed his dignity as outward chief of the tribe and he fell backward and fainted.

Mario's pride was so great that today he reproached himself for that weakness as for a lack of courage. That was why he was now anxious to avoid us.

Pierre ran after him and took him by the arm, leading him away from the village and talking to him all the while. He explained to him that we feared that we too would have to undergo the ordeal of the ants, and that we should certainly have been unable to withstand the pain because, like him, we had not drunk enough to blunt our senses. Gradually Mario recovered his self-possession. He grew less reserved and his old foxy smile returned to his lips and wrinkled the corners of his eyes. Pierre brought him back to our hut and he accepted a cigarette. We were burning with impatience to question him about all the things that had happened after he had fainted, and he was the only one who could tell us.

He explained that it was the old sorcerer who had set his face against our undergoing the ordeal of the ants, because we had not taken niopo in the night as all the others had, and because we had not drunk enough.

"You see," he explained with a smile, "if you had died we should all have had trouble with the white men."

He then explained that the cries we had heard in the night had really been those of a young girl. In her dreams she had suffered the tortures of the stinging all over again.

"If the full celebrations had taken place, as they do on the Sipapo, you would have heard still more," he added.

"What!" exclaimed Pierre, "the celebrations weren't complete then?"

"No," he replied, "the old man didn't want to, because of you. There should have been twice as much to drink for one thing. And then in the morning, after the ordeal of the ants, the children would have been whipped in the village square while the masked priests moved around them in a circle in the dance of the whales. They dance round and round, and the palm leaves are pushed back from their faces. It is then usually that the children see for the first time who it is beneath the masks. Everybody gets whipped, and everyone drinks twice as much. But, you see, after that our men go mad for four or five days, and if they had turned on you and killed you we should have had trouble with the white men. That was why the old man didn't want to have the full celebrations."

We passed the rest of the day filming one or two scenes we needed to join up our previous material, and the next morning the time came for us to leave. Our things were loaded on board our canoe and we pushed off.

The inhabitants of the village were all assembled along the side of the lagoon to see us go. In the foreground stood the old man smiling. He was dressed in the new shirt and trousers we had given him in accordance with the terms of the contract he had drawn up. He was obviously glad that we were going. A child was pressed against his side, one arm round the leg of his new trousers. The old man's hand was idly caressing the child's cheek.

A few hours later we sailed out into the Orinoco. Mario was with us and when we came in sight of his house he began to rummage around in his basket. Then he came to me with something in his hand.

"Do a deal with me now," he said. "Give me your clay pipe, which is no good to you, and I'll give you this for it."

It was his niopo outfit. Before leaving the village I had obtained the maraca with which the old sorcerer had robbed me of so much sleep. I had given him a tablet of soap perfumed with violets in exchange. Now I handed over my pipe to Mario in exchange for his niopo outfit. I remembered having bought that pipe in a tobacconist's in the Rue du Bac in Paris. Our canoe put into the bank and Mario, his wife, his brother, his sister-in-law, and their children alighted. The outboard motor started up again and off we went. As the Sama Canyon, where Mario lived, disappeared behind us in the blue horizon of the forest, I carefully packed the little wooden mortar, the breathing tube, and the maraca away in the case containing our exposed films and the notebooks in which I had jotted down the strange story of the "harvest festival"—our first intimate experience of the world of the Indians. A few days later the case with its contents was flown from Puerto Ayacucho to Bogotá, and it was a year or more before I opened it again. It was in Paris and when I took Mario's niopo outfit in my hands a strange odor pervaded the room, a stale bittersweet smell, cold and strange and worn. Quickly I packed the things away in a box and I have never touched them since.

OCTOBER 1949 TO MARCH 1950

PART 3

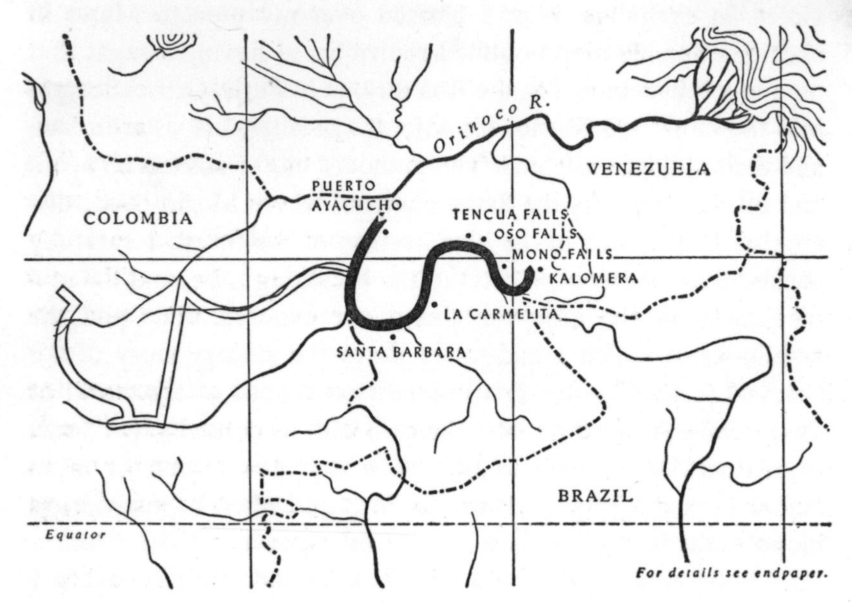

The World of the Sierra Parima—First Contact with the Maquiritares and the Guaharibos—Reverse and a Fresh Attempt

---

THE WORLD OF THE SIERRA PARIMA

AT PUERTO AYACUCHO we were rejoined by the fourth member of our expedition, Luis, and for a very long time after he alighted from the plane which had brought him back to the Orinoco he had to listen to enthusiastic descriptions of the adventures which had befallen us since he had left us. The item of information he had for us was that the 35mm camera had been successfully repaired and worked as well as ever. It was now mid-October and the waters of the Orinoco were falling. The time could hardly have been more favorable for us to make our attempt to go up river toward the Sierra Parima, and finally to justify the name we had chosen for our expedition by establishing the first contact across that *terra incógnita* between the basin of the Orinoco and that of the Amazon.

Before the time for the great departure, which we thought would be the last, we had to stay for a few days in Puerto Ayacucho to make the final preparations for our plan of action. We were well aware that we were now setting out on a much more serious adventure than any we had so far undertaken, and that the slightest mistake on our part might well prove fatal not merely to the hopes of the expedition itself, but even to us personally.

There are numerous legends about the Sierra Parima, the last western branch of the Guianas chain, and naturally Puerto Ayacucho, the capital of as much of the upper Orinoco area as was already known to civilization, was the main breeding ground for such rumors.

On the first maps of South America, drawn up by the Spaniards and the Portuguese in the sixteenth and seventeenth centuries, the Parima is represented as a vast lake, bigger than the Caspian Sea. On its banks, in the middle of a virgin forest full of monsters and savage Indians, was a great city of stone, the enchanted and mysterious residence of *El Dorado,* the "Golden One," the great Indian chief who was richer even than all the Incas of Peru. Every year this chief, his body covered with gold dust, was said to rinse himself in the waters of the sacred lake, as an offering to the Sun God, while his people cast thousands of other rich gifts into the waters of the lake: cups, vases, dishes, and statues of precious metal studded with countless rubies, emeralds, and diamonds as big as hen's eggs.

The feverish imagination of the conquistadors subsequently placed the site of this legend in a more accessible and more plausible spot, among the mists of the high Cordilleras of the Andes, in the vice-royalty of New Granada, which is now Colombia. Gradually the dimensions of the famous lake of *El Dorado,* Lake Parima, shrunk on the maps until in the middle of the nineteenth century it had become just an ordinary mountain pool. And after Alexander von Humboldt's expedition through the upper Orinoco area it disappeared entirely. Today, on modern maps, it appears as it really is, a chain of unexplored mountains completely covered with thick forest, a blank spot in the middle of equatorial America. But the imagination of man continues to work upon the Parima, and thus all the rivers that flow down from it carry with them many diamonds and grains of gold, and they are dredged both by Venezuela and Brazil.

The climatic conditions which are known to exist in the Sierra Parima, however, are such as to make it highly improbable that any civilization sufficiently far advanced to work in metals, even gold, has ever known it. I have said that it is completely covered with thick forest, in fact the highest and thickest forest in all the Amazon. Observers who have flown over it have seen only very rare and small patches of savanna, where men might conceivably live and develop their world despite the hostility of the elements. To those who have studied it, the Sierra Parima seems to be a complete collection of all the natural conditions most hostile to the development of man. Even in its foothills the local fauna becomes more dangerous and more numerous, with mosquitoes, spiders, and ants swarming in the forest and over what little land is left by the forest. And the nearer the approach, the more rain there is, until near the mountain itself the rain is almost continuous throughout the year, creating a climate which favors the development of the most dangerous bacterial and other forms of life in the equatorial area.

"The Sierra Parima is an impenetrable green hell." We were first told this in Paris, then in Caracas, and finally in Bogotá.

"The Sierra Parima is an absolutely impenetrable green hell." We were reassured by all the officials, colonists, rubber seekers, diamond seekers, gold seekers and wood cutters of Puerto Ayacucho.

The climate is quite sufficient to discourage most people, and some who are prepared to put up with that cannot face the superabundance of mosquitoes and savage beasts of the upper Orinoco; while the rest, who do not fear either the climate or the wild beasts and know how to protect themselves against the mosquitoes, give up in face of the men of the mountains. "Guaharibos," they said sagely, putting their glasses down onto the table and nodding their heads. What they said was enough to damp the ardor of the most enthusiastic explorers, but we had already heard so much of it during the past six months since we had first descended the Cordilleras of the Andes, in fact for the past year since we first left Europe, that we were immune.

The two peoples known to exist in "the green hell" are the Maquiritares and the Guaharibos. The latter have made themselves feared and detested, while the former, on the contrary, enjoy the esteem of everyone, not only in Puerto Ayacucho but throughout the whole Orinoco area through which we passed. They are hardy and industrious, we were told, and in all the work they do they display a level of civilization infinitely more advanced than that of any Indian tribe we had met so far: Guahibos, Piapicos, or Piaroas. Certain groups of these Maquiritares living along the higher tributaries of the Orinoco maintain regular relations with the colonists and the rubber seekers of the forest, hiring them their services from time to time, as the Piaroas do too, and there is unanimous praise for the Maquiritares. The others, the majority of the tribe, still live around the sources of the rivers which flow down from the Parima, going about naked, bedaubed with paint, and wearing feathers according to their ancient customs. But they have never at any time shown any hostility toward the rare white men who have fallen in with them in the course of their journeyings.

Finally we learned that the Maquiritares of Venezuela and the Mayongongs of Brazil were two names given in these two countries to identify the same sub-group of the linguistic family of the Caribbean Indians. More than forty years before our arrival in these parts, this family was studied by the German explorer and ethnologist Koch-Grünberg, who in the years 1911–1912 carried out an expedition somewhat similar to the one we now proposed, from one country to the other across the Pacaraima, which he explored, but leaving the Parima, which still remained the last virgin branch of the Guianas.

It was not really surprising to us to discover that the Maquiritares were on a relatively high level of civilization. After all, they are among the sole descendants of the men who, before the time of Christopher Columbus and with merely the resources available during the Stone Age, were able to cross the north of the continent from the Amazon to the sea which still bears their name today—the Caribbean Sea—and to cross the sea in simple canoes made out of hollowed tree trunks. They conquered first the Antilles, where the Spaniards made their acquaintance, and then the south coast of what is now the United States, from Louisiana to the peninsula of Florida. It was no more surprising to discover that the Maquiritares had retained something of the vigor and the spirit of adventure of their remote ancestors the Caribbean Indians, who were cannibals according to the chronicles of the Spanish conquerors, but who were also great conquerors themselves according to their own history.

"The Indians you have met are poor, backward people," we were told. "You must go and see the Maquiritares; they're quite different. They know how to weave fine hammocks and to make wickerwork baskets and so on, ornamented with designs and patterns of animals and men, arabesques and decorative borders. They can dance and they have beautiful decorations of feathers. The men are armed with bows and arrows, blowpipes and impressive cudgels. The women make decorative pubic girdles ornamented with the colored glass beadwork introduced at the time of the Spaniards. They build immense clay huts with proper doors and windows, and they are the greatest hunters in the whole of America. They lack nothing and they make the best cassava loaves you can possibly imagine, every bit as good as wheat bread."

Thus although the Sierra Parima was unexplored, everyone knew the Maquiritares. The Sierra Parima was a green hell, but the land of the Maquiritares was described to us as a paradise of savages. More than once we asked ourselves, during the few days we spent in Puerto Ayacucho before launching out on our great adventure, whether all those people with whom we ate or drank beer were talking about the same thing.

But while what we heard about the Maquiritares was most reassuring, what we were told about their neighbors the Guaharibos was certainly not. This tribe lived in the heart of the Parima and were the masters of the Orinoco sources, which still remained unknown after expeditions from all corners of the world had attempted to reach them. The Guaharibos were cannibals still. They killed and ate men. They were troglodytes who had remained on earth by an anthropological anachronism. The mention of their name was invariably followed by a long silence even among the most scarred and weather-beaten of the adventurers we met.

"They live in the heart of the forest and they go around completely naked," we were told. "They have no implements of any kind either of iron or stone. They are so backward that they don't know how to build huts or make canoes. But at the same time they are the most dangerous beasts in the forest. They are armed with very large bows about six feet long and their arrows have tips of bone or of bamboo wood hardened by fire. They attack everyone they meet, whether white or Indian. Many people who have disappeared in the forest without trace and have never been heard of again have either been killed by the Guaharibos or captured and carried off to slavery in the more remote parts of their territory."

And in support of these hair-raising statements would be quoted hundreds of facts, and hundreds of adventures which had happened to men mentioned by name. There was the story of a semi-civilized Indian woman who had accompanied a collector of balata into the forest where she had been captured by the Guaharibos and raped by a great number of warriors in succession. By a miracle she had succeeded in escaping and, after wandering around in the forest for two weeks, she had managed to reach a civilized outpost where she had told her story. Then there was the quite recent story of a wood cutter who had ventured too far up the Orinoco looking for cedar wood. Surprised by the Guaharibos, he had managed to escape, but had been forced to abandon not only his merchandise, his provisions, and his tools, but also his clothes. We actually saw the arrival of this unfortunate's canoe at Sanariapo, the advanced port of Puerto Ayacucho above the Maipures Rapids, and the man was half naked. He told us that the Guaharibos had captured him and taken him along with them for several days, and that he had had to take part in a dance together with all the tribe, both men and women. They had danced round and round in a small forest clearing. The Indians had used this pretext to rob him of his clothes. It appeared that in order to take part in the dance everyone had to be naked, the captive included.

The relationship between the Maquiritares and the Guaharibos seemed to be that of latent warfare.

We were also told many stories about the Guaicas, the neighbors of the Guaharibos. Some said they were more peaceable than the Guaharibos, but others insisted that they were even more ferocious, and lived in an equally primitive state.

We also had other information about the Guaharibos and the Guaicas, and this was based on historical facts recorded in the accounts of various travelers. For instance, there was the history of Esmeralda, which was for a long time the farthest point up the Orinoco inhabited by civilized men. In 1937 Esmeralda was a little outpost consisting of two or three houses. It was captured by Guaharibos in a surprise attack, pillaged, and razed to the ground. Since then no one had dared to live there. The story of the last expedition which had attempted to reach the source of the Orinoco was equally edifying. This expedition was led by Hamilton Rice, an American, and it was attacked at a rapid and forced to retreat in face of the number and ferocity of the Guaharibo aggressors. After this experience Hamilton Rice took the Brazilian slope of the Sierra Parima, and from there he made a series of reconnaissance flights in a hydroplane during which he succeeded in gathering material for the first and only map of the Amazonian tributaries of the Parima.

In short, from all the information in our possession it seemed impossible to talk to the Guaharibos with anything but a Winchester. Now we had no Winchesters, and in any case such methods were incompatible with the fundamental aims of our expedition. Our proposed crossing of unknown mountainous territory was to serve above all as a means of getting to know and studying the unknown men who inhabited it.

It suggested to us that we must take a different route from that followed by our predecessors in order to make contact with Guaharibos who had never seen a white man and might, therefore, be less inclined to adopt an aggressive attitude toward him.

We decided to abandon the Orinoco, properly so called, and to go up to the Parima by another river, to establish ourselves at its source with the assistance of the Maquiritares, and then to enter Guaharibo territory from this base, branching out in various directions, and making contact with the Guaharibos as late as possible through the mediation of the Maquiritares only after we had learned as much as we could about their customs and, if possible, their language, so that we could conduct ourselves in a manner least likely to alarm or provoke them.

We decided on the Rio Ventuari, the biggest tributary of the upper Orinoco. The Ventuari rises in the Sierra Parima about three hundred miles from where it joins the Orinoco, and a series of falls forms the frontier of Maquiritares territory and the north of Guaharibo territory.

Those few men who knew something about the district, either at first or second hand, were always talking about a big chief of the Maquiritares, whom some called Kalomera and others called Kalorinia. No one knew exactly on what river his village was situated, but everyone insisted that he was the only man who knew the secrets of the Indian tracks which led from one slope of the Sierra Parima to the other. He was obviously the man we needed, and the best way to get in touch with him seemed to be to go up the Ventuari with our motor until we came to the first fall, and then to get into touch with the nearest Maquiritares and persuade them to guide us further to the village of Kalomera, or Kalorinia.

Once we had decided on this plan we immediately set about the material preparations for its execution. First of all we had to collect sufficient provisions to see us through a stay of three or four months in the heart of the forest away from all contact with civilization. We also had to see to it that the equipment we took with us was light enough and handy enough in size to be transported by canoe and by porterage. We therefore reduced our provisioning to a strict minimum, limiting ourselves to a case of condensed milk, several pounds of chocolate, several pounds of coffee, but a great number of cigarettes, not only for our own consumption but to serve as a means of exchange with the Indians. We completed our stock-in-trade with lengths of plain red cotton cloth, which, we were assured, was the only kind used by the Maquiritares to make their guayucos, and a large supply of shot, black powder and primers for their muzzle-loaders.

THE SETTLEMENT OF THE VENTUARI

On the way up the Ventuari there are three settlements from which the immense area of savanna and forest bordering the river along its three-hundred-mile navigable length is exploited. The first of these is Santa Barbara, which is situated at its confluence with the Orinoco, a delta about twenty miles long by six miles wide through which the tumultuous waters of the Ventuari pour into the Orinoco round hundreds of small islands. Santa Barbara was founded by the Jesuits in the eighteenth century, and in all probability it was a very prosperous settlement, for contemporary records describe it as a colony of several thousand souls. I don't know what the good Jesuit fathers who had ventured so far away from their native Spain actually did with these thousands of souls, but I have no doubt that they opened the way to paradise to them in exchange for more profane riches, if we are to credit the legends about the place which still tell us of chests of gold and of diamonds now lost forever in the impressive circle of rapids and eddies which surround it. But with the disappearance of the Jesuits, the thousands of Indian laborers and the great avenues lined with fruit trees also disappeared, and today Santa Barbara is nothing but a little outpost consisting of three straw huts around which a dozen or so goats browse on the sparse growth amid a debris of black rocks.

The next settlement is La Carmelita, two days' journey by

outboard motor up river, and here the situation is rather more favorable. It is the only settlement along the Ventuari which almost merits the name of village. La Carmelita, in fact, has a population of about fifty, mestizos and civilized Indians, and there is a shop for the adults and a school with a blackboard, duster, and chalk for the little ones. Under the leadership of a capable man who knows the surrounding forest well, the inhabitants cultivate cassava, which is then exported to Puerto Ayacucho, hunt jaguars and cayman alligators, and, when there is any demand from New York via Caracas, they collect rubber, gutta-percha, and chicle from the neighboring forest.

It was at La Carmelita that we enjoyed the luxury of a laid table complete with cloth and ice water, with the ice taken from a frigidaire worked by a gasoline motor. It was the last time on our expedition. After having given us a good deal of new and very valuable information about the Maquiritares Indians, with whom he maintained commercial relations, the master of the settlement produced a bottle from a cupboard to drink with us and wish us *bon voyage*. It was a long time since we had seen a bottle of real French cognac, and we drank together to the Sierra Parima and the fierce Guaharibos who infested it.

Eventually we arrived at the last of the small settlements up river, Marietta, so called from the name of the tributary which empties its waters into the Ventuari there. Marietta was a settlement of the wood cutters we had heard so much about in Puerto Ayacucho, and we knew that it was in charge of two Brazilians, veterans of the virgin forest, Alexandre Marat and Helios Amazonas.

"We are almost natives here," said Marat offering us his hand with a friendly smile. "It seems that I bear the name of a famous French general, isn't that so?"

He was a tall and angular young man with yellow skin suggestive of malaria, and his jet black curly hair enhanced a quite youthful aspect. Amazonas was a different type, fat and rosy, and sporting unexpectedly a small moustache *à la* Dali. He was gentle and sentimental, despite the enormous matchet whose weight dragged his belt down at the side. He, too, was proud of his name, and he explained to us confidentially that his Christian name meant the sun.

"The sun of the Amazon," he declared complacently. "What do you think of that for a name?"

When we explained that we wanted to meet not only the Maquiritares but also the Guaharibos, his face darkened.

"You want to be careful with those dirty dogs," he said. "You don't know what you're up against. And how should you? They all talk about them at Ayacucho, of course, but none of them know the Guaharibos as we know them, we Brazilians of the Rio Negro. Do you know that it's on account of them that I'm here at all? They ruined my father by pillaging his fazenda. It was on the other side of the Parima. They destroyed what it had taken him twenty years to wrest from virgin forest. I was only a boy at the time, twelve years old perhaps, but I can remember it as though it were yesterday. But that wasn't all. My older brother gathered a few men and went into the forest to revenge the family. He was as strong as two men and he was armed with a Winchester automatic and two revolvers. But the Guaharibos attacked unexpectedly in the night and killed him with an arrow in his heart, and then they pulped his head with cudgels. Believe me, it's better to pick a bone with ten starving jaguars than two Guaharibos. If you ever do meet them, see that you shoot first, and God and the Blessed Virgin be with you."

We stayed for twenty-four hours in Marietta, during which time the talkative Brazilians told us the story of their lives. The surroundings in which we listened to the strange adventures and the dreams of these lumbermen of the virgin forest were no less strange. I remember that they had just killed two tapirs, and their hut was full of great pans of dark red meat sparkling with coarse salt.

For four or five months of the year the motley garrison of Marietta—and there were all possible degrees of cross-breeding to be met with in a continent in which whites, blacks, and Indians live side by side—worked to open up the forest, felling gigantic trees, cutting them up into thirty foot logs, and getting them to the river without the assistance of any machinery. Once in the river these logs were made into great rafts weighing as much as several hundred tons. It took them thirty or forty days to float down river to the sawmills at Ayacucho. A few men would remain behind to guard Marietta, and the rest, numbering between ten and twenty, would make themselves at home on the rafts like gypsies in a caravan, and off they would float down stream, eating, sleeping, dreaming for about a month, with nothing but the forest sliding away on either side and the sky and the stars above them as the river carried them gradually toward civilization.

At Ayacucho, Marat, Amazonas and their Negroes, Indians, Brazilians, Colombians, and Venezuelans would spend perhaps a fortnight, buying themselves new shirts and trousers, reading the newspapers brought in once a week by plane, drinking beer and rum, dancing to the music of the juke box, talking with shining eyes about the big towns with buildings twenty stories high, and swearing that one day, when they had felled enough timber, they would go there and settle down for good. But such forests are perhaps even more jealous than the sea itself, and very, very few who once enter them ever come out again for good.

From their base in Marietta, Marat and his men often pushed up river as far as the Tencua Falls, about two days journey. These falls marked the end of their territory and the beginning of Indian territory. There they would meet José Catire, the chief of a local group of Maquiritare Indians, and provide him with tools, cotton goods, and ammunition for his guns, which were good French, Belgian, and English muzzle-loaders dating from the time of Fenimore Cooper at least. They had been brought there from the Guianas along one of those mysterious paths whose secret we now proposed to learn from the Maquiritares. In return José Catire gave the men from Marietta cassava from his own plantations and trunks of "cedro" cut down in his territory above the falls.

We could have asked no better way to get into touch with José Catire, and we proposed to exchange the Oram with its outboard motor for trading goods. In any case we should be unable to use the boat above the Tencua Falls, and the goods would come in handy. The next day a tall yellowish fellow wearing an elegant grey sombrero planted himself in front of our hammocks.

"This is Louis XV," said Marat. "He belongs to the Yawarano tribe and he knows José Catire intimately. He will go with you in your boat as far as the falls. Then he will climb up to the village. With all due respect, you'd never find the path on your own. He'll explain your intentions to Catire and come down again with him to meet you. If it doesn't work all you need do is to come back here again in your boat, hand us over the goods, and then you can have your boat back. If all goes well, then Louis XV is capable of bringing your boat back here again on his own. That all right, Louis XV?"

The Indian Prince Charming grunted *"Sí, señor,"* and the deal was concluded.

We set off in the Oram the next day and slept a last night on board. On the afternoon of November 10th the calm and shining water of the river was rapidly covered with tossing froth, and from the distance we could hear a roaring sound which gradually grew louder and louder as we went forward, until finally, when we turned a last bend, the river suddenly ended at the foot of a wall of falling water three hundred feet wide and about ninety feet high. It was the Tencua Falls.

The imperturbable Louis XV put over the tiller and shut off the motor, and the Oram turned its nose into a stretch of fine sand where we landed safely.

A few yards from the bank were three small huts or ranchos which an invisible hand seemed to have prepared for us on this last stage of our slow journey from the world of the white man to that of the Indians. We slung our hammocks there while Louis XV carried a large cooking pot from the boat. It was full of fillets of tapir meat, a last gift to us from Marietta. All around us clouds of great blue and white butterflies as big as the palm of a man's hand fluttered up and down. They seemed to be the sole inhabitants of the place and their gyrations completed the impressions of enchantment conveyed by the golden sand against which the limpid water washed gently and by the enormous walls which enclosed the place, the one of roaring, sparkling water and the other of green somber forest, thick and silent.

But it was not long before we noticed that the enchantment, here as everywhere in this virgin forest, was deceptive. The air began to resound to a growing humming which we quickly recognized as that of swarms of anopheles mosquitoes. They set up such a furious dance around us that before long we were content to enjoy the beauty of the spot only from the safety of our mosquito nets.

In the meantime Louis XV had lit a big fire and prepared our dinner.

Night fell and relieved us for a while of these undesirable companions. We came out again from our mosquito nets and I attended to Luis's wound. A week before when disembarking from the Oram one evening he had stepped out into about six or eight inches of water and had been unfortunate enough to tread with his bare foot on one of those horrible brutes of the fresh water, the rayfish of the Orinoco. It had instantly stung him in the sole of the foot with a barbed and poisonous sting about an inch and a half long. He had collapsed on the bank, writhing in agony while the blood spurted out of the wound. I had no morphine at hand that evening so I gave him a dose of barbiturate which would have made the most optimistic medical man's hair stand on end. He had bled so much that we hoped all the poison had been washed out of his veins, but the next morning his foot had swollen to twice its normal size, and around the wound the flesh was puffed, black, and evil-smelling as though gangrene had developed. Every day I dosed him with vast quantities of penicillin. The malignance of the poison injected by the ray-fish is terrifying, and after a week of constant treatment there was still quite a large round place on the sole of his foot like a burn.

Luis could hardly walk, and that worried us a good deal, because if everything went well with the Maquiritares we should have to circumvent the Tencua Falls on foot, and according to Louis XV that would mean a march of several hours. That evening therefore I decided on a little surgical operation in the hope of expediting the cure. I took a pair of tweezers and a razor blade, which represented the total surgical equipment of the expedition, and while Luis stoically bellowed a samba I cut away the lump of black flesh which covered the wound. Beneath it was a shallow oval depression about an inch and a half across. The flesh around it was pink and looked healthy, but at the bottom of it was an oyster-like spot, dark green in color, cold and without odor. It looked dead, but it must have been living, for I was unable to remove it.

That ray sting remained in our memory as the strangest of all the accidents that happened to us during our fourteen months in the Amazonian forest. It was more than a month before that horrible, cold, greenish spot finally disappeared.

JOSÉ CATIRE SAYS "NO"

The next morning at dawn Louis XV plunged into the forest, matchet in hand. He returned just before nightfall accompanied by three Indians who took their places by the fire without saying a word. It was José Catire, his son Emiliano, and another Indian from the village. All three wore the washed out shirts and trousers we had seen on all the Indians we had come across so far, but only the chief, José Catire, was wearing a hat in European style. The two other men were bare-headed and their glossy black hair was bowl-cut low over their foreheads and the tops of their ears.

"What is it you want?" asked Catire after he had greeted us. He spoke Spanish with a slight lisp, running the consonants into each other, and his voice was soft and gentle.

We explained to him that we wanted to be guided to the source of the Ventuari and from there to the big chief Kalomera.

He shook his head and then began to talk rather impatiently and without looking at us.

"That's impossible," he said. "Kalomera no longer lives where he used to when the Frontier Commission came as far as the Ventuari and met him. He lives very high up in the mountain now. It would take several months to get there. You would have to pass the two other big falls of the Ventuari, the Oso and the Mono, and they are both bigger than the Tencua. Then you would have to go still higher to where my cousins the naked Maquiritares live, and I never see them. And even then that's not the end of it. You would have to go a long time on foot through the forest. Do you really want to go as high as that?"

He indicated the Oram.

"No, it isn't possible," he went on. "I haven't enough canoes for that, and there aren't enough men in the village. No one has been as high as that for years now. I don't know whether there are relay canoes at Oso and Mono. No, it's quite impossible. It would take months. Perhaps even years."

He went on shaking his head from side to side, repeating all the time: "No, it's impossible. It would take months, perhaps years. No canoes, no Indians. We never go that high. We don't know the way. It's impossible."

Louis XV was standing behind him, as motionless as a statue. He said nothing but he smiled as he looked at us. What had he said to Catire up there in the village and on the way as they came down to our camp?

We repeated for the fifth or sixth time:

"But if it is possible you find the men and the canoes and we'll pay you well. All those cases you see there contain matchets, red cloth for making guayucos, *coroto,* you know what that is, José, good *coroto:* iron, fire, cloth, combs, fish hooks."

The *coroto* certainly interested him, and he asked questions about the kind of fish hooks and matchets we had brought.

"And have you got cloth with flowers on for the women?" he wanted to know.

Oh, yes, we had cloth with flowers on.

"And have you got fine combs for the fleas?"

Yes, we had fine-tooth combs for the fleas.

"And powder, too?"

Yes, powder too.

"And shot?" This time he looked doubtful.

Of course we had shot.

He was silent for a while, looking at his feet, but then he began to shake his head again.

"No, my friend. It's impossible. No men, you understand. No canoes. Too far."

He was suspicious. We recalled our first contact with the

Piaroas and our first difficult talks with Mario: "Celebrations?" he had demanded. "What celebrations?"

It was not good to insist. The passivity of the Indians had to be answered with passivity. A tactic of attrition was the appropriate one. Talk about something else. And wait patiently. Never seem to accept the other's objections. Go on with your own ideas as they go on with theirs. Bring the matter up again a little later. Say white again when they say black. And keep on gently saying white until they come round.

Night fell, which meant that the three men would stay with us till morning at least. They slung their hammocks and Louis XV prepared the dinner, making a great *pot-au-feu* of the tapir meat. We decided to make the biggest possible spread in order to impress our man. From the boat we took out our last sack of rice, some coffee, and a tin of condensed milk. Then Pierre unloaded his battery and his sound recording apparatus and set it up under one of the ranchos. That was a good idea. After dinner we would give the Maquiritares a surprise. Mozart had introduced us to the Piaroan initiatory rites, perhaps Louis Armstrong would open up the Sierra Parima for us.

We also set the table as grandly as possible. Jean went to the boat and brought back new aluminum dishes and cutlery and a large milk can to serve as a pitcher for the river water.

Catire didn't turn a hair. He disdained the fork we laid for him, but he demonstrated that he could shift a small mountain of rice and about a couple of pounds or so of tapir meat with nothing but a spoon. As for his son and the other Indian, they hadn't spoken a word since their arrival, but they polished off their food as rapidly as Catire did. When the dishes were finally empty they rose, went to their pack, and produced an enormous round of cassava bread which they crumbled into their bowls, added water to it, and then drank it off as Burgundians drink a wine soup. Then we all stretched ourselves out silently on the sand and I passed the cigarettes round.

For about a quarter of an hour we lay on our backs looking at the stars. I was lying near Catire. I had an idea.

"Tell me, Catire: your cousins who live beyond the Mono and go around naked, are there very many of them?"

"Oh yes! You see there are very many women, and that means a lot of children. It's a long time since I last saw them, but there must be very many of them now. They don't want to come down. They would rather be quite naked."

"Do they know how to make canoes up there? Have they got plenty of them?"

"Canoes? Oh, yes. They've got plenty of canoes."

I said no more for the moment.

"If he really hasn't got any canoes and any men, we could always go up there and see if we could find some," Pierre said to me in French.

Nothing further was said about the matter for the moment. First of all they must have their surprise. Pierre got up and went toward the rancho where his sound equipment was waiting. He began to fiddle around with it. Above the steady roar of the waterfall we could hear the crepitation of the glowworms flying around among the bushes behind us. I began to talk again. I explained to Catire that our object in traveling so far was to get to know the Indians. We had come a very long way, and we had been many, many moons traveling. We had already visited a number of Indian tribes. We had with us a machine for taking down music we heard. We had already heard the Piaroan music, which was very beautiful, and we had taken it down with our machine. We wanted to do the same with the Maquiritares music if it was also beautiful.

At that moment Pierre started up a record. It was Sousa's "Stars and Stripes." José Catire listened in silence.

"Was that Piaroan music?" he asked when it was ended.

"No, that was American music."

Then came Louis Armstrong. Apparently he had no more effect on José Catire than Sousa had had. So Pierre resorted again to Mozart's symphony. Catire turned to me eagerly.

"What music is that?" he asked.

I explained to him that it was music from where we came,

music played with many instruments. He considered this for a moment or two, and then he spoke again:

"Up in the mountains the Maquiritares also make music. You must go to them and hear it and put it down in your machine to let the people in your country hear it later on. Then you can say: 'That's the music of the Maquiritares. The best Indians.' I'll come with you there. But we can't take all your cases. I haven't enough men and canoes. So first of all we must go to my cousins to get help. We can start tomorrow. Is that all right?"

THE THREE WATERFALLS OF THE VENTUARI

It was on November 10th, 1949, below the Tencua Falls, the barred gateway to the Sierra Parima, that Mozart registered his second victory and dissipated Indian suspicions once again.

We came to an agreement with the Maquiritares, and the next morning Louis XV left us and went off in the ex-Oram, which had now become the property of Marat. With the help of his son and the other Indian, Catire built a large woven frame in one corner of the strand. It was about three feet high and intended to hold our material while we went off with him to get assistance from his "quite naked cousins." The work lasted several hours and in the meantime we calculated how many men and canoes we should need to transport everything. Catire decided that we should require at least twenty men and six canoes.

Then we discussed who should go with the expedition to the savage Maquiritares to get help. It would take at least a couple of weeks. Luis Saenz was out of the question on account of the state of his foot, and so was Jean Fichter because he was then suffering from an attack of malaria complicated by boils. Thus there were only Pierre Gaisseau and myself, and it was agreed that we should go with Catire and his men and that Luis and Jean should stay behind and wait for our return in Catire's village above the falls. Once the decision was arrived at, Pierre and I made ourselves convenient bundles containing our hammocks, reserve provisions, a supply of cartridges, and a few presents from our stock in trade for the chiefs of the Maquiritares "higher up," and then, having taken leave of our two comrades who were to remain behind, we went off behind Catire and his men along the little path which went up to the top of the falls.

It was about one o'clock. The side of the hill up which we were moving was very steep and we went on for about an hour in silence. The path seemed to make a wide detour away from the falls because the farther we went along it the weaker grew the sound of the falling water, until finally it ceased altogether. Later on we heard the noise again, but it sounded different, and then we came out into a small creek where a superb canoe was swaying gently in the water. It was very high in the prow and of a type we had not seen before. Fifteen feet from the bank the water boiled, swirling from rock to rock. José Catire indicated that we should take our places in the middle of the canoe. His two men armed themselves with poles of some light colored wood between twelve and fifteen feet long and then took their places in the prow. Catire rolled up his trousers, stepped into the water and pushed the canoe along for a few steps; then he jumped in the stern and, taking up from the bottom of the canoe a large paddle shaped in the form of a heart, he began to paddle with all his might. The canoe, whose sides where we were sitting were not more than about four inches above the level of the water, shot forward and soon reached the rapids. The two Indians in the prow stood with their legs rather wide apart and their knees a little bent to give them balance and thrust their poles into the water together. As soon as the poles touched bottom they pushed away vigorously. Catire was no longer paddling. He was using the paddle behind him as a rudder, and with powerful movements he trimmed the canoe and righted its direction. Within a few seconds we were in the middle of the river. All around us as far as we could see were swirls and eddies with here and there the sharp points of rocks jutting out. The least false movement on the part of our crew, and our canoe would have been smashed to matchwood against them. But the three Indians were as calm and confident as though they were paddling in a park lake. They knew every rock and every trick of the river, and the steady arms of José Catire guided the canoe safely past every reef and around each whirlpool. It was our first navigation lesson in the racing waters of the Parima. After that we could very well appreciate the truth of what we had already heard on the Orinoco, namely that no one could hope to journey beyond the Ventuari falls without the assistance of the Maquiritares.

This dangerous and exciting voyage lasted for two or three hours and at the end of that time the waters of the river were growing calmer. Finally we came in sight of Cordoval, the village of José Catire and his tribe. At first sight there was nothing to distinguish it from any mestizo settlement on the banks of the lower Ventuari or the Orinoco. There were the same rectangular huts with clay walls standing side by side facing the river, and near by there was a plantation of cassava and pineapples and a little patch of bananas.

As soon as we had disembarked Catire pointed to a large rancho with a roof made of palm leaves supported by six pillars. A muchacho was conscientiously sweeping up the floor of beaten earth, and another one brought up two small stools. This was the visitors' quarters, and later on we were to find the same hospitable tradition honored in all the Maquiritare villages we visited.

Catire's village seemed to be practically empty. There was hardly anyone to be seen, but from time to time we got a glimpse of women passing to and fro rapidly in the background. There was nothing for us to do but to sling our hammocks and await developments. Before long Catire reappeared carrying a splendid stem of big bananas with golden skins and a haunch of cured peccary. Without saying a word he put them down on the bamboo structure which served as a table at one end of the rancho and then returned to his own hut. Immediately afterward he came back carrying two large loaves of fresh cassava bread. This time we insisted that he should stay and eat with us and so the three of us sat round the table and ate the cold meal he had improvised, which, incidentally, struck us as very much more attractive than the meal we had given him the evening before.

Gradually the ice which seemed to have formed on our arrival in the village began to melt. The children appeared first, peeping out from behind trees or round the corners of the huts.

Then they grew bolder and leaped forward to closer hiding places —I almost said perches. You saw their little naked bronze bodies for an instant, and their round heads, which consisted chiefly of two very wide-opened eyes under an enormous mass of black hair. They did not take long to get used to us and by evening they were playing in and around our hammocks. The women re-appeared too, coming and going from the huts to the river and to the place where the cassava bread was baked, which was in a rancho near ours, and generally behaving as though we were not there at all.

After we had eaten, Catire went off and we did not see him again until nightfall, when we had a long talk with him. Not only did we succeed in getting on much more confidential terms with him, but he gave us a great deal of new and valuable information about the Maquiritares and the Guaharibos. Catire counted seriously on his fingers, and as a result the months, and even years, which separated us from his "naked cousins up there" were reduced in the calculation to four days' journey up river to the next falls, which was *El Mono,* or the Monkey Falls, and then two days march up the mountain to reach the first of their huts. From there we should be only a day's journey to the source of the Ventuari, and a path led toward the north which would permit us to reach Kalomera's village in a couple of days more. This village was at the source of the Erebato, a sub-tributary, through the Caura, of the middle Orinoco.

The nearest Guaharibos it appeared were probably to be found on the other bank of the Ventuari, to the south two or three days journey from the huts of the Maquiritares of the uplands.

"Those Guaharibos are peaceable," Catire said. "Ten years ago Kalomera went to war against them. He set out with thirty warriors all armed with guns, and they killed lots of Guaharibos. Not only the men, you understand, but also the women and children. Like that there would be fewer of them later on. Since then they have kept quiet and they don't try to come anywhere near the Ventuari."

We asked him questions afterward about the Maquiritares festivals, and he told us that they wore garments of palm leaves and headdresses of feathers for the dancing, which was accompanied by large drums with two membranes made of monkey skin.

"And what about the *chicha?*" I asked. "Do you have that too?"

His eyes lit up.

"Ah!" he exclaimed. "You mean the yaraké? Drink made out of cassava. And how we make it! Yaraké is 'pure Maquiritare.' We make the best in the world, my friend."

The matter seemed to be one that concerned him deeply, for a little later he returned to the subject without encouragement.

"Is it true that you like that sort of thing, yaraké?" he asked with a maliciously knowing air.

Pierre and I sat up in our hammocks at once to assure him earnestly that we had nothing but praise for it. To this he said nothing, and after a moment or two he discreetly retired. When he came back his eyes were shining. He sat down in his place and then three women appeared with calabashes of something that looked like *café au lait.*

Catire was quite right: the Maquiritare yaraké was very much superior to the chicha of the Piaroas. We were imprudent enough to drink up our calabashes quickly. The women kept coming up out of the shade with more calabashes of it. They seemed to think we were capable of drinking it like real Maquiritares, and they pressed calabash after calabash on us. After having drunk about six pints of yaraké we began to feel a little uncomfortable, but we dared not refuse point blank to drink any more, so we took advantage of a moment when we were alone to pull down the curtain of our mosquito nets, lie back and pretend to snore. But our ruse was unsuccessful. When the women returned they just opened up our mosquito nets and shook us into wakefulness. We had to drink still more, until it became a tragicomic Chinese torture. But in the end they took pity on us and went away to leave us to go to sleep in real earnest.

However, it turned out that we had not suffered in vain that night, because the villagers of Cordoval had been won over by their first real contact with us and they became our faithful friends, so much so that later on they were to rescue us from more than one tight spot.

The next day at dawn we set off. In addition to his son and the other Indian who had come down to our camp below the Tencua Falls, Catire completed his crew by the addition of a curious sort of fellow, much bigger than any of the Indians we had seen so far. We unanimously christened him Marguerite because of the striking resemblance he bore to a certain well-known and rather mannish French actress.

Marguerite's powerful form worked steadily just in front of me and for hours I was fascinated by his ear decorations. Large holes had been pierced in the lobes of his ears to secure two flat pieces of wood perhaps half an inch across and ornamented in the center by red copper fuse caps. I wondered whether this was the fashion among the Maquiritares "higher up." Only the future could tell.

That evening we arrived at the second Ventuari falls, *El Oso,* or Great Anteater Falls. We worked round them along a small path through the forest, and after about half an hour we came out into a savanna dotted with clumps of palm trees. We went across this savanna for another half hour. A good deal of it had been recently burnt bare, leaving large leprous-like patches of bare earth of a somber violet color amid rolling stretches of golden herbage extending to the horizon. After a while we came to the forest which bordered the river above the falls, and the path led us to the small quay at which there should have been relays of canoes to take us on our voyage up river. There was only one canoe there. It was a large one, but it was damaged.

"I'll see about that tomorrow," said José Catire.

We pitched our camp, and that evening he talked to us about the Ventuari, which he said was the real river of the Maquiritares. I took out my notebook and began to jot down the everyday words of his language. We wanted to learn them as quickly as possible because the Maquiritares "higher up" did not speak a word of Spanish. For every Spanish word I mentioned, Catire told me two Maquiritare words, each differing slightly from the other. In general they were the same, but the sound of "d" in the one was represented by the sound of "y" in the other. I inquired the reason for this.

"Well, you see, we don't talk in quite the same way down below as they do up here," he explained. "We are the Dekuana and the Maquiritares up here are the Yekuana."

It was the first time that I had come across any oral indication of the linguistic map which Koch-Grünberg had drawn up forty years previously when he made his journey from Brazil to Venezuela, passing through these regions.

The next day Catire told us more about the history of the Dekuana and the Yekuana. We had been going up river for some hours when the forest on the right bank of the river gave way to savanna. In the center of it was a large ridge of flat grassland perhaps a thousand feet high.

"Do you see that?" asked Catire, indicating the ridge with the end of his paddle. "That's the Bare Mountain. During my grandfather's time, when there were very many Dekuana, we lived along the whole of the Ventuari from Marietta to here. And the Yekuana also came down as far as here from the sources of the Ventuari, the Erebato and the Caura. The Dekuana and the Yekuana weren't on very good terms then. They used to meet every year on the Bare Mountain and fight with spears and cudgels, because they hadn't got guns in those days. My grandfathers always won because they were stronger. But they were also the worst because they ate the men they killed. This went on for a long time until one day a canoe with Macus went past on its way up the Ventuari to trade, to exchange curare for the blowpipes and the cassava rasps of the Maquiritares. My grandfathers received them peaceably, but afterward they killed and ate all the Macus except one. And he managed to escape and hid himself in the forest. When my grandfathers had finished eating the Macus they had killed they got into their canoes and went home. Then the Macu came out of the forest where he had been hiding. Now you must know that the Macus are all great sorcerers, even worse than the Piaroas. So this Macu started to work his sorcery. He collected the bones of his brothers and breathed on them in order to make them ill. But as the victims were already in the bellies of my grandfathers, my grandfathers fell ill and almost all of them died.

"And that's why there's no one here now," concluded José Catire in a melancholy tone. "The Yekuanas are still very numerous, but there are hardly any Dekuanas left. And it was all our fault too."

After that he was silent, giving his attention to guiding the canoe, because we were now entering into a dangerous series of rapids. In the meantime the savanna had developed into a large plain. José Catire spoke again.

"This is where Captain Cardona pitched his camp for the airplanes. There were a tremendous number of things here: houses, drums of oil, like those you had below the Tencua Falls. Many, many things, and it took a great deal of work to get them all up here."

He was referring to a Venezuelan commission under the command of a Spaniard, Captain Cardona, which had made the last expedition to the edge of the Sierra Parima before our arrival and probably the only one since Koch-Grünberg. During our travels we were often to hear the Indians talk about this "Captain Cardona."

"Is there anything left of all those things?" I asked.

"Not likely," he replied with a laugh. "Everything's disappeared since then.

"Higher up there never was anything," he added. "No one ever went that way."

Ahead of us somber shapes began to rise along the horizon. They belonged to the northern extremity of the Sierra Parima, the country of the Yekuanas, the beginning of the unknown.

We pressed on for several hours and Pierre and I kept our eyes on the mountains ahead, which grew larger and larger.

"Cerro Mono," said Catire.

This was Mount Mono, where the last of the Ventuari falls was situated, the last natural obstacle which formed the frontier between the country from which we had come and the country which we were determined to penetrate. Our hearts began to beat harder. Each paddle stroke seemed to bring us nearer to the objective toward which all our efforts had been directed since we had left Paris more than a year ago.

But we were not to reach the foot of Mount Mono so quickly. There were three days of navigation ahead of us, during which time the river seemed to play tricks with our impatience, sometimes turning away from the mountain altogether. And when it turned toward the mountain again it was still far away in the distance though perhaps a further hour or so had passed.

We did not waste our time, however, and José Catire replied to question after question while our notebooks filled up with new and valuable information about the Maquiritares and their life.

By the evening of November 15th nothing was left of the smoked peccary meat we had brought with us from Cordoval. The following morning Catire decided to leave us for a while.

"You go on with the canoe," he said. "Don't bother about me. I'm going to get food and I'll rejoin you later in the day."

I gave him a rifle and six cartridges and he disappeared into the forest. Marguerite took Catire's place in the canoe behind me and we went on. Toward five o'clock in the afternoon, having gone forward steadily since morning, we heard someone call out from the river bank. It was José. The canoe put into a little creek whose entrance he had already cleared with his matchet. All we had to do was to pitch camp. I noticed the rifle carefully propped against a tree but I could see no sign of any game. José looked a little drawn and he delivered a long speech in Maquiritare to his men.

"What's the matter, Catire?" I asked. "No luck? You didn't kill anything?"

"Oh yes," he said producing the six spent cartridges from his pocket. "I bagged some peccaries. I've just been explaining to my men where they are. They'll go and fetch them."

"How many did you get?"

"Five."

The other Indians each took a matchet and went off into the forest at the trot. They returned at about six when night was falling and we had just finished our work setting up the camp. With them they brought three of the animals.

"Where are the others?" Catire asked.

"The jaguars have had them. But we've got enough as it is."

We dined late, but royally that evening. After having drawn and cut up the peccaries the four men lighted an enormous fire over which they built a sort of grate of green wood about three feet above the flames. Then they singed the haunches and the filets of peccary, cleaned the skin with their matchets and spread them over the grate to cook. The rest was cut up into strips and boiled in our biggest cooking pot. This was the Maquiritare recipe for cooking peccary. The pieces on the grate roasted slowly over a low fire in their skin all night while the fat dropped down into the fire. Every hour the Indians got up, poked up the fire and turned over the pieces of meat. In the morning they were done and all we had to do was to load them into the canoe. We were provisioned for several days.

LOST IN GUAHARIBO TERRITORY

On November 17th the forest closed in on both banks of the river, and at about five o'clock in the evening we sailed into a much narrower part of the Ventuari, about half its previous width. On both sides were mountains. This was the Cerro Mono. José Catire was examining the right bank of the river very closely, and finally he exclaimed:

"That's it!"

As far as we could see there was no opening anywhere in the forest, which formed a wall of dark and compact vegetation right along the bank. But Catire, Marguerite and the two muchachos slashed an opening with their matchets and we made our way into the undergrowth. It was obviously impossible to go on until the next day. The Indians cleared a space and we pitched our camp. Catire was rather preoccupied. His attitude was readily understandable, for, as he had said, he had not made the voyage here for ten years, and he could no longer find where the path began. Late in the night we heard him discussing the matter with Marguerite, who seemed to be well versed in everything connected with the forest.

The next morning, which was November 18th, the two men began to explore the neighborhood of our encampment. At last José found an old mark on a tree.

"This is the way," he declared.

We drew the canoe up onto the bank.

"We must hide it," said José. "You never know."

A recess was cut out in the undergrowth and the canoe disappeared. Marguerite climbed up into a tree and hid the paddles and half our provisions in it, then we set out one behind the other. Several hours passed and we passed on in silence, each of us busy with his own thoughts. Ahead of us we heard José's matchet striking as regularly as a clock as he cut away liana and felled small trees every few yards on our way, not so much to clear our path as to blaze our trail. I was following behind Marguerite, and my eyes went from his ears to his feet. He seemed to go forward more easily than the others through the forest. His feet were enormous and very dark in color, almost indistinguishable from the earth he was walking on. He was only one shape more amid the fantastic confusion of vegetation which peopled this gloomy belly of the virgin wood through which we were making our way.

Our first real contact with the forest of the Parima soon showed us that it was very much according to the descriptions we had been given. It closed so completely above our heads that we could hardly see. Hundreds of different kinds of trees and liana intermingled all around us in such a way that one had to be within a step or two of a tree perhaps six feet round before you noticed it. Some of the liana swayed like enormous serpents, sometimes eighty or ninety feet off the ground, sometimes at face height, and as big as trees. Now and again, but without turning round or slackening pace, José would exchange a word or two with Marguerite in their own tongue. I could not understand what they said, but from the tone of their voices I could gather that they were increasingly anxious. We went on more and more quickly and now José's matchet was at work almost without ceasing as he went forward.

Something was worrying them, not only José and Marguerite

but the others as well. The ground under our feet was beginning to rise. We were going up the mountain. My heart was beating faster, and soon I was panting like a gun dog. Cold sweat was sticking my eyelashes together and running down my back. My heart seemed to be leaving my ribs and slowly mounting into my throat. At last we came to a flat stretch and the beating of my heart gradually returned to normal and I breathed more easily. Then we came out into a small clearing. There were four small and decrepit ranchos there of a rather unusual form. The classic Maquiritare rancho is rectangular in shape, but these four were triangular. The poles which formed their ribs had not been cut with a tool and their ends had been crushed.

Pierre was walking behind me. So far he had not said a word, but now he spoke softly in French into my ear:

"What the deuce is that? Do you think it might be a Guaharibo camp? The Maquiritares never build their ranchos like that. I believe José doesn't really know the way after all. It looks as though we've been going along a Guaharibo path."

He did not say Guaharibo, but Polish, which was the word we had agreed to use when talking about the Guaharibos among ourselves in order that the Maquiritares should not understand what we were talking about. The same idea had just crossed my mind.

"I shouldn't be surprised," I replied.

Suddenly José stopped dead as though he had run up against an invisible wall. His matchet flashed in the air as he used it to cut down something in front of him. He turned and looked me in the face. His own was drawn and anxious.

"Guaharibos, my friend!" he exclaimed.

He pointed with his matchet at something on the ground in front of him. It was only a palm tree branch he had just sliced off, but it was the tip he was pointing to. It had been torn off by twisting only a few hours previously and the drops of sap were still oozing out of it. I realized what it meant. Pierre was right: we were in Guaharibo country. The torn palm leaf was one of their track marks. It had been twisted off by hand because the Guaharibos had no iron implements. The tear was quite fresh, so the

Guaharibos could not be far off. I pretended not to understand the situation.

"Isn't this the right path then?" I asked José innocently.

"No, it isn't, my friend. We're lost. I don't know where the devil my cousins go when they come down from the mountain. This track was made by those damned savage pigs the Guaharibos. I didn't know that they came as far as this, but they obviously do. There's no doubt about it. This is Guaharibo country."

He spat furiously onto the ground and then began a long discussion with Marguerite. In the meantime Pierre and I discussed the situation. Our mishap opened up interesting possibilities. Not that we wanted trouble with the Guaharibos; quite the contrary. We felt—if only as a reaction from all the hair-raising stories we had been told—that we might be able to establish peaceable contact with the Guaharibos straight away. After all, one of the main aims of our expedition was to establish friendly contact with these savages from another world. And now we suddenly found ourselves in their territory. Our long bottled-up impatience burst out: we were determined to see whether we could really approach them as calmly as we wanted—and hoped. In this situation each new indication of anxiety on the part of our Maquiritare guides enhanced our enthusiasm. We also wanted our first savages to be real savages. The whites and the mestizos of the Orinoco had told us rather too much about the Guaharibos. They had insisted so much on their savagery that we were beginning to doubt it. But when men like José Catire and his henchman Marguerite, who could not be suspected of having taken their knowledge of the forest and its inhabitants out of books, showed such lively signs of anxiety, we were almost reassured. This was, incidentally, by no means our only illogical reaction during the months we spent on our expedition. But it was certainly one of the most valuable.

We now insisted that our guides should lead us directly to their enemies, but they were not at all in agreement. José and Marguerite discussed the matter between them and then they put down their matchets, caught hold of the trailing liana and pulled themselves up into the trees. They were soon on the roof of the forest a hundred and fifty feet above our heads. Five minutes later they were on the ground again.

"There's smoke over there," José said, "but I don't know whether it's from Maquiritares or Guaharibos."

"Very well, let's go and see," said Pierre.

José never directly opposed anything with which he was not in agreement; he merely evaded it. He certainly didn't want us to think he was afraid of Guaharibos.

"It's too late now," he said. "It will be dark in less than an hour. Let's look for some place to camp, and tomorrow we can start off again."

We pitched our camp a few miles away on the other side of the hill we had climbed. There was a little stream of clear water hard by and we all took a bath.

"Where does this stream run to?" I asked José.

"I've no idea," he said gruffly.

We really were lost.

On thinking the matter over, José came to the conclusion that the stream must flow into the Ventuari, and so the next morning we all went off down stream one behind the other, with the water up to our knees as we went along. At midday we saw the sun shining through the forest ahead of us. It was the upper Ventuari. Catire put down his bundle on the bank and we all sat down together at the side of the stream.

"We must be below the nearest hut of my cousins," José said. "We'll cut a path along the bank and go and look for them. You wait for us here. We'll be back this evening or tomorrow morning by canoe along the river."

"Right, but leave your son behind with us," I replied. "You don't need more than three of you to carry the guns and the cassava."

The other Indians then went off and José's son Emiliano took to his hammock. He didn't seem very pleased at the idea of staying with us, but I regarded his presence as a guarantee that José would actually return. Not even the most ferocious Guaharibos imaginable would keep him away. Pierre and I also got into our hammocks and hours passed without anyone saying a word. The forest was every bit as silent as we were.

Suddenly there was a loud baying sound not far away. Emiliano sprang out of his hammock and stared at us with glassy eyes.

"Guaharibos!" he exclaimed in a fright.

We cocked our ears and listened intently. There was no further sound from the great wall of forest that surrounded the little clearing where we had slung our hammocks. After a while Emiliano got back into his hammock again. Some time passed and then from the other side of the river, right opposite where we were sitting, came a concert of yells. There was nothing to be seen. Pierre and I jumped out of our hammocks and ran to where a long branch extended over the surface of the river. Opposite us the enormous curtain of bottle-green foliage was impenetrable to the view. The yelling came from behind it and we could see nothing of its source.

We went back to our hammocks. We had taken off the clothes in which we traveled the day before, a shirt and drill trousers soaked in sweat and covered with mud from the marshland through which we had toiled before climbing the mountain, and we were wearing pajamas. They were grimy with dirt, but at least they gave us a change and a little freshness on our bodies when we pitched our camp in the evenings, and despite the state they were in they were still very precious to us.

A little later we heard the rhythmic sound of paddles from the river. Emiliano sprang out of his hammock and ran to our vantage point.

"It's my father come back with our cousins," he cried excitedly.

While running after him both Pierre and I had the same presentiment: supposing he was wrong? According to all accounts the Guaharibos had no canoes and wouldn't have known how to use them if they had. But what if these paddlers were Guaharibos after all?

The carefully collected facts of ethnography and all the technique of rational thought seemed out of place to us at that moment. Absurdity was more likely to triumph in such an odd situation. And we were quite prepared to let it—in fact we wanted it to. And in any case it was surely very strange that in all this immense forest there was not a Guaharibo with a canoe while the Maquiritares had been building them and using them from time immemorial, from the days when they had first come to live in the Sierra Parima.

All three of us were perched close up, one behind the other, as far out on our branch as possible above the rapidly flowing waters of the river when the canoe appeared. There were three men in it: one in the bow, another in the stern and the third amidships. As far as we could see they were quite naked and liberally bedaubed with red and black paint. Their hair was not cut pudding bowl style round their heads but in a crown, and the tops of their heads were shaven as though they were monks with large tonsures. From all we already knew of the matter this was the hallmark of the Guaharibo. Their ears were decorated with little bunches of black feathers. In front of us Emiliano stuttered:

"Guaharibos, my friends. Guaharibos!"

FRIENDS OR ENEMIES?

Emiliano's voice was hoarse and his throat was dry. He wanted to climb back off the branch and hide himself in the forest but we refused to let him. Here was living proof at last: we were in the country of the Guaharibos. The whole tribe probably surrounded us. If they hadn't already discovered our presence it wouldn't take them long to do so. The one thing we must not do was to hide ourselves. To begin with it would be impossible, and for another it would make them suspicious of us from the start. It was much better for us to take the initiative.

"Shout out something to them," urged Pierre.

"What!" exclaimed Emiliano in horror. He had to stay where he was: we wouldn't let him go back along the branch.

"Shout out that we're friends."

Emiliano opened his mouth and a frightened voice shouted: *"Atchika! Atchika!"*

Pierre and I took up the shout:

"Atchika! Atchika!"

At the same time we beat our chests vigorously where the heart is generally assumed to be.

The three Guaharibos turned their heads in our direction. They must have been as shocked as we were, for their canoe almost collided with a rock and nearly turned over. But their faces showed no vestige of expression. They plunged their paddles into the water as powerfully as they could and disappeared down river. The spectacle of two bearded men in pajamas clinging to the branch of a tree over the river Ventuari and shouting Indian words must have struck them as unusual.

Going back to our hammocks we discussed how they would go home and report the incident to their fellows. Emiliano was quite certain about what would happen.

"They'll come back and kill us all," he groaned.

The Spanish jargon of the mestizos of the lower Ventuari stuck in his throat, and got mixed with his own tongue of which we understood absolutely nothing any more.

"They won't kill us, Emiliano. Don't get upset."

We talked to him as one might to a nervous dog frightened of the wind or the darkness, and gradually he calmed down.

After a while we heard the noise of paddles again, and we went back to our observation post. It was the same canoe, but this time it was making its way up river and there were only two men in it. One of them was quite freshly bedaubed with black and red paint, and his hair was dotted with tufts of white down. The other man was not bedaubed and he wore no ornaments of any kind. His skin was light yellow in color and rather unhealthy in appearance. The canoe drew in to a rock on the far side of the river opposite our perch, perhaps sixty feet away. The bedaubed savage picked up a very big bow of some black wood and jumped out onto the rock where he dropped to one knee, chose the longest of his arrows, fitted it carefully into his bow, pointed his weapon in our direction and drew it taut. With his arm drawn back to its fullest extent he knelt there as motionless as a statue. It looked as though he were aiming at the center of Pierre's chest.

In the meantime the canoe swung round and came slowly

toward us. The yellow-skinned savage managed it rather clumsily, half standing and half crouching in the stern. Once or twice it almost turned over before he managed to get it to our branch, to which he then held on with one hand. He seemed to be very excited. We understood the situation: he was, so to speak, the bearer of a flag of truce, while the other man was the covering force—just in case. If we were to make the slightest gesture of hostility that tensed bow would be loosed and the arrow would flash silently over the river and land in Pierre's chest. The next minute was of excessive length. We tried to smile, being anxious to receive the delegate amiably.

The man in the canoe put down his paddle. It was not a well-made paddle in the form of a heart like those of the Maquiritares, but a plain piece of wood clumsily flattened at one end. He stared at us with wide-open eyes. It was an important moment not merely in our lives, but also in his. He wriggled and waved his free arm, gobbled like a turkey in his excitement, and tried to talk at the same time. He was so beside himself that he hardly seemed to know what he had come for; but after a while he calmed down and delivered a long and vehement speech of which, of course, we did not understand a word.

Pierre had a packet of cigarettes in the pocket of his pajamas. Slowly and carefully, in order not to give the warrior on the other side of the river the slightest cause for alarm—the man still had his bow stretched and the arrow pointed toward us—Pierre took out a cigarette, lighted it and offered it to the man in the canoe.

"Ugh! Ugh!" said the savage, and taking the cigarette he made a clumsy attempt to smoke it, bit off part of it, and lost the rest in the river.

He began to bob up and down in excitement, laughing heartily and making signs with his free hand.

"Ugh! Ugh!" he exclaimed.

"What's he saying?" I asked Emiliano.

"He wants the whole packet, and the idiot doesn't even know how to smoke a cigarette."

Emiliano had never been so indignant in his life, but Pierre handed over the packet.

"Ugh! Ugh!" said the Guaharibo.

I handed him a box of matches.

"Ugh! Ugh!" he exclaimed again.

What did he want now? He had thrown the cigarettes and the matches into the bottom of his canoe where they were already wet. We looked at him for a moment or two in silence. We were a little disconcerted. He began to wriggle and jump about even more than before. He got furious at our lack of understanding and pulled himself along the branch to get closer to us, stretching out his hand toward Pierre's leg. Finally we realized that he wanted our pajamas. We might have thought of that before. Pierre took off his jacket and handed it over. The anger immediately disappeared from the man's face and he began to laugh again.

"Ugh! Ugh!"

I took off my jacket and gave it to him. Then we took off our trousers. The warrior on the far side of the river had now relaxed his bow. The man in the boat bundled up our pajamas and continued to laugh heartily. He became almost delirious with joy. But we were now naked and we spread out our hands to indicate that we had nothing else we could give him. He seemed to understand and approve.

Now the moment had come to turn the tables, and Pierre and I took our cue energetically. We leaned forward toward the canoe shouting "Ugh! Ugh!" in concert. The fellow understood that too, and bending down he picked up a bow from the boards and handed it to us obediently.

"Ugh! Ugh!" we went on.

He picked up three arrows and handed them to us. The biggest was tipped with bamboo. It was a war head. The second was very much the same; it was an arrow for big game hunting, and the third was smaller, and bone tipped for hunting smaller game.

"Ugh! Ugh!" we continued to shout.

He raised his arms in the same sign as we had used. He, too, had nothing left to give, apart from our pajamas. Then it occurred to us that we were hungry. Catire had gone off with the last of our provisions. We had nothing left to eat. We hollowed our stomachs and beat a tattoo on them, shouting:

"Miam! Miam!"

He seemed to understand.

"Say 'bananas,' " Emiliano advised.

At that the savage made sweeping gestures with his hand, describing a circle round the forest and returning to us. Then he pointed to the sun and then to the east. Finally he let go of the branch to which he had been holding since the beginning of this memorable interview and pushed off his canoe and made his way toward his companion waiting on the rock.

Before long the canoe with the two savages in it disappeared round the river bend and we returned to our hammocks.

"Well, what did he say?" I asked Emiliano. "Are they going to bring us something to eat?"

"What a chance!" he replied gloomily. "He said they'd come back tomorrow with the whole tribe. But it won't be to bring us bananas, you can be sure of that. They'll take all they can find in the camp here and leave us without a stitch. And we'll be lucky if they don't kill us into the bargain."

He took his matchet and the blanket we had given him a few days previously and went off to hide them in the forest. They were his most precious possessions.

Night fell and we felt cold, but the thought of putting on our ordinary clothes soaked with sweat and very muddy from our march was not pleasant, so Pierre and I got into the same hammock, my head at one end, his head at the other, and shared our cover, a beard stuck out at each end. We must have looked like a playing card. Our situation was undoubtedly grave, but it was also comic and we began to laugh heartily. Emiliano looked at us gloomily. Our reaction to the situation upset him even more. We stuck a stake into the ground at the side of our hammock and fixed a candle on top of it to give us light. Then we began to jot down the chief events of the day in our notebooks.

In the meantime the depressed little Maquiritare rolled himself in his hammock, and we heard him muttering hopelessly:

"I wonder where Father is?"

Then he went to sleep and we were left alone at the end of the world in the little patch of light that flickered around our candle. I thought of the curious fate of my pajamas, with the label of the Paris firm from which I had bought them just before we left. What a story could be spun around them if their remains were found one day in a Guaharibo camp! Sometimes it's a pity that things can't write their own stories.

The silence gradually became alive. The forest and the darkness began to crepitate, to sigh, and to whisper. We had only three candles and we lit them one after the other as a nervous man chain smokes. We were divided between a feeling of excitement which tended to make us laugh at everything, and an indefinable anxiety which rose slowly like a tide and threatened to turn into fear. We felt disinclined to sleep, and we probably should not have been able to sleep in any case. Our Maquiritare friends might return, and it was therefore necessary to stay awake and keep the light burning to guide them to our encampment.

Pierre and I talked for hours. When the forest around us made too much noise we raised our voices to overcome it, to expel it from our presence. But it returned again and again. It was as persistent as a bad dream.

We talked of Paris, of our friends, of our childhood, and of our past life. We spoke of the future, and of the expeditions we should like to make another time. We wondered whether the Papuans were really as savage as they were reported to be. We talked and talked and talked. Our voices were like two babbling streams, and it seemed almost as though they dared not cease on pain of death. The more that fear rose up around us the more we sought to deny the plain evidence of it. It was November 20th, 1949. I had left Paris over a year before, and the adventure on which we had set out had taken on form at last. Everything was now at stake in every minute that passed, and we both knew it.

Suddenly Pierre started up.

"There they are," he exclaimed. "The Guaharibos. Did you hear? They have surrounded us. They're creeping up to take us by surprise. We're done for. We might get away still by making a dash for the water. Because we could escape by swimming down river."

In all good faith I sought to calm his fears.

"That was a troop of monkeys you heard springing from branch to branch, and the wind is shaking the trees."

I sat up abruptly in my turn, my heart beating hard, the blood hammering in my temples.

"There! There! Can't you see. There's something moving."

"No, I can't see anything. It's just the shadows dancing in the candle light."

I lay back again in the hammock and breathed slowly. I was thinking quickly. Supposing Pierre were right? Supposing the Guaharibos were there, creeping up on us to attack? Well, all right, supposing they were: what could I do about it? Nothing, as far as I could see. There was no defense against the forest and the men of the forest. Either you set foot in the forest or you don't. Either you go into the forest or you don't. And if you do it's because you wanted to. Therefore you must accept the forest world and all that goes with it. Otherwise you will have been cheating, just pretending. I realized that I could not defend myself whatever happened. The move had been made and there was no going back. The thought calmed me at once. I thought of the power of confidence. Up to then it had mastered all situations. My heart was beating normally again.

"They said they'd come back at dawn, Pierre. If they really wanted to attack us they could have done it already. They know there are only three of us and that we aren't armed. We shall have plenty to do when they do come. Let's get some sleep now. We must have confidence. It's our only chance."

We talked for some time about the next day, and then I blew out the candle and we went to sleep like children.

MEN THEY CALL "SAVAGES"

At about six o'clock the forest awoke in real earnest and there were yells and shouts. Above our heads a troop of monkeys chattered away, but there was no doubt at all that the voices of men were sounding in the forest from all sides.

We were sitting on our branch again above the river when the canoe arrived. It was so full of savages this time that it could hardly keep afloat.

A gnome-like creature with frizzy hair stood up in the stern and crawling over the heads and shoulders of the others he made his way forward to our branch and hoisted himself up. All he was dressed in was a tuft of black feathers attached to his left arm and a strip of liana around his loins. He grunted, laughed, shouted and jigged up and down. He caught hold of first Pierre and then me by our beards, pulling them vigorously to see if they were firmly fixed on, at the same time uttering great "Oh's" of admiration. He had four hairs on his own chin, something rare for an Indian, and so we were able to return the compliment. He slobbered a greenish sort of saliva onto our hands. It seemed to ooze permanently from the corners of his lips. A great black mass deformed his lips, extending them forward in two flat shapes. We were just wondering what shocking disease had so distorted his mouth when he put up his hand and took out the cause of the trouble, a lump of greenish tobacco about the size of half an orange. This he subsequently deposited in my hammock.

Behind our hammocks about fifteen savages had come forward out of the forest. They were bedaubed with paint all over their bodies and they drew their bows in our direction. They must have crept up to our encampment before daylight and watched us without betraying their presence or attempting to disturb our sleep. Perhaps it was these men we had heard in the night when I thought it was the wind in the trees. Our Emiliano looked like a condemned man about to be led to execution.

"The old man who pulled your beards is their sorcerer. He's in charge and he's the big chief of all these swine," he said.

We began a grotesque pantomime with the old sorcerer. We did our best to keep on laughing all the time and he began to laugh too, and soon all the others were laughing. In the meantime the canoe was going backward and forward between our camp and theirs, which was obviously quite close. More and more groups of gesticulating, hopping, gnome-like creatures piled out of it, brandishing bows as big as they were little. Their average height was probably about four foot six. After a while women appeared as well. They were smaller still, perhaps a little over four feet. The old women were quite naked, but the younger ones wore a small fringe of ocher-colored cotton suspended rather coquettishly over the pubic area. There was so little of it that it tended to draw attention to what it was supposed to conceal. Their costume was completed by large round tufts of white down below the ears and a small ring through the nose. They had large empty baskets on their backs and their intention seemed to be to fill them as quickly as possible at our expense. They were not in the least timid and they came forward in a crowd to examine us in detail, uttering little exclamations of surprise and making comments in shrill voices or whatever seemed to strike them as surprising in our anatomies.

In the meantime the men had opened our bundles and unrolled the lengths of printed cotton goods we had brought with us for the Maquiritares of the uplands. Our beards and the hair on our chests were momentarily relegated to second place in the general interest. A loud discussion was going on among the men while the women busily filled their baskets. We made as though to intervene. We did not want them to take all our treasures at once for fear of what they might do afterward. And we were also anxious to create the impression of a fair exchange as we had done the evening before with their delegate.

I handed our aluminum cooking pot to the old sorcerer, but in return I took the bow and arrows of one of their warriors. One young woman who was holding a length of material pressed to her bosom I deprived delicately of the balls of white down at her ears. But we could not keep the brake on indefinitely, and the moment came when the women's baskets were full and our stock was empty. But still they made no attempt to go. They seemed to be waiting for something. What else was there to give them?

Above all, they must not be allowed to get bored. Already some of the warriors had picked up their bows and arrows again and they seemed to be growing fidgety. While they were playfully pulling our beards they could as easily have hit us over the head with cudgels, or transfixed us with arrows just to amuse themselves.

Pierre was making trials of strength with the men, lifting them up with outstretched arms one after the other. They felt his muscles and then tried to lift him up in their turn, laughing heartily.

I led the old sorcerer over to a tree on which I had hung my Leica. I was burning with impatience to take photographs. They would be the first photographs of Guaharibos ever.

"Careful!" Pierre cried.

I knew what he meant. He was thinking of what had happened to an American minister. The story had been told to us by an old rubber gatherer of Puerto Ayacucho. This minister had had an experience something like ours but in Brazil. He had unexpectedly fallen in with a group of Guaharibos in the forest. They had stripped him and he had made no attempt at resistance, but he had unwisely raised his camera and pointed it at them. At that moment an arrow had transfixed his chest. His Boy had managed to escape and when he found his way back to civilization a month later he had told the story.

But I had an idea. I took the camera out of its case and I showed it to the sorcerer while focusing it.

"Atchika! Atchika!" I exclaimed, slapping the old man heartily on the back. He repeated the word without understanding but with amusement.

"Atchika! Atchika!"

I pointed to the men standing around us and I tapped my heart. He was at a loss. I showed him Pierre in the view-finder and he was astounded. I tried to convey to him that my magic apparatus made all the people I liked quite small so that I could carry them next to my heart. Then I took a photograph of Pierre. The old man was highly amused.

"Get him to stand with you," I said to Pierre, "and I'll take the two of you together."

I handed the camera to Pierre and I put my arm round the old sorcerer's neck. He seemed still very happy and he addressed a speech to two of the men who were holding their bows and arrows. Obediently they put them on the ground. We were dripping with sweat. I put one of the young women between Pierre and the old sorcerer and took a photograph of them.

"Why not make the presents all over again?" I thought, and I took an aluminum pot which was on top in one of the baskets and gave it to the young woman. She rewarded me with a delightful smile. Then I went close to her and took a photograph of her alone. I handed the pot to the old sorcerer and then took a photograph of him standing by the side of the young woman. They were both delighted and they looked like a barbarian Adam and Eve.

In this way we took a whole roll of film without untoward incident. At about four o'clock in the afternoon the Guaharibos gave signs of departing, and then, with the assistance of Emiliano, who was a little more confident by this time, we explained to them that we wanted to get to the nearest Maquiritare village. They explained that it was higher up the river, and, without being asked, they offered us their canoe. Then they disappeared into the forest on foot, advancing as adroitly as monkeys.

Silence fell after their departure. After so much excitement we found ourselves exhausted and, after so much noise and shouting we found nothing to say. We realized that we were ravenously hungry. We had not eaten for two days. There was a buzzing in our ears and our heads began to whirl. We went to the stream and dipped our faces in the fresh, limpid water. It seemed to take away our fatigue and to relax our nerves after the acute tension of the past twenty-four hours. The cool, murmuring water was like a sedative. We took off what clothes we had left, little more than shapeless rags. My trousers had only one leg, because before leaving the old sorcerer had insisted on taking along the other to make himself a hat and I had cut it off with my matchet, which he had also taken along with him.

Our encampment looked like a battlefield. All we had left was our hammocks, but strewn over the ground was an arsenal of bows and arrows.

Pierre and I got into the same hammock again as before and

Emiliano brought us a packet of cigarettes and a box of matches which he had somehow managed to save. We lay back in the hammock. It occurred to me that unless José Catire came back pretty soon that box of matches was likely to be our most precious treasure for quite a while.

There were patches of sunlight around us and a bird was singing in a tree near by. The smoke of our cigarettes rose straight up above us toward the roof of the forest. We had seen and talked to the Guaharibos. A used roll of film was our evidence. And we were not dead, but very much alive still.

The atmosphere was hot and damp and rather oppressive. I remembered that in Europe it would be the first day of winter. For a moment or two I thought of the primeval forest of the Gauls in my own country, and of the men who were there even before them. It was probably much worse than this. Words and visions became confused in my head. I glanced at Pierre. He was asleep with his mouth open. His cigarette was burning away slowly on the ground by the hammock where he had dropped it, the smoke rising into the air. The Guaharibos might come back. I went to sleep as well.

"THE COUSINS FROM HIGHER UP"

The peaceful pause was not to last long, perhaps half an hour, and then we were awakened by new shouts from the river. Was it the Guaharibos again? No, this time it was the three Maquiritares who had come back for us. They had marched for twenty-four hours almost without halts and they had found nothing but three abandoned huts. They had come to the conclusion that their cousins had gone higher up the Ventuari when the Guaharibos arrived in the neighborhood, because the latter would certainly have destroyed their crops. In order to get back as quickly as possible to where we were waiting for them, the three had felled trees and made themselves a raft.

When we had finished telling our adventures to each other, we decided that the following morning José and his men should go up river again in the canoe without us. In any case, the canoe which the Guaharibos had given us was too small and not in good enough condition to hold us all. In the meantime we would go on foot to the nearest of the three abandoned huts and wait there for their return, as we should be better off there than alone in the open forest.

The canoe the Guaharibos had given us was really not in a very good state. They had torn away the front half of the boat to make a seat and the vessel leaked like a sieve. The next morning José and Marguerite patched it up as well as they could, covering up the leaks with flattened bark and tying the bows together with strips of liana. Then they shaped rudimentary paddles out of some soft wood and transported us one by one across the river, because the abandoned hut we were to make for was on that side. Then they paddled off up river while we started our journey on foot, Emiliano taking the lead and clearing a path with the one matchet he had been wise enough to hide from the Guaharibos.

We did not feel too secure and we had the impression that we were being invisibly escorted by Guaharibos hidden behind the trees. The forest was full of them, and if they encircled us again and closed in we should have to laugh and joke and play the famished clowns for hours on end again. However, toward midday we arrived without incident at the abandoned hut José had described. It was a great round hut with a conical roof and walls of dried clay set on the summit of a cleared hill, and we could still see vestiges of a cassava plantation. There had also been a banana plantation and we immediately explored it in the hope of finding something to eat. All we found was a stem of small green bananas. We picked them all the same and took them back to the hut.

While we were slinging our hammocks Emiliano made a small fire and we put the bananas in the embers in the hope of improving them. At the third banana we had had enough. They almost choked us. However, even that poor meal was sufficiently restoring to give us the idea of washing our clothes. We had no soap, but the river bank was covered with a red ocherous sort of earth which was enough to remove the smell of dirt, sweat, and mildew from the garments even if it didn't clean them properly.

We treated shirts and pants with this earth, rubbing very gently in order that they shouldn't fall to pieces altogether; then we spread them out on the grass in front of the hut and retired to our hammocks.

Emiliano was already asleep when we heard a noise from outside the hut. Pierre and I ran to the door. Two colossal Indians, naked and colored red, stood on the path about twenty paces away and their eyes went from our clothes spread out on the ground in front of the hut to the pile of Guaharibo bows and arrows leaning against the wall of the hut. We looked at each other for a moment or two in silence. Then Pierre spoke.

"Let's get out of it."

Almost mechanically I restrained him while I searched desperately in my mind for an Indian word to say to them. Finally I remembered the word Emiliano had shouted to the Guaharibos.

"Atchika! Atchika!" I cried, and both of us beat our breasts vigorously to indicate friendship. The two savages continued to look at us in silence and obvious astonishment. Then the nearest one repeated *"Atchika!"* as though he were turning it over in his mind, and then both of them turned round and slowly made their way back to the river.

"They're Guaharibos all right," said Pierre, "but a good deal more frightening than the others. Did you notice their build? They're athletes, proper warriors. They've certainly gone off to fetch others. This time we've had it, I'm afraid, like rats in a trap."

I hid our one remaining matchet and our clothes in the bushes and then we went back to our hammocks. We didn't know what else to do. We were at the end of our tether. The weather had been wonderful for a week, but now it chose this particular moment to start pouring. The rain came down in such sheets that it was impossible to see for more than five or six feet through it.

"We mustn't make a fire this evening," Pierre said. "At least we needn't guide them to where we are."

"And we could climb up into the roof and sling our hammocks there," I suggested.

All we could think of were senseless, useless suggestions.

Then Emiliano woke up and we told him what had happened.

"The other one had a queer sort of sack like a bandolier over his shoulder," said Pierre.

I had not noticed that detail, but apparently it was important, for Emiliano was keenly interested at once.

"A little sack," he repeated. "Then they weren't Guaharibos at all, but Maquiritares, our cousins from higher up."

He almost shrieked the last words in his delight, and before we had recovered from our surprise he had sprung from his hammock and was dashing off down to the river, quite oblivious of the pelting rain.

Pierre and I looked at each other and hardly knew what to say, so we burst out laughing in our relief. We had quite forgotten that the Maquiritare Indians we were looking for also went around practically naked and painted red. And if they really were Maquiritares, what must they have thought at the sight of two white men, quite naked, in their old hut; white men who had apparently fallen from heaven and whose only visible equipment was a pile of Guaharibo bows and arrows; white men whose only word was "*Atchika!*," incidentally a Guaharibo word!

But perhaps they were Guaharibos after all. Emiliano came back from the river disconsolately. He had not found them.

"It's enough to make a fellow throw his hand in," said Pierre.

I had nothing to add to that summing up of our situation, so we turned in and went to sleep again.

The next morning between nine and ten there was again the sound of footsteps outside the hut. Whoever it was saw no need for stealth, and then a big and shaggy head appeared in the doorway. It was Marguerite, with his pierced ears and his impassive expression. Our reconnaissance group had returned again, but this time victorious. Two splendid canoes were waiting for us at the river bank, and José, who was in one of them, immediately handed us a large flat loaf of cassava bread, white and fresh and as appetizing as though it had just come out of the oven.

Five minutes later we were in the canoes and making our way up river. However, we had not gone more than perhaps five hundred yards when a burst of shouting and yelling sounded from among the foliage and undergrowth along the river's edge. It was the Guaharibos again, but this time they had arrived too late. José spat demonstratively into the water and went on paddling vigorously with great sweeps of a magnificent heart-shaped paddle.

A few hours later we arrived at a quay where there were many other canoes like ours. A much-used path led away from the river bank up through a plantation of thriving cassava to a big ocher-red hut like the one we had left, except that it was not dilapidated and a plume of blue smoke rose up through the roof. At last we had arrived among "the cousins higher up."

José led us behind the big hut to a guest rancho like the one in which he had accommodated us in Cordoval. His own hammock was already swinging there. While we were engaged in fixing up our hammocks, more and more men emerged from the big hut and came up to watch us silently, leaning with folded arms against the posts of the rancho. They were all young men, quite naked and of athletic build. Around their loins was a large red guayuco, one end of which hung down almost to the ground along one thigh. Round their upper arms were leather straps embroidered in a check pattern with white and blue beads, enhancing the curve of their biceps and the breadth of their shoulders. At the end of a necklace of beads of the same color hung a triangle of polished silver in the middle of the chest, and like their bodies these silver ornaments were painted with red arabesques. Round their ankles were narrow bands of plaited black hair.

They smiled as they stood there looking at us, and occasionally they exchanged a few remarks. They were quite motionless, apart from raising a hand to their lips from time to time to smoke long cigarettes of green tobacco rolled in very thin rose-colored bark almost like rice paper. Women also came out of the hut, depositing a number of black earthenware cooking pots discreetly in the middle of our rancho. They contained a steaming dish of pimentoes and fish. There was also a large basket of black and white wickerwork with fresh cassava bread. The women were naked to the waist, and below that they wore a little apron embroidered with beads and with a fringe which swayed gently as they moved.

An old man came and crouched in front of the pots. He was the master of the house. The young men followed his example, and José invited us to do the same. Lunch was served.

When the pots were empty, the women brought three large calabashes of some warm liquid, and they passed from mouth to mouth. In one there was a sort of yam soup, and in the others banana juice and yaraké.

The whole meal was over in a quarter of an hour and we retired to our hammocks well satisfied.

"I've already begun to make arrangements for men to go down river and get your stuff," Jose explained, "and there will be others. All the huts along the Ventuari have been informed too. These are good muchachos. You see, they'll work well, and, of course, you must pay them well. And should we meet those dirty savages on the way down you can be sure we'll get back all they stole from you."

Our departure was fixed for the following morning. In the meantime, the Maquiritares, excited by the story José and Emiliano had told them about our adventures, were preparing an armory to take with them in case of an encounter with "the dirty savages," our friends the Guaharibos. When the time came for our departure, the six splendid canoes which awaited us at the quayside literally bristled with arms. There were bows and arrows, ancient flintlock muskets, blowpipes and quivers full of curare tipped arrows, and, finally, great spears of hard wood, metal-tipped and perhaps ten or twelve feet long. In the hands of the athletic Maquiritares such a spear was a redoubtable weapon, and certainly the handsomest of all.

MORE SETBACKS AND LUIS' SACRIFICE

The descent of the Ventuari was as agreeable as the ascent had been disagreeable. In four days we were at Cordoval again, and Jean and Luis were hardly able to believe their eyes and ears when they heard the sound of conches from around the river bend and saw our six magnificent canoes appear one after the other. A couple of dozen dark-skinned athletes were paddling in unison, while in the stern of each canoe stood a helmsman blowing away at his conch. Incidentally, Pierre and I were every bit as enthusiastic as Jean and Luis. Our present magnificent state might have been sufficient to let us forget the grimmer moments of our adventure but for the precious package wrapped in banana leaf we had with us. It contained our first roll of film with the photographs of the savage Guaharibos. It was now the evening of November 28th and we had left on November 12th, so that our whole journey there and back had occupied sixteen days. But it had been sixteen days very well spent.

The next day José and his twenty-five warriors went down to the foot of the Tencua Falls to get our baggage. After that another few days passed while we checked over our equipment, distributing the weight and opening and re-nailing our cases.

In the meantime our Indians were not idle. Every morning two or three of them would go out hunting, and in the evening there was much drawing, cutting up, and preparing of peccaries. The women occupied themselves with grating cassava roots and making piles of cassava loaves. On December 1st we put away our saws and our hammers in the neighboring rancho, and José packed away the meat and the cassava loaves in four large baskets carefully lined with banana leaves to protect the food from the rain. Everything was ready once again for our departure, which was fixed for the following morning.

Now, José was a wise man who always showed a proper respect for traditions, and he had not caused so much cassava to be prepared merely for our journey. When night fell the women appeared with calabashes. Cordoval was offering a grand yaraké in our honor before we left. The son of the chief and one of the "cousins from higher up" appeared each carrying a bamboo tube perhaps three feet long, and they sat down on our threshold and began to play for us. The bamboo tubes were "uanas," a kind of large clarinet, which is the traditional instrument for making music at the feasts of the Maquiritares. All night they two treated us to a shawm-like duet which reminded us of two snorting, grunting boars about to engage in a duel. It was a new kind of music to us and we listened to it with interest, though from the standpoint of melody it left a great deal to be desired.

We went off at dawn, and before the end of the first day we had reached the Oso Falls. But as powerful as our Maquiritare companions were, even they could not carry both baggage and canoes over the five miles of path which went through the forest and over the savanna to the top of the falls, so they contented themselves with unloading our baggage that evening and leaving the journey to the next day. The weather was threatening and so they built a rancho for the night. They worked so quickly that we hardly had time to film the main stages of the job before it was finished. Within half an hour they had built a shelter sufficient to hold the thirty members of our party and all our equipment. The main supports of the rancho were as thick as a man's thigh, and the great roof of leaves, sufficiently thick to resist even the worst storms, was at least ten feet from the ground.

We didn't miss a single detail of these building operations, and more than once such a Maquiritare rancho proved a great boon to us in the heart of the Sierra Parima, where it rains practically all the time. I would gladly pass on the working instructions to those camping enthusiasts who would like a change from their canvas tents, but I am afraid they would be of little use, because the operation requires materials which are very difficult if not impossible to obtain in Europe and the United States or Canada, such as six or eight feet long banana leaves, tough yet supple liana for fastening the supports and the beams, and, above all, tree trunks as tough as oak, as straight as poplar, but infinitely more easy to work than most of the timber that grows in our climate.

Two days later we embarked once again, above the Oso Falls. The Maquiritares had carried the six canoes and our two tons of baggage from the lower level of the Ventuari to the upper level. For another couple of days our voyage proceeded without incident. We took detailed shots of the extraordinarily skillful paddling and poling which was necessary to get us safely through the rapids, and our notebooks recorded a generous harvest of ethnographical information. From six o'clock in the morning until about four o'clock in the afternoon the canoes were driven steadily forward, and then, when the sun began to sink, the paddlers slowed down and all eyes began to examine the river banks. It was the time of unexpected encounters and of surprise meetings, the time when large numbers of birds and animals came down to the river from the forest.

Slowly we would move along the bank in the tremendous silence with bows and muskets ready for instant use. At a sign from the helmsman one of the canoes would glide gently into the bank and come to a halt under one of those many great trees whose branches spread out over the water.

He would look up into the tangle of branches and foliage reaching perhaps a hundred and fifty feet into the air above his head. We too would look, but we would see nothing until the arrow he loosed brought down a bird, a wild turkey, or a paujil, one of those big aquatic birds of the forest, the size of a domestic goose, or perhaps a grey and yellow or red and green iguana, looking like a fairy-tale dragon. Or another time perhaps the Indians would begin to laugh as one of their number struck at something in the foliage a few feet away from us, and only then would we see the boa, as big as a fireman's hose, beginning to uncoil its rings one by one as the blows drove it away into the forest.

It takes weeks, perhaps even months, of living in the forest to spot motionless birds, animals, and reptiles at once as the Indians do, particularly when they are half-concealed in the foliage and the mimicry is almost perfect.

Already the general plan for the great film we were going to make was taking shape in our minds. We already had the title: "The Crossing of the Sierra Parima." The first part would consist of the slow and calm voyage up the Ventuari with these superb Indian watermen. We had already filmed not only their superb prowess with their paddles and their poles as they drove their frail canoes through rapids and round whirlpools, but also their life in the encampments mornings and evenings. We had shots of them making the camp fires, building the temporary ranchos, cooking the meals, with menus always different and always improvised: one day an alligator's tail, another day fried monkey with a brace of roast parrots, soup made of piranha, and so on. And afterward we had shots of them singing and playing reed-like flutes, either squatting around the fire or lying in their hammocks.

We came nearer and nearer to Cerro Mono and the last falls before the Maquiritare territory proper. There we would establish ourselves with "the cousins from higher up," using their village as a base from which to go out into the surrounding country in various directions, to lift little by little the veil of mystery which still hung so closely over the life of the Sierra Parima. First of all we would visit Kalomera, the chief of chiefs. We were already quite certain that he would receive us well, and why not? All the other Maquiritares had made us welcome. He would hold a great feast in our honor, and after that we should visit the Guaharibos again to get to know their villages and their way of life. Our first encounter with them had gone off so well that we no longer expected hostility from them. Of course, they would steal some more of our goods, but it would be well worth it. And finally Kalomera would lend us some of his best warriors and they would show us the secret of the tracks that led across the Parima so that we could arrive triumphantly in Brazil along a route that no white man had ever previously traveled.

On December 4th at about four o'clock in the afternoon my canoe was ahead and I noticed for the first time that we had left the other canoes so far behind that they were out of sight. I ordered the helmsman to turn round and go back, and an hour later at the outflow of a great rapid we found the five other canoes lying alongside a large rock on which Pierre and Jean were engaged in sorting, cleaning, drying, and dismantling the remains of three of our cases. Fifteen hundred feet of film were lying in a puddle near them. One of the canoes had overturned. Our generating set had been fished out as though by a miracle after it had been under water for about half an hour. All its coils had to be attended to. A case of discs had been lost altogether.

It was the first cloud appearing in a clear sky. It was not the storm itself, but the preliminary rain. The storm itself burst a couple of days later.

The next day, which was December 5th, the 35mm camera which had been so carefully repaired in Bogotá jammed again in the middle of a take. Jean took the thing to pieces and got it in order again.

On December 6th it jammed once more. Jean took it to pieces, but this time he could not get it to go. Several cogs had been broken and were now useless. The accident to our truck on May 6th, the first day of the expedition, must have imperceptibly bent one of the axles in the mechanism; not enough to reveal the damage at once, but in course of time and use the thing had become hopeless. The mechanic in Bogotá had not seen it any more than we had, and we had no spare parts.

"It wouldn't help us even if we had," said Pierre. "It's a proper bench job. Only the manufacturer could do it."

But the camera had been made in Chicago. We were now about six hundred miles from the upper Orinoco, where two or three planes a month left for Bogotá. What on earth were we to do?

We called the little creek into which we put that evening Black Harbor. Catire's men built a rancho as usual and he sent off some of them to hunt for our supper. When we had slung our hammocks we explained to him just how serious the situation had become. We held a regular council of war and it was twenty-four hours before we were able to arrive at a decision. It was fifteen months since we had left France, and for the past seven months we had practically lived on equatorial rivers in equatorial forests. We were all more or less exhausted, both physically and morally. Luis could still only hobble around owing to the ray-fish sting in the sole of his foot. Pierre's body was dotted with sores and ulcers, the kind the equatorial forest brings up on a man's arms and thighs to drain his strength and energy in the long run. Jean was troubled with malaria, and almost every week he suffered a recrudescence of the fever which often took him two or three days to get over despite all the quinine we dosed him with. And I had to admit that I was not in much better case myself. In addition, the state of the treasury was discouraging. In fact, we had all but exhausted our credits.

To go on with our expedition would mean that first of all we must return to civilization, perhaps go to New York, and then come back here again, which would mean further months of travel and further heavy expenditure on an adventure whose upshot was still uncertain, despite all our enthusiasm and our faith in ourselves and in our Indians. Further, we should lose the benefit of the dry season. In what state should we find the Ventuari and the other rivers of the Parima if we tried to navigate them when they were in flood? Yet they were our only means of entering the heart of the country and leaving it again. And what about the Guaharibos? If we left the almost miraculous chance which had put us into peaceable touch with them too long without following it up, we might not find it so easy the next time.

Night fell and found us still discussing the situation. We were still talking animatedly, but the only possible conclusion was forcing itself upon us as we talked. We all knew it already, but no one dared say it outright.

It was the only thing to do, we told ourselves, but for all that, we were very unwilling to give up now. And yet it was the only reasonable, wise course.

The Indians returned with a fine cayman alligator. They lighted resin torches and set to work. They cut off its tail and passed it through the flames, scraping it with their matchets. Then they cut it into pieces and made a big *pot-au-feu* of alligator flesh. The Indian we called "The Sioux," chief of the uppermost of the Ventuari huts, had abandoned the wickerwork which he did patiently every evening, and he now sat by the fire waiting for the soup. He was a dreamer. Another we had dubbed "The Eskimo," who had three wives and two hats, was not singing for once, but lay back in his hammock wiggling his toes. Sanoma, the inquisitive, no longer cared to fiddle with the leg of my pajamas to find out how it was made. José was sitting all by himself on the bank of the lapping river, smoking. The dogs were asleep curled up. The pot began to boil and from time to time drops of the alligator soup spilled over into the fire and hissed and steamed.

Far above us in the immense crown of the forest we could hear a pair of monkeys calling to each other.

The sky began to spangle with stars, and constellations formed. On the other side of the river the Southern Cross leaned to the left and looked much too close. The moon made its way toward the zenith, carrying Venus, shimmering bluishly, in its wake. The yellow mirror broke in the upstream waters and the glistening fragments were carried down by the plashing water. The horizon, Cerro Mono, was black and high. It was the unknown Parima inhabited by the Maquiritares and the Guaharibos, naked men without money and without cameras. That other world was so close at hand now. All we had to do was to push forward energetically, put our shoulder to the last barrier and force our way in with one final effort.

To go forward now would be easier than shooting the rapids.

And yet the wisest thing to do would be to give up. Or would the wisest thing really have been to stay in Paris, in London, in Chicago, in Bogotá, in Caracas or Yokohama?

The thread which went from the orchids of the airport and the glass cases of the museum, the caciques, and the sorcerers squatting in the Calle Trece and the Carrera Octava had wound its way up river and awaited us there in the darkness we wanted to transform into light.

Bernard Palissy had not been wise either. He had "groped in the dark" too, but he had never given up, and in the end he had succeeded in making his enameled dishes.

"I own a little property not far from Bogotá," said Luis, the Colombian member of our expedition, quite calmly. "It's worth a few million pesos I should think."

And then the good fellow added:

"Of course I shall make the journey back alone because you can be doing useful work above the Mono while I'm gone. I'll try to get a new camera sent down from New York, and if that isn't possible I'll go there myself. After all, it's only forty-eight hours from Bogotá. It's hardly much farther than from the Oso to the Tencua Falls. I'll get some more trading stock, too, because as things are we shan't have enough to see us over the Parima. I reckon to join you again in about forty-five days, and you can wait for me above the Mono."

After that we began to talk about a 16mm film we could make of the Guaharibos while we were waiting for him. We were engaged in a wild discussion of lunar and solar mythology when the sky began to lighten.

Our dog fancier, a giant of a man with a red striped face, was crouching near my hammock, a puppy in each hand. He was making them drink in turn out of the same calabash.

Sanoma cut up alligator flesh with vigorous blows of his matchet to make our breakfast. The weather was fine and I got out of my hammock and took a header into the river.

"We'll leave after breakfast," said Pierre to José, who then briefly gave his orders. In the meantime we seized pencil and paper: if we wanted our New Year good wishes to arrive in Paris in time there was not a moment to lose.

Our Sioux had a son who was about the same age as my own boy, between seven and eight years old. I gave him a new knife and pointed to his cotton hammock, red with the paint he left behind every night. He seemed to find the bargain satisfactory and so I took down the hammock, rolled it up and handed it to Luis who was preparing his traveling kit: there were presents to be thought of as well.

Our letters joined the hammock in Luis's kit. Luis himself added the film we had shot and the famous roll of Leica film which recorded the events of our first reconnaissance trip. He rolled up everything in his cover and his mosquito net and took a matchet and a small cooking pot. Then he was ready. Breakfast was ready too, and we squatted around the pot of alligator flesh. José brought up the cassava bread and the pimento seasoning passed from hand to hand.

Luis's canoe left first, gliding down river like an arrow. Luis paddled in the bow and José's son Emiliano paddled and steered in the stern. They disappeared from sight around the next bend in the river just as our remaining five canoes turned their backs on them and put their noses upstream. We pressed on our way through a dream day. Not a cloud was anywhere to be seen in the blue sky. Along the banks boa constrictors slept above the water, coiled round and round the thicker branches of the trees which leaned outward over the river. Flamboyant macaws and little green parakeets flew across the water shrieking as they went. We grew sluggish in the silence and the heat, and our minds were on the many days, and perhaps months, which were to come before we were likely to see Luis again.

That evening the only place we could find to pitch our camp for the night was a small island, and there was not a banana tree or a palm anywhere on it, so it was impossible for the Indians to construct a rancho. We slung our hammocks between such trees as there were and rolled ourselves up in our blankets. The rain waited until we were fast asleep, and then it came down in a sudden rush, splitting the sky and thrashing through the leaves of the trees. We leaped out of our hammocks, quickly unhooked them and rushed for shelter beneath a big tree, where we crouched together holding leaves over our heads and pressing close to each other to keep our bodily warmth. In this way we passed the night, half awake, half dozing, occasionally exchanging a word. Pierre smoked stoically on my left and talked about wood fires in the country enjoyed within walls of stone while the elements raged outside and a stew simmered on the hob. On my right Jean kept his spirits up by singing:

"Deux éléphants ça trompe énormement . . ."

All around us the forest drummed and cracked, and no doubt it was steaming in the darkness. My mind went round in a circle from the rain to the night, and from the night to the rain, to the cold, to the Indians, and back again to the night and the rain, the rain which pelted down on us like a pack of snarling dogs, cold and ruthless in all climes, cold and ruthless like death with his scythe, rain which insinuated itself pitilessly between the flesh and the dream, dispelling the warmth, seeking the central hearth of man's being to extinguish it with cold, clammy fingers. I thought of the first man who discovered fire and thereby set an impassable frontier between him and the animals and the rest of creation for all time. I thought of the little Guaharibo crouched in the rain over the pitiful little fire it had taken him many centuries to light, sheltering it from the elements with his own body, until such time as he had learned to construct his miserable little triangular rancho and cover it with banana leaves. And one day he would interest himself in the bigger, rectangular, better-built hut of his cousin the Maquiritare with its carefully plaited roof.

I thought of the day which must come after this night, however slow the seconds. I thought of the sun, worshipped by the Piaroas and the Maquiritares, but perhaps not yet by the Guaharibos, because they had not yet left the womb of night, the mother of all things, the great night of man's origins, without heaven and without hell, without height and without depth, and without hope because it was without despair.

And then the sun dispersed the night and the clouds, and once again the paddles began to move rhythmically to right and left, forcing the canoe on through the current and leaving Luis farther and farther behind us as he went off on his own to sell his property, his trees and his peons, and the sun on his patch of earth in order that we might still press on toward the summit of the mountain which was now beginning to loom up ahead of us. And as we pressed on the river grew narrower and its banks grew higher and higher above the water. We were approaching the Cerro Mono again.

AT THE EDGE OF THE SIERRA PARIMA

We arrived that same evening.

José Catire, the Sioux, the Eskimo, and two other chiefs came to me and said:

"We can't carry all those cases up there on our own. The Maquiritares are watermen, not porters. And, in any case, you must remember that there aren't enough of us, and that a single journey from here to the river above the falls takes two days. It would take us a week you must consider."

Oh yes, I realized that all right. None of us had any desire to hang around the Cerro Mono for a week.

"Yes, I see," I said to José, "but what do you propose?"

"Me!" he exclaimed with a nonchalant gesture. "I don't propose anything. You must remember that I'm not at home here. It's my cousins who have to propose. They say that they'll get hold of a group of Guaharibos in the neighborhood. The Guaharibos aren't much good, but at least they can climb up a hill with a case on their backs. It won't cost much. You just give them a little present, nothing at all worth mentioning, and they'll be quite satisfied. And if they're not . . ."

And if they weren't I had no doubt that the score of Maquiritares would quickly convince them that they were mistaken owing to their lack of education.

"Right you are," I said, "but how long will it take before they can be got here?"

"Not more than a day. You know, Sanoma isn't a Maquiritare at all, but a Guaharibo. Of course, he's not a Guaharibo like the others; he lives with my cousins, and you'll have to pay him just like them, but he's a pure Guaharibo all the same. He talks their language and he knows where all those dirty little dogs live. He'll go and look for them, and he'll be quick; you can rely on that."

I accepted the proposal. The Indians had already built a magnificent rancho with two compartments, and all we had to do was to sling our hammocks, crawl into them and go to sleep to forget the rumbling of our empty bellies, because all the food had gone.

The Sioux, the Eskimo and their companions had painted the affair in over-bright colors. Not only were the Guaharibos not there the next day, but only a very small advance contingent arrived on the following day.

"The others will be here tomorrow with Sanoma," José assured me.

The newcomers rapidly constructed one of their own little three-cornered ranchos next to ours and slung their hammocks in it. Silence and somnolence descended on the camp and we were left to hunger, boredom, and lassitude. Almost all our Maquiritares had gone off at dawn to hunt in the forest. They all returned empty handed and went to sleep. There was nothing to be done about our empty bellies, except wait and sleep—if we could.

"Haven't you even got a little rice left?" asked José.

Jean sprang to his feet.

"We're dumbbells!" he exclaimed. "Of course, I'm quite sure there must be some of the rice we brought from the Orinoco still there somewhere."

He ran to our cases and opened them one after the other furiously. In the end he produced the remainder of a sack of rice triumphantly and handed it over to Catire.

"It'll have to be ground though," he said.

"That's all right," José replied and nodded his head toward the rancho of the Guaharibos.

He shouted something and one of the Indians left his hammock and came toward us. José gave him the sack and a stout stick and told him what to do. The Guaharibo crouched down to the job. He was a fat little man with a brownish yellow skin, a dirty little Buddha wearing nothing but a bowstring round his loins.

A great quid of tobacco turned his lips into a tulip of flesh and tobacco juice dribbled constantly from the corners of his mouth, giving him a kind of greenish moustache. He jabbed away at the rice, and from time to time when he thought we weren't looking he shot us a short, ironic glance from under his lashes. He could have been torturer-in-chief at some university of savages, or perhaps even master of wisdom. Once our eyes met and from behind his quid he muttered something unintelligible. His feet were fixed firmly on the ground like two trees and his torso swayed as he worked. He smiled a little. What was going on in his mind? Was he perhaps calculating our weight in meat? He was a gnome, a man of the forest, a being of the twilight. Was he really thinking anything at all?

To right and left I heard the cracking of branches. His fellow Guaharibos had left their rancho and had gone out into the forest. They reappeared after a while with our axes over their shoulders. Their cheeks were distended and they were chewing. They must have found something to eat. Their children followed them with their arms full of pieces of white, fleshy wood. Now and again they bit pieces off and chewed them. We were nonplussed.

"Cogollo," grunted a Maquiritare warrior contemptuously.

It was the pith of the palm tree. They came up and offered us long pieces of it. It proved fresh and tender but tasteless, and after a little chewing it seemed to dissipate hunger without satisfying it. In the end so much insipidity turns boredom, hunger, and headache into a gradual and definite feeling of nausea.

"It's all right for those swine to eat it raw like that," said José contemptuously.

He filled a cooking pot with the pith and boiled it up with salt and pimento.

"Like that it's tolerable," he said.

The Guaharibos watched his performance with obvious disgust.

I have often recalled that scene. It summed up the fundamental difference between the Maquiritares and the Guaharibos, and between us and the Guaharibos as well. It can be expressed in two words: salt and pimento. Sacks of coarse salt are carried from the Orinoco into the heart of the forest. No Maquiritare ever goes on a journey without a hollow piece of bamboo or a bottle containing dried and crushed pimento and salt mixed. Food without seasoning would be as insipid to him as it is to us. The Guaharibos, on the contrary, have a horror of salt and they detest pimento. They like only the natural insipidity of the forest itself. If they kill game they eat it raw or half cooked and without either drawing or skinning it. Sometimes they plant banana trees because it is sufficient to take a few cuttings and thrust them into the soil in order to have bananas in a few months, but they have no proper agriculture because they feel no need for it. The stomach of a Guaharibo is satisfied with whatever its owner happens to come across in his ceaseless wanderings through the forest. We saw Guaharibos eating wild berries, marsh flowers full of earthworms, caterpillars and insects, and even earth if it seemed rich enough. The ability to make fire and their upright stance were about the only things which distinguished them from the animal world. To be really men in the sense in which we understand the word they lacked the taste for salt, the taste for pimento; they lacked the desire to transform their food, to transform the world in which they lived, to intervene in the workings of their fate.

The Maquiritares, on the other hand, organized proper hunting expeditions; they cooked their game, cured it, and seasoned it. They reformed the forest in which they lived; yesterday they felled its trees with stone axes, today they use steel axes. They burned down stretches of the forest and planted cassava shoots in the warm ash, or bananas, or pineapples, and yams. They sowed, they harvested, they pressed, they peeled, they grated, they ground, and they cooked. They cleared spaces in the forest; they built their own houses, and very gradually they transformed their own world into the image of man's own desire, into an affirmation of his own will.

The Maquiritare transforms his environment; the Guaharibo suffers it.

The gap runs not between us and the savages, it runs through the world of those we call savages, between the Maquiritares and the Guaharibos, between the active principle of salt and pimento, and the passive principle of nature's insipidity.

Revolted by work which, in the course of our inordinate evolution, has often ceased to bear any recognizable or tangible relationship to our needs, themselves transformed out of recognition in their own evolution, many a white man dreams fondly of a return to our origins. But our origins lie further back than the Maquiritare. He is still a savage and he goes naked, but he is our younger brother, our brother all the same. He has the same fundamental needs and the same fundamental problems as we have. He is a man in the same sense that we are men. He works and he goes forward just as we did, or are perhaps still doing.

Our origins lie with the Guaharibo, who still lives in the belly of the forest, in the twilight of the world, in the twilight of space and time. The Guaharibo does not work, he merely exists as plants and animals exist, and there is very little difference between him and them. Those who want to return to our origins forget one thing: to be like the Guaharibo one must accept the original commandment of life without enhancement, life without salt or seasoning. And I don't think that any men, from the

Maquiritares to ourselves, could do that any more. Time has gone in one direction and it can never be put back. That gap can never go forward. And finally, man has changed organically. He is changed; he is alone against the world around him. He has been born a second time, and now there is no alternative for him but to follow his destiny.

On the following day the second group of Guaharibos arrived. On December 12th we set off, and on the evening of the next day we reached the upper source of the Ventuari, where other canoes were awaiting us. The Guaharibos Pierre and I had met on our journey had still not shown themselves. Before these other Guaharibos took their departure, after having each valiantly carried about ninety pounds up the mountainside, we had to pay them. I left it to José to settle with them, not wishing to offend the susceptibilities of the Maquiritares. He gave each Guaharibo two boxes of matches and a small piece of flowered cotton cloth about a yard and a half long and perhaps a hand's breadth wide. I gave a thought to our ethnographical collection.

"Tell them that if they would like to bring some of their own things up to us, I'll give them more coroto," I told José.

Sanoma translated what I had said to the Guaharibos, and all the Maquiritares burst out laughing.

"What do you want with their things?" they asked. "They haven't got any things. Do you know the only sort of knife they possess? An agouti tooth fastened on to a stick!"

The Guaharibos listened to what Sanoma had to say to them; then they shrugged their shoulders and turned away. One after the other they disappeared into the forest without using the path.

"They're not interested," said José.

The following evening found us installed with José's Yekuana cousins above the falls in the same guest rancho in which we had been accommodated two weeks previously on our first arrival. But this time we had our two tons of baggage with us, and we had no intention of ever going down the Ventuari again.

Our first aim while awaiting the return of Luis was to get into touch with Kalomera. He was to be found not more than a day's journey away, we were told. The day after our arrival we sent off a messenger to him. In the meantime we chatted with our hosts. We had been astonished at the almost civilized fashion in which the Guaharibos who had acted as our porters had behaved themselves, and we were equally astonished at having seen no sign of the other Guaharibos we had met. We then learned that Diego, the housemaster, and the Indian we called "the dog man," had been beset by the little savages when they had gone up to the hut for the first time to fetch cassava bread. The Guaharibos had contented themselves with a part of the provisions.

It appeared that the relations between the Maquiritares and the Guaharibos were much more complicated than one might have supposed. In the last resort it was a question of colonization for the Maquiritares: either the Guaharibos were hostile, for example the Yavani tribe, those who had mobbed us on our first journey, or they could be pacified and made into vassals, for example the Kamishavani tribe, those who had carried up our cases. But none of the Guaharibo tribes were at a stage of development which would make it possible to make an agreed peace with them on a footing of equality. Only a few particularly intelligent individuals, wanting to improve their position, came to live with the Maquiritares, gradually learning the Maquiritare technique and the Maquiritare language, thus transforming themselves and establishing themselves in the Maquiritare community. Such was Sanoma and one other man, whose name was Saudi and who, we learned, had been a Guaharibo chief.

Saudi disappeared shortly after our arrival, and when we asked what had happened to him we were told that war had broken out somewhere beyond the source of the Ventuari between two Guaharibo tribes. The trouble threatened to extend as far as the first of the Maquiritare plantations, but the Maquiritares wanted peace, and so Saudi had been sent off to mediate between the two tribes.

"What are they fighting about?" I asked.

"It's over women as usual. The men of the one tribe have stolen two women belonging to the other tribe, and there you are."

We learned from this that war is endemic among the Guaharibos themselves, and that it is liable to break out again at any minute, always over some dark-skinned Helen. They told me about the final episode of a war which had raged for a long time between our friends the Yavani and another tribe of Guaharibos living at the source of the Orinoco.

"At that time the Yavani lived to the south of the Ventuari a few days journey away from the territory of their enemies. The latter penetrated into Yavani territory right up to the village where the Yavani were well established. The enemy began to shoot arrows into the village. No one replied. The flight of arrows continued, and still no one replied, but while the shooting was going on the Yavani collected the arrows fired at them. When the shooting finally stopped they began to shoot back, not only their own arrows, but also those of the attackers, of whom they then killed two. With that the war came to an end. They're funny monkeys, those Yavani," José concluded.

At last our messenger returned from the village of Kalomera. He had gone to ask for men to transport our baggage to the village. José interrogated him and then translated the message the great chief had sent back. It was clear and precise:

"Let the same men who conducted the white chiefs up the Ventuari now conduct them here. I will undertake to guide them over the mountain."

There was nothing to be done but to bow to the great chief's wishes and to go to him ourselves and explain that we did not wish to cross only the mountain, and that, in any event, we could not do so before the fourth of the "white chiefs" had returned. Having decided this, we set off the next day.

BY FOOT TO THE VILLAGE OF KALOMERA

José went ahead and I went behind him followed by Jean and Pierre and then a number of Guaharibos carrying our baggage. The journey was dull and monotonous, and the path went through a forest as high as that of the Mono. At first the path was just a straight line. Then the terrain ceased to be flat and the path began to rise and wind along the chain which separated the valley of the Ventuari from the valley of the Erebato. Although the way was straight it took us several hours to reach the ridge, which was perhaps sixty feet across. José went at a trot along this narrow plateau. I followed his example, preferring that gait because it seemed to shorten the way and because it helped me to forget my fatigue and muscular stiffness after our long march. The sky now seemed nearer, but on either side of the path precipices of forest fell away into a bottomless pit. Then we went down for a mile or two before the path rose again to the top of a new ridge.

Hour after hour passed in silence. All I could hear was the thudding sound of bare feet on the ground ahead of me and behind me. Looking back over my shoulder, I saw that we had outdistanced our companions. There were only four of us now: José, two Guaharibos, and myself. I knew that José would stop only in his own time and so I said nothing. At last, after a new and long descent, the endless twilight of the forest began to give way to a pale greenish light that seemed to be filtering through the trees.

Then we emerged altogether from the trees and came into tall bushland, and here the path forked. José sat down and I sat down with him to wait for the others to come up. The two Guaharibos sat down near me and freed their foreheads from the bark straps with which they carried their loads. I offered cigarettes round and lay down on my back. Now I could feel fatigue stealing along all my limbs like a slow current. It seemed to me that I could hear the beating of my heart in the silence as it gradually returned to normal.

The somber blue line of a mountain ridge formed the horizon. Gradually the sun sank toward it. Of a sudden a loud barking sounded from the verge of the forest we had just left, and a pack of slavering dogs shot out from the trees along the path. They were enormous beasts, their bodies taut like bowstrings, and they panted as from a long run. They halted a little distance away from us, keeping close to each other, lowering their heads, growling and baring their teeth as though they were about to attack us.

"Humans around," said José, but without turning his head.

At the sight of the dogs the two Guaharibos had made off in a panic.

"Come back!" shouted José. "Are you afraid of dogs?"

His voice had cracked like a whip, and at the sound of it the two men turned round and came back. They sat down again without a word.

There were sounds in the forest behind the dogs and then a man appeared. He was tall and naked apart from his guayuco, and his body was covered from head to foot with red markings. In his hand he held a large musket. He was in the full paint of a Maquiritare warrior. Three plump young women, also painted red, followed him at a little distance. Large bands of light blue and white pearls ornamented their wrists and their ankles. They stopped at the edge of the forest behind the dogs. The man stood in the middle of the path leaning on his musket and looking at us. We did not move. He turned his head and said something to the women, who went along the path with their eyes to the ground. They disappeared ahead and were followed by the dogs.

José and the man spoke to each other with deliberation, first one and then the other, and without exchanging glances. They made gestures frequently, indicating with hand or a nod of the head, the path and the thick forest which began again at the other side of the clearing. They raised their arms toward the sun and followed its course across the sky toward the horizon. Finally the Indian shouldered his musket and went on his way.

"It's still a good way to go," José said. "We must pass two canyons and then we shall come to the old house of Kalomera. After that we go over a small mountain and then we shall be there."

"Do you think we can get there before nightfall?" I asked.

"Who knows?" he replied.

The remainder of our little expedition came up. Pierre's face was drawn and he was limping. His boots had been cut to pieces on the way and he had hurt his foot. I was the only one of us three now who was not barefooted.

"Those damned Guaharibos tried to lose us on the way,"

Jean said, and he told me that Pierre had had a bad time and was now hardly able to walk.

José's face broke up into myriads of lines and he laughed. "Let's get going," he said. "We must hurry."

We started off again slowly. José didn't seem to care in the least about Pierre's state. We had to keep on shouting to him not to go so fast for fear that he would disappear from sight. The path became muddy and slippery, and we could see the imprint of many feet. It looked as though we were approaching some forest capital. The idea was obviously displeasing to our Guaharibos and their faces began to darken. The sun was almost down to the horizon and there was perhaps about an hour of daylight left. Pierre was moving along with difficulty.

"We'll try to reach the old site," I said to José, "and there we'll spend the night."

He mumbled some reply. We still went forward in silence, as first one and then the other canyon appeared. We passed them over narrow trunks laid from one side to the other, managing to keep our balance. Once again the green shade grew lighter and the vegetation became less somber. Then we came out into a vast round clearing. Quite suddenly the forest withdrew to the horizon, and the terrain changed abruptly to great rolling green plains. Above us was a blue sky dotted with clouds. Two great black ridges formed the horizon to the north above the forest. We were in a great plain between the two mountains. Before us were the ruins of what had once been the tribal hut of the great chief Kalomera. Fire had destroyed the roof of palm leaves, but the clay walls were still standing. The hut was about ten feet high and perhaps a hundred and twenty feet in diameter. It might have been the ruins of a Roman arena quite recently destroyed by fire and abandoned. The fire had cracked and whitened the walls, but here and there were pinkish areas with vestiges of the original ocherous color.

The main beams of the roof were only half consumed, but their overhead joints had given way and they had subsided into the center of the arena like the black spokes of a gigantic wheel.

The central support still remained standing upright to the sky as though nailing the enormous wheel to the ground.

The air was grey-blue, and the forest began to suck in the night like blotting paper as the sun gradually declined below the horizon. We had no time to spare whatever we did: either set up our camp here or try to reach Kalomera's village if we could. But the grandeur of the sight impressed us so much that we remained standing, lost to the passage of time and held by the enormous silence of the abandoned site. All around us in the great clearing and in what had once been the tribal headquarters of Kalomera and his men, among debris of all sorts—bones gnawed clean by the dogs, drinking calabashes, eating calabashes and so on—grew the same high grass which overgrows everything man abandons anywhere in the world, whether it be his house or his corpse.

We tried to reconstruct in our minds' eyes the funnel-shaped roof that had once crowned the gigantic building. We could no more do it than we could imagine the sea or a great river in the heart of a forest. This hut of wood, clay and palms must have been as big as a house of stone. It surpassed all we had seen and all we had imagined of the Indians' architecture.

The Guaharibos had sat down and were mechanically chewing a piece of sugar cane they had come across on the way.

"Let's go on," said Pierre. "I feel a bit better. I think I can hold out to the end now."

We started off again. We had not been in the forest for more than perhaps ten minutes when a light appeared ahead of us and advanced toward us along the path. It was carried by one of three Indians who had been sent out by Kalomera to meet us. Three messengers from Rome or Sparta who came toward us armed with bows and arrows—and an American battery lamp. Between his two companions, each as handsome as he was, walked the mysterious man with the musket we had met in the afternoon. Now he carried the lamp and smiled as he turned its beams toward us.

In the light of his electric torch we could see that the path had widened very considerably and taken on almost the proportions of an avenue. This time we really were approaching a forest capital. We clambered up the "mountain" José had mentioned. Fortunately for us it was no more than a hill, and as soon as we crossed the brow the path was lit up by a reddish glow.

WE FIND OURSELVES AMBASSADORS OF FRANCE

At the foot of the hill we came out into a clearing where the new headquarters of Kalomera was established. It was very different from the old. It had not the character of an area definitely wrenched from the forest by man and transformed according to his own scale. It was nothing but a vast clearing around which the menacing sea of trees was merely provisionally held up. The reddish glow which lit up the latter part of our way came from a large bonfire of branches burning in one corner of the clearing. The flames leaped up and flickered in the wind and filled the whole space with reddish light. Here and there gleamed fresh gashes where trees had been felled. They were almost the color of flesh in the firelight. The ground was covered with chips and slivers of wood, and mingled with the leaves, dead, half dead, half rotted, they made a strange soft carpet under our feet, a brownish violet carpet touched with pink. There was as yet no tribal hut. For the moment the tribe sheltered itself under long, grey ranchos, squat like fortresses and covered with logs laid closely together. They were arranged in the form of a U around the clearing with their backs to the forest. The scene was immediately impressive, with its suggestion of ordered, confident power and its almost military arrangement. The feeling I had had on the old site of discovering a forgotten yet living detail of Roman history returned to me here with redoubled force. I almost expected to see some centurion advance from the shadows.

A small light flickered in the center of the cleared space from under a roof of palms without walls. It was there that our silent escort took us. We immediately recognized the guest house of the Maquiritares, the visitors' rancho.

A gigantic chorus of barking saluted our arrival. I knew that Kalomera's men were great dog fanciers and that they traded with them throughout the Guianas, but I did not know that they went in for dog breeding on such a scale. As soon as we had come into the clearing, a barking and a baying arose from all the ranchos of the village, and there was such a tremendous noise of dogs that by comparison what we had heard in the afternoon had been nothing but the snarling of a few curs. But we looked around vainly in the clearing to see the animals which caused the noise. Not one was visible. Nor a human being either. Even our guides had disappeared as soon as they had led us to the visitors' rancho. Between our hammocks, which were already slung, burned a resin torch, smoking and sputtering, but throwing light over the immaculate earthen floor. Without that evidence one might have thought that no one had passed this way for ages. Obviously it would be indiscreet to show any curiosity in the village of Kalomera, and so we followed the example of José, who had already got into his hammock. The light from the great bonfire in the open space suddenly swung round to us like the beam of a lighthouse, reddish and bordered with smoke, making us blink.

Then an arm became visible between two hammocks and put a dish of cassava bread on the floor near the torch. A naked form disappeared into the gloom as we heard the faint clicking of a beaded fringe. Gradually the silence was peopled with forms. Modest young faces became visible in the light, and, with eyes cast down, their owners quickly put new dishes of cassava bread on the ground and two, three, four, eight, ten little black earthenware pots steaming with dishes of various colors. What strange beings these Indian girls were with their doll-like faces! Their timidity in the presence of such bearded giants as we were to them did not prevent them from appearing with their cheeks and foreheads covered with blood-like paintings of tigers or panthers.

A piquant and tempting smell arose from the cooking pots. All the women had gone back to their own hearths, but the men were there now, squatted around us on the edge of the night. Ten, twenty arms stretched out, breaking off pieces of cassava bread and dipping them into the pots. We jumped out of our hammocks and did likewise. They ate, laughed, and chatted, rubbing shoulders with us happily, squatting down on their heels. Their shoulders, backs, and arms were splendidly muscular, and as they moved, their muscles rippled under their glistening brown skin with its red stripes. Our rancho had abruptly ceased to be in the desert, and night had been pushed back. It was now crowded, warm, and alive. It was a real house, full of familiar noises and odors.

And there was nothing violent or vehement about it all. In everything these men did and said there was the same abiding principle of tact, discretion, and moderation which seemed to preside over the whole life of the Maquiritares.

Great calabashes of warm drinks now passed from hand to hand. Banana syrup and yaraké were drunk in large quantities to appease the clean and lively prickle of the Maquiritare pimento.

When the meal was at an end the women appeared again to take away the empty dishes, calabashes, and pots, and we went back to our hammocks. The men remained with us. They examined our clothing with interest, looked at us amiably, and asked us questions in their language. We replied to them as well as we could, mixing Spanish with the inadequate resources of our Maquiritare vocabulary.

But I was impatient to see the man of whom we had heard so much, and who presided over this friendly reception without being present. When we arrived at the village, I had asked José where Kalomera was.

"Don't bother your head about that," he had replied. "He will come. And he, too, knows that you have come."

I looked round at the men. Perhaps he was already there, somewhere at my elbow. Perhaps it was that little dried-up man with the winking eyes who spoke in a voice which was pitched higher than the voices of his companions? He never seemed to address his remarks to anyone in particular, but all other conversation ceased when he raised his voice. It must be he. We had been an hour in the village now. It was about time to do something, but what? José seemed to have forgotten us altogether. He was lying back in his hammock, smoking peacefully and looking at the roof.

I turned to the old man.

"What are you called?" I asked.

He took a long cigarette wrapped in very thin bark from his lips, smiled, and looked me straight in the eye:

"Kalomera," he said simply.

"Ah! So you are Kalomera! I am Alain. This is Pierre, and this is Jean."

Slowly and with some difficulty he repeated the names after me, and then after him everyone else present repeated our names too, in a sort of nocturnal speaking chorus. I became the soloist and Kalomera the coryphaeus, and the night edged with all these smiling, friendly faces was the chorus. Behind them in the middle distance the dogs growled, as though they were not yet altogether reassured at our presence, as though they were the expression of everything in this world that had not yet accepted us.

A youngster approached. He carried long lighted cigarettes between all the fingers of his hands, and he blew upon them as he came. He gave one to Kalomera, one to me, one each to Jean and Pierre, and one to José.

Jean and Pierre were very tired and soon went to sleep, but I chatted on with Kalomera, who was squatting on the floor next to my hammock. My conversation was chiefly in answer to his questions.

"What have you come to do here? Are you going to stay a long time? Where is your coroto?"

Above all he was anxious to know who we were. He had never before heard the language we spoke to one another.

"You know," he said, "I have met a lot of people. There aren't only Venezuelans among the whites. I know that. Do you know Captain Cardona? He came to visit me too. He is a Spaniard. I also knew a German. But that was a long time ago and I was very young. He had dozens and dozens of cases with him. And what beads he had in his coroto! When a muchacho brought him a paujil or an agouti for food, he would take a calabash and scoop it into one of his cases and bring it out full of beads to the very brim. 'Open your hands,' he would say to the muchacho, and when the man did so he would pour out the whole calabash filled to the brim with beads into his hands. That was coroto if you like! He was a German. A great chief. He had come a very long way to see the Indians."

Captain Cardona had crossed the Sierra Parima in 1940, and before him there had been only one white man in this neighborhood: Koch-Grünberg, who had been sent out by the Ethnographic Institute of Berlin. That was in 1911. Apparently it was Koch-Grünberg Kalomera was talking about.

"I know the Venezuelans because I have gone down to them several times to sell them canoes or cassava, but they have never come to visit me. No, before you only the German and the Spaniard have been here."

"The German is dead now," I said, "but the Spaniard is still alive. They both came from the same part of the world we have come from to see you. You know that if you go down the Erebato to the Caura, and then down the Caura to the Orinoco, and then right down the Orinoco you come to a very big lagoon without trees, and its waters are blue and green and very full of salt. We call it the sea. The land ends at the sea. But there are very big ships that float on the sea, which is bigger than the earth. They find their way across it by the skies: the sun, the moon, and the stars guide them on their way. They sail on for many days and nights without ever seeing anything but the waters of this sea and the skies above them. Then gradually a new land comes in sight, where the men, the animals and the things are not like those here. That's where our country is. It's called France. People there don't know the Indians or the country of the Indians, but they are interested in anything that concerns other men. We crossed the great lagoon and came up the rivers in canoes to get to know the Indians. When we return to our own country we shall tell the French people that there is a different land here and that different people, called Indians, live here."

Kalomera listened to me with keen interest.

"France, French people," he repeated slowly.

I knew that those words were now engraved irrevocably in his memory, like the Germans of Germany, and the Spaniards of Spain. The choir of male voices around him repeated:

"France. French people."

Now Kalomera wanted to discover the importance of the country we came from.

"Do they make guns in your country?" he asked.

"Certainly they do."

"Well why haven't you brought me any then?"

At this point I should have had to explain to him about the customs procedures, which would have been difficult, but fortunately he wasn't really interested: he had so many more questions to ask me.

"And these steamboats?" he asked. "Do they make them in your country?"

"They certainly do."

"And what about airplanes?"

That France built steamboats was natural enough, they seemed to think. But airplanes! A great silence followed my affirmative reply.

When Kalomera and his men retired soon after that and I remained behind awake in our rancho, I found it none too easy to realize the improbable situation. We had become ambassadors of France to this small Indian people who lived months away from the civilized world, and it had never before occurred to us that we were anything but individuals without specific allegiance. But for Kalomera the great chief of the Maquiritares we were not individuals: we were the representatives of a people he did not know. I, Alain Gheerbrant, was a member of the French family just as Kalomera was a member of the Maquiritare family.

That was my first contact with a great chief whose people still lived in the stone age.

AND HEALERS OF THE SICK

The next morning Kalomera arrived to visit me very early.

"You are a medicine man," he said. "You must therefore come and see our sick."

An Indian was instructed to carry our medicine chest, and we went off from rancho to rancho and from hammock to hammock. Before each door Kalomera indicated that I should wait outside for a moment and then he entered on his own. I heard him giving orders and through the walls I could hear the sound of objects being hurriedly moved. After a while he would reappear and beckon me in. A feverish child would be lying there, or a man. One child had slashed open its foot with a matchet. An old woman complained of pains in her back. Throughout our visit Kalomera served me as interpreter and assistant. Each time I bent down over a patient a circle of interested heads surrounded me in the gloom. Each time I produced an instrument, a thermometer or some medicament, the laughter and the conversation ceased. Ten or twenty eyes would be silently fixed on me, wide open to receive something of the science they ascribed to me. And Kalomera himself was not the least attentive. I could feel that he was watching and judging all my movements.

There was something theatrical about the scene. I had to impress him and all of them. When I had to make an injection, I demanded that all doors and windows should be closed and that everyone apart from Kalomera, the patient, and myself should go away. The patient shook with malarial fever and his hammock swayed and trembled. Kalomera held the phial of quinine. I removed the thermometer from the patient's mouth and looked at it. It was above 105 degrees. I lit the blue fire of the alcohol in the gloom, and its flame danced on the chrome of my instruments, of which I paraded as many as possible. That was part of the theater too, but it was serious, for it was performing with the life of a fellow human being. I had to do more than merely try to cure the patient. I had to create a favorable impression with the science I used to achieve my cure. I had to impress them with my art and with the theater I created. I snapped off the top of my phials of distilled water. I mixed yellow and white powders. I made bandages. I raged because the boiling water I had asked for was only warm when it arrived, although I knew very well that it would never be aseptic. I handed a satchet of permanganate to Kalomera and explained gravely that each time the water must be boiling. He understood perfectly, and he never omitted dipping his finger into the water before the next dressing to assure himself that the water had really been boiled.

When the visits were at an end, Kalomera wanted to know exactly what was in each jar and each phial, and I explained to him as well as I could.

"The things you know!" he exclaimed admiringly.

Once again we went from rancho to rancho and workshop to workshop, for all the men worked. Some of them went off into the forest at a trot with their spears on their shoulders and their white and red dogs at their heels. Others cut down trees on the edge of the clearing and turned them into logs to make the roof of some unfinished rancho. The women came and went, their baskets of roots on their backs, and through latticework walls we could hear the sound of grating as the cassava flour was prepared. Kalomera inspected the work of everyone on his rounds, his little mongol eyes looking keenly between his wrinkled lids. He said a few words here and a few words there, and his orders were immediately carried out.

There was a certain childlike and very real pride in what he did. He would swagger a little, and then suddenly he would turn to me and murmur something almost touchingly naive. He was in turn the great leader of centurions, the king of savages, the Red Indian of legend, noble and haughty, and then an almost timid little man anxious to learn the secrets of the whites.

We went afterward to his own rancho, where he sent away the women and tied up the dogs. Taking a little stool, he offered it to me and pulled me by the arm tyrannically to make me sit down. A great variety of objects are often hanging from the inside roofs of Maquiritare huts: reserve calabashes with a golden patina from the rising smoke, blowpipes, bows and arrows, hatchets—a whole stock of strange objects covered with dust and soot from the smoke of the fires.

Kalomera clambered easily up to the cross beams which go from wall to wall in a Maquiritare hut, and he got down two fine cedar-wood boxes from above my head, the sort owned by the watermen of the Orinoco. Taking a key from a necklace of trinkets dangling on his chest, he unlocked the boxes and opened their lids. Then he proceeded to show me his treasures. There was a large ball of American fishing line, not so strong, but brighter and whiter than the twine the Maquiritares used; five or six pounds of black gunpowder, "native brand," in neat enamel canisters; three lengths of cotton cloth for guayucos, of which he unrolled a few yards on the floor to show me; a pot of ointment against the itch; and a yellow bottle with a label declaring the contents to be "the authentic Capuchin remedy" and a sovereign cure for all insect stings and reptile bites, and an unfailing specific for colics, fevers, and colds.

Kalomera took one article after the other from the two chests, and there was soon a heterogeneous collection of all sorts of odds and ends piled up between us. Finally he produced a shiny leather cap like those worn by the bootblacks of Bogotá, which he placed on his head, a pair of steel-rimmed spectacles, which he placed on his nose, and a dagger which was quite new and which he sheathed in a little case of imitation leather after having made me feel the edge. He hung the dagger on a nylon belt which he fastened round his waist. He then stood up in his queer panoply. It formed such a strange and astonishing contrast with his red and muscular body and with the thick black hair that emerged from under the leather cap that I was lost for words and searched in vain for the compliment he obviously expected. But from behind his glasses he gave me such a commanding and authoritative look that finally I managed to blurt out:

"You are a great chief, Kalo."

"I am the great cacique of the Maquiritares," he replied with dignity. "I am he who makes war on the Guaharibos; he who brings salt, powder, guns, iron, and guayuco to all the Indians of the mountain. And when our new hut is built you will see that I will sing too. I am the great singer. I can sing for five days and five nights. All the muchachos will be dressed in crowns of feathers and robes of palm leaves. But I shall be dressed as I am now because I am the great chief and the great singer."

He fell silent abruptly and remained motionless for a moment or two.

"But you must bring me a great deal of coroto," he said then, "and now give me a cigarette."

He put all his treasures back into the two chests, shut the lids and locked them, and then sat down on one of them. He seemed to be thinking. After a while he rose, undid one of the chests, and with great care took out something about the size of a matchbox and wrapped in dry leaves. Then with two small sticks, held one in each hand, he opened the little package, taking great care not to touch it with his hands. A small piece of reddish brown stone or hard earth was revealed. This he lifted up with the two sticks.

"Do you know what that is?" he asked.

I confessed my ignorance and he laughed happily.

"You're a great medicine man," he said, "but you don't know what that is! Perhaps you think the Indians don't know anything at all? Now you can write it down in your little book and tell it to your friends in France: you have seen the great Indian remedy. With this I can cure all pains. I touch the bad spot with this and the evil goes. It's the sun stone."

He wrapped up the little stone again, put it away, and locked the chest, sat down on it, and looked at me happily.

"One day you may learn why," he concluded.

I realized that he was going to tell me no more and so I changed the subject. I did not want to show curiosity about things he was unwilling to tell me. That would make things too easy for him. I decided that the preliminaries had now been concluded, and I could broach the matter which had brought us here.

"Kalo, in about a month my third comrade will be back, and then we will all come here to see the celebration of the new hut. We have not many guns with us, but I will give you one if you get your men to prepare many feather ornaments, drums, dance clubs, Maquiritare trumpets and flutes, and all the things you know about as a great chief, but which the young men have forgotten. If you make us these and many other things I will give you pieces of red guayuco bigger and better than those you already have in your chests, and knives, matchets, cooking pots, beads, powder and lead. We could be here in one or two moons. Agreed?"

He repeated this shining promise of coroto in detail:

"A lot of powder, a lot of lead, a lot of guayuco, a lot of knives, cooking pots, and beads. Very well, I know you are great white men. But why do you want to see our celebrations?"

When I spoke of taking photographs and films his face clouded over.

"I know what photographs are," he said, "and I don't like that sort of thing."

"Why not?" I asked. "There's no harm in photographs. They're simple, ordinary things, not bad things. Why don't you like them, Kalo?"

He made no reply. Obviously he was thinking. Through the half-open door I could see my two companions in the visitors' rancho surrounded by the men of the village. Our baggage was on the ground, opened, and the men were rummaging through it without embarrassment, even putting their hands into the pockets of my friends' clothes. I drew Kalomera's attention to what was happening.

"Look, Kalo," I said. "My friends might just as well say: 'I don't like that.' But why should they? Your men want to see what we've got with us. There's no harm in that. It's like our photographs. That's why we want to see your celebrations."

Apparently there was nothing he could think of in reply so he changed the subject.

"Why do you want to cross the Parima?" he asked.

"Because no white man has ever crossed it before. We want to get to know it."

"No," he said, shaking his head. "It isn't possible. I can take you across the mountain, but not across the Parima. I can take you to Brazil with your friends and your cases, but not that way. A little further on I can, across the Paraguas, across the other mountain."

He meant across the Sierra Pacaraima. I knew the route he had in mind. Two white men had already gone that way. It was beyond the territory of the Guaharibos, beyond the fascinating blank spot on the maps, beyond the great question mark.

"No, that won't do, Kalo. We want to go over the Sierra Parima. That's why we have come here to you."

"It isn't possible," he declared. "There's no path that way."

"Oh yes there is, Kalo. There's a path to the south of the Ventuari source."

He showed anger and exclaimed: "No! I won't go that way. And no other Maquiritare will either."

"But why, Kalo? Is it because of the Guaharibos?"

"We haven't enough weapons. They would kill us all. I don't want my men to be killed on your account. If you really want me to take you that way then you must give me fifty guns."

"No, I won't give you fifty guns, and I don't want you to kill Guaharibos. We have four guns, and that's quite enough to do all the hunting we need on the way. I want to go that way peaceably, not fighting Guaharibos."

He looked at me in stupefaction.

"Then you'll go alone," he said. "No Maquiritare will go with you, neither from here nor from anywhere else. And you'll be drowned in the waters that flow to the east if you go over that mountain. You'll fall in the rapids before you get to the Brazilians and the piranhas will eat you because you won't have any Maquiritares to paddle your canoes. But we won't go. No one has gone that way for fifty years. It's too dangerous. My father had cousins on the great river Parima which flows toward the east on the other side of the mountain, the river which leads to the white men in Brazil. They are all dead with their wives and their children. The Guaharibos killed them and ate them. There are too many Guaharibos there. It's the land of misfortune. No, we won't go there."

"We shall come back in one moon," I said. "We shall bring with us ten cases, twenty cases, with cooking pots and cloth, powder and lead. You will have built your hut, and prepared all the things and the drums for the celebration. You will have made us Maquiritare hammocks and cudgels. And we will give you more coroto than you have ever had before. I will tend to your sick and I will give you the white man's remedies. And then we will see which way we go. We are friends. We shall come to an agreement."

And with that I went back to the visitors' rancho.

"UANADJI," THE SON OF THE SUN

Pierre had prepared a little package of coroto which we had brought along for the chief. I gave it to José and told him to take it to Kalomera. A few minutes later a woman came bringing us a stem of ripe bananas and three pineapples. When mealtime came, Kalomera arrived to preside over the feast, which included a great dish of antelope meat. I was lying in my hammock writing.

"Well, doctor," Kalomera cried gaily, "are you coming to eat?" And he handed me a large calabash of meat.

After the meal he brought his stool of office and sat down by my hammock. I got my notebook ready and began to question him about "Uanadji," the son of the sun and the father of the Maquiritares. He explained to me that Uanadji's mother had lived three times and that each time she had had a different name. She had created all the four-legged beasts, and that was the moment at which the whites had been favored by comparison with the Indians.

"She made two dogs," he said, "and she put one on each of the two mountains that face each other across the water. One mountain was the home of the first whites, and the other mountain was the home of the first Indians. The whites and the Indians fed their dogs, looked after them and educated them, and built little houses for them to sleep in. But the dog of the white men grew and grew and finally became the horse on which they mounted and set out to explore the world, conquering country after country and discovering the land of iron where your knives and your hatchets come from. But the dog of the Indians did not grow like that. It remained a dog. It was useful only to hunt, and all we discovered was the land of stone where my fathers and my grandfathers got their hatchets and their knives of stone. That wasn't fair, my friend. Give us horses and we'll give you stone.

Agreed? No, clearly you don't agree. That's what's wrong between the Indians and the whites.

"There are many gods, many spirits, and many people who live above the earth and below the earth. I know them all because I am a great singer. There is the one who created the baskets, and the baskets began to walk, and they entered the water after having eaten many Indians. They are the cayman alligators—you've only got to look at their skins to see that. An Indian doctor saw this spirit creating the first basket, and he managed to escape in time to avoid being eaten. It was a Maquiritare. That's why our baskets are better made than anyone else's."

He told me that the first Maquiritares were wild boars, and that it was the fault of another doctor that they had since lost all their bristles. In consequence they had to make a long journey to the foot of heaven, which was far away in the mountain, beyond Brazil. And there they went up to the shop of Uanadji where at last they were able to buy other bristles. He described how on the way they met the birds, who were also Indians and who were going to the foot of heaven and on to the home of Uanadji on the banks of the great lagoon which is in heaven to buy themselves more feathers.

"You ought to know the paths of the mountain better than I do," he concluded, "because what you call the sea is the great lagoon, and the path of your country goes that way."

He did not leave me until the night was far advanced. He took great care to see to it that I noted down all he told me. At the same time his story grew more and more confused, and he mixed legend and geographical reality in the same way that he mixed Spanish, Maquiritare, and the ritual language of his tribe, of which I did not understand a word. Gradually the obscurity of a strange human, animal, and divine world was peopled with all the beings of creation amid a cloud of feathers, pelts and furs. Desperately he tried to arrive at some sort of synthesis, but it escaped him, although a whole dream filled his mind: a dream as old, as complete and as coherent even to the point of absurdity as all the world's legends and all the cosmogonies. When he finally went he carried away our largest aluminum cooking pot, which I had refused to give him outright but had agreed to advance on our contract against a hammock and a ritual cudgel to be ready for us on our return.

A murmur awoke me a few hours later when the day was already near at hand. We were to leave that morning to reach the village on the Ventuari in one day's journey. Kalomera was squatting beside the hammock of José Catire. They were smoking and talking to each other.

José was becoming more and more my friend, but I never discovered what it was they had talked about that night when all the world was sleeping around them.

As the sun rose the village awoke with the precision of a military encampment, and shortly the women, wearing their beads, brought a steaming soup of bananas to the middle of our rancho. Our Guaharibo porters emerged timidly from the shade and ate their rations after the men of the village and before the dogs were fed. José detached his hammock.

"Time to get moving," he said.

The Guaharibos fell in behind him, but at that moment a voice shouted something and the last in the line put his case down. It was the case containing the medical kit.

"You must go and see the sick before you leave," Kalomera said to me.

It was a good hour before I arrived at the old site. It was raining a nasty little European drizzle and the great deserted arena steamed into the sky. I stopped for a moment or two among the ruins, and I noticed that the interior walls were ornamented with great white designs. There were tapirs, peccaries, and horses surmounted by the silhouettes of their riders. And there was an airplane too. Then I went on at a trot and a little later caught up with my companions, and with José and the Guaharibos.

As I walked behind José we chatted.

"Pierre is going better now," he said. "That's because I laughed at him the other day when he was hurt."

He laughed again and turned to look at me over his shoulder.

All that was lacking was a helmet of beaten metal. He, too, was a Roman. From time to time he would shout a few words like whiplashes to urge on the little barbarian slaves who were carrying our cases and his hammock and matchet. They were terrible slackers. Then he asked for cartridges and went on ahead with a rifle to see if he could find any game in the mountainous area through which our path wound.

By nightfall we had arrived at the village of his cousins. Fortunately he had succeeded in shooting a bird, but for that we should not have eaten. Famine time was beginning on the upper Ventuari, and things grew worse as the days passed. There wasn't a root left in the cassava plantation, and, after the peccaries and the tapirs, most of the birds too deserted the forest. We ate parakeets, waders, and forest rats.

Finally the village sought the assistance of the Guaharibos, who still had bananas. In exchange for a few matchets they brought us in basket-loads of them. Before long bananas were our only nourishment: raw bananas, cooked bananas, pulped bananas. I need hardly describe how heartily sick we very soon became of them.

Sanoma served us as our only intermediary with the Guaharibo tribes spotted about the Ventuari. In the evening we would give him a small package of coroto and off he would go, returning the next day or the day after with ten or twenty Guaharibo tribesmen, dribbling greenish juice from their chops, jumping around, gesticulating and shouting. They would dance around us and pull our beards playfully, or dance and sing in front of our rancho while we filmed them with our 16mm camera and recorded their songs on our discs.

They danced a war dance with six men defying each other, flourishing great arrows with bamboo tips. They danced a "trading" dance, with two men smothered with trinkets squatting down opposite each other. They had feathers in their hair, feathers in their ears, feathers on their arms, and on their chests over the daubing were little puffs of white down everywhere, stuck onto the bare skin. In one hand they held three arrows, a bow, and the large red stick which is the Guaharibo cudgel. They talked, swaying their bodies to right and left. The rhythm of their movements grew more and more rapid. They wagged their heads violently like dolls whose fastenings have broken; they shouted great throaty cries; they beat themselves on the chest vigorously and thumped the earth with the flat of their hands. Finally their growing excitement reached its utmost pitch. Then they flung away their bows, arrows and cudgels, and tore the feathers out of their hair and from their ears, despoiling themselves even of the little blue feathers which transfixed their lower lips. The mime of this vehement "business discussion" ended when one of the two adversaries rolled over on the ground dead beat.

Before long we had not a foot of unexposed film left.

Our hosts looked at the spectacle from a distance, rather jealous to see that we were so much interested in it, but the baskets of bananas which each new Guaharibo group brought along helped them to bear the burden patiently.

Saudi returned from the war and served us as assistant along with Sanoma. We asked him how the war had ended. He laughed heartily.

"Two of the young men were killed and then the women were returned," he said.

"And what about your people?" we asked. "Were any of them killed?"

He laughed even more heartily.

"Just imagine," he said. "One day one of our men got an arrow right through the chest. The whole point went in, as big as your fist. He fell dead. But the old man who knows all drew it out again, did something with tobacco and breathed on him, and then the man got up and lived. But he still has the hole in his chest and every time he breathes a big pinkish something comes out and goes back again with a squelch. You understand?"

We got acquainted through Sanoma and Saudi with the seven Guaharibo groups which lived around the upper Ventuari and were on visiting terms with the Maquiritares.

I kept the calendar of the expedition on the back of one of my notebooks, crossing off a date each morning. Soon it was December 24th, and then December 25th, Christmas Day. In honor of the great day we made ourselves a present of our last but one tin of condensed milk.

December 27th, December 28th, December 29th. Messengers came from other Maquiritare villages to fetch me to attend to their sick. I would go off in the morning and return dead tired at night. Undernourishment made us so weak that in the end I refused to leave the village. In all the other villages I visited it was the same story: famine. Whole groups began to emigrate, seeking refuge in the richer territories of Kalomera.

On December 29th Sanoma brought us two pineapples. Jean thereupon asked for one of the remaining pints of medical alcohol we still had left in the medicine kit. He put chunks of pineapple in the alcohol and poured in sugar-cane juice. Pierre and I were more than doubtful about the performance.

"Don't worry," he said. "I know a thing or two about liqueurs. My mother used to make them in the country when I was a little boy."

He regarded that argument as unanswerable and was quite surprised to find that neither Pierre nor I were convinced.

It was rather difficult to decide the exact moment at which we left the old year behind and advanced into the new. For months now we had had no watch. However, on the last day of 1949 we dined again. José had succeeded in shooting a rather stringy white wader after hours of stalking through the forest.

"It's inedible!" exclaimed Jean. "It tastes of *eau de cologne*."

Perhaps it did, but all the same it was flesh and there was hot soup.

We waited until we were hungry again and then we decided that it was New Year's Day. We lighted a candle and amid an almost religious silence Jean opened our last tin of condensed milk. We also had a little Nescafé left. The water had been hot for a long time. We were surrounded by about fifteen Indians all observing us with great interest, because we had explained to them more than once that this evening was one of the greatest festivals of our tribe.

"Navidad!" said José gravely.

They were impatient to see how we were going to celebrate it.

We drank the rich *café au lait,* dipping pieces of cassava bread in it and consuming them hungrily, for we were as famished as stray dogs. Then Jean produced his terrible bottle of liqueur "like mother made."

It didn't go down at all well after the *café au lait* and dunked cassava bread.

"When are you going to start laughing and singing?" an Indian we knew as the Colonel asked impatiently. Colonel was a slim young man, very impatient to learn the secrets of the *"cocovani,"* as our hosts called us. The word "colonel" was the only Spanish word he knew, hence the name we had given him.

Poor Colonel, he did not hear us laughing and singing that night. The liqueur like mother used to make caused us to fall irretrievably into a state of melancholy. Each of us recalled New Year's Day 1947, the last time we had celebrated the New Year in Paris. Then I took out a sleeping draught from our medicine chest: the best thing to do with the night was to make quite certain that we slept through it.

On January 3rd José approached me. His face was lined and drawn and he looked like a walking skeleton.

"I have just bought a wife," he informed me. "I can't stay here any longer. We shall all die of hunger. Why don't you come with me? I am going down to Tencua. Perhaps we shall meet Luis there. Of course, I shan't be able to look after you on the way on account of my wife, but I'll lend you my son and a canoe. Colonel will certainly be prepared to go along too. In that way you'll have a crew."

We felt that we couldn't go on any longer either, and José's proposition made up our minds. We left on January 6th after having carefully stored our cases away in the tribal hut of José's cousins. All we took with us of our equipment was the 16mm camera, the Leica, and the Rolliflex, our used films, and the discs on which we had recorded the sounds made by the Guaharibos.

"Goodby for the present," we said to the Indians. "We'll be here again in a moon."

BACK TO MARIETTA—I ALMOST DROWN

For some time I had suffered from a mild form of *sabañón*. It is a strange infection known to all the mestizos of the Orinoco. It is a sort of fungoid growth which attacks the feet, scoring red and yellow lines round the toes, and these lines develop like a network of roots. If treatment is not begun in good time the lines become deep grooves in the flesh and offer a breeding ground to a multitude of secondary infections. In addition, the glands of the groin swell and walking becomes a torture.

I did not know how to treat myself, and I was particularly apprehensive of the two days march required to outflank the Mono Falls. And, in fact, toward the end of the first day the infected area around my feet burst. We were all marching barefooted along a soaked path made difficult with long, sharp roots, thorns, and liana. Right at the beginning Pierre had torn off a toenail in that dangerous terrain. Our morale was low and our stomachs were as empty as ever. At four o'clock in the afternoon we could go no farther. José himself was quite willing to make a halt, and so he built a rancho for himself and his new wife, a mountainous woman of fat and muscle and well suited to increase the production of cassava at home in Cordoval.

José's son Emiliano and the Colonel built our rancho a few paces away from that of José, and we crawled exhausted into our hammocks. José's huge wife brought us a little calabash of cassava soup. José had bought her together with all her supplies and her personal belongings.

"He wasn't born yesterday, that fellow," commented Jean.

That was all that was said during the evening. Before long night fell. I lay stretched out in my hammock as stiff as a corpse and unable to sleep. I had lead weights instead of feet and fever coursed through my veins. Dreams and reality mingled round me in the darkness. From time to time I heard Pierre turning over in his hammock. Occasionally he seemed to have a choking fit and then he sat up so violently that the whole rancho shook. For myself I created a great Second Empire ballroom in which suffering almost turned into joy in the midst of ornamented chandeliers and fluted glass, lace jabots, and graceful bows. I don't know whether I actually slept that night or remained awake the whole time experiencing nothing but my dream.

Our awakening was every bit as lugubrious, and the dawn took almost as long to dissipate the darkness as it does sometimes in darkest Europe.

As soon as it was light enough our march began again, as inexorably as a machine.

"Hurry. Hurry," urged José. "It's still a long way from here to the river."

He went on ahead followed by his new spouse. Both of them were loaded with calabashes and cassava graters. As the light grew stronger, so my fever increased, and soon each step was a perilous enterprise as though I were walking the tightrope. I began to lose my sense of balance and had to cut myself a stout stick to lean upon as I walked, which I did with short steps like a sick old man. The way seemed endless. We had to go up and then to go down, and after that there were straight stretches hundreds of yards long before there was any turning, and then only to show a new climb ahead, which made my heart beat against my ribs, or a new descent during which my bare feet, red and yellow with festering wounds, were torn open by thorns and slid helplessly in the slimy mud. Was I really awake? My dream went on. It was my safeguard and my talisman. I thought so intensely of lovely women in crinolines and I could distinguish so clearly every step of the minuet they danced that I ended up by distinctly hearing the sound of violins coming through the forest.

Toward midday we came to a stream which ran across our path and I sank down on the pebbles along its edge. I took some aspirin and bathed my face with the fresh water. I remained there, lying on my back, for perhaps a quarter of an hour, motionless, my arms crossed over my chest, and above my head the crowns of the trees waltzed slowly round and round. The sky was beyond reach. It was too far for me. I opened my mouth wide in the hope of getting a breath of fresh air, of stealing a little freshness from another world.

Jean had gone on ahead, but he returned.

"Cheer up," he said. "We're in the valley now. The river isn't far ahead."

He looked greenish.

"You look all in too," I said.

"I'm starving," he replied.

We started off again, and it took us three hours to reach the river. The canoes were waiting there and all we had to do then was to get on board. I stretched myself out in the middle of our canoe on the baggage. Automatically I placed a rifle by my side. It was as well to be prepared for surprises where the river widened.

There was a surprise. About thirty wild duck flew low over our heads at the first bend. I fired and brought down two of them. I put the rifle back again at my side. I felt quite resigned. Let what must come, come. At least we had something to eat. I closed my eyes and listened to the splash of the paddles. We went down river steadily and without effort, sliding along rapidly with the current.

That evening we could reach the Oso Falls, and the following day we could be in Cordoval. Perhaps on the way we should meet Luis in a new canoe, with new Indians, with a new camera, and with letters from Europe. Or perhaps we could go on to Marietta to the lumbermen there. They would take me down with immense care to the Orinoco, where Doctor Baumgartner would attend to me. I would tell him about the Guaharibos and he would be astonished. Then Luis would arrive.

It became steadily hotter. The waltzes in my head grew slower and everything became confused. No doubt I went off to sleep. In the distance I heard someone say that we should be at the Oso Falls by evening. And then the river swirled into the canoe and I found myself treading water under an enormous black roof. It was the overturned canoe. We had upset. Suddenly I was sucked downward, head first. I rolled and spun round. I must have been seized in a whirlpool. Then I could breathe again, but at once I was dragged down. My body did not turn and roll this time, but went through the water like an arrow. Then my body turned and automatically I passed under the whirlpool. My head rose above water again and I gasped for breath.

Again I went under. Time seemed to accelerate. I distinctly saw its end ahead. Perhaps there was no beginning to time, but there was an end. It was a great wall, smooth and vertical, and it came toward me rapidly.

"It's very simple, after all," I thought. I was quite resigned. "Soon I shall be nothing but a thing in the water."

A new eddy sent me to the surface instead of forcing me down. I shot through the water like a meteor through the sky and suddenly the sun blinded me. Then I could see the black shape of a canoe dancing in the froth of the rushing water. I recovered completely and turning toward it I swam as though I were exercising, using long, supple strokes and compelling my lungs not to pump too hard.

"So it's not to be this time," I thought. "Not this time."

Soon my head was near the bow of the canoe. José's face was above the water and his distorted mouth was shouting something in Maquiritare. I got hold of the side with both hands and hoisted myself over the gunwales with difficulty. I tipped over and slid into the canoe on my stomach. My face was in a pool of yellowish water. I wondered why the water was so dirty.

I found it difficult to move my body, but I managed to lift my face out of the water. To my right one of the wild ducks I had shot floated peacefully on the surface of the river like a small boat. Was I still dreaming?

"The duck," I shouted.

The canoe swung to the right and José retrieved the duck.

At least we've got something to eat, I thought.

The canoe made its way toward the bank and I was helped out onto a rock. Then I saw my two companions on another rock higher up the river. Between them and me there were five hundred yards of rapids. They were the great rapids of the Oso. Coming toward me bottom up, like a whale, I saw our canoe. Colonel was sitting astride its keel. He had managed to save himself and now he righted and emptied the canoe of water. José got into it with him and slowly they made their way up the rapids on the favorable side. They came down again as gracefully as the flight of an arrow with Emiliano, Pierre, and Jean.

"We thought you were drowned," my companions said.

"So did I," I replied.

We pitched camp a little further on and my companions checked up on our things. We had lost our last camera, our last photo-electric cell, all the film and all the discs of the Guaharibos—the war dance and the trading dance—our two last rifles, our change of clothes, and our cooking pots.

"If we don't meet Luis on the way we shall have to go as far as the Orinoco and send him a wire," Pierre said.

We arrived in Cordoval the following evening, January 10th.

"Marat has just left here," we were told. "He is leaving Marietta the day after tomorrow to go down to Puerto Ayacucho."

It was two days journey by canoe from below the Tencua Falls down to Marietta, and so there was no time to lose. But we were also told that there were no canoes in reserve below the falls and that all the men had gone off with Marat.

The only males left in the village were an old man, Horacio, José's brother, and three boys. Could we get José's heavy canoe below the falls and reach Marietta in time to take advantage of Marat's motor?

We went to sleep exhausted and overwhelmed by our misfortunes.

The next morning at dawn the old man and Colonel came to wake us up. Everyone was ready to take a chance and help us, apart from José himself, who was suffering from a serious inflammation of the ear and was unable to move.

We went off toward the falls.

I was unable to give much help to anyone because I was still very weak. I went down the path ahead of the others, leaning heavily on a stick. I had not gone far before the fever had me again. At last we arrived at the little stretch of sand along the river bank where I had first made José's acquaintance two months earlier.

How many things have happened since then! I thought. We held victory in our hands and still it evaded us.

By four o'clock the canoe was in the water again and we embarked. We were all members of the crew, the whites, the Indians and the three Indian boys. We kept paddling day and night, and at dawn on the following day we could see the grey smoke of Marietta rising in a clear, hard sky beyond the next bend in the river.

A GUITAR IN THE JUNGLE

We returned to the outposts of civilization like specters. As soon as our canoe was sighted all the lumbermen of Marietta ran down to the river bank to welcome us, headed by our friends Alexandre Marat and Helios Amazonas. They knew already that we had made contact with the famous Guaharibos, but they were quite sure that we were dead by this time. They shook our hands with a mixture of respect and sympathy, and then we went to their house.

We were offered a cup of coffee, then a second, and a third. The Sierra Parima was now only a blue line on the far distant horizon. Cigarettes were passed round. Soon we were drunk with coffee, with speaking Spanish, and with being again in a white world, even among these half-colored men. A woman busied herself with plates and glasses, forks and spoons, and through a half-open door came the smell of cooking.

Marat postponed his departure to the following day, and all we had to do was to eat, to sleep, and to recuperate.

The day passed like a dream and night came again, the first night we had slept well for a very long time.

I had slung my hammock in the middle of the stores. All around were the piles of merchandise with which the settlers paid their Indians. It was a sight we knew well. Up above there, in the cases we had left behind in the care of savages, there were also iron and aluminum, cloth, matches, fish hooks, and little mirrors for the ladies. Behind a partition Helios Amazonas was tuning his guitar. It was a fine new guitar, almost unreal here, where even nature herself seemed old and worn. To my right behind another partition the pigs were snorting and snuffling. Helios finished his tuning and began to sing. All day long he had been felling trees, but now his voice was soft and sentimental as he sang a love song.

Parole de femme,
Que j'écoutais
Auprès de toi.

A lamp was burning, or rather, smoking, above the pigs. It was made of an empty can which had once contained American beer. There was a hole in the cover through which a wick had been inserted. It smoked. I breathed in the air in mouthfuls as it came through the latticed wall. I could not distinguish the pigs in the engulfing darkness, but they were there, crowded together, their snouts obstinately raised toward the flickering light of the oil flame.

Each time the singing and the guitar accompaniment stopped the grunting and snuffling of the pigs rose again. Above my head hens were clucking and tripping over the palm leaves on the roof.

Madame Marat had borne a pink and rosy infant, and he was to accompany us on our journey so that the bearded priest of Puerto Ayacucho could baptize him "Edison" with holy water.

At midnight twenty-four hours ago I had been part of a crew with Colonel. Everyone except us and the helmsman were asleep. The silence flowed past us with the stream to the rhythm of our paddles and the sound of wood against wood. In the sky above us great masses of milky stars disputed mastery of the heavens with the clouds. Colonel raised his head and spoke:

"*Joje konoyo, coneda!*" which meant, "Many clouds. That's bad."

Then followed renewed silence. After a while he added:

"Many stars. That's good."

He looked at me over his shoulder and a great smile lit up his face. I repeated the two phrases. A new constellation became visible and he told me its name. I said nothing. He repeated the name twice and indicated the design of the constellation with his finger. I repeated it after him clumsily, and he laughed. I laughed too.

Our paddles sounded in unison against the wood of the gunwales, and the night around us was alive and moving.

For a moment or two I removed my paddle from the water and placed it in front of me. Before we left Cordoval José had given me a few leaves of green tobacco. I dried them now in the heat of a match and rolled two cigarettes with two pages I tore out of my notebook. The moon went down behind us. In front of us the three boys slept, leaning over their great heart-shaped paddles which they had placed from one side of the canoe to the other. Jean and Pierre were stretched out asleep behind us. With their waxen faces they might have been two figures on a tomb. Horacio, our helmsman, went to sleep too. He was lying back in the stern, his head low and his feet high. His legs formed a sort of lyre against the dark blue of the night sky. The wind rose and we passed the first stretch of savanna. Then we no longer paddled, and the canoe drifted forward slowly. Colonel and I smoked our cigarettes to the end.

The boys, Pierre, Jean and Horacio woke up and took their paddles again. The sky above us began to tremble with the first premonitions of the dawn. I felt cold, and I now took my turn in the bottom of the canoe. A number of things went round and round in my mind: the names of the stars, the price in Swiss francs of the camera we had lost, the sickly sweet smell of death at the bottom of the river. Gradually my eyes closed. . . .

The guitar began to sound with muted strings, and there was no voice accompanying it. A chord followed a chord and died away. A human snore rose and was lost in the dark roof. The pigs grunted and snuffled. The guitar slept too.

PUERTO AYACUCHO, MEDICAL TREATMENT, AND NEWS OF LUIS

We left Marietta on the morning of April 13th, and on the evening of the 15th we arrived in La Carmelita. Our friend Nestor, the man with the frigidaire, welcomed us amiably and, seeing our condition, produced his bottle of French cognac to raise our morale. Then he spread out a Venezuelan magazine on the table before us. The double page was covered with a map of the world divided into two zones. One was black and the other was hatched. The caption informed us that the black part was the "Russian World" and the hatched part the "American World." Nestor put one finger on the Caucasus and demanded:

"Is that where the Russians are making the bomb? You ought to know, you come from Europe."

But we were anxious to know whether he had any news of Luis. He replied politely that he had no news, but that we should certainly be able to find out in Puerto Ayacucho because a revolution had just broken out in Colombia and about five hundred families of political refugees had sought safety by crossing the llano into Venezuelan Orinoco territory.

Once again we slept in the school, between the blackboard and various government posters urging the virtues of literacy and reafforestation.

"If all the world could read and write," one of them proclaimed, "there would be no wars."

And another one raised a threatening voice:

"A match flung away in a forest could spell Venezuela's doom."

The following evening we reached Santa Barbara, at the mouth of the rapids where the Ventuari pours its waters into the upper Orinoco.

"Have you heard anything from Luis Saenz?" was our first question when we disembarked.

"Luis Saenz?" said the man we asked. "He was almost drowned here about a month ago. He shot the rapids on his own and his canoe struck a reef and shipped water. It was I who managed to arrange for him to go on. He seemed to be in a devil of a hurry."

We breathed again. Luis had with him all the 33mm film we had taken on the upper Ventuari and our first photographs of the Guaharibos. In short, he had everything which now remained to us of our months of toil and trouble, since we had lost all the rest in our canoe mishap in the Oso rapids.

"Did he lose any of his baggage?" asked Pierre.

"Oh no," the man replied. "He looked after that as though he had a load of diamonds. No, he didn't lose anything, I can tell you that."

He winked solemnly. Some time later we were to learn why.

At last we arrived at Puerto Ayacucho, and Doctor Baumgartner immediately took my infection in hand. He bandaged up my feet so thoroughly that I was unable to walk at all.

"When you leave I'll give you a packet of salicylic acid to use," he said. "You'll be all right with that. By the way, when you were a little boy didn't they make preserves in your family?"

Yes, I could certainly remember an aunt of mine who had a passion for making preserves.

"There you are!" exclaimed Baumgartner triumphantly. "And do you remember that she used salicylic acid in her preserves to prevent mold forming? Now the *sabañón* is really nothing but a sort of mold. All you've got to do is to shake salicylic acid powder into your boots and everything will be all right."

"The only thing is that I'll have to wear boots, my dear doctor."

Baumgartner looked after us and coddled us like children.

"Gentlemen," he insisted. "Only the French and the Germans understand this country and the Indians."

When we told him of the worst difficulties we had encountered it only made him all the more enthusiastic. If he had not been tied down to Puerto Ayacucho by his professional obligations, I am quite certain that he would have come with us when we went back to the Sierra Parima. He continued to study the Piaroas, and every day his waiting room was crowded with nervous little Indians dressed in civilized garb who had come in from the hills to consult "the great white sorcerer," as he had become for the whole tribe. Despite his white hairs he radiated youth and enthusiasm.

"Just think of it," he would say, "there are people wasting

their time on the atomic bomb when the forest is full of Indians."

We found that we had already become legendary in Puerto Ayacucho as "those who lived with the Guaharibos," and the governor of the district placed his wardrobe at our disposal, for our clothes were no longer presentable. We appeared dressed as Venezuelan officers.

But we still had no news of Luis. Then a Catalina arrived from Bogotá. However, it brought neither Luis nor news of Luis. We had already sent three radio messages to Bogotá without getting any reply, but at last one came:

"Arriving by next Catalina. Luis."

And on the day that Catalina should have arrived in Puerto Ayacucho the radio brought the news that it had crashed against a mountainside near San Carlos, the last village to the south of Venezuela, about three hundred miles away. So Luis was lost and the new camera. Our expedition was now definitely at an end.

We tried to get in touch with San Carlos by radio. It took us forty-eight hours, and then we asked for a list of the passengers who were aboard the wrecked Catalina.

"None" was the laconic answer.

Then we received a further telegram:

"Take-off delayed. Arriving by next Catalina. Luis."

JAILED!

January came to an end, and February wore on. On February 28th we drank so many bottles of beer that I have difficulty in remembering the exact facts.

Another telegram arrived:

"Had enough of planes that don't arrive where they ought to, or dump me on the way. Arriving March 3rd by private charter plane. Luis."

And he arrived punctually on March 3rd with eight cases of new material. The final phase of our expedition could now begin. Unfortunately, however, the dry season was approaching its end.

"It would be madness to go up there now," we were told by those who knew the forest and the hills. "You'd be bogged down in the rains and you wouldn't be able to get back again before next year."

But we refused to let ourselves be put off. We'll see for ourselves, we thought.

To go up to the Tencua Falls again we needed a boat with a motor, and we managed to hire a little *falca* of much the same type as the former Oram. All that we needed then was gasoline, so we applied to the governor for help.

"Gentlemen," he said with a smile, "I will see that you get what you need. I can also place a truck at your disposal to take you and your baggage to Sanariapo."

He could hardly have been more amiable, and then he added:

"But there is one matter I should like to talk to you about. No doubt you will have guessed that I have a fair idea of what you are going to do in the Sierra Parima. Well, why not do it officially on behalf of the government I have the honor to represent?"

"What exactly do you mean?" I asked. "Do you mean that we should organize an international ethnographical expedition?"

"Come, come," he said chidingly. "I am not talking about ethnography. I mean the real aim of your expedition. Understand me. We are talking together as reasonable men."

At that we understood even less what he was after.

"Ah!" exclaimed Pierre with sudden inspiration. "You mean the films?"

"No," said the governor gently, and still with a smile. "I don't mean the films. You are intelligent men, Parisians, and you are risking your lives on this expedition. You don't really think I believe that you're doing that just to visit the Indians and take photographs of their mud huts, do you?"

"I am afraid that we haven't the faintest idea what you mean, sir."

Then he exploded.

"Diamonds, gentlemen! Diamonds, that's what I'm talking about. All the diamonds found in the rivers of Venezuela and Northern Brazil come down from the Guianas, you know that."

"Yes," we said blankly in chorus. We were utterly flabbergasted.

"Very good. Now the richest part of the Guiana is the least known, the Pacaraima and the Parima, just the regions you propose to explore. Now don't tell me that all you want is to study the Indians there. Let's put our cards on the table. I propose that a group of miners I have here at my disposal should join your expedition. We can stake our claim together at Caracas. If you refuse, you will not be allowed to leave the country."

We talked over the matter for two hours. What on earth could we do with miners on the upper Ventuari even if there were diamonds there? But the governor refused to abandon his idea. In the end we promised to prepare a detailed geological report on the regions we explored when we returned to Puerto Ayacucho, and we were allowed to retire.

We were now ready to start. All we had to do was to transport our baggage to the river in the truck the governor had placed at our disposal.

The next day we were in Sanariapo. A big vessel was tied up at the port by the side of the little *falca* we had hired. It was the Venezuelan packet steamer which went once every two months from Puerto Ayacucho to the military post of San Carlos del Río Negro via the upper Orinoco and the Casiquiare Canal, and it was about to put off. It was a good opportunity to economize on gasoline, so we decided to let it take us in tow as far as the mouth of the Ventuari. We slung our hammocks that night in a deserted hut.

We slept like logs, but before dawn we were awakened by the glare of electric torches in our faces and by harsh voices shouting "Police! Police!" At the same time rough hands shook our hammocks to complete our awakening. At first I was quite convinced that I was dreaming and I turned over to the other side grunting irritably. But it was not a dream. There were fifteen armed policemen around us.

"Orders of the governor. You must come back to Puerto Ayacucho at once. Get a move on. Be a bit quicker than that."

They compelled us to load our cases into their truck, which was the same one in which we had traveled to Sanariapo the previous morning. When we arrived at Puerto Ayacucho they took us straight to prison, a fine place with bars as thick as a man's arm, behind which three or four local agitators were incarcerated. We couldn't decide whether to laugh or to be furious. We were angry at being compelled to bring our baggage back to Puerto Ayacucho, and we were afraid that we would miss the packet steamer. On the other hand, the adventure had its funny side.

"Ditched by diamonds," said Luis.

We threatened to write to our consuls to protest against our arbitrary arrest and we did our best to question our jailers, but they were frightened to death, and when we made the slightest move to approach them they hurriedly took down their revolvers and sabers, and even an enormous matchet, from the wall where they were hanging. Thus fortified one of them said politely:

"Excuse me, monsieur le Docteur, but you have no right to come near us."

How long was this farce going to last? After many attempts we managed to persuade one of the scared men to take a message to Doctor Baumgartner. That was at three o'clock in the morning, and we decided to go to sleep and await events. We were provided with a very good cell in which to sling our hammocks. We did so and settled ourselves as best we could to go on dreaming our dreams where we had left off.

At dawn we were awakened by the sound of voices and the rattling of an enormous bunch of keys. Our cell door was opened and outside we heard the indignant voice of our good friend Doctor Baumgartner.

"But Your Excellency! Think of the cause of science! Think of the Musée de l'Homme in Paris!"

The governor seemed repentant. He had come in person with Doctor Baumgartner to deliver us from jail.

"Believe me, gentlemen," he said. "This is all a mistake. I am utterly confused. I trust that you will bear me no ill will."

We demanded that he should immediately arrange to load our baggage into the truck again and get us back to Sanariapo as quickly as possible. Our jailers now became our zealous servants, and we went with Doctor Baumgartner to drink a cup of coffee while the truck was being made ready.

That was the end of our stay in Puerto Ayacucho. A few hours later we were in Sanariapo again, where we found the packet steamer waiting for us.

MARCH 7TH TO MAY 28TH 1950

PART 4

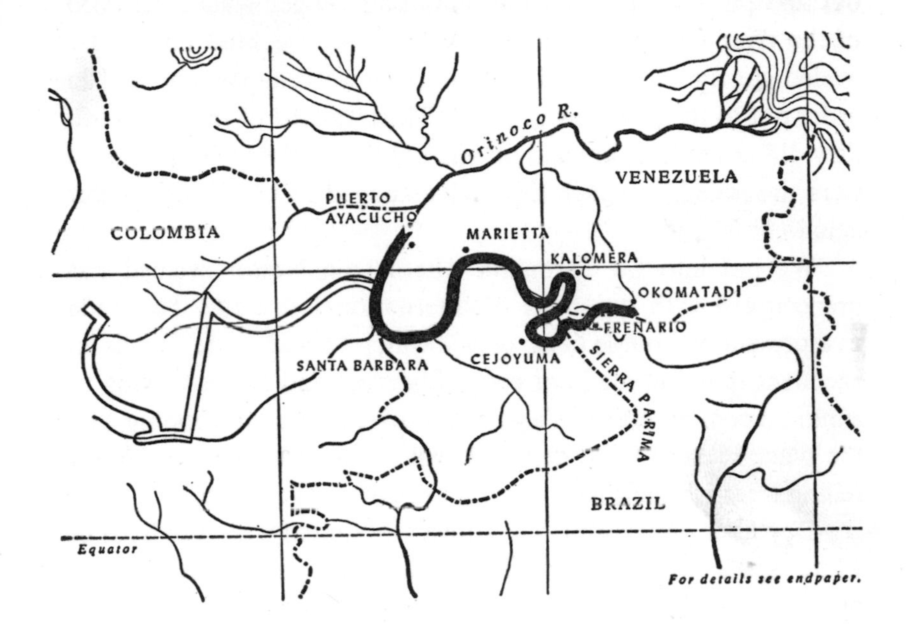

The Crossing of the Sierra Parima

OUR SECOND JOURNEY TO THE PARIMA

On the morning of March 11th the packet boat on its way to San Carlo broke down just before the Santa Barbara rapids. I cast off the rope that had taken us in tow that far and Pierre started up our motor. The helm went aport and we entered into the Ventuari, which sparkled ahead of us, immense and empty. Its water were still lower than before because this was the period of maximum subsidence, and in many places sharp black rocks like teeth jutted out above the surface. On either side the forest began to glide away behind us while we maneuvered our craft between the rocks. We had been warned to look out for mud flats which would hardly be visible in the turgid water, but despite the warning we soon grounded, and then we had to jump out and push the boat off the bank into deeper water. The bed of the river was full of ray-fish sleeping in the mud and as we waded slowly over it pushing our boat we dragged our feet in order not to tread on any of them. Thus warned of our approach they did not attack, but slid off silently like bad angels. Twice we were grounded, but each time we managed to reach deep water again.

We put into La Carmelita where Don Nestor seemed less preoccupied with questions of international strategy. He made us a present of a bottle of oil of *sejé* which he had made. It was an excellent table oil made of certain berries, and he was trying to exploit it commercially. We passed Marietta without stopping, and the place seemed to be deserted. All the men were in the forest felling trees for their next convoy to Puerto Ayacucho.

Day after day passed. The forest was dotted with hundreds of white spots where big white waders sat motionless in the branches. They hardly lifted their wings as we went by. It was the culmination of the dry season, and great numbers of animals had left the depth of the forest to seek a little freshness along the river banks. We kept our eyes open and our rifles ready, carefully studying the banks in the hope that some tapir or peccary might get the happy idea of varying our menu, which consisted chiefly of sardines in oil. We had bought a case of tins in Puerto Ayacucho for use on this stage of our journey. But the tapirs and the peccaries hardened their hearts, and not one of them put in an appearance.

"All the same," remarked Jean, "I should like to film some big animal."

He got his chance the day after we passed Marietta. It was neither a tapir nor a peccary, but a great anteater, and it thoroughly deserved its adjective, for it was really enormous. It appeared suddenly on the bank of the river about fifty yards away from us. That was the exact moment for me to discover that we had forgotten to unpack the buckshot so we had to use small shot. The bank rose several feet above the water and the beast tried to get back to safety by standing on its hind legs like a bear. Each time we fired it fell back into the water and then rose and tried again. It took us seven shots to finish it off, and then it fell back and remained still. We turned our boat into the bank and Pierre and I waded out into the shallow water along the bank. The beast was so heavy that the two of us had all we could do to hoist its carcass over the side into the boat. When we were under way again we examined our bag at leisure. A very long tongue hung out of the aperture which served as a mouth, and a sticky liquid dripped from it. This long, thick tongue with its sticky exudation served to trap the ants and draw them from the galleries of their hills. The hind legs, short and thick, were armed with enormous claws stronger than those of a jaguar. The whole body was covered with a sumptuous pelt of thick black fur circled with silver, a sort of boyar's mantle, and most strangely suited to the great heat of the equatorial forests in which the beast lived. At the other extremity was a great tail ending in a fringe of black hairs as long as a man's arm. But the most interesting feature of all was the head. About twenty inches in length, it was covered with short greyish fur reminiscent of the wig of a little marquis, the whole ridiculously surmounted by two small pointed ears no bigger than lilac leaves.

In camp that evening I decided to skin it. If we got to the Tencua Falls fairly quickly the pelt would not have time to go rotten and then José's men could prepare it for us.

First of all, I discovered that I had greatly underestimated the job of skinning it. It actually took me all night, working hard. Then it proved to be labor in vain, because by afternoon the cadaver began to stink so horribly that life in the boat with it became impossible, and I reluctantly decided to fling it overboard. We had become rather superstitious since the beginning of our expedition, and to our way of thinking the episode of the great anteater was an auspicious one. We felt that in killing that strange and fabulous beast we had also killed the evil genius which had caused the failure of our first attempt to cross the Sierra Parima.

"The evil spell has been raised," we said. "From now on things will go well."

On March 16th, toward midday, the blue summit of Tencua appeared on the horizon. It was as we approached it that our motor—which had been behaving admirably up to then—decided to give trouble. It coughed, slowed down, and then stopped. Was it the gears, the ignition, or the carburetor? Jean, the mechanic of the expedition, dismantled, cleaned out, inspected, and reassembled. The motor started up and went quite well for a while; then it went off again into spasms of coughing. Our boat drifted back several hundred yards while Jean had another go at the motor. By this time his hands were covered with grease. I dozed as I lay stretched out on the cases.

"Just about enough gas for another hour," he said.

"That doesn't matter," said Pierre consolingly. "We haven't far to go now."

I did not feel quite so optimistic.

The hour passed, and this time the motor coughed and stopped for good. Our goal was still not in sight. We had only one paddle on board, and there was no question of poling such a heavy boat along.

"What about the medicated alcohol?" Pierre asked.

We had about five pints of it and I sacrificed three of them. But there was still no oil. This time the brilliant idea was mine, and triumphantly I produced the bottle of sejé oil Don Nestor had given us. Jean poured the lot into the gasoline tank and stirred. We were a little apprehensive when he gave a vigorous tug on the starting cord, but oh joy! Our outboard motor consented to work on with its strange sustenance. It spat out an enormous cloud of black smoke, but it started up and it went on. A quarter of an hour passed and we were all in the bow keenly watching each new bend in the river. Still we weren't there, and then the motor stopped again. I handed over the last of our alcohol and the oil can for our small arms. Again the motor accepted what we gave it and started up.

When it finally gave out we were in the middle of a bend of the river, hugging the bank, and by pulling ourselves along by the trailing lengths of liana we managed to get the boat round the bend into a new straight stretch. Right at its end there now appeared a gleaming white wall of water, the Tencua Falls, and to the left of it, on the stretch of sand we knew so well, were agitated little ants in white shirts beside a *falca* which was no other than our old friend the Oram. The ants were men from Marietta who had come up river with the Oram and would certainly have gasoline on board. We were saved. With one accord we put our cupped hands to our mouths and shouted:

"Gazolina! Gazolinaaa! Gazoliiina!"

For a while there was silence and then we heard the beat of a motor and the Oram came toward us. On board were two men with black faces, shining white shirts and white teeth exposed as they grinned happily at us. We arrived at the strand in tow and there we immediately recognized two friendly familiar faces staring at us from beneath two fine and brand-new straw hats. One was José and the other was our old friend Colonel, the man who knew the names of the stars. No doubt he had stayed at Tencua during the whole time of our absence.

After all, we had said: "We shall come back." And he had waited there to take us above the falls again. But obviously neither José nor Colonel had been wasting their time. They had made up for the weeks of fasting they had spent with us as guests of José's "cousins," and they were now both as fat as bacon hogs. We concluded that our prediction with regard to José's new wife had come true: the cassava machine of Cordoval functioned wonderfully.

Luis opened our new cases as soon as we landed. There was a present for José and another for Colonel. We had decided that where they were concerned it was unnecessary to take the usual precautions when giving presents to Indians. Colonel received a wonderful red jersey with white stripes and José was handed a mysterious little cardboard box which he opened to produce a nickel-plated lighter as sparkling as the sun itself. He examined it without emotion and then said to Luis:

"You need flints and petrol with this thing, don't you? Where do you think I'm to get them?"

But he put the lighter in his pocket all the same, still grumbling. Luis was quite disconcerted. Indian logic is implacable.

A little later two canoes beached on the strand. A group of Yavarano and Curisicano Indians had arrived to do a little trading with the Maquiritares. They had brought feathered headdresses and small calabashes of curare, which they desired to exchange for blowpipes. As far as we were concerned they had fallen from heaven. Not only did we offer them fine new knives for their feathered headdresses and their curare, to their intense satisfaction, but José explained to them that they would be well advised to make the journey to Cordoval with our cases on their backs because then they would receive another knife, or something else that pleased them.

"These gentlemen are rich," said José. "You'll see how heavy their cases are."

I don't know that it was this last argument that made up their minds for them, but, in any case, two days later all our cases were safely up at Cordoval, where José immediately presented a new Indian to us, a man we had never seen before. He wore shirt and trousers, spoke Spanish passably, and answered to the name of Napoleon. He was to join us for the rest of our journey.

On the 21st we left for Mono in two canoes in charge of José and Napoleon respectively, with Colonel and Emiliano, and two Indian boys perhaps twelve or thirteen years of age posted in the bows. All the other men of Cordoval happened to be away at the time. We spent two days at the Oso Falls, the time it took us to transport the canoes and our baggage by land beyond the falls. We re-embarked up river, and by the 26th we were at the foot of the Mono Falls, having passed through the Oso rapids of unpleasant memory without incident. We established ourselves in the ranchos we had constructed four months previously. Maquiritare building is sound and solid and they were still standing. It was impossible for us to negotiate the Mono Falls with so few hands so José decided to send his son Emiliano and Colonel on ahead to look for reinforcements. They both went off the following morning.

Colonel was dressed for the part. That is to say he had divested himself of his shirt and trousers and he appeared again as we had first seen him three months before when we had christened him Colonel. He was now dressed only in his guayuco, which he had continued to wear under his trousers as a sort of talisman, and through his ears were pieces of arrow shaft. He did not leave at once, however, because there was apparently some detail lacking in his costume. He squatted down on the ground, took a small calabash of red coloring, and dipping the end of his finger in it, he began to decorate his naked body with arabesques. Then he loaded his bundle onto his back, took his matchet, and disappeared into the forest. We watched him go. There was no doubt about it, something had changed in him. He was not quite the same.

He was still only fifteen or sixteen years old, but he had filled out and his chest was deeper than before, and his gait and his gestures were more assured. It seemed as though he had suddenly become a man on his first journey away from his family and his native forest. We remembered his surprise at Marietta when he had seen a white man's house for the first time. He had hung back, looking at everything, taking everything in slowly: the walls, the tables, the steps, the improvised benches, the large mosquito nets which hung across the rooms, the kitchen with all its dishes and cooking pots. And when the first meal was served he had come up to us and with an expression of distaste he had said simply:

"Coneda, ed'de!" "It's lousy, all that."

And after the meal he had gone outside to squat down and wait for Horacio, with whom he then went back to Cordoval. The white man's world had not pleased Colonel. It had even frightened him a little. No doubt there was too much about it he did not understand, too much he had never seen before.

Unless you're used to wearing shirt and trousers from the beginning you'd be lost there, was probably what he thought.

But all the same he had waited until he was on the verge of his own country, at the high gateway of the Mono, with its thick, somber forest, before he had discarded the trappings of the white man's civilization and abandoned the mask he had worn there.

How much had he retained of that Odyssey? I recalled his stupefaction when the black pigs had come snuffling round his feet. He would probably talk of nothing else but his experiences in the white man's world. He would walk with an assured step into the tribal hut, which is the meeting place of the males. In silence he would sling his hammock, and only after a woman had brought him a calabash of yaraké would he decide to open his mouth, and then one by one the old men and the young would gather round him to listen to his story.

"The white men have boars living with them, very fat boars you have to kick before you can get into the houses. These boars are not tied up and they don't run away. They stay where they are. They wait until they are killed by the white man with a matchet. He doesn't have to run around after them in the forest."

And fathers and brothers would repeat what he said slowly, sentence by sentence, until finally all of them would burst out into the loud shout which serves as applause among the Maquiritares.

Once he had disappeared, followed by the invariably impassive Emiliano, there was nothing for us to do but wait. We made ourselves comfortable in our hammocks and then José came up and planted himself before us. His forehead was wrinkled and his whole bearing announced that he had something important, something he had thought over carefully, to say to us. He opened his mouth and spoke:

"You have no further need of me now, and I will go. I cannot go any farther than the Mono. I have work to do. I have engaged myself with Don Nestor. I have promised him canoes and cassava. I must go. I must go and do my work. I leave you my son. He will not come down again until you no longer need him."

What could we say to that? José was our only interpreter and the man in whom we had most confidence, and now he was leaving us. Many trials and tribulations, many hours on the march, and many nights in camp, chatting from hammock to hammock, had forged a bond of real friendship between us. He was irreplaceable. He knew that as well as we did. He regretted his decision just as we did, or he would not have displayed that somber and rather solemn air. The decision to go had cost him something, and he had thought it over carefully before deciding. But once he had made up his mind, his decision was irrevocable.

Nestor had come to him and said:

"Look, José: so many knives, so many matchets, so much cotton cloth, so many combs, so many mirrors in return for so many canoes and so much cassava within a month."

And José had been unable to resist the combs ornamented with glass beads on which his four wives had cast covetous eyes, the fine knives of polished steel, the pieces of cotton cloth. He had taken them and stored them in his hut, and with that his word had been given to Don Nestor.

When we arrived he had not been able to leave us in the lurch so he had found a way out by accompanying us this far and then leaving us his son.

"All right, José," said Luis. "Then we'll pay you now."

He opened a case and invited José to take what he wanted. José decided on powder and shot.

"That will do," he said.

Then he went off toward his canoe, his paddle over his shoulder. I followed him to the bank. Before getting into his canoe he turned round and looked me in the eye.

"You know," he said, "if I hadn't any wives I'd have stuck with you to the end."

He got into the stern of the canoe. The two Indian boys were already in the bow, and together they plunged in their paddles and set off.

AN AIRPLANE AND FEAR

We now remained behind with only Napoleon, our new recruit. Every three hours I made him sulphamide compresses because he had an abscess on the sole of one foot, but that did not prevent him from going off with Luis that same evening to hunt.

"I'm sure there's something to eat there," he said in explanation.

They returned in the night with two paujils and a wild turkey.

He had been right in his feeling: the forest game had returned to Cerro Mono.

During the three days we had to wait until Colonel and Emiliano returned, Napoleon never stopped talking to us about the people of the mountains, about the Maquiritares and the Guaharibos. He also told us that in order to cross the Sierra Parima the best guides were not Kalomera's men, but the men of Cejoyuma, who had lived to the south of the Ventuari source from time immemorial.

"There is a path which leads from where he lives and goes to the farthest of the Maquiritare chiefs, Frenario, who lives on the other side of the mountain on the Yavadehudi, a river which flows toward the east."

That meant that there was a path which led across the Sierra Parima to a river which was part of the Amazonian system. Napoleon also assured us that Cejoyuma was the greatest singer of all the Maquiritare tribe.

As a result of Napoleon's information we decided that as soon as we reached the village of the cousins which had served us as our base of operation on our last journey, we would separate into two groups, the one going to Kalomera and the other to Cejoyuma. Then we could decide which route we would finally take, either with Kalomera or Cejoyuma.

Napoleon also told us that the Guaicas, the Sajé, the Awake, and the Guademas of the Rio Parima on the Brazilian side of the Cordilleras were only the names of different groups of Guaharibos, and that they were not really separate tribes.

"But the worst of all," he added, "are the Waitchas, who live not far away from Cejoyuma, toward the source of the Orinoco. They aren't much bigger than children and they have fuzzy hair, but they kill and eat men.

"And when you have crossed the Parima," he concluded, "you'll meet other people there, different from the Maquiritares and the Guaharibos, and, it seems, more dangerous too. They're called the Kaserapi."

On March 30th our men arrived. They were accompanied by a number of Maquiritares and Guaharibos who had already worked for us, twelve in all, including Sanoma, more elegant than ever, Saudi, the Sioux and his son, called the "Warrior," and a new fellow as tough and muscular as a market porter, whom we later christened the "Burgundian" on account of his swollen nose and his unequalled capacity for stowing away food.

We broke camp and went on our way at once, and on the evening of the 31st we found our stored cases and everything exactly the same as it had been during our gloomy celebration of the New Year three months previously. It took us only forty-eight hours to organize our two expeditions, and on April 2nd Luis went off with Napoleon and the Burgundian to contact Cejoyuma, while I accompanied Pierre and Colonel along the path which led to the village of Kalomera. We were impatient to see the new tribal hut, which was perhaps completed by now, though that would be unfortunate for the continuation of our film. We therefore pressed on rapidly. Toward three o'clock in the afternoon we heard a drumming sound overhead.

A plane was crossing the Sierra Parima! Up there were men, men like ourselves, but in a few hours they would be in a town with shops and cafés, newspapers and moving pictures. They were probably yawning with boredom up there, flying for hours above a forest which was always the same to their view, close knit and monotonous. We stopped and looked up, trying vainly to spot the aluminum bird in the shreds of sky which were visible to us through the giant crowns of the forest. We saw nothing, but we were nonetheless quite moved by the incident. It was almost as though we had unexpectedly met other white men on our path. I turned toward Colonel and I was just going to say:

"That noise comes from a flying machine which is called an airplane and which is now passing over the forest. Inside it are men like us, men with white skins."

But when I saw his usually cheerful face downcast and somber I said nothing. He was frightened. The Guaharibo who was carrying our baggage went up to him and whispered something in his ear. We started on our way again and before long we passed the old site, then, at the end of the long avenue which led away from it, we came into the clearing where the new village was situated. Nothing whatever seemed to have changed since last we were there. The same frantic baying of dogs greeted our arrival. The same roofs of grey logs marked out the rectangle which had been won from the forest, and, just as they had done on the first occasion, our feet sank into the thick carpet of chips and dead leaves. We went to the visitors' rancho and found Kalomera waiting for us there sitting in a hammock. We slung our own hammocks and settled ourselves in them. He made no sign whatever, and his face was overcast and somber. A little boy came up and offered us cigarettes, and then a woman brought calabashes of yaraké.

Finally Kalomera leaned toward me and said:

"So, Doctor, you want to kill Indians?"

"Kill Indians?" I repeated. "What with?"

His voice grew vehement.

"Do you think we didn't see your airplane as it passed over? It wasn't half an hour ago."

I breathed again. So that was it! I lit a cigarette to give me time to think. Obviously, white men did not penetrate into the forest more than once in twenty years, if then. And airplanes were rare too. So that it must be my airplane which had flown over. I should lose face if I denied it. We should no longer be "great white chiefs." On the other hand, I knew that during the war military planes had machine-gunned Indian villages in reprisal for the death of soldiers who had fallen in the forest and never been found. Thus an airplane was a machine to kill Indians. The logic of the thing was very simple.

"Listen, Kalo," I said. "If we wanted to kill Indians do you think I would have tended to your sick the last time I was here? And do you think I would have sent our airplane here the very day we arrived at your village and thus risk being killed ourselves? It is quite true that our airplane passed over just now, but it was only to find out if we needed anything, or if we were having any trouble with the Guaharibos. I told them that everything was in order and so they flew away. You won't see them any more I can assure you, so be calm."

"Let's hope that damned plane doesn't come flying back this way after all," said Pierre.

Kalomera seemed reassured and he delivered a discourse to his men who had gathered around, listening to our conversation with an anxious air. However, I felt that he was not altogether at ease.

I then spoke to him about the object of our visit this time.

"Where is the tribal hut?" I asked. "Where are the things you were going to make for us? When are the celebrations to begin? We have brought nine cases of new coroto with us along the Ventuari. We don't want to lose any time. We want the celebrations straight away, and afterward we will go off together to the Brazilians over the Parima."

"We have not begun to build the hut," he said softly, "and I don't want you to come here with your machines."

And a moment or two later he added: "And I don't want to talk to you any more about Uanadji and such things, because that would be the death of us all."

Then he fell silent.

That was something of a facer, and I was nonplussed. Could anything be done? Was it really the passage of the airplane which had so upset him, or was there something else? I never discovered.

"Let it go," said Pierre. "We'll go back to the Ventuari and go forward on the other side. Cejoyuma's tribe will probably be even more interesting than Kalomera's. They've never seen a white man before, and no doubt Cejoyuma knows as much about Maquiritare traditions as Kalomera does."

That seemed about the only thing to do, but I was unwilling to give up without another attempt. Luis would not return from his reconnaissance expedition for a few days and so we had a little time to spare.

We said no more about our projects that evening, but the next day, I broached the matter again.

"Tell me, Kalo: which is the best way for us to cross the Sierra Parima into Brazil?"

He mentioned a path along the source of the Ventuari, the one Koch-Grünberg had taken forty years before, but it went across the Pacaraima and not across the Parima, and we were not interested in it. He then admitted that there was another path which went past the village of Cejoyuma and that of Frenario on the Yavadehudi. We did not know much about this Yavadehudi, although Napoleon had mentioned it to us, but we did know that it flowed toward the east and that it must therefore be one of the unknown tributaries of the Amazon running down from the Sierra Parima. That was the route that interested us; it passed through the heart of the unknown territory.

"But I don't want to go that way," said Kalomera. "It's infested with Guaharibos, Guaicas, and Kaserapi. It's much too dangerous, my friend. No Maquiritare would go with you there: neither my men nor those of Cejoyuma either."

I wondered whether he knew that Luis had gone off to get into touch with Cejoyuma, and whether he and Cejoyuma were rivals as far as we and our coroto were concerned, since obviously this material benefit would be the most tangible result for the Indians of our passage through their territory. *Quien sabe?*

"I'm quite willing to guide you to Brazil by the Caura and the Paraguas," he said.

And he explained the itinerary to me in detail, with all the stages and the time necessary for each. The whole route would take twenty-four days, and it would bring us to the first village of Brazilian civilization. It was the traditional path of the Maquiritares across Venezuelan Guiana, the way they must have brought their Guaharibo slaves to Dutch Guiana in the eighteenth century, as contemporary chroniclers record, and, later on, their gold dust to British Guiana, where they exchanged it for the muskets which made them famous as far as the Orinoco. Historically it was interesting enough, but we did not want to go that way because for one thing we should meet no Guaharibos at all, and for another we should not be passing through the unknown territory of the Sierra Parima. However, I made a note of what he said just in case it should prove impossible to cross the mountains further south. We should soon find out. Luis's return from Cejoyuma would let us know whether it was really true that none of the Maquiritares would venture to cross the Sierra Parima with us.

VEILED THREATS FROM SAVAGE CHIEFS

Kalomera waited for our reply and I didn't give it to him, but contented myself with describing in detail the treasures we had brought with us on this journey and which were now waiting on the Ventuari for whoever accompanied us on our journey to Brazil. I also asked him various other questions about Cejoyuma and Frenario, the man who lived farther on than anyone else, in the heart of the Parima on the other side of the mountain.

Finally Kalomera spoke:

"One day a white man went up into the Parima. It's twenty years ago now. Frenario lives so far away because he killed that man. He killed him because the white man got to know the Indian paths across the mountains too well."

That seemed to be a warning. He told me the story without special emphasis while we were having a meal.

We gave no indication of what we felt and we left him without having decided one way or the other.

Back in the village of the cousins we had to wait another two days before the canoe returned with Luis and Napoleon.

A stranger was with them, a superb Maquiritare wearing splendid feather ornaments at his ears. Luis was obviously in a state of great excitement.

"Fantastic!" he exclaimed as soon as he caught sight of us. "I've seen wonderful things."

And he began to describe the land to the south of the upper Ventuari and the site of Cejoyuma's village, which was on the summit of a mountain covered with cloud, as a sort of Indian Shangri-la, where all the ancestral traditions of the tribe were kept alive.

"After two days of paddling through a narrow canyon with high banks, we marched for two more days up the side of a mountain, and on the summit, a sort of sugar loaf without trees, and surrounded by clouds, we came to a large hut, and on the threshold a man was waiting for me with his arms crossed over his chest, and around his neck was a great collar of peccary teeth. We slung our hammocks in the middle of the hut itself, in the round space where the men meet. Then Cejoyuma himself appeared, a man much older than anyone here. He was a little man with a cunning look, and so old that there were four white hairs on his chin. He sang for me in a high-pitched voice extraordinarily thrilling to listen to, and he told me through Napoleon that he was very glad to sing for me because the gods had told him that a white man would come to his hut one day and that that would mean good fortune for his people. I questioned him all night and he told me that he could have us taken across the Sierra Parima in a fortnight via the Yavadehudi where Frenario lived. He would himself accompany us as far as Frenario's village, where a great celebration would be made in our honor and he would sing at it. He fiddled with my beard for about a quarter of an hour and then he called all his women for them to do the same. Napoleon then informed me that they wanted me to take off my shirt, which I did. They then stroked the hairs on my chest and made little exclamations. Napoleon then asked Cejoyuma if I really ought to take my trousers off. I was a trifle uneasy about that, but fortunately Cejoyuma was against it."

The man who had accompanied Luis back had a head like a Mohican brave and he squatted on the ground beside us, smiling and listening to what Luis said. He seemed to understand it all and to approve indulgently of Luis's enthusiasm. Luis opened his pack to show us a magnificent necklace of peccary teeth he had brought with him.

"That's the man who welcomed me at the entrance to Cejoyuma's hut," he said, "and this is the necklace he was wearing. But that's not all I've brought back. Look at this."

And he took out a long wooden instrument whose oblong sound box and the unusually long pegs holding its three strings at the neck made it reminiscent of a Chinese fiddle.

Luis was enjoying our amazement. His new companion took the instrument and began to play it. The sound was rather weak, but there was no doubt about its relationship to a violin. The sound box was pierced by two slots in the form of an "f" in just the same way as European violins are. The belly was not made in one piece, but assembled and fastened with black gum. There was a proper bridge, and a small piece of wood raised the strings above the sound box.

For a time we forgot our expedition and our itinerary, and with some excuse. No white man had ever ventured to the south of the upper Ventuari, and no ethnographical work had ever mentioned a violin as highly developed as this one among any of the Indian tribes throughout America. Where did it come from? The instrument is now in Paris, but the mystery of its origin has not yet been solved. All the other musical instruments we came across, not only among the Maquiritares but also among the other tribes we had come in contact with, were extremely primitive. So where did this violin of the Sierra Parima originate? Finally we formed a theory according to which one day in the seventeenth or eighteenth centuries, a monk, or some other Spanish missionary, had set out to conquer souls for God, taking his violin with him. An ancestor of Cejoyuma had staved in the good man's skull with a war club in order to examine the instrument at leisure, and when the instrument finally got broken another one was modeled on it, thereby establishing a tradition of violin-making which had persisted in this one spot, unknown to the whites and unknown to all other Indians, until Luis met the enigmatic music lover with the head of a Mohican.

Luis's enthusiasm was catching. Pierre and I were not in a position to compete with his story by telling of what had happened on our trip. We decided on the spot that the expedition should cross the Sierra Parima by the Cejoyuma-Frenario route. All that remained was to persuade "the cousins" to accompany us that far with our baggage.

"Cejoyuma told me an interesting story about Frenario through Napoleon," Luis mentioned. "It would seem that about twenty years ago he killed a white man who knew the Indian paths too well . . ."

What was the use of paying too much attention to that? We should never know all the secrets of the Indians. Whether it was sheer coincidence, or due to some secret understanding between Kalomera and Cejoyuma, the two big chiefs of the Maquiritares, the fact remained that the same edifying story had been told at the same time to two different groups of our expedition far removed from each other—and that all in all it sounded like an indirect threat.

Our departure was fixed for April 12th and we checked over our baggage while Diego, the head of the hut, who was now to be our lieutenant in place of José, got together his crew and his porters.

We went over our knowledge of the Maquiritare idiom as carefully as though we were preparing for an exam, and in fact it was an examination which would go on day after day when Napoleon and Emiliano had gone back to Cordoval, because then there would not be anyone left with us who could speak even a single sentence in Spanish. It was true that Diego, our new lieutenant, had once gone down as far as the white man's civilization, but all he had brought back with him of the white man's language was "Yes, sir; no, sir."

We sorted out the contents of the old and the new cases, and we succeeded in emptying three of them. They were big wooden cases soaked through and through from our canoe mishap and the general humidity of the air, and they were now about twice as heavy as they had been when they were dry. We offered them to Diego. He looked at them from all sides and then he took them back to his hut, returning to us joyously.

"Well, are you satisfied, Diego?"

"Oh yes!" he exclaimed. "I'm going to keep them because they'll make lovely coffins for me and my wife."

Unlike most of the chiefs, Diego had only one wife, and he was very much in love with her.

On the 11th the two last men in trousers took their leave, and on the morning of the 12th Diego had our baggage loaded into the canoes and we embarked. Colonel stood on the bank with folded arms watching the others at their work.

"Well, Colonel," I asked, "aren't you coming?"

He shook his head.

"What's the matter?" I asked Diego. "Why isn't Colonel coming with us?"

"He doesn't want to because he's just gotten married," Diego answered with a smile.

We were sorry about that because we had come to like Colonel very well, but we had not been mistaken: he had very definitely become a man. When we pushed off he remained on the river's edge with folded arms and watched us until we were out of sight. He gave no sign of any emotion, and he made no gesture of regret or hesitation.

A DUNKING AND A CASE OF PETTY LARCENY

We soon reached the Ueyeto canyon, which flowed into the Ventuari from the left bank between the village of the "cousins" and the abandoned hut in which Pierre and I had slept during our first trip.

After that every paddle stroke became a conquest of unknown territory. We had never known such disparate crews on a journey before. Diego had not been able to get together sufficient Maquiritares to man all the canoes, and so one of them was in the hands of Guaharibos, members of a group we knew well.

"They aren't quite so mad as the other Guaharibos," Diego had said to reassure us. Installed in their canoe they looked rather like a crew of comic drunks. They paddled so badly that they were quite unable to keep their canoe in a straight line for more than twenty yards at a time, and each time they dug in their paddles or withdrew them they drenched themselves with water. Not wishing to share in the inundation, the Maquiritares watched their performance from a distance.

On the second day of our voyage the river narrowed between high rocky sides and the water began to boil as we came to rapids. At this point the Ueyeto poured from a higher to a lower level in three stages. At the foot of the cascade a path led up the rocks and along this we could transport our baggage to the top of the falls. But first we had to get there. The Guaharibos in particular were hopeless, and their canoe was caught amidships and turned round and round in the current. A Maquiritare canoe went to their assistance and was upset. Four cases were pitched into the water. The water was shallow enough to allow us to recover them, but the contents were soaked. We got them ashore and opened them up. Three of the cases contained nothing but tins of unused film. Here and there the solder had broken and we were not at all sure that they were really watertight. We had to examine them reel by reel to make sure, and that was some hours work. Jean got busy and examined them all with the aid of a so-called charging bag, which was a sort of portable darkroom made of canvas with two apertures for the operator's hands. In this bag he could safely examine the tins of film, opening them and touching the film with his finger. If it was sticky then the water had got into the case and it would have to be thrown away.

The accident cost us more than three thousand feet of film. When the job was finished we had to light a fire, melt down paraffin wax, and close up and solder all the tins once again. It was a sensation for the Indians. They crowded round us, squabbled over the tins of film that we discarded, and unrolled the spools while prancing along the river's edge with the film and shouting with enthusiasm and astonishment. Some of the lengths were three hundred and fifty feet and they had never held anything so long in their lives before. The unexpected game rapidly became the pretext for a hundred and one drolleries on their part. One of the Indians, rolling a length of film around his body, looked like an Egyptian mummy. Another one, pushing up the middle of the spool, made himself a comic hat with a tall point. Two of the Guaharibos, wildly excited, plunged into the river and swam to the other side, risking their lives in the swirling water, in order to stretch a bridge of film over the water from one bank to the other. And finally, they piled all the discarded film into a sort of disordered bed over several square yards of rock and then, all together, they wallowed in it with joy. In the end some of them went to sleep in it. Between the roaring cataract of water and the somber green walls of the forest, which rose to a height of perhaps a hundred and twenty feet, the sight of all these naked savages, jumping and shouting with joy around our dripping cases, exceeded anything Hollywood had ever imagined, even the famous scene where the Sioux attack and loot a train in the Far West and then ride along the track unwinding bales of cotton cloth fastened to their horses' tails.

When we finally set off again each Indian carried on his back, together with his hammock and his bow and arrows, two or three tin cases which had once contained film and bore the well known inscription in white letters: "Eastman Kodak Co., Rochester, New York." They treasured them henceforth and it would not surprise me in the least to learn that movie film had become an important means of exchange among the Indian tribes of the Amazonian forests.

But our troubles were not over with this one accident. From then on the rapids became more and more numerous, the banks of the river grew more and more steep, and the forest seemed to reach higher and higher into the sky on both sides. We were going steadily up into the mountainous heart of the high Parima itself. In addition, we had to keep a very close eye on the Guaharibos now, and our progress grew slower and slower. The day of the accident happened to be Luis's birthday, and that evening we celebrated his thirty years on this earth by opening the only bottle of rum we had with us. In the meantime the Indians had gone off to hunt by lantern. We emptied only half the bottle, but that was not on account of our natural wisdom or innate sobriety, but because in a few days, Jean, the youngest member of our party, was to celebrate his coming of age.

On April 14th we left the Ueyeto Canyon and branched off into a little tributary on its left bank, the Tuna Uaritcheta. We had not been paddling for more than an hour when the canoes grounded, and we had to clamber out to allow them to float again, and then to push them the rest of the way to our destination, which we reached at nightfall. A mountain higher than any we had yet seen rose far and high away from the river toward the south. It was so high that its summit was still spotted with grey and blue in the night, though down by the river it was already dark. Parakeets flew along the river in pairs, shattering the silence with their hoarse shrieking, which echoed and re-echoed through the river valley.

"That's where Cejoyuma lives," said Luis. "Up there."

Without bothering about the rapidly gathering darkness, Kometante, the man with the Mohican head, took his matchet and his hammock and went off into the forest. He was going on ahead to inform the old chief of our arrival and to get reinforcements for the porterage. For the three days or so we should have to wait until he returned we made ourselves comfortable in a series of large ranchos which some unknown hand seemed to have erected along the river specially for us. Faithful to the principle of discretion which marked all his tribe, Diego constructed a family rancho at a little distance for himself, his wife, and his little four- or five-year-old son, who had come along with us. The Guaharibos also settled down on their own, with the exception of our old friends Sanoma and Saudi, who slung their hammocks with the rest of us.

Incidentally, since the departure of Emiliano, Sanoma had become one of the most important members of the expedition, because he was now chief in Emiliano's place. It was he who now skinned and cut up the alligators' tails and the agoutis, which formed the bases of our meals. It was he who made the soup and afterward washed up the dishes and the plates, though perhaps we had better pass over this latter part of his activity. In this respect he was still a trifle too Guaharibo for our taste. However, he did not lack good will. At each new thing that he did he would ask us eagerly:

"*Atchika?*" Which meant was it good, were we satisfied?

And if we were compelled in the interests of truth to answer "*Coneda,*" which meant that it was by no means good, he would try again as often as was necessary to earn our approbation in the end.

His only fault was that he was a trifle too curious about everything that concerned us, and that very evening Jean suddenly noticed him holding something, a piece of colored cardboard which looked very much like a carton containing a spool of film from our reserve stock. Jean leaped out of his hammock and a strict interrogation followed, conducted largely in dumb show apart from the stern *"Conedas!"* of Judge Jean, repeated in an astonished, interested, and satisfied tone by the accused Sanoma. The court requested him to produce all his personal property for the purpose of examination. This latter was all contained in a small rectangular sack made out of the leg of a pair of old pajamas and carried across the shoulder like a bandolier with the assistance of a bowstring. The accused handed this sack to Jean, who, keeping a straight face, opened it and sorted out the contents, placing them on a banana leaf laid out on the ground.

The results of the investigation were surprising and amusing, and quite conclusive from the standpoint of the investigation. First of all there were a few leaves of green tobacco, then a box of matches, a piece of engraved wood for stamping designs on the face, a red guayuco from the last porterage, and finally a mysterious small package done up in tissue paper and carefully tied with a strip of liana. When this was undone a smaller package still was inside, wrapped in a banana leaf, and within that was a third. The accused watched the unwrapping with an air of the keenest interest, but as the last package was opened Jean rose to his feet with a red and furious face:

"The thief!" he exclaimed. "The wretched little savage! My Ansco 57 and the anti-dazzle filter of the camera! *Coneda amade! Coneda!"*

"Coneda!" agreed the accused obediently.

Jean looked at us in such despair that we burst out laughing, and finally he cheered up and joined in.

"There's nothing to be done about it," he said finally, putting away the anti-dazzle filter. "And all the same, I'm very fond of them. They go for anything bright. Like magpies."

A STRANGE SORT OF HUNT

The next morning Sanoma and Saudi came to us with a resolute air and demanded rifles. They had decided to try hunting the white man's way. Before giving them the rifles we carefully and at some length explained how they worked. It was the first time the two had gone hunting with rifles and they listened to our instructions carefully, their eyes shining. In the end they seemed to have understood quite well and off they went with great dignity, ignoring the laughter and mockery with which the Maquiritares greeted their initiation. They had only gone a few steps when Sanoma's rifle suddenly went off with a loud report, and he stood there amid the smoke looking at it rather sheepishly. It appeared that he had found it convenient to carry the rifle by the trigger. Fortunately no one was injured.

"What do you think they'll come back with?" I asked Diego.

"Who knows?" he replied. "Perhaps some worms or caterpillars."

Two hours later Sanoma returned as the first of the hunters. He was inordinately proud of himself, for he had killed a toucan and a paujil. Pierre asked for the black crest of the paujil and the red and white jabot of the toucan, which represent the classic ornamental feathers of the Guaharibos. Sanoma carefully skinned the two birds, using the point of a knife, then he came and squatted down beside us, the two morsels of bloody skin stuck to his thighs.

"Ashitsha?" he asked with shining eyes—his tribe's word for *atchika.*

"Ashitsha," Pierre agreed.

Sanoma appeared as though he felt happy to be alive. He looked at us for a moment or two and stroked the feathers of the toucan spread out on his thighs. But he was unable to stay still for long and he got up, removed the skins from his thighs and stuck them on the bottom of a pot.

Then Saudi also returned. We were interested to see what, if anything, he had killed. He held his rifle in one hand and in the other he carried a pretty little basket of woven wickerwork fastened at the top with liana. He sat down near us, all smiles and handed the basket over.

"Akuri," he said.

I looked through the wickerwork. It was a cage more than a

basket, and inside I saw two little reddish animals sleeping rolled up close to each other.

"Akuri," Saudi repeated.

No doubt it was the name of the animals. To judge by their pointed noses and their big black ears they might have been rats, but against that there were their beautiful glossy pelts of long chestnut hair.

"Are you going to eat them?" I asked.

He laughed and shook his head.

"Pets," he said.

He had brought them back to amuse himself and to amuse us.

He got into his hammock, which was slung next to mine, and I heard nothing further of him. The little animals in their wicker-work cage began to scratch around in the silence. We had nothing to do but rest until the emissaries of Cejoyuma arrived.

An hour passed silently. Then I looked up and happened to notice Saudi talking to himself in an undertone and studying something in his hand which looked like a picture post card. A picture post card? I raised myself on my elbow to see better. It was a photograph of my son with his fringe of fair hair. I had believed it safe among my notebooks at the head of my hammock. I was so indignant that I shouted out in French:

"Saudi, what's that you've got there?"

He was not in the least embarrassed and leaned toward me, holding out the photograph with a smile.

"A nice little Indian," he said. "Very nice."

"That's not an Indian," I said. "That's my son," and I put the photograph away again.

Night fell and Sanoma left his hammock to prowl around near the camp. After a while he could be heard laughing loudly, and then he came up to the fire where all the Maquiritares began to abuse him roundly.

"Pig!" they exclaimed. "Throw that away."

He was holding a big rattlesnake by the head. Diego was indignant.

"He's going to eat that, the pig," he said.

A little Guaharibo from the canoe which had overturned had noiselessly taken his place in a hammock slung above mine and next to Saudi's. He was fat and yellow with the face of a girl. Through the meshwork I saw his bright, almond-shaped eyes following the movement of my pencil over the pages of my note-book. One of his small fat feet with toes like little sausages hung over the side of the hammock, like a brown flower against the dark green of the foliage around us. He soon got tired of looking at me, and he produced a piece of white string from somewhere or the other and began to tie and twist it between his fingers and his mouth, producing squares, lozenges, and triangles. This naked little savage with his brown skin, who ran about in the forest eating flowers and worms and catching little brown animals asleep in their burrows, was playing the same cat's cradle game we had learned as children.

It was pitch dark now and voices were heard in the night. One by one, six men slid to the ground from their hammocks. Diego was making up a Maquiritare party to go out looking for food. He came to me to ask for two electric torches. They were going to hunt for alligators along the river bank.

Saudi had waked up and was squatting near the fire making such a disagreeable grinding noise that he was told to amuse him-self in some other way. He was systematically scraping down a bone to use as an arrow tip. As nothing else seemed to interest him at the moment, he went back with a disgusted air to his ham-mock to sleep.

Hardly a quarter of an hour after Diego's party had gone out on the hunt, two men burst out of the forest and entered our rancho. The one was Kometante and the other Cejoyuma's "in-terpreter," who had come to bring us a message. It was extremely difficult to understand what the fellow was saying, and he was so proud of his Spanish that he refused to talk anything else with us. However, he knew no more than a dozen words and these he repeated indefinitely strung one after the other. The result was very striking but not intelligible. At the end of half an hour's hard work we managed to understand that ten men were coming to our encampment the following morning to help us transport our cases and that we could leave them all safely to the men and set off ourselves at dawn. Our baggage would follow us. In addition, Cejoyuma asked us to dismiss our Guaharibos, as he was unwilling to have them in his village.

Having done his work at last, the "interpreter" retired to the neighboring rancho and slung his hammock among the others. The news had caused a sensation in the camp, which came alive in the twinkling of an eye. The Burgundian had got down from his hammock and was looking for something among the baggage in one corner of the rancho. He produced a Maquiritare drum which we had bought on the Ventuari, and soon the whole camp was singing to the rhythm of his beating. The fire had died down and now it was little more than a red glimmer. In its light I could just distinguish the forms of the singers, and against the darkness the lighted points of their cigarettes showed up, occasionally describing a sudden arc.

The singing went on indefinitely, low and monotonous, and gradually we fell asleep. When the hunters returned I automatically opened one eye. Diego was leaning over my hammock and there was delight and satisfaction in his face.

"Two caymans and three lapas," he said, showing the five fingers of one hand before my face excitedly. "*Ashitsha!* We shall have enough to eat until we get up there."

I went off to sleep again, not to the sound of the drum, but to the thudding of matchets as the men cut up their bag and prepared the frame on which to cure the pieces through the night.

AT LAST THE SIERRA PARIMA!

The next morning we set off at about seven o'clock after having made a big breakfast of alligator meat. About a hundred yards away from where we had been camping, the path began to rise and from there on it went up steeply right to the end. We went in silence, saving our breath for the difficult climb. We were accompanied by only two or three men who carried our camera and our sleeping material. The others were coming on behind with the heavy cases. Before long we met Cejoyuma's men, coming down the steep path at a trot. They were every bit as handsome and powerful as Kalomera's men, and they had the same square, clear-cut faces which made me think of Roman soldiers.

"Uitchakono! Uitchakono!"

"Friend! Friend!" they called out as they trotted past without slowing their pace.

The Sierra Parima was closing in around us now. Through occasional clearings in the forest we could see an immense fall of crystalline water hurtling down into the valley from a height as great as the summit of the mountain we were climbing. It was the Ueyeto Canyon, and the volume of rushing water was so great that somewhere higher up there had to be a plateau where the waters gathered from various sources before plunging down into the valley.

We were feeling just about all in when at three o'clock or so in the afternoon our men at last gave signs of stopping. We emerged into a *conuco,* or cassava plantation of the Maquiritares, in the middle of which was a rancho. There we installed ourselves. Before night fell a number of porters had joined us.

All of us went to sleep at once, dog tired with the strain of our climb. At dawn we went on again and the path rose more and more steeply ahead of us. Cejoyuma's men, who had now joined us with the cases, were tremendous mountaineers, and despite the weight they were carrying on their backs, between ninety and a hundred pounds per man, they made quicker progress than we could.

Several times I was obliged to stop and stretch myself out on the ground to calm the rapid beating of my heart and dry the icy sweat on my face.

In the middle of the afternoon we finally reached the summit. To judge by the vegetation, which had grown steadily less and less like the thick, luxurious growth of the equatorial forest, and was now no more than a high thorny bush, we must have been well over six thousand feet above sea level. After crossing a short plateau we went down into a valley perhaps a thousand feet lower and suddenly came out by a river. Where it came from and where it went to we could not tell, but the main thing was that a large canoe was waiting there to carry us to the village of Cejoyuma. Were we to go at once?

"No," said one of the men. "We must wait for the porters."

At this information we quickly took off our clothes and plunged into the water. It was wonderfully refreshing and we immediately felt very much better. While we were dressing after our swim a number of the porters arrived, and there were sufficient of us to justify a first boatload. We sped along for perhaps half an hour and then we landed at the foot of the sugar-loaf hill Luis had described to us. From its summit the smoke of the tribal hut rose up through the clouds. We were there.

CEJOYUMA'S VILLAGE

The sky was like lead. Great stretches of blue forest formed the horizon in all directions. It was raining a fine drizzle.

Our seasons don't exist at the equator, one is inclined to say lightly. What an error! They change their dimensions, that's all. One no longer meets them in time, but in space. December is not winter, and July is not summer, or the other way round, as they are in the southern hemisphere. The lowlands, the llanos of the Orinoco, and the Amazonian forests are nothing but petrified summer out of due time and clinging forever to the sap, the resin, the damp leaves, to the tree trunks rotting yet still alive, and to the cracked and burned earth of the savanna. On the heights of the Cordilleras of the Andes, around the smoky little cabins where men and llamas sleep huddled up to each other, it might be Christmas every day of the year.

Autumn comes to the watershed of the Sierra Parima in chill and rain, insidious, and evil cold, the weather of illness, mists, and organ-like winds that sing of space and adventure and shake the trees of the parks and the forests with systematic fury, the weather of little, clear fires whose flame is like a comforting look or word in the solitude, the weather of naked grief and the flight of ducks.

At the most not more than thirty people live in Cejoyuma's village, but there might be only two or a hundred and it would make no difference: they would always be alone. Each man, each dog, each of the stringy chickens swept across the village square by the wind, every living being on the summit of the Sierra Parima is alone and has always been alone. He is alone during the day under a cloudy sky and surrounded by damp mist. He is alone at night, clear and hard like a knife of steel, and pierced by cold stars. He is alone in the eternal autumn of the mountain tops.

Famine on the upper Ventuari empties the forest of its animals and the *conucos* of their precious roots once a year. But here no one knows the meaning of the word famine because here the forest is always bare of animals with warm, red blood, animals that can be transfixed with one swift blow of a spear, whose flesh can then be cut into pieces and roasted for food and eaten to the heart's content in warmth and well-being, and packed away in banana leaves fastened tightly with liana to hang from the high crossbeam of the tribal hut against barren days. Up here all the days of the year are barren days, and that is why no one is astonished or very much worried by the fact. Cejoyuma and his men work harder than any other Indians. They have perhaps won eight or ten *conucos* away from the virgin forest, representing perhaps twenty or twenty-five acres of land, an enormous area for their numbers. It is not to sell cassava to the white man, as José Catire does at Cordoval, and it is not to feed the inhabitants of several villages as Kalomera does; it is just to prevent Cejoyuma's own men from starving, because the earth up here is so poor that it yields only an eighth, or perhaps even only a tenth, of the harvests at Cordoval or in Kalomera's country.

We remained a fortnight with Cejoyuma, and not once did we see either him or his men eat anything but boiled worms with the remains of cassava, dry and several months old.

But I am going too far ahead with my story. It is now only April 19th, 1950, the day after our arrival at Cejoyuma's village. It was raining a fine drizzle and we were stretched out in our hammocks around a small fire that was producing more smoke than heat. Although the tribal hut, the center of beaten earth, and the one rancho which sheltered us were actually at the summit of a hill, we had the impression that we were at the bottom of something—at the bottom of a funnel of icy cold the top of which was formed by the mountain crests around us—and surrounded by a wall of opaque, thick, curdled air full of humidity.

We had put on our thickest shirts, buttoned at the collar and the neck, and we were rolled up in our woollen blankets—but we were cold. An absolute silence weighed on the village. But we were not alone. Not far away from us there were other hammocks bulky with human forms, and in the doorway of the tribal hut we could see naked children with bedaubed faces and dilated bellies. A little farther off, squatting on the ground facing each other, were two men discussing something. They were too far away for us to hear their voices, but we could see their lips moving, and from time to time they made gestures to underline their words. One of them was so old that he had a few white hairs on his chin, and his eyes were almost hidden under an old pointed and colorless felt hat. His torso was clothed in an extraordinary collection of rags sewn together to form a shirt. From below the shirt the fringe of a guayuco hung down over his naked legs.

It was our host, Cejoyuma himself, the greatest singer of the Maquiritares, the man who knew every detail of the creation of the world and its animals, all the metamorphoses through which the son of the sun had passed, and all the adventures, all the marches, and all the wars which the Maquiritares had undergone to take the form of men, to discover fire and the cassava root and learn to construct the great circular huts with their carefully sewn roofs, to make wickerwork in two colors, to make pottery, to spin the raw cotton of the forest, and, finally, to make blowpipes, cudgels and hatchets of stone.

The man facing Cejoyuma was a very different type. He was bigger and more upright, and in the best years of his life. His head was also that of a chief, but harder and colder, more determined than that of old Cejoyuma. He was also more hairy than most Indians. There were sparse brown hairs on his chin and the vestige of a moustache on his upper lip. The hair of his head was not straight like that of the other Maquiritares, but frizzy like that of the Guaharibo sorcerers. His eyes shone keenly from under his heavy, wrinkled eyelids as though secretly from the depths of some loophole. He looked like a man who knew very well what he wanted, a man who would never surrender, a man who would always have reserves of strength in his body barricaded behind the defenses of his knowledge and his experience. At the same time he radiated a strange attraction, due perhaps to a sort of immense melancholy which began with his consecration as a leader. The melancholy seemed to be not fundamental but imposed by life, a role to be played to the end, but one not altogether in accord with his real impulses, with the dreams of his childhood, or with the desires and ideas he had harbored before he had one day finally withdrawn into the depths of his being, that day when the world had wounded him while at the same time making him chief.

The man was Frenario, the chief of the Marquiritares in the upper Yavadehudi, the most remote of them all, the man who actually lived on the farther slope of the Sierra Parima, on the Brazilian side. It was the man who, according to both Kalomera and Cejoyuma, had killed a white man because he had known too much. Had we been told that story by chance or because of some secret understanding between them? Who could tell? Frenario had arrived alone the evening before. He had trotted into the village naked and with nothing but a matchet, a hammock, a bow and three arrows, and the traditional satchel-like receptacle over his shoulder.

He had squatted down opposite Cejoyuma in the same position as he was now, and someone had said:

"That is Frenario, the chief. He has just arrived."

We had squatted down beside the two and listened while Frenario spoke rapidly in a low voice, almost as though he were anxious that we should not understand what he was saying. A little boy had brought the usual cigarettes of welcome, and afterward a second and a third little boy had come. Frenario had taken the cigarettes, one after the other, without turning his head and without interrupting what he was saying or moving anything more than his hand. When he had a cigarette in his mouth and cigarettes between the fingers of his left hand, two other little boys had come up. We had thought that with so many cigarettes already he would refuse. But that would have been a grave lack of politeness, so he had taken three more between the fingers of his right hand and gone on talking, while puffing away in turn at the eight lighted cigarettes.

He had directed all his remarks to Cejoyuma, and as we had felt unwilling to wait there until he was ready to give us his attention, we had gone back to our rancho. However, later on in the evening he had come to the rancho and slung his hammock next to ours, and in the darkness he had begun to talk. We had assumed that he knew no Spanish, but to our surprise we had found that he spoke it fluently and even rather elegantly, much better than José Catire could speak it, and better than many of the mestizos of the Orinoco. We had explained to him that we wished to go to his village and then from there down to the white men of Brazil. He had said neither yes nor no, but grunted and mechanically repeated the last part of what we had said.

Soon I got up and went off to give Cejoyuma's old wife an injection. I had been chiefly a medical man since our arrival. On the day after we arrived Cejoyuma had sent his brother, a giant of a man, specially down to the river to carry up the medicine chest. He did the whole journey there and back in forty-eight hours. I had been awaited in the village rather as a Messiah is awaited. As soon as I arrived I had to go straight to the hammock of the old woman, who had probably been lying there moribund for many months. There was nothing specifically wrong with her. She was slowly dying of old age, that was all, and there was not very much I could do for her. I therefore spoke to Cejoyuma about Uanadji, the chief god of the Maquiritares, telling him that the fate of his wife depended more on Uanadji than upon me or any human aid. Uanadji was calling her to his side at the Great Lagoon above.

"I will not attend to her unless you absolutely insist," I said. "You see, I am not sure that I can cure her, and I do not wish her to die after I have tended to her because I might then be blamed for her death."

Cejoyuma smiled gently.

"Tend her all the same," he said.

And so I had to stage my piece. The patient was no more than a decrepit old bag of bones, a balloon which had been partly deflated. All that was really left alive of her were her yellow, shining eyes which darted here and there like frightened birds as I bent over her. Her body was covered all over with a thick network of swollen veins and ropy arteries. Treatment was quite hopeless. I began by forbidding her to take pimento or salt, and I informed Cejoyuma that she should eat no other food but boiled mashed bananas. Then I decided to try a course of liver extract and vitamins.

Turning the old woman over in her hammock was a difficult job, but I had to deploy all the theatrical arts of a white sorcerer. My first attempt at giving her an injection was a failure. Her tough skin resisted the needle and the contents of the syringe went over her body and ran into the hammock in full view of all the eyes watching me intently out of the darkness. I began to sweat as I recharged the syringe, but the second time I was successful.

Afterward I went back to my hammock, and Frenario, who had come with me, began to ask about our coroto as though he were resuming an interrupted conversation. How many hatchets? How many matchets? How many lengths of cotton cloth? And so on. I told him that Cejoyuma had proposed holding a great celebration in his village and that Cejoyuma himself had promised to come and sing at it.

"Cejoyuma will not come unless the old woman is cured," he objected.

So the fate of our expedition was made to depend on the life of an old woman, a frail life which was already hanging by a thread.

Cejoyuma and Frenario concluded their discussions. The older man got up, and taking a hatchet he went off into the forest alone. It was midday and the porters were arriving in the village with the last of our cases. They moved slowly and their faces were drawn with fatigue and exhaustion. Climbing the mountain with a load of about a hundred and ten pounds was no easy matter. There were more loads than porters, and each man had had to make more than one journey, but now everything had been brought up.

Saudi and Sanoma were able to stay with us despite Cejoyuma's objection to Guaharibos in his village. They were not ordinary Guaharibos, but almost Maquiritares, almost civilized men. They were converted barbarians and therefore admissible. However, they had to pay for the favor by working twice as hard as any of the other men. For the third time they came into the village with cases on their backs. Each of them had carried about three hundred and thirty pounds up the steep side of the mountain. Sanoma was very glad to have finished the work, and he showed his white teeth in a broad grin, rubbing his back and thighs and looking at us.

"*Tamunioto!*" he exclaimed. "*Tamunioto!*"

Heavy work it certainly was.

Diego was moving around busily among the porters, giving orders and superintending the placing of our cases on two great logs near our hammocks. He was completely intent on his work and fully conscious of his responsibility. I don't know how many times he had gone up and down the path leading to the river, and his body was steaming with sweat. He turned toward us and counted on his fingers.

"*Toni, ake, adouaou, aketshima . . .*"

"One, two, three. . . . All the cases are there now."

He asked us to check the number and we did so.

"The men are tired now," he said, "and you must pay those who have to go down."

Very few of the men from the Ventuari were to follow us beyond the village of Cejoyuma.

We got up and opened the cases. I became the accounts clerk and Luis the treasurer. Diego stood at my side and supervised the accounting as I explained each item to him.

"The Burgundian: nine days of labor at ten bolívars a day, equals ninety bolívars. He has already received one cooking pot and two lengths of guayuco in advance to the value of thirty-nine bolívars. Leaves a balance of fifty-one bolívars. Right, Diego?"

We went through the account again in the Maquiritare fashion: ninety, that is four times twenty plus ten, or four times the two feet with their ten toes, and four times the two hands with their ten fingers, plus the two hands with their ten fingers once more, making altogether four and a half persons. The biggest single Maquiritare unit is "one person," or twenty, being the sum of his ten fingers and his ten toes. Thirty-nine is much more difficult to express because it means subtracting a finger from the sum of fingers and toes of two persons.

The Burgundian stood there smiling until Diego confirmed my accounting of what was due to him, then he said:

"Guayuco. A lot of guayuco."

What did he want with all that guayuco? He had already received six yards on his last accounting, and another six yards as an advance on this. All Frenario's men would want guayuco as well and we hadn't brought miles of the stuff with us. No, the Burgundian would have to modify his demands in the matter of guayuco. It was up to Luis and his assistant Pierre to interest him in the quality of our fine-tooth combs, our knives, our American fishing line, each ball of which was accompanied by a dozen hooks. . . . Jean had quite a different job. He was strolling around with his camera taking a film of the proceedings.

Two hours passed in this fashion, devoted to the discussion of two and a half persons of guayuco, two persons and a quarter of journey, three cooking pots, two packets of needles, one canister of black powder. Then the Indians packed away the treasures they had acquired at the cost of so much sweat and so long a journey, while we closed up our cases. Cejoyuma's men came to watch the payments being made, and we allowed them to go through our cases and discuss at leisure the merits of the goods we had brought with us. We hoped that this foretaste might encourage them to come a little farther with us.

Pierre then carefully checked his sound-recording equipment to discover whether any damage had been suffered on the way, for we hoped to be able to use it before long. For an hour he screwed and unscrewed, made adjustments and tested the generating set.

MOZART IN THE JUNGLE

The sound of it as it started up brought all the other Indians out of the hut to see what was happening. As the whole population of the village was now surrounding us and looking at our apparatus with lively interest, we thought it a good opportunity to stage a concert.

At the first notes of a minuet by Rameau the clouds which had covered the sky since the previous day rapidly began to clear, leaving a sky so pale and blue that it might almost have been over Paris. A gentle sun lit up the forest and the high blades of cassava on the plantation beyond the village square. The violins played a gay and cheerful air well suited to the scene around us, and the Indians came closer, listening to the music and watching the disc turning. The power of music seemed to have transfixed them and they stood there stockstill but with smiling lips.

When the minuet was over Pierre put on "The March of the 87th Regiment of the Line." The faces of the Indians lit up at its lively tune and they began to beat time with their heads. Luis insisted on trying to explain what a military march was, and taking two aluminum pots he banged them together and marched round the square in an exaggerated imitation of marching men, lifting his knees almost up to his chin. I don't think the Indians understood much of this pantomime, but they enjoyed it, and three or four of them, headed by Sanoma, began to follow him round and imitate his movements. It was rather like a burlesque of an Indian dance, and it ended only when Cejoyuma came out of the forest again, his hatchet over his shoulder. In one hand he held a large piece of hard wood which already had something of the shape of the cudgel he would carve from it.

After the march, Pierre put on a record of a Maquiritare song we had recorded on the Ventuari. The old man had put away his hatchet and his piece of wood and he now squatted down near our apparatus. Automatically his men closed in round him. At the first notes there was complete silence and our audience listened gravely. It had amused them to hear strange music coming from our apparatus, but this was their own music and their own voices. At first it was little more than a whisper, then the volume increased, filling first the rancho and then the whole village and the funnel of air and forest that surrounded it. It might have been the voice of Uanadji himself.

The preliminary surprise and astonishment gradually gave way to a sort of religious fear in the minds of the listening Indians. Cejoyuma stared at our apparatus without blinking, squatting there as still as a statue while his men anxiously studied his face to anticipate the judgement he would pass on the miracle, for he was "the man who knows." Quite a time seemed to pass and then Pierre reduced the volume as he had previously increased it.

At last Cejoyuma's eyes grew softer, his lips opened, and he smiled. Then he began to hum the sacred couplets the invisible Maquiritare was singing. At that a great cry of joy arose from the men around us and they took up the verses with their chief. One of them ran off to the tribal hut and returned with a drum to accompany the singing.

Pierre put on a second Maquiritare record. This time Diego was almost bursting with pride, for he recognized his own voice. Eagerly he explained to Cejoyuma's men just how it had been recorded in his little hut on the Ventuari, showing them the electric wires and the discs. He had an appreciative audience and they listened to him with deep interest.

The women now came out of the hut in which they had concealed themselves since our arrival—intimidated by our beards, our size, and our white skins. Perhaps, too, their fathers and their husbands had threatened them with all the punishments of heaven if they dared to come anywhere near the white strangers.

The first to appear was an old woman with bold eyes. She was old enough to have almost the same rights as the men. In any case, she had nothing to lose. She squatted down at a little distance from our apparatus and listened to the explanations Diego was still eagerly making. Before long she was joined by a little girl. Diego's voice was stilled as Pierre put on the next record. It was our beloved Mozart.

Mozart seemed to exercise some magic influence on the

Indians, and his music dissipated the last misgivings of the younger women, who now came forward from the hut one after the other and sat down with the old woman who had first taken courage. Diego's wife made a spot of bright color among the rest of them, with their dark bodies and their little beaded aprons, for Diego had given her a flowered cotton dress from his previous payment.

The performance was not new to her; she had seen and heard it more than once on the Ventuari, but she was a real Maquiritare and she would never have come out of the hut if the other women, her sisters, cousins, and sisters-in-law, had not kept her company. Now she was at liberty to share the pride of her husband, and she too delivered herself of long explanations about the miracle. They were discussed in considerable detail by the old woman who had first come out and who had listened very carefully to what Diego had to say.

Then Diego's wife produced another treasure her husband had got for her: a pair of chromium-plated scissors, and under the admiring eyes of the other women she began to snip away industriously at a little plaque of thin metal.

In the music of Mozart there is a strange charm in the widest sense of the word, some magic influence to which no Indian could remain insensible. On them as on us the music seemed to exercise a soothing influence: it relaxed the body and allowed the soul to expand gratefully. It was a sort of oxygen, the very gentlest of balms. It dissipated fears, melancholy, and the fatigues of the journey. It solaced our loneliness and gave us comfort in the primitive life we were leading. Above this somber countryside eternally closed around its secret the music placed a trembling forest of clear-toned violins that made the hairs of the skin move as the bluish cassava shoots moved in the wind on the hill slope. Such music did not stiffen the body nor clamp down a mask of fear on the faces of those who listened. It opened up the secret places of the heart; it made a thousand hidden voices surge up from the hidden center of things, a thousand colors, a thousand unsuspected forms.

Cejoyuma's younger brother and right-hand man, known to

us as "the Centurion" came from the direction of the village carrying a small stool in one of his enormous hands. He sat down on it at a little distance from our apparatus and went on with some wickerwork he was making. His fingers moved swiftly and skilfully backward and forward among a maze of black and white strips of osier. He was weaving a wickerwork tray with complicated decorative motifs. There were human forms with upraised arms, a frieze of monkeys running and jumping, and intricate patterns of arabesques, crosses, lozenges, and dots. His swift fingers moved like those of a harpist to the rhythm of a classic allegro, and the black and white figures took shape rapidly as he worked.

Two Indians were stretched out beside me smoking, occasionally scratching themselves and shifting their feet, their heads lifted to watch the triangle of light on the polished black disc as it turned.

I do not know if music is really the universal language people often say it is, but I shall never forget that it was the music of Mozart to which we owed the rare moments when the chasm which centuries of our evolution had dug between us, civilized white men of the twentieth century, and them, the barbarians of the stone age, was almost completely filled.

Only Frenario and Cejoyuma maintained their reserve. They were afraid to open up their hearts, afraid to surrender themselves to the magic of our music. They were unwilling to forget that we were and must remain "others," for they were chiefs and they had charge of the souls of men. They were not individuals but the conscience of the group, the leaders of the men, women, and children who followed them along the road of life amid ambush and treachery and the dangers which lurk behind all unknown things. The music ended and night fell.

We ate boiled cassava roots and a little smoked tapir as hard as leather, and then we went to our hammocks. Luis, whose idea of a meal always included a sweet, swallowed a dose of cough medicine to give him the familiar taste of sugar.

Before I turned in I went to see my patient. She was wailing like a baby, raising her fleshless arms above the hammock. With some difficulty I gave her an injection of liver extract in the buttock. Her condition was unchanged. Indeed, why should it change? I felt like cursing the fate which compelled me to disturb her on the verge of her last, long sleep. I hated anyone to shake me or touch me just before I went to sleep, and on the verge of death such interference must be even more disagreeable. But what could I do? I dared neglect nothing in my efforts to persuade Cejoyuma to come with us and sing in the hut of Frenario.

It grew cold, and Sanoma lit a fire between our hammocks, slinging his own above it and sleeping there like a ham in the chimney corner. Our civilized ways did not impress him very much, and in particular he could never understand why we disliked smoke so much. Pierre talked longingly of a big white bed and then went off to sleep like a child. Before going to sleep Jean arranged his usual collection of heavy English keys within reach of his hand. Each key was attached to a piece of twine. When dogs came nosing around and disturbing us in the night he would bombard them with these keys, and when the keys had served their purpose he could retrieve them on their lengths of twine without getting out of his hammock.

Somewhere behind me a puppy was scratching something and whining softly. Then he obviously dug up a bone, for he began to gnaw it and crack it between his teeth. My left side, which was toward the fire, was burning; my right side, which was turned away from the fire, was freezing. Frenario began to talk. He started off in the middle of a phrase where he had left off the night before. It was a habit of his to resume a conversation hours and hours after it had been broken off, and at the exact spot. It seemed to him the most natural thing in the world.

"If you want to see Guaharibos in my territory you will see them. There are very many of them. The forest and the surrounding countryside are swarming with them. If you want to talk to them or to make your images, you need not trouble to go to them; I will make them come to you. But they're not really very interesting, you know. They sing perfectly idiotic things, and they have neither flutes nor drums. Nothing at all."

I already knew this kind of talk.

"Do you know what they do with their dead?" I asked.

"Their dead? Why, they burn them on big bonfires in the heart of the forest, and their women dance around and cry and shout. When the bodies are consumed they collect the ashes and mix them with onoto and paint their faces and their bodies with it. They say that in this way there will be more and more Guaharibos in the world. But as for me, I find there are too many in the world already. There are three times as many of them as of us. That's because they can eat anything and nothing ever does them any harm, the little pigs."

So the Guaharibos burned their dead and used the ashes to make a paint with which to daub themselves? There were many Guaharibos in the forest, and many more in the mountains. We should never get to know them all, just as we should never get to know all the Maquiritares. Before this expedition little or nothing had been known of the Guaharibos, and yet hundreds and thousands of them had been taken as children to work as slaves for the Dutch of Guiana in the seventeenth and eighteenth centuries. But once there they had ceased to be Guaharibos. They were just chained human beings who worked until they died without ever opening their mouths.

On all sides we were about a month away from civilization. The men of the upper Ventuari were to leave us tomorrow, except Diego, Sanoma, and his small and very humble brother Mamai, who was little more than a pair of shining eyes, a shaven head, and a backbone always ready to receive a heavy case, thus to gradually become the straight back of a man.

The Burgundian, the Sioux, Saudi, and their brothers were going down as far as Marietta. They had told us so a little while before. José Catire had engaged them on behalf of Marat. He would lend them shirts and trousers if they had none of their own, so that they should be able "to hold their own in the world." No one would ever know again that they had never seen a white man until our arrival in their village. No one would ever know that Saudi was a Guaharibo. They would all go down to Puerto Ayacucho when they had worked to earn enough, and there they would buy shirts and trousers of their own. They would then be able to take their place in the white man's world without José's assistance. They would learn to drink iced beer taken from the gasoline-driven refrigerator, and in their memories the new life would soon oust the old in which they had once chanted the story of the first son of the sun, drinking calabashes of yaraké and painting their bodies with the ashes of their fathers. Who will ever really know the Indians we call savages? When they meet us in civilized surroundings they will always do their best to evade us.

A fit of melancholy overcame me at the depressing thought. The old woman began to whimper softly. The noise woke up a dog, which growled and then went to sleep again. My heart beat hard. I was afraid she would die between one of those little whimpering sounds and the next. But gradually she fell silent and my heart returned to normal. I thought of her eyes as she lay there in a hammock too small for her: they were the eyes of an old animal, dark brown and flecked with yellow and grey, sad and dejected eyes looking out from the parchment-like skin that covered her bones. Her life was approaching its end in the same autumnal surroundings in which it had begun. She was and always had been the head wife of Cejoyuma, and to protect her against the obscure forces of evil he had slung his own hammock above hers, and there he slept, only a few inches away, like a shield and armed with the knowledge of chants that lasted six days and six nights. Thrust into the roof within easy reach of his hand were two strong bows and six arrows with sharp steel tips, so that if the dreaded powers of evil appeared the old chief would have weapons of wood and bone to try conclusions with them.

What did the old woman know of life, the life of the earth, of the forest, of the dome of sky which pressed down on all things? What did she know of the world and of the other seasons which preceded and followed the eternal raw, damp, and cold autumn here? What did she know of the men and the women who peopled the vast world? And what did the old chief above her think when he heard her whimper? She had ground him a very great deal of cassava. She had brought him a calabash of pimento and a calabash of drink at each sunrise and at each sundown for many, many years. And she had given him the four children of whom he had spoken to me the previous day:

"Two males and two females."

PREPARATION FOR THE MARCH TO THE EAST

On April 20th Frenario decided to start. He gave orders to the men who, we learned then, were from his village, and to us he said:

"It will take at least a week to carry all your material from here to my village. It is far away. We have to march until we come to the Yavadehudi, and then march along it until it becomes large enough to be navigable. And then I must organize relays of canoes because it is not possible to do the whole journey in one stage. At certain spots the river is barred by impenetrable rapids, and at others it disappears altogether underground to reappear a quarter of an hour's march further on. And then I must organize the fetching of baskets of cassava from my village, because otherwise we shouldn't have enough to eat on the journey. Cejoyuma will not give us enough provisions for a journey of eight days."

Our new expedition was rapidly organized. Since the majority of the men from the Ventuari had gone down again, there were not enough porters left to carry all our cases, so it was arranged that they should make several journeys to the halfway mark, where Frenario's men would come to their assistance. A detailed plan of operations had to be worked out, and Frenario did the planning like a general preparing a military operation. He never lost his equanimity and he never had the air of being worried or harassed. Most of the time he spent in his hammock, but every time he spoke something new was done. A native in full Maquiritare dress, with large earrings of bamboo decorated with feathers, a fine collar of beadwork round his neck and newly painted designs from his calves to his head, came to ask us for a matchet.

"Give him one," said Frenario. "He is my runner. He must go off to my village and organize the canoe relays and the transport of cassava, and he will need a matchet."

We handed the man a large matchet which was quite new. He rolled up his hammock, fastened it over his back, took the matchet in one hand, and started off into the forest at a trot. In three days he would cover a distance that would take us perhaps eight or even ten. After that he would come back at once and shoulder one of our cases. . . .

At dawn on the 21st six men started off, each of them carrying a heavy case. The next day it was our turn to move off with other men and further cases. We still did not know whether old Cejoyuma was coming with us or not, and whether we should have to leave the Sierra Parima and return to our own world without having seen him perform his office or heard him sing his songs, without having filmed him or recorded his voice. His wife's condition was unchanged. Each of us sought in turn to persuade him, but without much hope of success, and he listened to us all with the same patience and in the same silence.

In any case, the die was cast. If he refused to come we should have to go without him. The machinery of our departure had been set in motion now and the weather permitted no delay. It was on the day of our departure that the first real rain fell. When I say "real rain," I mean the first of those downpours whose monotonous violence shows beyond all question that the dry season is definitely over.

Before long it would be raining every second day; then two days out of three; and, finally, twenty-four hours out of the twenty-four for months on end throughout the whole of the Sierra Parima. Torrents would pour down the mountain side to the Brazilian plains beneath. And every day they would grow bigger. The rapids would rise beyond their rocks and form an impenetrable barrier of tossing water, and the force of the current would increase tremendously. We should have to go forward quickly if we wanted to leave the Sierra Parima. We had entered it, but that was only one part of the task.

That afternoon we had tried to record the performance of a flute player, but the result was not very satisfactory. We hardly felt how tired our bodies were because we were sustained by hope and enthusiasm, but our instruments and machines had nothing to sustain them. They were tired of so much forest, so much humidity, and so much mildew. The microscopic mushroom growths of the forest which had given me such disagreeable memories did not confine their attentions only to the human body; they attacked inanimate things as well, developing and infiltrating wherever they could. They had already made our field glasses and two of our camera lenses unusable. White networks of frost-like patterns had spread out between the cemented layers. These mushroom growths also attacked the winding mechanism, the condensers, and all the vital parts of our electrical equipment. And, finally, our two storage batteries had dried out so often during porterage, because despite our instructions the porters preferred to carry them the wrong way rather than the right way up, that now they contained not more than perhaps a quarter of an hour, or, at the utmost, half an hour, of strength. Our oil reserves, too, were practically at an end.

From the 21st to the 22nd of April we did not sleep at all. We discussed the pros and the cons very carefully and in the end there was no doubt about it: our situation and the state of our resources demanded that we should lose no time. And above our heads the rains of heaven beat down steadily to underline the need for haste.

"Tomorrow we shall give up the ghost and go silent for good and all," said our machines.

"Tomorrow you will no longer be able to get out of here at all," said the rains.

We smoked incessantly, perhaps because we knew that in a couple of weeks, or even less, we should have no more tobacco. We were not very much disturbed about that. We felt a desire to cut ourselves adrift from everything that might give us a false sense of security. The day was fast approaching on which we should meet our final test and justify our journey across this unknown world. But for that it would be too simple to cross the areas still blank on our maps.

Sanoma turned over in his sleep. His hammock was so slung as to divide the smoke of our fire in two halves. The rain grew heavier and splashed down on the whining dogs, on the fire which gnawed rather than bit into the circle of mildewed logs it was made of, on us and on our reasonings, and on our vain but inevitable efforts to control the course of events, to decide our own destiny, to give orders to the invisible Power which held us in Its hand and would decide our ultimate fate without reference to our wishes. There was nothing left for us but to withdraw into our dreams in the heart of the night and await the daylight when our bodies and our spirits would once again take control over our lives. Then we would set off toward the east, against the direction of the sun.

ADVENTURES IN AN UNKNOWN LAND

On April 22nd at dawn our march toward the east began. For a few days we went along the crest of the mountain through that same inanimate and inhuman terrain that we had discovered on arriving at Cejoyuma's hut and that seemed to characterize the whole of the upper Sierra Parima. There was nothing but trees, leaves, liana, and the earth, not even the call of a bird, not even the track of some animal on the ground. Then we descended into a valley. We pitched our camp beside a small water source, and a rivulet ran toward the east, but it was so small that it was not easy even to drink at it.

"That's the Yavadehudi," said Frenario.

"*Tunake, tunake, ed'dhe adaie,*" added Sanoma.

"Little stream, little stream which grows large down below."

It was thus that we passed a frontier that no white man had ever passed before us, the frontier that separates Venezuela from Brazil at the summit of the Sierra Parima. Our fate would now mingle with that of those drops of water which rolled on and on from river to river to arrive in the basin of the Amazon and reach the sea at Pará (Belém), where the biggest river in the world empties 157,000 cubic yards of muddy water per second into the Atlantic with such force that ships sixty miles off shore can find their way in merely by following the yellow track in the blue sea before them. We had reached the halfway mark between the Orinoco and the Amazon, the fascinating spot we had once marked on our map.

Sanoma was right when he said:

"Little stream, little stream which grows larger down below."

"May we be there to see," we felt inclined to add.

The next day and the day after that, and for several other days we followed this new thread of Ariadne which was to lead us, we hoped, out into our own world. It was a strange feeling: there was so little to take us to so much; and while we went forward, we found ourselves frequently glancing at it with involuntary misgiving. That thread was so frail and narrow, we should not have been surprised if it had broken off and disappeared for good.

But as the days passed it grew stronger. Other waters joined it and it grew wider. Before long it was a small river with high, bushy vegetation of a light green color growing along both banks. To our joy it hurried on toward the east faster and faster and with more and more noise, and with a systematic persistence that nothing could prevent. Every day we watched it moving swiftly toward the sun, which we saw born ahead of it as though from a chrysalis. The mountains to the right and to the left receded and dipped toward the earth. The highest summits of the Sierra Parima now occupied no more than half the horizon behind us.

And then we reached the first and highest of the relay stages where men with canoes were waiting for us. Our voyage began, but it was not easy. The bigger the Yavadehudi grew, the more wildly it hurtled downward on its way to the valley; and for the first few days we met with numerous mishaps. First of all there were trunks of trees which obstructed the river bed, and then there were rapids and falls through which our canoes shot like black arrows in the white spray and foam, or rapids and falls that we had to outflank on land, going forward slowly and with difficulty, carrying our cases and our canoes one after the other.

The mornings were damp, grey, and cold, and there were no birds to be seen. The days were wet and the rain fell from the sky in torrents, lashing the surface of the river so furiously that sometimes we were at a loss to tell which was up and which was down in this liquid world which surrounded us and soaked us through and through.

Where were the days when the chrysalis of the dawning sun developed regularly into a radiant circle in the center of a blue sky, up there in the realms of Uanadji and the gods of his fathers? Gold and azure blue were both excluded from our color scheme in that full season of the rains when we crossed the Sierra Parima. There was nothing but the dingy white of the sky, the water, sparkling or dull, and the eternal green of the forest. It was ideal weather for colds, influenza, bronchitis, mildew, and all the other pests of the Indian world. Suddenly we understood how it came about that the Maquiritares had only one word to describe the color green, dampness, and suffering. In their tongue the rainy season was the time of water, but it was also called the time of sickness. In truth, a religion sternly male and solar, such as theirs, was needed to help them survive the terrible hostility of those long months of suffering and insecurity, both moral and physical, which the rains brought with them every year.

One rapid, two rapids, three rapids—before long we were negotiating a dozen every day. As soon as the surface of the water ahead of us began to be cut up as though with saber strokes from bank to bank, our canoes would come to a halt side by side, the men in charge of them would spring out together on a rock, and while the air trembled with the distant noise, they would carefully study the dangerous passage ahead. After a few words they would get back into their canoes and on we would go. Our course had been decided: we had to skirt that rock, go ahead at top speed toward that whirlpool, then swing round it to one side. . . .

The canoes would dart forward one after the other, half covered by the foam whipped up by the swirling, tossing water, shooting the rapids like skiers through snow or skaters over ice, until finally, and with hardly a paddle stroke, just using the momentum of the water rushing swiftly between the rocks, they would glide out surely into calmer water. Then they would be guided into the bank and lifted up while their crews used the flats of their paddles to scoop out the many gallons of water they had shipped in the passage.

After such excitement a more tranquil descent would begin again. A gag seemed to have been fixed round our mouths and no one spoke. The silence was complete. We had not yet returned to the real country of man, though the first birds were beginning to appear again. But the parakeets in pairs and the families of migratory birds were not the real doves our arks were seeking. They were more like flamboyant and terrible archangels, or silent black crosses sweeping across the sky at such a height that they did not really belong to our world. No, we could not cry "Land!" yet.

Our troubles were by no means over, and on more than one occasion the whole Yavadehudi just disappeared altogether—not as though the earth had swallowed it up but quite literally because it had.

Its mighty power, its anger, and its thunderous growling as it thrashed its way through the rapids, or between those chaotic assemblies of sharp rocks were suddenly gone. Gone too its broad calmness, its assurance, and its confidence as it gathered its forces and grew steadily larger while the whole world around it was nothing but a backcloth, just the valley through which it flowed. All that was gone, was ended, had disappeared, was swallowed up. The earth opened its lipless mouth and the whole river vanished with all its ninety feet of breadth and all its great mass of clear water.

The absurd impulse which had made us cast sidelong glances at it when we saw it being born and gradually growing bigger was no more absurd than that. There are many rivers, really big rivers, which suddenly disappear without trace, and the Yavadehudi, which the Brazilians call the Auari on their maps, was such a river. Their cartographers indicate its reputed course by dotted lines, and they are very wise to do so. Even if they had known the river as we knew it, they would not have mapped its course accurately throughout its whole length. Those dotted lines would still have been there.

A few miles further on beyond such points the Yavadehudi

would reappear as suddenly as it had disappeared. In the meantime our canoes and our cases had to be laboriously manhandled over the intervening distance before we could take to the water again.

One day—I was in the leading canoe—I saw three birds on the river a little ahead of us. They were black divers, and although their flesh was not exceptionally good, at least it was edible. For days we had eaten nothing but cassava, and so I eagerly reached for my rifle. But Diego laid a restraining hand upon my arm.

"No," he said. "Don't do that. It's unlucky. There will soon be plenty of animals, and tomorrow we'll shoot peccaries or alligators."

Soon after that we entered the real valley of the Yavadehudi. At the same time the weather grew warmer and birds began to sing once again behind the green walls of the forest. The next day we did, in fact, dine off peccary meat. Sanoma shot the beast with one of our rifles, and he was not a little proud of his feat.

One day Luis was sitting on one of our cases in the middle of his canoe and dreaming, when suddenly he was flung backward as the canoe unexpectedly encountered an unseen obstacle. To the great amusement of all of us he went head over heels backward into the water. We had come into Guaharibo country again, and the excuse of Luis's mishap was a great bridge of liana across the river a little below the surface. Animal life appeared again first, and then human life. We passed a second and then a third of these bridges, and on shore we saw ocherous paths leading from the banks and disappearing into the darkness of the forest.

One morning after we had already been compelled to land twice in order to get round dangerous rapids on foot, carrying canoes and baggage, the men produced the small calabashes in which they kept their red onoto paste; and taking the pocket mirrors we had given them, they began to decorate their faces and their bodies before re-embarking. This was something they had not done since we had left the village of Cejoyuma. Then they put little pieces of bamboo wood through their ears to hold tufts of black, red, and yellow feathers, which are the colors of the Maquiritares.

The preparations were a sign that we were approaching the end of our journey. Not long after that the helmsmen of the canoes put down their paddles and, standing upright, they blew loud blasts on their conches. The sound echoed and re-echoed through the valley from hill to hill. The river turned to the right, and round the bend we saw a hill which had been cleared of trees and was now covered with superb cassava waving in the breeze. And just at that moment we heard the sound of drum and trumpet come to answer our signals. The village had heard our fanfare and was greeting us in its turn.

IN THE VILLAGE OF FRENARIO

The village of Kalomera was like a Roman encampment. The village of Cejoyuma, the great singer, reminded one of nothing more than the hermitage of a Tibetan monk, lost in the autumnal mists of the mountain peaks.

The village we were now reaching had a character all its own. The brow of the hill dominated the Yavadehudi at a height of more than three hundred feet, and one could see over a great expanse of forest and far down the valley, which opened out in the distance. Under the blue sky the view was calm and majestic. The size of the village, its wealth, and its organization made it into an authentic Indian settlement in the same way as Carimagua was an authentic white settlement. After many years of labor, Frenario had won a space away from the forest just as the brothers Solano had won a space away from the llano, and if the results differed the difference lay only in the inequality of the resources of the two settlements.

But when we saw the enormous tribal hut with its green walls and its white drawings of a whole hierarchy of animals from the agouti to the tapir; the great mortar for pounding cassava root, fixed in the ground to one side of the village square; the rancho workshop containing all the village's reserves of arms and tools in wood and stone; and when we saw the perfection of that living oasis many, many days' journey away from any other center of human life, we were moved by a very real emotion: to us it was an earnest of the faith of man which had erected all human edifices, from the Indian huts to the pyramids of Egypt and the great cathedrals of the Western world.

When we told Frenario warmly that the site on which he had set his village was more beautiful than any we had seen, his eyes filled with tears. They were the first tears we had ever witnessed in the eyes of an Indian. It was shattering for him that we had moved him, because it meant that henceforth he must like us, and he was unwilling to like us—his experience of white men had warned him against such weakness. On our long journey together he had told us how he had made the acquaintance of our civilization, and how he had left it to hide himself in the thickest and most impenetrable fastness of his native forest, and what he had wished to hide revealed itself so clearly in what he said that it was quite easy for us to guess what it was. When he was quite young Frenario was taken away from his people by collectors of rubber somewhere on the upper Orinoco. He traveled around with them for many years and went with them to Colombia. When he was older and more experienced, speaking Spanish fluently and not forgetting that he was the son of a chief and that he would one day be a chief himself, he returned to his own people. Then he went on his own to Villavicencio, the capital city of the llano, from which our expedition had set out.

In Villavicencio he had quickly realized that for white people he was nothing but a menial person, often compelled to beg his bread, and always miserable, wearing clothes which suited neither his body nor his soul. He lived in Villavicencio for a few months, earning his living by chopping firewood in the nearby forest and selling it in bundles from door to door. Then he went back to the Orinoco. Going up river, he penetrated into the forest, followed a path he discovered, and came in this way to a Maquiritare village. But he did not stay there for long. He wanted to go still further into the interior. Then he came to the Yavadehudi, where no white man had ever set foot in Indian memory. There he gathered his men around him and built his hut. And the day he saw a white man—who it was we shall never know—he killed him without hesitation in order to preserve the peace it had cost him so much to gain.

Many years passed, and in the meantime a whole people grew up around him as vegetation grows up in the shade of a large tree. Then one day a secret messenger arrived to warn him that four white men in rags were in the village of his nearest neighbor, the high priest Cejoyuma, that they knew many Maquiritares, spoke their language, and desired to visit him too. Frenario took his bow and arrows and went out to meet us. He met us, observed us closely, spoke to us, and then brought us here; and the first thing we had said to him was that his village was the most beautiful of all the villages of the forest. He had almost wept, and yet he had wanted to hate. He should have killed us, and instead he had guided us.

There will always be something inexplicable in a man's feelings, something inaccessible to ordinary reason. Frenario liked us and detested us at one and the same time because through us he feared the obscure danger essentially attached to the world of white men. He would no longer attempt to kill us, and he would not even drive us away, but on the other hand, he could not welcome our presence; and in his heart he longed with all his might that we should go on our way without contaminating the work he had done and was still doing here so far away from our world, from our haste, from our rapacity, from our *"codicia,"* as the chroniclers of the Spanish conquest used to say of Cortes or Pizarro, far away from the absurd and monstrous genius of our kind which had compelled him to receive us here.

Once we had gone, Frenario would soon forget that he had felt regard for us, and once again there would be no feeling in him toward the whites but hatred, the sentiment that had always informed that proud head and that muscular body according to the imperative law that had made him a chief, a colonizer, and a builder.

The sky was immense and blue over our heads, and flecked with white clouds. The frieze of forest animals running across the vast wall of the new hut sang in the sun of the joy of man who defied the fates and gained his first victory over his own origins. It was May 1st, and the sun that shone down on us was worthy of May day. It was warm but not hot, and it filled the valley with life-giving oxygen just as it did in Europe. Frenario's men were gathered in the rancho workshop. Cords were drawn tight between posts, and on these cords they were weaving garments of green and yellow palm leaves. Others were making crowns and tiaras of delicate wickerwork and decorating them with the red and golden feathers of the toucan. Others still were arranging great necklaces of peccary teeth round their necks. Hanging from these down the back was a length of red cotton cloth. Still others were suspending dead birds from a ring of osiers. The plumage colors were dazzling: wine-colored stripes on a grey background; a mixture of orange as luminous as the sun on water; bottle green, uniform and soft; jet black with white or red throat—sumptuous colors without end. The eyelids of the dead birds were closed and sewn up, and their bodies were plumped out with forest cotton as though they were still alive.

The tribal hut was lighted from a sort of skylight in the roof through which the sun poured in a great beam as though into the nave of a cathedral. Along the walls were ten hearths, and at each of them a woman was busy cooking cassava in the embers. The sun had ripened the cassava roots in the earth, and the women had picked, washed, grated, and dried them. Baked in round loaves, the cassava would become bread; and the bread, broken up and fermented in water, would become wine with which to celebrate the inauguration of a new tribal hut. The chief would bless the habitation of his people and chant the litanies of the Sun God: first toward the east—where the sun rises and on to which one door opens—and then toward the west, where it sets and toward which the other door opens.

And all the men would dance and drink the cassava wine and chant the litany in their turn. And they would wear garments of palm leaves, which are the vestments of the forest, carry aloft the bodies of birds, which are the emissaries of the gods, and be ornamented with the teeth of wild boars, which are their ancestors and from whom they have inherited their strength.

The life of man originated in the forest, and in order to understand the significance of Indian celebrations one must always keep the forest in mind as a clammy, obscure haven for man. The forest was the only haunt of man until he decided on his own accord to leave it.

For the first man the forest was not on earth; it was earth. It was not a vegetable growth; it was something fundamentally given. It was a universe of its own, without form, contours, or limits. The forest was a world of softness, a universe of osmosis governed by the invisible. It was a mortar in which life and death were closely mingled in a gigantic mixture of all kinds and all species.

Forest man has no individuality. He is hardly differentiated from everything around him. The Guaharibo is the first man. He still sleeps in this dark, damp haven, curled in on himself like a foetus. He is as yet immune to those feelings which make a man shiver and inspire him to go forth into the outer light. He sees the world of light only when the chance that governs his vagabondage leads him to the banks of a river, and it frightens him as it frightens all dwellers in the gloom. He flees from the light at once, hiding himself in the thickest part of the forest, where his body will be almost the only shelter he can give to his fire, as yet his only conquest. He flies from the light and the sun because he does not yet know that one day his real world will develop there. The first step will be taken on the day he decides to leave the womb of his forest mother, to control his own life, to be born again, to rise above those things which merely permit him to exist.

The Maquiritare has already made that first and definite step. He distinguishes between night and day. He has weighed good against evil, and he has set out on his journey, choosing the light, as at one moment or the other in their history all men must. First of all he searched for a hill. It was invisible to the eye, but he felt its presence in his legs, his muscles, and his nerves. He felled the trees on the hill he chose, and the sun and the air dried up the dead foliage and the branches. Then he burned them, for he was already master of fire, and his wife planted cassava seed in the warm ashes. To crown his work he cleared the unseen earth for the first time, compressing it with his hands and feet to be hardened by the sun and the air, and finally he built the hut to protect the fire and the harvest and to guard the body and the spirit from the evil forces of the night.

Such a triumph demanded celebration, and Maquiritare tradition has ever since ordained that all those who build themselves a new habitation shall celebrate its completion. It was such a celebration that we were to witness the next day.

Not that Frenario had told us all this. He did not even know that we knew anything about such things. Earlier in his life the whites had despised him because he was an Indian, and the old, forgotten shame now rose again in him as we busied ourselves taking photographs and films of his men as they went about the preparations for their festival, and asked them the meaning of this or that detail. The old, forgotten, and abominable shame rose in him again even here, on the soil that he had won from the forest with his own hands, in the village of which he was chief. It was truly enough to make a man tremble with rage. And he reacted by refusing to know anything about what was happening. He was naked and covered with daubings when I spoke to him, but he shrugged his shoulders:

"You know that I have always lived among the *castellanos*. I know nothing about these Indian things. The *muchachos* do all that, not I."

A STRANGE CEREMONIAL AND A CHANGE IN PLANS

The next morning the weather was cold and damp, and great nebulous curtains of mist hung down from the mountains into the valley. A file of muchachos dressed in their full-skirted robes of palm leaves and wearing all their ornaments were moving round in a circle, each man with his hand on the shoulder of the man before him. Their dance was accompanied by uanas of bamboo, and the leading man in the file held a staff with the hooves of deer suspended from the top. This he used to thump upon the ground and mark the time. All the heels rose together and stamped in unison, and the little hooves of horn at the top of the staff rattled against each other in a dry crepitation.

The thudding feet made a dull and muffled sound, the uanas whistled and grunted like the voice of the wild boar they were supposed to represent, and a drum made from the stretched skin of a monkey throbbed rhythmically throughout the dance.

The young men sang and laughed, and each time they circled round the village square they passed quite close to us with a great rustling of palm leaves. Frenario was sitting near by on one of our cases, apparently completely absorbed in carving the neck of a paddle. I could not understand what the young men were chanting because they were using their ritual language, which is to Maquiritare what Latin is to French.

"What are they singing, Frenario?" I asked.

"How should I know?" he returned with a shrug of his shoulders. "I have already told you that I know nothing about these Indian affairs."

And obstinately he lowered his eyes to his work again. But after a while I noticed that each time the dancers came near us his lips moved almost but not quite imperceptibly, and that each time the leader of the file looked toward him expectantly. And then I realized that Frenario was speaking soundlessly. He was muttering the verses of the chant and the man at the head of the file was watching his lips and repeating what he said in a loud voice for all the others to say after him. Frenario was acting as prompter.

"Frenario!" I exclaimed. "That young man is your pupil. You are the real singer."

"Well," he said casually. "What of it? The older men must pass on what they know to the younger ones, or else how would they know? They do that in your country too."

"And what is it you're passing on to them now?"

"The tributaries on the right bank of the Orinoco from Puerto Ayacucho right back to the source."

So, among other things, the celebration of the hut's completion was the occasion for a lesson in local topography for the young men of the tribe.

The class learned its lesson while dancing round in a circle. And after topography came the art of the chase. And after that the art of war. In this way the whole sum of Maquiritare knowledge was passed on to the young men morning and evening, day after day, throughout the celebration. It would seem that these people, who have no written language and therefore no books, and whose traditions are preserved solely in the memory of the old men of the tribe, cannot pass knowledge on from one generation to the other without the mediation of the physical body and its movements.

History alone was excluded from these daily lessons, and that was because the history of the Maquiritares is also the history of man's origins, the history of genesis, the history not so much of the visible as the invisible. Frenario taught it to his young men in the darkness of the night which closed the last day of the celebrations, and in a ceremony which was infinitely more solemn than all the other ceremonies which had taken place previously.

A great fire was burning in the middle of the village square, and Frenario stood upright and motionless beside it, his arms crossed over his chest. The circle of men turned around this center, forming the perfect hieroglyph of the sun, a moving circle with its glowing center immobile. No instrument accompanied this final dance. Frenario no longer pretended not to be part of the ceremony. He chanted in a high, nasal voice, and his men repeated each verse of the chant after him. Little children crouching at his feet kept up the fire. It was no longer Frenario who was speaking, but the Sun God speaking through his lips, telling them how he had dispersed the darkness, fashioned the earth, and established man upon it.

We flung a pinch of magnesium on the fire and as it flamed up the camera recorded the image of his face, impassive amid the sudden leaping light battling with the surrounding darkness.

This time Frenario was unable to evade us. He was compelled to play out his role to the end. As the hours passed, his body seemed to grow tauter, and he continued to speak, revealing in our presence all he knew of the fathomless mysteries of the universe. He did not move, but gradually his voice changed so as to become almost unrecognizable. He chanted in a lower and lower key, and his voice broke, and phrases followed of which we were unable to understand a single word. At last he fell silent and crouched down at a little distance from the fire, his face turned toward the east.

The men had formed two parallel lines, one before and the other behind him, and they now began a new dance which alternately brought them closer and took them farther away from the fire. The only accompaniment to this dance was the dry rattle of the maraca staff with its little horn hooves, as the man at the head of the file thumped it on the ground to mark the time. One by one the men discarded their robes of palm leaves and their crowns of wickerwork, and flung them into the fire. A small boy blew on the flames, and several yards away we heard his breath distinctly. The fire crackled and rapidly devoured the palm leaves. All other noise had now ceased, for the file leader had thrown away his maraca staff. There were only the two files of naked men coming almost imperceptibly closer to the fire. Only the rhythmic thud of their heels on the earth continued to sound like the steady beating of a heart. By now the palm leaves had been consumed in the red glow of the fire, as red as the bodies of the two files of men dancing round the village square, separated from each other only by the dying fire which cast deep shadows over their faces.

Then the beat of their naked feet accelerated and the files came close together over the fire, their faces almost touching; and now their heels drummed out the last vestiges of the fire, crushing the embers beneath their feet. Darkness closed in on the last sparks and the last noises, filling up the void into which the Maquiritares had disappeared.

We remained alone with the somber earth and the dark sky in which star after star was now beginning to appear. The festival of the new hut was over, and slowly we returned to our hammocks. We were dog tired, for we had filmed and photographed from early morning on, and the only thing we wanted to do now was sleep. But Sanoma and his little brother Mamai had felt themselves humiliated earlier, and now that all the Maquiritares had disappeared into the tribal hut after the conclusion of the festival, the solitude drew them toward us.

The fine costumes of the Maquiritares and their thrilling dances had fascinated the two Guaharibos, and they had done their best to deck themselves out in the same way. Closely watching the sons of Frenario, they had copied the palm-leaf garb for themselves, and they had painted their bodies all over with the same designs. They had no palm and feather crowns, so they had fashioned themselves red turbans from the last remnants of our red guayuco.

In this get-up they had tried to join the dance, but after a few clumsy steps they had been compelled to give up. Of course, they could not dance like real Maquiritares. They were unable to remember when they had to take three paces forward and two paces back, or when they had to bow and stamp on the earth five times or six times, and they could not follow the lead of the uanas when they marked the pause.

The Maquiritares had not liked their attempts to join in, and the men had interrupted their own chant to rebuke the interlopers angrily, while the women had gathered round to jeer at them. In the end the two Guaharibos had fled, abandoning their fine costumes and seeking out a dark corner in which to hide themselves and watch the rest of the celebrations in aggrieved silence.

Sanoma now climbed into my hammock, rolled two cigarettes, and asked for a light. He lighted them both and handed one to me.

"Could I go to your country," he asked, "or should I die if I went there?"

He had no idea of the burden he imposed upon my tender conscience.

"Yes, I think you probably would," I replied. "It's better that you shouldn't come to my country. You would very likely fall ill and die."

Mamai now came up as well. He asked me to let him look at my watch. He had known about it for some days now. When I had first arrived at Frenario's village, I had been suffering with tonsillitis which had given me a temperature of 104° for a couple of days. Only Sanoma and Mamai of all our Indians bothered about me. Sanoma had noticed that I always took a patient's pulse when I was acting as medicine man, and he attempted to use this procedure of the white man's medicine on me. Each morning he arrived to take hold of my wrist and to place his two palms on my forehead and on my chest. After a moment or two he would ask, as he had asked after cleaning a cooking pot:

"Atchika?" Is that all right?

And he would go off happily if I replied: "Yes, that's all right."

Mamai had squatted for hours at the head of my hammock, smiling and making designs with his fingers. One day I had an idea and I took out my watch to show him something he had never seen. It was not easy for me to hold any conversation with him, because he knew about as much Maquiritare as I knew Guaharibo. I put the watch to his ear to let him hear the ticking, and then I opened the case to show him the pendulum switching backward and forward tirelessly for all the seconds of all the hours of the day. His eyes opened wide and he whistled softly between his teeth. Then he went off to find his brother, with whom he talked long and earnestly in a low voice. After that it was a joint amusement for us to look together at the moving pendulum and listen to its ticking.

Night doesn't exist for Indians without dogs. In Diego's hut on the Ventuari, on New Year's Eve, at a time when near famine prevailed, a big yellow dog had landed suddenly on my head. The beast had somehow succeeded in clambering up onto the roof, attracted by one or two stale pieces of cassava bread we kept there and guarded as one of our most precious possessions. But before he had succeeded in reaching the basket in which they were concealed, he had slipped on the crossbeam and fallen onto my head. In Cejoyuma's village the dogs did not fall out of the roofs on our heads because Jean kept his bunch of heavy English keys ready to drive them off, but for all that, hunger kept them on the prowl all night, and they would bump into us violently as we lay asleep in our hammocks and they were scratching around to see if we had left any food near our fire.

Here, in Frenario's village, there was a dog which bayed to the moon. It woke up late, after the moon had already completed a great part of its trajectory. That was just the moment when Sanoma and Mamai had decided, after having studied my watch for a long time, to go to their own hammocks. First of all, the dog seemed to be clearing its throat, carefully and scrupulously, until the preliminary whufflings became almost insupportable, then it seemed to stretch itself tremendously in one mighty yawn, and after that it burst into song. I don't know any noise more hair-raising than the sound of that dog as it howled to the moon over the Sierra Parima.

After all we had seen and heard at the festival, I wanted to think, to reflect and ponder, to sum up all we knew definitely about the Indians, and to think about our return to civilization, which would begin in a few days' time, as soon as we left Frenario's village. But this dog with its howling distracted me. He had escaped from the world and the laws which laid down the place of dogs in the world. He had gone off on his own and I was being compelled to follow him. Together we barged around in the night air, describing loops and spirals in the ether. The beating of my heart followed the rhythm of his baying; my heart slowed down when the baying slowed down, and quickened when it quickened. In the end I could stand it no longer, and, leaving my hammock, where I had longed so much for sleep, I seized a matchet and went off toward the demon dog. For one moment I spotted him in the darkness and hurled my matchet at him. I missed and he disappeared into the night, yelping, this time, like a dog.

I went back to my hammock. It had begun to rain, and the drops pattered softly onto the roof of palm leaves above me. I tucked myself in and optimistically hoped for sleep at last, but no! Above my head the cocks and hens now began to stir and cackle and refused to let me sleep. All Indians kept them, but why no one knew, for they never seemed to get the idea that they could be eaten. Keeping chickens is a luxury to the Indians, as keeping peacocks or deer is to us. They say that man has a sense for utilitarian things before he thinks of luxury, or what are called unnecessary things. They say that the needs of the body prevail over the needs of the imagination, of man's soul or spirit. I don't believe it. The chickens kept by these Indians are answer enough to that. I also recalled "the devil's wife," whose acquaintance we had made earlier on, the mysterious little terra-cotta pot which served as an instrument of sacred music among the Piaroas. Before the Piaroa women obtained cooking pots from the white man they had cooked their food wrapped up in leaves or in calabashes, but at that time, which was not so long ago, the men of the tribe knew the secret of making terra-cotta pots to serve as "the devil's wife." It would have been a very useful thing to apply that knowledge to the kitchen, but that, so they thought, would be contrary to their religion, and so the men had kept their secret and left their womenfolk without cooking pots.

The silence and stillness which descended on the village of Frenario after the festival left us without an occupation, and our hands were idle. We had worked intensively for days on end, but now there was nothing left for us to do. All the essentials of our film were completed and we seemed to be encumbered by unnecessary impedimenta. We had no more gasoline, and so we gave our generating set away. To another man we offered our accumulators in exchange for a bow and some arrows. Frenario had always been in a hurry to see the back of us, but now he was becoming positively anxious. He set all the women of his village to work and prepared six great baskets of cassava bread for us on our way. He sent out his messengers through the forest to organize the stages of our journey, and yet he was unwilling to let us go by the route which chiefly attracted us and which looked the most normal and obvious way to reach the Brazilian plains.

His men had grown quite used to us by this time, and in his absence they would draw the map of the Yavadehudi and the Uraricuera into which it ran, using the points of their bows to make marks in the dust, and indicating the route from there to civilization, which could hardly be more than a month's journey away. But as soon as Frenario reappeared they would fall silent. When I put the matter point-blank to him he definitely refused to assist us if we tried to go down the Yavadehudi. That settled it, for we were not in a position to do without his assistance. We needed canoes and men, and he was the only man who could let us have them.

That was the general situation when one evening a Guaharibo appeared in the village square to obtain cassava for his people, who were camping in the forest a few days journey away. In exchange for the cassava he was offering great balls of cotton. The Guaharibos can spin the forest cotton, but that is as far as they have got. All they can do after that is to trade it for other things with the Maquiritares, who know how to make hammocks and so on with it.

"If you want to get to know the Guaharibos, why don't you go to those people?" Frenario asked. "The way there isn't difficult. I'll help you to get there, and once you're there you'll find that a path exists which leads beyond their territory to the Uraricuera."

That would lengthen our expedition by crossing back over the crest of the Sierra Parima, which, as we already knew, was very difficult to negotiate, in order to link up again with the Orinoco system in which these Guaharibos lived, and then retracing our steps over the crest of the Sierra Parima a third time to get back to the Amazonian side and go down the Uraricuera in order to reach civilization in Brazil. It would mean setting off on a new expedition which would be long and at the same time dangerous and difficult, particularly as our supplies, our trading goods, and our medicaments were approaching exhaustion.

However, at the same time it would mean penetrating into further unknown territory, and at the end of it all we should be certain of being able to return to civilization via Brazil and not via Venezuela as we had been compelled to do six months previously. It would mean going on after all, and not going back, and in the end we should complete the west to east crossing of the Sierra Parima, which was the main object of our expedition. We should have preferred to go down the Yavadehudi and reach Brazil that way, but if Frenario refused to help us then we had no choice in the matter. We adopted his suggestion and on May 16th we set off.

AMONG THE GUAHARIBOS

Having crossed the crest of the Sierra Parima a second time, but in the opposite direction, we pitched our camp on the banks of a river which flowed down the slope toward the west. Sanoma came up to me and declared with vigorous gestures:

"Entovare amonche, amonche," which meant that the Ventuari was a long way away, a very long way away. And then without having given me a chance to say anything, he added:

"I am going tomorrow morning. If you come back one day to the Ventuari, then bring me an electric lamp and batteries for hunting alligators. It's much more practical that way than with torches."

Diego had already left us to return to Cejoyuma's village, where his wife with the chromium-plated scissors was waiting for him, and thus Sanoma and his brother were the only remaining companions of our first adventures in the Sierra Parima. The river on whose banks we were camping would allow them to get back to the Ventuari without any very great difficulties. There would be no one else now to replace Sanoma, and both he and Mamai knew it as well as we did, but it was useless to insist.

They left us at dawn the next day. Above his hammock each of them carried a few cases marked "Eastman Kodak Co., Rochester." These had once contained film and were now filled with various extraordinary oddments which remained to them as souvenirs of our adventures in common and would probably serve them for a long time on the upper Ventuari, where perhaps they might even become chiefs by virtue of the experience they had gained with the white men in the forest and along the rivers.

Then we went off in our turn. Frenario escorted us as he had promised, carrying the heaviest of our cases on his own shoulders and forcing the pace of our column as much as he could in his anxiety to be able to leave us as far as possible from his own people. Ten men accompanied him, but alas! they were almost all to leave us before long.

The man with the shaven head acted as our guide into the territory of the Okomatadi, one of the most savage and barbarous groups of all the Guaharibo tribe. A small group of their warriors came to meet us and bring us into their camp, which was still a few days march ahead, and we drew our canoes ashore before following them. (We took to the river again later, when it became necessary to reach the crest of the Sierra Parima for the third and last time on our way east.) Then we marched resolutely northward through the thick forests of the Okomatadi. We went on for four days without seeing anything but the very narrow path, blazed here and there by a branch twisted off by hand, which led toward the lair of the Guaharibos. The foliage around us was so dense that it might almost have been night all day long.

At last we came out into a small clearing in which there were six clumsy and lopsided huts with their backs to the forest. The encampment stank. Altogether the impression was one of unspeakable poverty, and our hearts felt sick at the sight. Not even the ground itself had been wholly won away from the forest, and it was still covered with a variety of rotting vegetation. The general atmosphere was very gloomy, and a stale smell brooded over everything. Half collapsed trees leaned together over the small huts with their roofs of leaves. They had no proper doors and the walls were made of palm leaves just propped against the eaves. A spectral population of old men, women, and children lived in this sinister place. They were pale and emaciated, and their skin, eaten by mildew and pests, looked as though it had never seen the light of the sun.

Guaharibos have neither hatchets nor knives, and to clear a little space in which they can live in the forest they have little else but their hands and their teeth. To fell a single tree is a more difficult undertaking for them than to raze a whole forest is for us. The only tool they have invented is what the Maquiritares contemptuously call "the Guaharibo knife." It consists of a small piece of wood with an agouti tooth lashed to one end of it.

Such was the Guaharibo encampment. I hardly dare call it a village, and yet it represented the fullest form of social organization we ever encountered among them. At the sight of us, the women and the children cowered close to their tumble-down huts, standing there motionless, their eyes fixed on us, as though some unholy terror had petrified their limbs. The old men slowly raised their arms and opened the palms of their hands toward us. Among Indians this sign means: "Come no closer."

We sat down in the middle of the small clearing on the first of our cases, which the porters had just brought in. We sat there for half an hour, perhaps three quarters of an hour, in silence.

The old men, the women, and the children with their distended stomachs which suggested internal parasitism—horrifying children with unnaturally fixed and staring eyes full of midges—watched us in silence from the shelter of their primitive huts. We had arrived first, having all four outdistanced our column. Now we had to wait and not move in order to give these people back a feeling of confidence. The ground at our feet was sticky, slimy, and covered with filth and half-rotted debris of all kinds, and there were swarms of buzzing flies, fleas, and other insects.

Above our heads thousands of winged termites flew around, and as the evening approached they died one after the other in full flight, dropping to the ground, falling into our hair, our beards, and our eyes. At the moment of death their big black wings detached themselves and floated for a while after the bodies had fallen, filling the air as though with ashes. It almost seemed that nature had deliberately decided to add a macabre touch to the desolation around us.

Gradually the women and children grew less fearful, and they crept out of their shelters, coming toward us slowly and by short stages, pausing for a long while after each, and deciding to venture a little further only when they were quite sure we were not going to move. Then I realized that even in this tragic and lowly state man still had something of the principle of beauty which is the very fundament of all his hopes, of all his faiths and of all the staunch beliefs in the future of his kind. After a while we grew accustomed to our depressing surroundings and to this primitive village of the Okomatadi, prehistoric men who by some strange chance had persisted in this blank spot on our planet. The sudden and unexpected contact with such eerie reality had first tightened our chests and stretched our nerves, but slowly the feeling of tension left us, and our eyes, which at first had looked away as though from some unspeakable horror, now looked at the scene with greater understanding.

Behind so much filth and so much sickness, behind those skeleton-like figures eaten by all manner of leprous diseases, behind those faces hideously deformed by the filthy Guaharibo habit of chewing a large quid of green tobacco mixed into a paste with ashes which pushed the underlip forward grotesquely, behind those eyes only gradually losing the veil of fear which had descended over them, banishing all other expression when they saw us emerge from the forest, we began to discern gentle curves, tender gestures, naive curiosity, and strange wishes and desires—unformulated and perhaps incapable of formulation—all signs of a reality as absolutely human as our own.

It was something apart from race, geographical place, or position in time. It was an unforgettable earnest of the fraternity which bound us to these strange beings despite the thousands of years that separated us.

When all our porters had come in, and after they had talked for a while to the women, we opened one of our cases and took out boxes of matches. It seemed to us that quick fire would be the best gift to offer them. Some of the women had crept back to the shelter of their huts, and we beckoned them forward again, calling out:

"Hua'to! Ed'he!"

Fire! Come and take!

At that they came closer again. On her hip almost every woman carried a baby supported by a coarsely made band of bark strips passed bandoleer-wise over her shoulder. Each put one hand over the child's eyes to protect its vision, and half extended the other toward us. The first woman who took a match put it into her mouth, much to Frenario's superior amusement—he had just joined us. He took the box from her and showed her how to strike a match. None of the women could resist the magic of these little sticks of fire, and they all closed in eagerly.

The chief of the village was a puny little fellow, but tough for all that, since he had carried one of our cases weighing over a hundred pounds the whole way to the camp. He made a sign to the women and they brought up a large calabash full of banana liquid, the ceremonial drink of the Guaharibos. Taking the calabash, he drank from it himself, no doubt to show us that it was not poisoned, and then he handed it to us. Frenario made a gesture of disgust, but we took the calabash and drank without hesitation. The warm liquid flowing into our stomachs was comforting, and it brought us closer to our hosts.

Now it was the turn of the old men to grow less timid, and they too came and squatted around us. Pierre quickly obtained his usual facile success with his double-jointed thumb and his trick of rolling his tongue round and round inside a distended cheek.

Then suddenly a great clamor arose in the forest behind the huts, and everyone turned round and looked toward the path which led into it. About a dozen naked and muscular men covered with daubings rushed into the clearing. They were the hunters of the tribe, who had now returned from the chase. Without hesitation they rushed toward us, shouting and waving their bows and arrows over their heads. One of them was carrying a great armadillo on his back and he now flung it down beside us. Frenario's face clouded over, but we knew the Guaharibos sufficiently well by this time not to be disturbed by these noisy demonstrations. They began to pull our beards and we lifted them into the air, and they tried to do the same to us, grunting tremendously with the exertion. They pulled at the rags in which we were clothed and beat themselves on the chests vigorously, their eyes shining and their mouths open. Green tobacco juice ran down their chins. If the Maquiritares had not come to our assistance, we should have found ourselves naked again as Pierre and I had on the occasion of our first encounter with Guaharibos on the upper Ventuari six months earlier. But the Maquiritares seized them roughly, shook them vigorously, and made them understand that if they hoped for presents they must behave themselves a little more calmly, and this they soon did.

"They want to give you bows, arrows, tobacco, sugar cane, and bananas," said Frenario, and he planted himself beside the case we began to open. He had already told us when we left the

Yavadehudi that if he accompanied us personally to "those monkeys" it would be to see for himself what we gave them. He was reassured when he saw us hand a length of flowered cotton cloth to the Guaharibo chief. The Maquiritares much prefer the red cloth from which they make their guayucos. The flowered cloth they regard with amused contempt as fit only for "monkeys," that is, Guaharibos.

When night approached, the Guaharibos offered us a hut in the center of their village, but the thought of sleeping there horrified us, the whole place being smelly and full of vermin. On the other hand, we were loath to refuse for fear of offending them. Frenario saved the situation by ordering his men to construct a large rancho a little apart from the Guaharibo huts. He was not concerned with the feelings of any Guaharibos. He began to bargain with the chief for a piece of the armadillo the Guaharibo warriors had brought in. After a while he broke off the discussion with obvious annoyance. Coming toward me, he took me by the arm.

"Come on," he said in Spanish. "The man's meanness makes me sick. Let him keep his armadillo."

We walked toward the rancho that his men were just completing. In the middle of the path was a large tree whose trunk had a swelling like a buzzing abscess. It was a termites' nest, but its occupants had just previously performed their dance of death around our heads and now there were no more warriors left to defend the citadel. Four columns of ants were now marching up the trunk waving their feelers. They disappeared into the empty nest, reappearing after a while carrying all the treasures the termites had laid up for themselves in years of labor.

Although the air was stagnant under the three-hundred-foot high ceiling of forest, it seemed pure and fresh in the rancho by comparison with the Guaharibo village. We were short of food now, and all we had to eat was a little of the cassava we had brought with us. The Guaharibo chief's avarice had deprived us of our supper. To have argued with him any further would have lowered Frenario in his own eyes. When we had eaten our frugal supper, we stretched ourselves out in our hammocks. Once again we passed a night within enormously thick walls of vegetation to the accompaniment of all the usual forest noises, cracklings, crepitations, soughings, and rumblings.

After dark it began to rain, a heavy and monotonous equatorial downpour, warm and persistent as though it were never going to stop. The hammocks of Frenario and his men and our own hammocks were slung in the middle of our shelter. The rain formed gutters along the roof and the water poured off to the ground on all sides.

Then I heard a different noise, and looking in the direction of the village, I saw a small point of light glowing in the darkness. It was a human noise and it went on as persistently as the rain itself, coming to me monotonously through the foliage and the sodden air.

The Guaharibo sorcerer was chanting as he crouched over his fire. All around him and around us, around our two small and precarious human oases, was the omnipresent unknown. Among the hammocks of his sleeping people the Guaharibo sorcerer squatted by the side of his little fire which must never be allowed to go out, and there he chanted.

I do not know what chants the Guaharibo sorcerers intone, and I do not know why that particular sorcerer stayed up that particular night to intone them, crouching with his puny body over his small fire, a fire perhaps a foot across, not big enough to burst into flames. And how could it, for the forest wood of which it was made was more rotten than dead. Somehow as I listened I was impressed with a feeling of urgent necessity I can still recall today: some urgent need sent those words scattering into the night, words I could not understand, but whose alarm and appeal I could sense.

As the Guaharibo sorcerer squatted there by his glowing hearth amid the sleeping men, women, and children of his tribe and intoned his hurried invocations, a fire burned in his own belly. Inside him was a small sun and he identified himself with the fire before him. He was the receptacle and the guardian of the flame by which his people grew and multiplied. He exorcized. He labored. He wrestled with the monstrous forces of the unknown which crowded in on him—three feet away, eighteen inches away—jostling each other. The little sun in his vitals, like the one that burned at his feet, was his sole weapon: it preserved and quickened life.

He chanted there to secure the future of mankind. His breath radiated in all directions as though from the center of a star. At the points of the star his people slept, their bodies traversed by his breath. The forest all around him, and between him and me, trembled, cracked, writhed, and swelled. And I knew that over thousands of square miles of forest shrouded in the night, there were similar small fires flicked here and there. Over thousands and thousands of square miles of country, between sorrow and laughter, the life of naked man advanced slowly and almost imperceptibly, between heat and cold, good and evil, around such little men who chanted at the center of their stars.

Then behind me and very close I heard furtive movements and little scratchings. Noiselessly I half turned to see what it was: Frenario was stealing our cassava. It was all the food we had, but it was not for himself he was taking it. It was for his dog, and the beast squatted by his side and fed out of his hand. I turned back and closed my eyes. I did not want him to know that I had seen what he was doing.

Between us and the Guaharibo village there was now nothing but the nest of the dead termites. The ants had long ago finished their pillaging and returned in military order to their own citadel.

THE MONKEY DANCE

We remained with the Okomatadi for some time, and we were able to study the everyday life of a Guaharibo group quite closely. It was very different from the active busy life of the Maquiritares. It would seem that the simple notion of labor, so essential in the one group, is still unknown in the other, and it is this fundamental difference in the lives and habits of the two tribes that makes the Maquiritares look down with such contempt on the Guaharibos. As the Okomatadi women have no cassava plantations to cultivate, they spend a great deal of the day in their hammocks, playing with their babies and with the little animals that surround them, indifferently distributing their milk among everything still small. Thus more than once we saw a baby sharing its mother's breasts with a puppy, and on another occasion we saw two small monkeys which had been brought in by the hunters, being suckled at the breast like twin babies. And the little girls of the tribe would often try to imitate their mothers and offer their little nipples to their brothers and their cousins.

The Guaharibo men cannot really be said to hunt. They play with the forest much as their women play with their own bodies and their babies. They never organize real hunting expeditions as the Maquiritares do, nor track down big game with their dogs through many miles of forest. The Guaharibos do not wrest their living from nature as the Maquiritares do. They do not live by battles and conquests, but by a kind of pilfering. They are still at what ethnographers call the picking stage. When man has not yet developed adequate technical aids he prefers to trick nature rather than fight her in the open. Thus the Guaharibos rarely eat tapir or boar meat, but they often catch birds, rodents, and insects. They are not really hunters at all, but just bungling amateurs. They pick the berries off the trees like blackberries in the hedges. They steal the honey of the bees—something which arouses the particular disgust of the Maquiritares—and they often feed on unexpected and improvised dishes, for example, worms, caterpillars, and large flowers whose centers are full of maggots and other insects.

One day they learned that we had been present at the festival with which the Maquiritares had celebrated the building of their new tribal hut, and so, knowing that music and dancing interested us, they decided on their own initiative to show us "the monkey dance," which is the most important ceremony of their ritual. This dance lasts all day long and is performed, like the "trading dance" and the war dance we had already witnessed on the upper Ventuari, entirely without music. The men, bedecked with black and white feathers, run, jump, and contort their bodies, marking time with their heels on the ground. Their gait is obviously intended to represent that of a large monkey. Altogether the monkey seems to play a role in their ancestral mythology comparable to that of the wild boar in the mythology of the Maquiritares. Waving the fringes of palm leaves, the women sing and dance around the men during the ceremony. For the occasion they wear special skirts consisting of long strips of banana leaf.

Then one day the time came for us to think of departure. It was not only the Guaharibos we were leaving this time, but the Sierra Parima itself and the whole Indian world in which we had now lived for so many months. We were to attempt the final stage of our adventure, and at the end of it civilization awaited us, with its haste and its rapacity, but also with its power and its glory. We had grown so used to the life we were leading among the Indians that we found ourselves almost doubting the real existence of what we called "the other world," just as today we call the world of the Indians which we left behind us "the other world."

MAY 28TH TO JULY 2ND 1950

PART 5

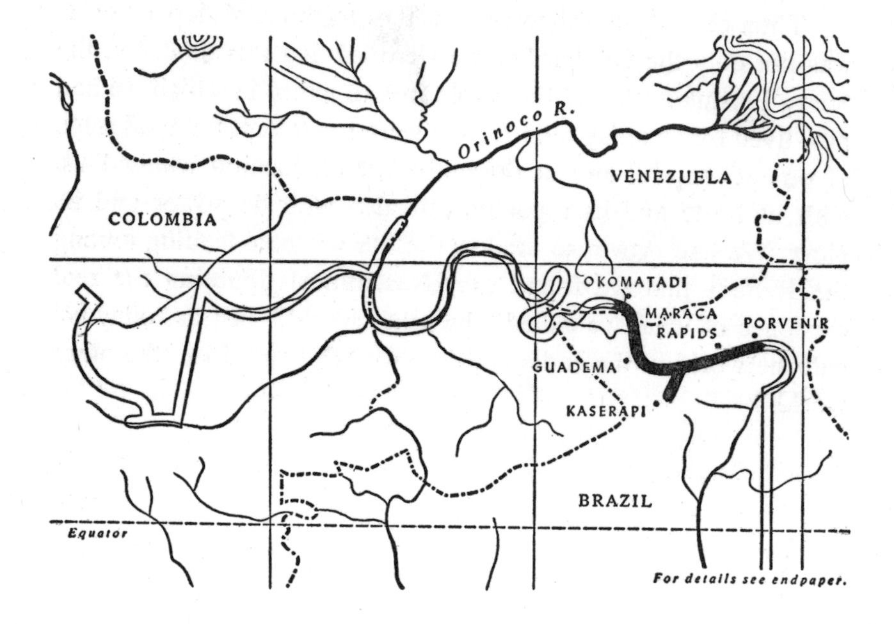

The Return

THE PRECARIOUS THREAD OF A NATIVE'S MEMORY

OUR MISSION WAS ACHIEVED. We had reached the center of the Sierra Parima; we had gotten to know its inhabitants, the Maquiritares and the Guaharibos; we had shared their lives; and, safely stowed away in our cases, there were precious evidences of what we had seen and heard. It had not been easy to get to the center of the Sierra Parima, but now it was proving even more difficult to get out.

We were still on the western slope of the mountains, and we

now had to climb up to the watershed again and find a river on the other side which would take us to the Amazon.

We had gradually come to realize that this eastern slope of the Sierra Parima was universally feared by all the Indians. Frenario had been absolutely opposed to letting us go down the Yavadehudi, which ran at the foot of his village, although by doing so we should have saved at least a month of our time and the arduous necessity of recrossing the summit of the Sierra Parima twice more. His refusal had been quite uncompromising, but his reasons had never been made fully clear: one day he would say that it was because of the difficulties of finding provisions on that slope; another day it would be on account of fierce, unknown tribes who would attack us and eat everybody; a third day it would be because there were numerous dangerous rapids which were impossible to negotiate in the rainy season. In short, he presented us with a variety of excuses, some of them quite ridiculous, others quite reasonable, but we were never able to discover the real reason, or reasons, for his refusal.

The American Hamilton Rice flew over the mouth of the Auari—the river known to the Maquiritares as the Yavadehudi —and, on the map of the eastern slope of the Sierra Parima he drew up as a result of his numerous aerial reconnaissances, he indicated the presence of what looked like ruined stone bridges at the junction of the Auari and the Parima, or the Rio Padamo of the Maquiritares and the Guaharibos, which formed the Uraricuera, which we were now attempting to reach. Civilization began again at about three hundred, or five hundred miles from this center of mystery and speculation. Hamilton Rice gave no further details, but legend speaks of "the ruins of a town built of stone" to be found along the lower Yavadehudi not far from its confluence. Now the distance from Frenario's village to that spot could not have been much more than a hundred and twenty-five miles. If this mysterious ruined town existed so near to him he must certainly have known of it. Was it some secret Maquiritare capital? And was that why he refused so obstinately to let us take the route that led to it? It was easier to ask the question than to find an answer to it.

At any event, when we finally left the Okomatadi Indians, Frenario and the majority of his men refused to accompany us any further. Only four men remained with us, three Maquiritares and the Guaharibo slave of one of them, and he had no alternative but to go where his master went. Thus we parted from Frenario very much as we had met him: without having solved any of the mysteries which surrounded his person or the country into which he had withdrawn.

After he had departed with his men, we too set off. We had to reach the Merevari, as the upper reaches of the Caura were called. The Caura was a tributary of the Orinoco, which meant that we must then turn up stream. Not far from its source we should then find a small tributary called the Uania, and from there, Pancho, the Maquiritare with the Guaharibo slave, knew a passage through to Brazil. That was the northern extremity of the Sierra Parima, at the spot where the mountains swung eastward to form the chain of the Pacaraima, the oblique continuation of the Sierra Parima itself.

A number of Guaharibos accompanied us on our trek to the first river. Very few of them arrived there. As we proceeded eastward, most of them were seized by the same inexplicable fear as our former guides and they deserted us, sometimes abandoning their burdens in the middle of the path, sometimes stealing away noiselessly from the rancho at night. In this way our little force diminished in numbers every day. When we arrived at the Uania Canyon there were only eight of us left: the four of us (members of the expedition proper), Pancho and his Guaharibo slave, and "Monsieur Non" and "The Italian," two men from Frenario's village who were obviously bolder than their companions and who had made a good impression on us.

We had promised each man a gun and a supply of powder and shot on the day we reached civilization. All four men were tough, robust types, and Pancho, Monsieur, and the Italian were experienced watermen. Pancho's special mark of distinction was that he knew more about the country through which we were passing than the others did. He was the last survivor of a group of Maquiritares who had onces lived along the Uraricuera on the other side of the Uania Canyon, and who were mentioned by Koch-Grünberg in his reports. He had made the crossing as a child but he was confident that he could find the way again.

Our fate now depended on the precarious thread of his memory.

According to his calculations, the journey would take about a month. On the way we should not come across a single village where we might reprovision before reaching the Brazilian plains. We could expect no sort of human help so long as we were in the mountains, and we would have to rely entirely on ourselves for food: partly on the food we took with us and partly on whatever opportunities for hunting and fishing presented themselves on the way.

There were not thirty pounds left of the five or six baskets of cassava we had brought with us from Frenario's village, and as for hunting and fishing, although they were relatively rewarding in the lowlands, they were very uncertain in the higher mountainous regions. We should in all probability find the same conditions of life up there as those under which the Maquiritares of Cejoyuma lived, and their main sustenance consisted of boiled worms.

The only weapons we had left were two single-barreled sporting guns, and they were so damaged by the forest, the rain, and the various canoeing mishaps we had suffered that cartridges could be inserted into the breeches only with the aid of a hammer. And the breech closure had to be consolidated with a piece of wire for fear of an explosion.

We were not much better off for ammunition, either. We had only five metal cartridge cases for the two guns, and they were so battered and rusty that they had to be filed and oiled after each shot before they could be used again. And despite all the precautions we had taken, our powder had got so damp that we had to halt during the rare lulls in the downpour and put out the powder in little heaps in the sun for it to dry.

As for shot, there was so little of it left that we had come to regard it as precious, and so we preferred to use odd bits of lead cut up from the elements of an old storage battery we now no longer required for other purposes.

Our baggage had to be carried over mountains. We had seventeen cases and Indian baskets full of films, notebooks, and our ethnographic collection. All in all they weighed over three-quarters of a ton and they had to be carried in the three canoes we had managed to obtain—not without difficulty—with the last of our stock in trade.

Before embarking on the Uania, which we knew was broken by numerous rapids, we all four undressed and wrapped up our precious "Orinoco-Amazon" film in our clothes for its better protection.

To the great delight of our men we adopted the same little red guayuco to cover our nakedness as they wore. Henceforth we and they were more alike than we had ever been before, for now only our beards and the rather lighter shade of our skins prevented us from passing altogether as Indians. Our naked feet were as bruised, blotched, and scarred as theirs were, and on the morning we set off, Luis and Pierre had to make heroic efforts to use their paddles properly, because their hands were covered with the type of festering sore caused by the mildew of the twilight forest, which only a change of climate and a different way of life could cure.

On the morning of May 28, 1950, we took down our hammocks from under a small shelter of leaves, and the eight men of our company embarked in our three canoes and set off through the unceasing and monotonous rain of the Parima. Jean was forbidden to touch a paddle or a pole. The skin of his hands was still intact, and he had to film the interesting incidents of our journey to the very end, so he sat with his camera in the center of the largest of our canoes. Our three Maquiritares took the helm in each of the canoes, while Pierre, Luis, the Guaharibo, and I wielded the other paddles.

For the first few days the voyage up the Uania was easy enough. The river ran lazily and quite enchantingly between curtains of drooping liana which hung down and trailed in the water from amid the green foliage of trees perhaps one hundred and fifty feet high on either bank. Flocks of blue parakeets crossed the sky from time to time, while great yellow and silver fish leaped out of the water here and there, seeming to pause for a moment, balanced miraculously on their tails, before falling back again in a shower of spray.

Pushing the water behind us with the flat of our paddles, we advanced yard by yard up the river, singing anything and everything that came into our heads, including the sacred chants of the Indians and old French songs. The three Maquiritares tried to join in, laughing heartily at their failure when the song was not in their repertoire. But when we did our best to sing Indian tunes, it was our turn to laugh at our awkwardness.

We set off in the mornings very early, before the sun had properly risen, and we halted for the night an hour or two before darkness set in. In that two hours a couple of our men would set off wordlessly into the forest, a matchet in one hand and a rifle over one shoulder in the hope of finding something to stay our ever-present hunger. While they were gone the rest of us would build the rancho. At other times we would wait for nightfall and then all go off together along the river bank carrying resin torches and looking for some unfortunate little alligator asleep near the bank, or a lapa, the big agouti of South America, whose flesh tasted succulent to us. The animal would be fascinated by the glare of the torch and would stand motionless, staring at the light, while we approached and planted a spear in its back. Then for a couple of hours we would lie in our hammocks near the cooking pot, whose contents were boiling over a star-shaped fire. We waited for the moment when Pancho, our very learned chef, would give the signal that the feast was ready.

THE FINAL BARRIER AND A COMPROMISE

Days and nights passed in this fashion while we pressed on for miles up river. At last one evening, when we were strenuously poling our canoes forward because the strength of the current had very greatly increased, a huge mountain face rose white and bluish on the distant horizon, its summit surrounded by wisps of white clouds. It was the final crest, the barrier which separated us from the other world for which we were making, the barrier we still had to cross.

Our progress became increasingly difficult. The river was enclosed in a gigantic fault in the mountain face, and in the rock the somber red of porphyry alternated with the light blue color of some scintillating stone. The surface of the water, which had previously been like a mirror, was now ruffled and broken, and white with spume. The rapids were ahead. We had to jump out of our canoes and push them yard by yard up stream against the current, bending forward with the water up to our armpits. Before long, even this method of progress became impossible as the current increased in violence. What lay ahead of us was no longer a river, but a mass of tossing water pouring with a tremendous roar down the steps of a great staircase of stone.

"We shall have to go on by land," said Pancho. "A day's march from here the river is calmer again and we shall be able to paddle for two or three days more to where the path leads across the mountain."

Pancho's day turned out to be over a week. We had to open up a path along the river bank, and then push, pull, and carry our canoes along it one after the other, and our seventeen cases as well. And all this time we ate properly only once. The growing altitude made game scarce and the cascading water depopulated the river banks of animal life. When we finally arrived above the falls we were so exhausted that we had strength enough only to sling our hammocks and crawl into them. We slept for something like eighteen hours on end, and when we woke up Pancho was missing.

"He's gone on ahead," Monsieur Non informed us. "He wants to spy out the land. He's taken a gun with him to shoot some meat."

That night Pancho returned empty-handed and obviously worried. He turned in and went to sleep without saying a word. We hardly had any cassava left. For several days now we had been rationing it strictly: each man received a handful morning and evening, the equivalent of a rather small piece of bread. Our stomachs had to be content with that. When he awoke the next morning, Pancho told us that he had seen no game of any kind and that he had not succeeded in finding the path.

We were sitting in our hammocks, our feet dangling over the sides. Pierre, obsessed with the thought of a real cigarette with real tobacco in it, took the next best thing and rolled up a little piece of light-colored bark which he prepared to smoke. Luis scratched himself with a vague air. Jean hummed a tune. But none of us got out of our hammocks; instead we lay back in them again and stared vacantly at the foliage over our head.

The whole day passed like this, and when the sun was just going down Pancho came to shake us. He wanted a nail and a file, the precious file necessary to prepare our cartridges. Jean got up and went down to the river with him to our cases to get him the nail and the file. Pancho took two stones from the river and squatted down by the fire. He worked until nightfall, heating the nail in the fire, bending it, cooling it, and filing it to the shape he wanted. Then he took one of the strings that held up his hammock and went off again toward the river.

In the middle of the night we were awakened by a great to-do. We looked toward the center of our rancho and there we saw our four native companions crouching round the cooking pot which was simmering on the fire. Beside them was a bloody knife, and on a leaf of the false banana tree the half of a fish as big as a salmon. We got out of our hammocks and went toward the cooking pot with such astonished faces that the four Indians burst out laughing. We learned that along the river's edge there were sometimes pools or pockets of stagnant water in which such fish were caught as though in a trap.

"They're very stupid fish," Pancho explained.

He had fashioned the nail into the kind of fish hook required and had baited it with a certain kind of flower. The only inhabitant of the torrent-like rivers of the Sierra Parima that we knew of was a sort of sardine without scales which clung onto the rocks by means of an abdominal sucker and could therefore be picked off by hand. This was the only form of fishing known to the Guaharibos.

The meal revived us and we decided to do something before we grew too weak with hunger again and lost the will to act. Pancho was to go off the following morning in search of the path again, while the rest of us spread out in all directions in the hope of falling in with game of some sort.

It was not surprising that Pancho had failed to find the path at the first attempt. After all, no Maquiritare had used it for the last fifteen years, and so the matchet strokes which blazed the trail had quite naturally become obliterated.

But for all our determination, the next day was another black one. We found no game of any sort. Although Pancho actually found the path, his face when he returned in the evening showed us at once that all was not well. It appeared that it rose so steeply to the crest that it would be quite impossible for us with our inadequate man-power to get the canoes and the baggage up it.

"We can't go on so heavily loaded," he declared gloomily. "The canoes are too heavy and there aren't enough of us to carry them to the other side of the mountain. We shall have to travel light if we are to get over at all. Let me and the others go on ahead and you stay here with the cases and the canoes and wait for us to come back. There must be Guaharibos on the other side of the mountain and we can bring them back with us to carry over the canoes and the baggage. It won't take long."

We firmly refused to countenance the suggestion. We had no desire to find ourselves alone again and without help. A rather acrimonious discussion ensued. Pancho dug his heels in obstinately because he was afraid. The bad weather and the lack of food made a threatening combination. The other men listened to the discussion wordlessly, but we knew that whatever Pancho finally decided to do they would fall in with. Our lives were at stake now. These Indians just had to be persuaded to do what we wanted them to do, but it was not easy. The temptation of coroto promised to them when we reached civilization was not enough to reinforce our arguments. And our urgent reasons for wanting to go on without our baggage were not sufficiently cogent for them. If we could not persuade them we should have to compel them. But how?

We thought of our revolver, the only revolver of the expedition. We had brought it with us as a concession to what our fellow whites had always said about the Indians, but for a year now it had been getting rustier and rustier at the bottom of one of the cases. Should we have to fall back on it after all? It might, of course, gain us a temporary material victory, but at the same time it would mean the breakdown of one of the chief resolutions of our expedition. We had not the heart to try it.

For some time the atmosphere remained tense.

"Leave all the cases here," Pancho said as though he were making a concession. "With two of the canoes, our hammocks and our matchets we might be able to do it."

A second time we said no very firmly. Pancho looked at us. He was puzzled and sad. He could not understand that the cases were almost as valuable to us as our very lives. We realized that it was very difficult for him. Apart from our films they contained nothing but ordinary everyday objects of Indian life, nothing in the least rare. There were pieces of wood and bone, feather headdresses, and so on, very common things. So why did the white men, who were, of course, rich, attach so much importance to them? Not even an Indian would risk his life for so little.

Then we made our proposal. We undertook, the four of us, to carry the heaviest canoe up the mountain side.

"The rest of the work we'll share, of course," I said.

That did the trick and the next morning we began our attack on the slope. There was little more than a mile of it but it was so steep that in our weakened state we had to use every root and branch we came across as a hold to pull ourselves up even without being burdened. It seemed very long odds against getting the canoes up.

It took us a week, but finally we managed it.

When the Indians observed the vigor and determination with which we went to work, they were put on their mettle. They were unwilling to be outdone by white men and soon our original arrangement was forgotten and we did everything together, panting, pulling, and pushing hour after hour and day after day up a slippery, muddy slope rising at an angle of forty-five degrees to the summit of the last mountain that separated us from the other world. Once we had crossed it, our path would go downhill all the way.

Pancho fastened a length of liana to the bow of each canoe, and then, from tree trunk to tree trunk, this line, perhaps thirty feet long, held the dead weight of the boat and prevented it from slipping back while we took a breather after every combined push got it up another few feet.

Our hands became so torn and raw that the pain kept us awake at nights despite our exhaustion. They were caked with dried blood and mud, and our pulses beat in them painfully like overburdened hearts.

But the human body is tougher than one thinks until some quite exceptional situation forces one to try everything in order to survive at all, and then it shows its real capacities. One develops a will of iron and one's attention is grimly concentrated on the matter in hand. One is impervious to all suggestions of danger. The flesh, too, rises to the occasion: wounds look after themselves and heal quickly on their own. Every morning we doubted whether we should be able to start work again, and every morning our stiff and anguished fingers closed round the liana with determination, and we pulled and pushed until finally all three canoes and all our baggage were safely at the top.

During all this time and during the many days that followed on our journey from the Uania to the Cuato, which is a tributary of the Amazon rising on the other side of the mountain and flowing down its face, we ate properly only once, and that was thanks to Jean's presence of mind. He woke up earlier than the rest of us one morning, and spotting a band of monkeys gamboling in the trees over his head, he automatically seized a rifle and fired, killing two of them.

At last we arrived at the Cuato. It was a small, muddy, yellowish stream trickling lazily through a marsh of spongy vegetation, bracken, palm, and arborescent growths. The evening on which our three canoes finally floated on its surface represented one of the greatest triumphs of our whole adventure. It was raining in torrents and we built a small shelter of palms by the side of the stream and slung our hammocks there.

After that, instead of sleeping, we passed half the night in singing. We were quite drunk merely to hear the sound of water flowing away to the west quite near us. Pancho talked without stopping.

"Tomorrow there'll be alligators and fish in the river," he said. "We'll have a torchlight hunt, and then we'll eat for three hours on end, and belch for another three after that."

The following morning we set off. I was in the leading canoe, and Luis was in the second. Pierre and Jean brought up the rear in the heaviest canoe. The day passed in swooping down the mountainside at an ever-increasing speed amid fantastic surroundings. In the full rainy season, the Cuato had overflowed its banks to such an extent that it was now nothing but a current threading its way through an immense inundation. There was nothing to be seen of river banks on either side. In all directions the water lost itself amid the vegetation, and as the altitude rapidly decreased the vegetation grew imperceptibly less harsh and more lush. There were no trees on the lower Cuato, but only arborescent growths, swollen with water, fragile but gigantic, a frail and fantastic tangle never lower than sixty feet.

Each of the obstacles that arose before us as the principal current of the river wound its way amid plants, liana, and foliage could have been pushed over with a shove of the shoulder, but at the same time it was bristling with invisible defenses—hard, black thorns, sometimes almost a foot long and as sharp as needles, and swarming with myriads of ants of all sorts, wasps, spiders, and a thousand and one other species of insect life. They fell onto our heads and down our necks, immediately stinging and biting the human flesh that chance had presented them as an unexpected feast. At each clash it was almost as though we had suddenly broken up a somnolent stillness consecrated by centuries of forgetfulness, and then this microscopic world of insects would pounce upon us instantly and organize a bacchanalia with our flesh and blood. On the evening of that day, I noted down that the neighborhood of the Cuato represented the most extraordinary proof of the reality behind the fantastic dreams of a Jacques Callot, a Hieronymus Bosch, or a Max Ernst. It was impossible to distinguish the vegetable from the animal there. I wonder how many species of insect still unknown to the entomologists of the world I brushed hastily off my neck and shoulders and disentangled from my hair and beard each time our canoe forced its way through one of the many tangles of vegetation.

Just as one sees a succession of lightning flashes on a summer's evening, so I saw a succession of insects: insects like leaves; insects like fragments of half-rotted vegetation with spots of putrefaction for eyes; insects like pieces of dead wood, that suddenly revealed legs and began to walk; insects like moss moving along like a caterpillar and leaving behind an acid trail of slime quite capable of eating into wood.

Toward five o'clock in the evening the native who was with me in the first canoe jumped up suddenly from the piece of wood that served as a seat and exclaimed:

"Ed'dhe adimi! Aaké tuna coneda!"

"There's the real river! The bad water is over!"

I rose too, but my head was swimming and I nearly overbalanced. When I tried to focus my eyes on any particular point ahead, everything blurred and danced around me. With a tremendous effort I managed at last to see the horizon, which had suddenly withdrawn into the distance. It was true: we had arrived in the river proper. The forest had been left behind at last. Before us the river lost itself in an immensity of space, and clouds wandered over the sky at a distance we had not seen for ages. A great mass of scintillating water disappeared toward the east, while to the west rose blue and somber mountains. The Sierra Parima had been crossed. It now lay behind us.

A great river of silver sparkling water emerging from a thick forest into the open, a broad expanse of water reflecting the sky, the surface just ruffled by the wind as it glides through low banks —I know no more miraculous sight than that. It is like recovering both oxygen and the use of one's lungs at the same time. It is like recovering both the world and one's own body at the same time.

It was liberty. It was delivery from a green jail, the terrifying and yet so beautiful forest.

SUCCESS BRINGS FRESH DANGERS

The river must have been the Uraricuera, or Rio Parima, an upper tributary of the Rio Branco, a river which is to be found very clearly marked on all the maps of Brazil. Not so very far ahead of us it would broaden out tremendously and large steamers would move across its surface.

The canoe in which Jean and Pierre were traveling had not caught up with us, and we pitched camp for the night on the left bank of the Uraricuera not far from the mouth of the Cuato. The other canoe would arrive later, we were sure. We had only two hammocks between four men, because the others were in the third canoe, and so we slept two in a hammock, head to foot, in the shelter of four leaves of the false banana tree. It began to rain again. Our companions had lighted a fire. Monsieur Non got up in the middle of the night. No one could sleep. He went out into the rain and returned with a large leaf which he put down on the ground near the fire. Then he took our precious little hoard of buckshot and put some of it down on the leaf in the grooves made by the veins, and began to count the shot, pushing each small piece of lead to one side separately with his finger, intoning at the same time:

"Uno, dos, siete . . . no!
"Uno, dos, siete . . . no!
"Uno, dos, tres!"

He wanted to feel at home in the civilized world we were approaching, and he wanted to talk like the whites. He had therefore determined to learn Spanish—not knowing that in Brazil, for which we were making, people spoke Portuguese. He began by teaching himself to count: one, two, three, four and five. Every evening for weeks he had pronounced the words hesitantly after us. His vocal cords had a good deal of difficulty in pronouncing sounds which were so far removed from those of his native tongue, Maquiritare. That evening he had got a new idea to help him in his search for knowledge: he had re-invented the abacus.

Shortly after dawn the canoe of Pierre and Jean rejoined us.

We saw them loom up with the sun like a ship of specters amid a great mist which covered the whole surface of the Uraricuera. After a while the air seemed to tremble and the mist vanished. Then we went on our way. Pierre and Jean had been held up by the trunk of a tree across the Cuato. When our two canoes had passed the previous evening it was a foot or so above the surface and by ducking down we had managed to glide under it, but their canoe had been an hour behind ours and by the time they arrived the river had experienced one of those sudden rises which are quite common in the Amazonian system, with the result that the surface of the water was touching the trunk and making it impossible for them to pass. They had camped at the spot for the night, and in the morning they had got to work on the trunk with their matchets and had soon been able to continue their journey.

By the time we set out, the rising sun had completely dissipated the mist which had clung to the surface of the river. In the full light of the morning it was as polished and shining as a great expanse of silver. We had to paddle vigorously now, because the previous violence seemed to have exhausted the strength of the river: on leaving the mountains and entering the plain it had grown almost sluggish. It went forward slowly and gently, and it seemed to take us ages to get round each bend that appeared. To the right and left of us the forest was now so far away that it seemed little more than a low hedge.

The wind began to rise. We hardly knew what wind was any more, and we welcomed it now with an enthusiasm that was almost delirious. Gulls appeared from the horizon and passed swiftly over our heads. Then flocks of parakeets crossed the river from one side to the other, keeping high in the sky. And all around us rustled the noises and whisperings the wind brought to us from the forest.

Our Indians were happy. The evening before they had fed on caterpillars which they had picked from a tree and boiled up in our cooking pot. We had tried to follow their example, but in vain. Those caterpillars lived on palms and other oil-bearing trees, and this gave them a soapy taste which made us heave with insupportable nausea at the first taste.

Our Indians were happy. Every now and again they would shout: "Finished the mountains! We'll be eating soon. There are fish in the river and animals in the forest. We'll hunt and we'll fish. We'll eat great lots of meat."

We were all so undernourished that our bodies seemed as light as feathers, and we found some difficulty in telling the reality from the mixture of hallucinations both of vision and hearing which were provoked by the unaccustomed volume of oxygen in the air around us. At each puff of wind we instinctively clung to the sides of our canoes. From hour to hour the horizon down river grew lower, while behind us the mountains were crowded together very low and very distant. The first civilized settlements could not be very far ahead now, but we were hesitant to believe it: the forest was still too near and we were afraid that it would once again establish its ascendancy over us. We consulted Pancho on the point.

"That's right," he agreed. "The white men aren't far ahead. Three days perhaps, not more."

We found a very comfortable little camping place that evening. The swift rise of hope had overlaid our ravenous hunger.

The next day the river grew wider still. In the middle of the afternoon the Indians stood up in the canoes and asked us to keep quiet for a while while they listened. Silently they maneuvered the canoes into the side and asked in a low tone for the rifles. Their eyes were shining with anticipation. We understood when we were close to the forest again and the mosquitoes began to whine around our heads. Behind the enormous curtain of vegetation which masked the earth, something was moving, brushing through the vegetation and grunting. Sudden thumpings shook the earth, and we heard a concert of squeals and snortings —peccaries!

Our men slid like shadows into the foliage and the liana along the river bank and were lost to sight. We listened, our hearts beating almost hard enough to deafen us. Our hunger was reawakened now, and it made its presence felt throughout our bodies like an electric current. A series of wild sounds were heard receding through the forest. Then there were dull sounds and finally a stampede. Then at last the sound of a shot. We waited for something that did not come. They must have missed. Now they were no doubt gliding through the forest bent double behind our stampeding meat. Hours passed. The news of our arrival seemed to have spread in the mosquito world, and their swarms grew rapidly larger and larger around our canoes. We were no longer used to mosquitoes; there weren't any in the upper forest reaches from which we had descended. Now we found their stings intolerable. We killed hundreds of the wretched things on the backs of our hands, on our arms, and on our legs; and where we crushed them there were great smears of blood.

I couldn't stand it any longer and I felt like throwing myself into the river to escape their attentions. Their stings around my ankles were particularly irritating and so to protect at least my legs from them I swung them over the side of the canoe and dangled them in the water. I had been sitting for about half an hour in this more agreeable position when suddenly a stab of terrible pain caused me to fall over on my back with a shout of anguish. A lump of flesh was hanging off one of my toes as though it had been imperfectly cut with a pruning shears, and I sprinkled the front part of the canoe with a stream of blood. The surface of the water around us was ringed and pitted as a river can be in France in the height of summer when the trout chase after gnats. Reddish shadows became visible in the water. My dangling feet had attracted a shoal of piranha, the famous carnivorous fish of the Amazon, and one of them had bitten me. I sat up with some difficulty in the bottom of the canoe, and with both hands I held up my foot by the ankle. The blood continued to spurt from my toe like a fountain. I began to tremble as though with ague and everything around me became confused. In the distance I heard the voice of Pierre:

"Lie back," he said.

"It isn't worth the trouble," I heard myself reply.

Jean opened one of the cases and extracted a mosquito net, from which he cut a piece with his knife. We hadn't possessed gauze or cotton wool for a long time. Pierre lifted up my foot, and Jean put the hanging lump of flesh back into place, as though putting the lid down on a box, and then bound up the wound with his piece of mosquito netting. I lay back and stuck my knuckles into my mouth.

A piranha! When we had first set out everyone had told us:

"Take care if ever you should upset in the water. The piranha will eat you alive. They are so voracious that if a man falls into the water they leave nothing but a clean skeleton of him within a few minutes."

Since then we had got to know a dozen and one rivers and we had capsized several times, and instead of the piranha eating us we had eaten them by the shoal for our dinner. They had saw-like teeth as sharp as needles, but they had never once attacked us—until now. We had exploded sticks of dynamite in the rivers, and then I enjoyed plunging in with the Indians, seizing the fish by their gills and throwing them into the canoes. I knew how voracious they were by a little experiment we had made several times: taking two of these fish we had placed them head to head, and the moment they touched their immediate reflex, although they were dying, was to bite, and the head of the smaller fish would be bitten off by the needle-like teeth of the larger one like ham in a slicer. However, not one of the innumerable varieties of piranha we had eaten had ever made the slightest attempt to attack us, though it would have been different perhaps if an already wounded man had fallen into the water. Then the smell of blood would have provoked them to attack.

After two years in Equatorial America I learned on that day that there is a kind of piranha which attacks man unprovoked, even when he is not wounded. That is the red piranha, shaped something like a bream, and we had not made its acquaintance before reaching the Amazonian river complex.

At last our hunters reappeared, and they were beaming. They had shot two peccaries. The Guaharibo slave dumped the dead beasts in the canoes and our journey continued. I was unable to paddle and I lay back in the canoe next to one of the dead peccaries. It gave off such a horrid smell that I felt dreadfully sick and forgot for the moment the pruning shears which were still steadily opening and closing around my toe.

After journeying a few hours, which seemed to me like aeons, the sun sank down toward the horizon and our canoes put into the bank. While our Indians were clearing a spot for us to camp in, the mosquitoes reappeared and made a dead set against me. I was unable to move and they sucked my blood at their leisure until a form bent over me, took me round the waist, lifted me up bodily, and deposited me in my hammock.

"A barbiturate injection," I muttered. "I'm badly stung."

Night fell and a smell of cooking meat spread all around. Our biggest cooking pot was bubbling merrily, full up with peccary meat. I took no part in the preparations for the feast. There were still one or two barbiturate injections left in our medicine chest, and Jean bent over me, the hypodermic needle in his hand, and beside him Pierre's face glimmered in the darkness. We had no light left at all, not even a resin torch, and Jean made the injection by the red glow of a brand that Pierre took from the fire and held up by the side of my hammock. Then I fell into a deep sleep.

At dawn I put a great dish of meat and some hot soup inside me, and then I was helped into the canoe. My foot was numb but I managed to sit up and take my place at the paddle again. The two peccaries which had been killed the previous evening had been so large that, despite the incredible appetites of our famished group, there were still many pounds left. The Indians had smoked it in the usual way during the night and now it was piled up near me.

My canoe soon became jocularly referred to as the restaurant car, and frequently the other canoes would come up to allow their crews to help themselves to a leg, or a steak, or some chops. Then they would draw away again and go on, paddle in one hand, lump of meat in the other, chewing away happily. Between them the two peccaries must have provided us with something like two hundred and sixty pounds of meat, but within twenty-four hours there was not even a smell of it left.

Our Indians were still elated.

"In a couple of days it will all be over and we shall be in the land of the white man, where there's plenty of cassava, plenty of meat, and plenty of tobacco."

Our three canoes made good time, and gradually I forgot about my wound, just as we all gradually forgot the nightmare of those last few days before we were able to break our fast.

It became hotter and hotter as we went on, and new kinds of trees, typical of the lowlands, began to appear. Behind us the Sierra Parima grew lower and lower on the skyline. Farther down, on the left bank, a new mountain suddenly appeared, long and low, very blue, and divided in the middle by a great vertical line of shining silver, a gigantic waterfall at least twenty-five hundred feet high.

"*Marutani hed'de!*" our men muttered.

Marutani hed'de! The Sierra Marutani. Almost trembling with emotion we studied the only map we had left and which so far we had had no reason to use. It was a small map of Northern Brazil. For the first time we recognized a name on it: the Sierra Marutani, one of the mountains of Brazilian Guiana following on the Sierra Parima. Our two predecessors, Koch-Grünberg and Hamilton Rice, had both mentioned it. A mountain marked on the map and bearing the name our men had just pronounced! It was situated on the verge of the blank spot, on the edge of the unknown. We had now made contact with our own world. We now knew where we were and we could calculate the distance as the crow flies between us and the first town we were making for.

"*Soto, soto, Guadema,*" said Pancho. "There are people hereabouts. We can buy bananas from them."

On the left bank of the river we could see a path leading up into the forest.

"*Soto! Soto! Guadema!*" our men repeated.

When we had questioned the Maquiritares of the Sierra Parima about their neighbors they had often mentioned a tribe of Guaharibos with that name.

"The Guademas are not so much like monkeys as the others are," they had said. "They have canoes and they plant cassava—in fact they're almost men."

We put the canoes into the bank, and Pancho and Luis followed the path into the forest. They returned a few hours later escorted by a crowd of men with yellow skins. They were certainly Guaharibos, as could be seen from the inevitable quid of green tobacco and from the way their hair was cut, but they were more white and more slender than their fellow Guaharibos of the forest. Undoubtedly these Guademas must have had a different ethnic origin.

They brought us a few leaves of green tobacco and a stem of bananas, which we immediately began to eat raw as they were.

Pancho had often spoken to us of great falls further down the river near the island of Maraca, and these men must know where they were. We asked them to come with us. Their chief and a young man of the tribe agreed to accompany us. They produced two paddles from a near-by hiding place, and one climbed into my canoe and the other into Pierre's.

No sooner had we started on our journey again than a lively discussion began among my crew. I was in the stern of the canoe and I could hear only fragments of their talk, which was accompanied by many gestures and contortions as each man used his own language: Maquiritare for some, Guaharibo for others.

The Guadema spoke rapidly and pointed down river to the left bank, which was entirely closed in by very high forest. In the end I could hear the words "Waika" and "Waitsha," which I knew to be the names of other groups of Guaharibos. And then I heard the word "Kaserapi," and this was repeated insistently. I jogged my memory in an effort to recall when I had heard the word before. Of course! Kalomera had said:

"If you cross the Parima you will meet Indians much worse than any Guaharibos: the Kaserapis. They will kill you."

Up to the moment I had overlooked that detail. We had been told so many things about the unknown Sierra Parima. . . .

"Akene Kaserapi? Soto?" I asked my men.

What are these Kaserapis, I wanted to know. Are they people?

"Soto! Soto jojeconeda! Kunumai."

Oh, yes, they were people all right, very mad people. They killed everybody.

And to make the point clear our Indians pretended to stick arrows into their bellies and tapped the back of their necks with their hands as though they were bludgeoning themselves. The Guadema explained to me that the right bank of the river Uraricuera, or Rio Parima, around here was inhabited by four groups of Waikas and Waitshas who were at war with the Kaserapis. All the Guadema groups, with the exception of these, had been exterminated by the Kaserapis. On the upper river and into the mountains the Kaserapis had depopulated the whole forest, slaughtering every group, no matter what their race, including the few groups of Maquiritares who had once lived beyond Frenario's village. The Kaserapis attacked at night with bludgeons and arrows poisoned with curare.

It appeared that one of the mythical dangers of the Sierra Parima was to become a reality at last.

WE BLUFF THE FIERCE KASERAPIS

That night in the rancho the discussion became general. Our Maquiritares brought up the two rifles and demanded that we should prepare them for use at a moment's notice, We dried our powder, and once again we began to cut bits of lead off our storage battery remnants. Then we conscientiously charged our five metal cartridge cases, filing them smooth and oiling them. Our men followed these operations with the greatest interest.

This time we were not preparing our rifles for the chase, but for war. Was it really and seriously true? Although we did all that was required of us, we still doubted it. Later on, when we were trying unsuccessfully to go to sleep in our hammocks, we still doubted it. Was our pacific expedition really to end with the use of arms? If it did, the arms would not be used against the Guaharibos after all, but, at their request, against these mysterious Kaserapis whose very existence had previously been unknown to white men.

When we awoke the following morning we found our men still squatting round the fire and pursuing their endless discussion. They hadn't slept at all.

"Kaserapis," they repeated. *"Kunumai Kaserapis!* Kaserapis kill."

When we got into our canoes to continue our journey, Monsieur Non placed a loaded rifle ready at my feet, and then into the bargain he undid our bundled collection of bows and arrows and distributed them at spots where they could be seen. Altogether our three canoes were bristling with bone and bamboo tips. We must have looked like floating porcupines.

"We are in Kaserapi territory now," Monsieur Non informed us solemnly. "If you see any of them fire at once."

Then he fell silent and joined the others in studying the banks, while our three canoes took the middle of the river. All our Indians were now perfectly calm and their faces were serene. They no longer displayed nervousness or misgiving. Their attitude interested us. What good would our two rusty rifles be in the face of any real danger? They could hardly fire more than once every quarter of an hour. They were more for show than anything else, and our Indians knew that as well as we did, so why the appearance of confidence?

About an hour passed and we were beginning to think that the whole business was a myth, when they all stood up in the canoes and pointed toward the bank.

"Hem'ma Kaserapi!"

A Kaserapi path! Yes, there was a path where they pointed. It wasn't a Guaharibo path; it was too big and too well made for that. At the same time it could not be a Maquiritare path because the Maquiritares had abandoned the banks of the Uraricuera for at least twenty years. It was an excellent path and quite new. It was obvious that those who had made it were people of a civilization quite different from anything we had met among the Indians to date. So the Kaserapis really did exist after all, and it was astonishing to see, as we could from this small detail, that these terrible barbarians were more highly developed than our Indian companions. Our curiosity about them was tremendously increased, but at the same time we had to be prudent, so we continued to paddle in silence. The forest closed in again at the end of the path and from behind its impenetrable green walls we heard shouts which echoed along the river. I wanted our canoe to stay in the middle of the river out of arrow shot, but our men all turned to me together.

"No," they said, and their faces were angry: "The other side of the river."

Had they gone off their heads? I looked round at the other two canoes: they were both putting in toward the Kaserapi shore. "Very well," I thought. "We shall see," and I turned our canoe in the same direction, toward the invisible enemy.

When we approached the bank the air became full of the shouts of our men. They had put down their paddles and now they stood up in the canoes brandishing their arrows. Voices replied for a moment or two from the shore and then fell silent. No enemy showed himself. Our men began to shout even louder. The anger gradually disappeared from their faces and gave way to a sort of joyous triumph. Amid the welter of words they were shouting we could recognize some of the worst insults their dialects were capable of.

"Dirty Kaserapi pigs," they cried in effect. "So you kill everybody, do you? Come out and let's have a look at you. You've killed our cousins, our fathers and our grandfathers, but come out today and we'll see who does the killing. We are with great white chiefs and their guns, and we have hundreds of bows and arrows."

After this followed a long and astonishing explanation in Indian dialect as to exactly what a gun was and how much damage it could do to wicked Indians who got in its way.

This bluff seemed to succeed. Presumably the Kaserapis had fled in terror, or at least, discomfited, to their lairs in the heart of the forest, for nothing further was heard of them, and the following day the Guademas informed us that we had now definitely left their territory behind us. Our feelings were divided between relief and regret at having perhaps missed the opportunity for new and interesting ethnological investigations.

On that same day the first rapids of the Uraricuera appeared ahead.

"We are coming near Maraca," the Guademas said. "There

are many rapids, very bad rapids, but we can pass on the northern side. You come to a great falls twice as high as the forest. You go down by land, and below there the river is good, and the land of the white man begins."

They were referring to the Santa Rosa arm which carries off some of the waters of the Uraricuera round the northern side of the Isle of Maraca. Koch-Grünberg had taken that route forty years previously when he had set out on his journey but in the opposite direction. We knew that he had mentioned a high falls, and we also knew that no white man had ever traveled by the other arm which reached around the Isle of Maraca from the south and must therefore logically also descend one or more falls. But there must be no mistake about the matter.

"Do you know the way well?" I asked the Guadema chief.

"I know where it is," he replied.

"Have you ever seen the white man's country?" I persisted.

"No, never," he admitted.

Below the island the forest gave way, according to our map, to the great savanna of the Rio Branco, where Brazilian colonization was proceeding to the north and the west. That, at least, ought to be easy to see.

The river now began to flow around a great number of small islands, squeezing itself into hundreds of narrow arms with such violence that we had difficulty in retaining control of our canoes. Rapids appeared in increasing number, and the farther we went the more and more difficult it became to navigate our way through the watery labyrinth. At first it was difficult, and then it became dangerous. Shoals of piranha slid through the water around us. There were so many of them that it would have been easy for us to lean over the side and hit them with our paddles. Several times I saw the fish leap out of the water and snap at them. They bit deep into the hard wood of the hevea tree, leaving tooth marks perhaps a third of an inch deep. We had to be careful with our bare hands. In one of the canoes a piece of cloth was hanging out of one of the cases above the water. Two of the piranha leaped into the air and tore it.

At each bend of the river we expected to see the calmer water the Guadema had promised us, but the labyrinth of rapids grew worse and worse hour after hour. The faces of our men grew somber. In the meantime the Maquiritares had once again taken over the helms of the three canoes and we were in front with the other men. The Maquiritares needed all their consummate watermanship to prevent the canoes from capsizing in the boiling torrents through which we now had to pass. But for the presence of the two Guadema Indians, which meant four more strong and experienced arms, I don't think we should have been able to make it. Although we had shot a good many dangerous rapids since the start of our expedition, these rapids on the Uraricuera really alarmed us.

We were afraid of losing our precious films, but, more than that, we were even afraid of drowning. And, worst of all, we were afraid of being eaten alive by the piranha fish. Each of us knew that if one of the canoes capsized now among the piranha, the others would be powerless to help.

The lightest of our canoes was leading the way, manned by Pancho, his Guaharibo slave, and Luis. My canoe followed in second place. The canoe ahead disappeared round a bend and suddenly I heard wild shouts. Behind me the voice of the Maquiritare helmsman sounded in my ears:

"Luis neemai! Luis neemai!"

Luis is dead! Luis is dead!

Our own canoe swept on and immediately I saw Pancho on a rock, and a little further on I heard Luis shouting from the branches. Then I saw him standing on the bank of a small island, alive and apparently uninjured. Their canoe must have capsized in one of the rare stretches where there were no piranha fish and he had been able to scramble out of the water before they arrived. We passed down river like an arrow. It was impossible to stop.

"I've saved No. 7," I heard him shout.

Which meant that of the three cases in his canoe two were lost, but that he had managed to save the most important of the three: No. 7, one which contained some of our film.

"Bravo!" shouted Pierre, whose canoe followed ours at that moment. Then we both noticed one of the lost cases bobbing along ahead of us, visible from time to time amid the spume. Despite the shouts of our Indians we tried to paddle harder in order to catch up with it. Just before we were about to do so it was swirled into a small side arm of the river. We wanted to follow it, but the shouts of the Indians grew even more furious, and driving the canoes toward the shore they grabbed the branches and the trailing liana with all their might and so brought the two canoes to a standstill. Not twelve feet straight ahead of us the water shot down with a thunderous noise into a dark funnel-like opening. The case had already disappeared into it. We saw no sign of the second case at all.

In the meantime, Pancho had saved his canoe, emptied it, and got it floating again. He picked Luis up and then went on ahead to take up his original position as lookout man to our column. There was no change in the conditions by evening, and after a perilous maneuver we succeeded in beaching our canoes on a small island. While our men built a rancho for the night, we checked up what had been lost in the mishap to Pancho's canoe. One of the lost cases contained a collection of Indian objects and our mosquito nets. The other one contained our sound recorder, various items of electrical equipment, and all the records we had made since our final departure from the Orinoco, about fifty in all. Pancho chose this moment to inform us that all hope of finding the Santa Rosa arm must now be abandoned. We were lost in a labyrinth and no one knew the way out. The news was the culmination of our despair. Fate was once again conspiring against us. I cursed our map which pretended that civilization was so close, and I cursed our enthusiasm of the past few days and our cocksureness that our troubles were over and the expedition within sight of safety.

Night fell and we lay dismally in our hammocks.

"Looks as though we've had it," said Pierre.

And we fell asleep.

PIRANHA!

The next morning early we started off again. With strips of liana each of us attached some precious object to his person for fear of further capsizings. I emptied a bottle of sulpha into the river. It was one of the last items in our medicine chest: the container had now become more precious than the contents. Luis filled it with matches, carefully corked it, and tied it around his neck. I filled a little Indian sack with all my precious notebooks, containing perhaps two thousand pages in which I had scribbled down the whole story of our expedition to date, and then I fastened it bandoleer-wise over my shoulder.

We were silent. Each of us was troubled with evil presentiments but we said nothing in order not to discourage the others. Our canoes sped along in the center of the current. It was no longer navigation in the ordinary sense; it was more like an obstacle race. We shot down falls eight or nine feet deep like toboggans, and each time the canoes filled with water almost to the gunwales, but their speed carried them on. And then we had to bail furiously in order to be ready for the next drop.

In the afternoon my canoe just disappeared in an enormous wave. With each hand I seized a case by the liana strips that had been tied round it for the purpose, and, as good luck would have it, I found ground under my feet. The men saved the canoe and almost all the rest of the cargo. All we lost this time was our collection of bows and arrows and one of our two guns. Unfortunately my wound opened up and the water around me was stained with blood. One of the men lifted me on his back and carried me to the shore. There was not a palm tree, not a banana tree, nor any tree with large leaves on the island where we camped that night. As we were unable to build a rancho we just slung our hammocks between such trees as there were. For some days there had been no rain, but now it began to fall again immediately. It poured in torrents all night. We had one blanket left, and this we fixed up over our heads and went to sleep huddled together at the foot of a tree: Guaharibo with Maquiritare, and Maquiritare with White.

The following day and the day after that were spent in the sinister labyrinth we invariably referred to now as "The Maraca Hell." The last of the bananas we had obtained from the Guademas—we had been rationing them as carefully as we had rationed the last remaining pieces of Maquiritare cassava a couple of weeks earlier—had now been eaten. Every evening I marked off another day on the little calendar I had made for myself at the back of one of my notebooks. For a month now we had had no other means of checking the passage of time. Among the dates there were words, such as Christmas, Easter, Whitsun, Spring, but they had lost all real significance for us; they belonged to another world and another age. According to my improvised calendar a day dawned which called itself July 1st. I don't know why the idea impressed me so, but I sat in my canoe thinking of nothing but the fact that this was July 1st when my Indians began to shout wildly:

"Death! Death!"

And then I saw a white waterfall open almost below us and huge waves descended on my head. As the water swept me out of the canoe I grasped instinctively at the case nearest to me and managed to get hold of the liana strip round it. My grab was as much to save myself as to save the case. As we were thrown round and round in the torrent it almost seemed as though the case and I were clinging together for support. Somehow I managed to get hold of a rock which jutted out of the water. The bank was not far away, but between us was—apart from about eight or nine feet of water—a great mass of vegetation bristling with huge dagger-like thorns. About twelve feet farther on the river plunged out of sight over a new precipice. Through the spray I could see my two Indians clinging to a rock above the abyss. I saw them stretch out their hands vainly toward our canoe. Its bows reared over the falls for a split second like some black monster and then it plunged into the depths.

"Kudiera neemai! Kudiera neemai!"

"The canoe is dead" was their way of putting the disaster.

Each moment the wild current threatened to dislodge them and sweep them after the canoe.

"Caja! Caja!"

It was primarily the case I was interested in.

And from the bank came the voice of Pierre, shouting as anxiously as I was:

"Caja! Caja!"

I had saved the wrong case. My case contained our hammocks, our identification papers and I don't know what else, but in the other case we had lost all the photographs we had taken in the Sierra Parima, and half our films. It was all gone, and there was nothing to be done about it. Pancho approached with his smaller canoe, pulling himself along from liana to liana. The canoe danced on the water like a tightrope walker. He reached me and took my case on board. It was high time. I was about at the end of my tether, and in a moment or two I should have let it go or been carried away with it. I clung desperately to my rock. Pancho's own balance was so precarious that he had to push off with the case without attempting to take me on board. Pierre was out of sight now behind the thorny vegetation, but I could still hear him shouting:

"Caja! Caja!"

The sack with my notebooks was floating in the water beside me, but it was still fastened round my neck. I tried to cheer myself up with the idea that I had saved something valuable after all. Even if no other record of our adventure remained at the end of it, at least there were my precious notebooks. I clung there helplessly, not knowing what to do. The whole world seemed to be swirling around in the torrent of water, as though it would go under finally and disappear for good. Rain began to thrash down on the forest, on my head and shoulders and on the water around me. I was in the center of a battle of the elements in which all things human became smaller and less important than the smallest drop of water. The seconds which passed in this way remain in my memory out of relation with time and longer than centuries. My bandage came off again and the water around me was stained red.

I seemed in a dream. The voice of Pierre came to me urgently. He was no longer shouting. He was speaking in French, calmly but with emphasis:

"Alain! Come over to the bank and come quickly."

"I can't," I replied automatically. "It's impossible. The current's too strong. I can't get a hold on these branches; they're full of spikes. I should have to plunge into the water and I should be carried over the falls before I could reach the bank."

But Pierre just ignored what I said. He merely repeated what he had said:

"Alain! Come over to the bank, and come quickly."

I looked round. And then I saw in the distance the surface of the water being whipped up as something darted forward. I understood then: the piranha were racing toward me through the water, attracted by the blood from my wounded foot. Pierre had seen them too, but he hadn't wanted to frighten me. The danger had calmed him and now he spoke firmly but urgently, in a very different tone from his despairing accents a little before.

I hardly had time to realize the danger fully. Instinct made me forget all my fears and I plunged through the water toward the bank, striking out with all my remaining strength. I managed to reach a mass of twisted roots and by holding on to them I succeeded in pulling myself up the slippery bank. A strong hand gripped me and yanked me up bodily onto the bank, where I lay outstretched and exhausted. The water swirled furiously behind me. The piranha had arrived, but too late.

When I sat up, Luis, Pierre, and Jean were all three gathered round me and I learned that our biggest canoe had just managed to avoid being swept into the terrible side arm of the river that had swallowed us. They had found a calmer passage and had managed to reach the other side of the island without much difficulty, so at least the remainder of our baggage was safe.

The island was not much more than a clump of gnarled trees some fifty yards long. Apart from the little creek in which our two remaining canoes were floating there was nothing to be seen all around but a great cloud of falling water and spray.

Our two Guademas were standing together silently in the

rain, trembling like frightened horses. Rivulets of water poured off the banana leaves they had put on their heads.

"Guadema!" we shouted, and slowly they turned their eyes toward us with the look of patient beasts facing death and resigned to their fate. The three Maquiritares came through the foliage and joined us. Their faces were drawn and haggard. They looked like specters against the somber sky, the grey curtain of rain, the green and blue patches of forest and the masses of water boiling and tumbling around us.

"I've been all round the island," said Pancho, "and we can't get through anywhere for rapids. The canoe is dead, so we'll have to pack what's left in the others and try to get through by sheer speed."

Which meant practically: "Let's all die together."

"Land all the baggage," I said. "Build a rancho. We'll stay where we are until tomorrow, and then we'll see."

He nodded his agreement without argument and gave his orders to the Guademas. Everyone set to work.

The gunwales of our canoes were only about three or four inches above water as it was, but if now we loaded up the two canoes with the remains of our baggage and all piled into them they would be almost down to the surface. Even in a calm river that would have been hazardous. At first we thought of building a new canoe, but even if we succeeded in finding a trunk big enough on the island it would take us a week to hollow it out. We should have starved to death before then. No, as difficult as it was for us there was only one way out. We should have to abandon half the baggage that still remained to us in the hope of saving ourselves and what was left.

We began to sort out our things. Having got them so far we had become sentimentally attached to them all and it was terribly difficult for us to divide them into the saved and the damned, into a group whose fate was still to be linked with our own, and another group which was to be left behind. It seemed almost as though each item, having shared our troubles and our labors, had thereby acquired an individuality of its own and a right to live, almost as though it were a human being.

We spread a covering over the ground and unpacked the contents of our six cases on it. We were afraid that our Indians might collect the objects we decided to abandon, and so, one after the other, we threw them into the water. It was like an organized and systematic sacrifice, and we worked methodically for hours.

I felt as though we were in the labyrinth of Minotaurus. The monster was the hard fate which now demanded that we should sacrifice the material results of our long struggle in return for our lives. Our few remaining ethnographic books went into the water first, followed by boxes, bags, headdresses, wickerwork, magnificent ornaments, arrowheads, and calabashes of curare decorated with esoteric designs. The fate of each object was carefully discussed according to its size and weight and its importance for us on our problematical return to civilization. We hadn't the heart to deprive Monsieur Non of our remaining rifle, as we had already promised it to him, but the last few ounces of powder and lead went into the river. Five cases, from Bogotá, were of poor-quality timber, but the sixth was much better and more solid than the others. It still bore the labels of various railroad, steamship, and airline companies. Pierre had had it specially made in Paris to his own specifications to hold his sound-recording apparatus, and it was constructed of particularly tough wood. It now contained over a hundred pounds of expensive machinery made to order for our expedition in first-class Paris workshops. All of it was still in good condition, despite its long stay in the equatorial forest, despite the rains and despite immersions. It was worth many hundreds of dollars, and a good deal more than money, but it also happened to weigh about a hundred pounds, and so it was condemned.

Pierre and Jean lifted it up by its chromium handles, one of them on each side and carried it over to the water's edge and there they held it for a moment or two. Then their courage failed them and they lowered it gently to the ground—they did not want to break the filaments of any of the valves by rough handling. Finally they lifted it again, carried it a few yards into the vegetation of the tropical forest, and put it down.

And there it still lies. Stenciled on its sides are the proud words "Orinoco-Amazon Expedition," and the colors of France and Colombia. If any other expedition happens to pass through the watery hell of Maraca . . .

At last we had only three cases left, and then we fell, dead tired, into our hammocks in the large rancho the Indians had built. In the center of it they lit a fire and above and around it we dried out everything we had decided to take with us. Fortunately for us, a tortoise appeared on our wretched island, and the Indians killed it and cooked its flesh. It was nightfall before we each received a bowl of soup in which small pieces of meat were swimming. A tortoise of perhaps a foot in length divided between ten men doesn't provide much meat for each man. However, although the lack of salt and pimento made it very insipid, we ate it gratefully.

"The pigs haven't drawn it," an indignant voice declared.

We each had a closer look at our basin. It was quite true. All the digestive apparatus of the tortoise was floating around in the soup. Ah well, what did it matter? Offal, but hot, and presumably nourishing.

The darkness deepened and there was no noise but the sound of rushing water. I went to sleep thinking that the Indians were certainly right: death was near, close enough to touch.

THE LAST LAP

When we woke up the next morning the air was fresh and there was a blue sky without clouds. The night's sleep had done us good. I awakened out of a pleasant dream and felt myself suddenly filled with an inexplicable but firm confidence in the future. I sat up in my hammock and looked at my companions. Their faces were like mine, pale, muddy, and lifeless. It was the kind of complexion a man gets from persistent hunger, constant dampness, and the gloom of the forest. They were the faces of specters, but in their eyes was a certain sparkle, and I could see that they, too, were feeling more confident.

Our men loaded the canoes and we set off. Once again we

hurtled over falls and short rapids, but despite all the difficulties and dangers, the unreasoning confidence we felt did not desert us. For hour after hour we surmounted the one and escaped the other. It was almost as though our solemn sacrifice of the previous day had been graciously accepted by the gods of the place, who were now benevolently inclined.

Less than forty-eight hours later the river widened, and once again we were gliding along in the middle of a broad stream under a permanently blue sky. There were still boiling rapids and a succession of falls, perhaps five or six feet high, to negotiate, but our canoes skimmed over them all like skaters over ice.

Pancho stood up in his canoe and shouted enthusiastically: *"Shodi neemai! A'aké Maraca!"*

The rapids are over! Maraca is dead!

All our men talked about now was cows and bulls.

"If we're not going to die we shall see cows and bulls."

That was their one idea. Cows and bulls had become the symbol of the white man's civilization for them, containing all its power and its mystery. They had never seen cattle, but they knew that the white man kept big animals, bigger than tapirs, which did as the white man told them and worked for him. The idea that they would now be able to see such a marvel close up was fitting recompense for the nightmare weeks they had gone through with us.

The vegetation along the banks of the river began to change. Shrubs with smooth, thorny leaves began to appear, palm trees, long lines of cactuses jutting into the sky, all kinds that one never met with in the forest. That meant savanna. It meant Brazil. It meant civilization.

Pancho stopped his canoe at the foot of a big palm and handed a matchet to his slave, saying something to him. The Guaharibo sprang out and began to chop down the tree vigorously. It took him over half an hour, for the closely knit trunk of the palm is tougher than ordinary wood. At last he had it down. Then he went to work at one end, cutting through the outer rind along a length of about three feet and then peeling it off. He worked for perhaps another hour, and then he came toward us with a large piece of shining white fleshy-looking substance. It was the edible heart of the palm tree. All of us chewed away voraciously for perhaps a quarter of an hour and then we went on.

The distance between one bend of the river and the next steadily increased as it rolled more and more lazily through the plain. All along its banks the vegetation formed a green corridor, broken here and there to reveal yellow, savanna-like countryside stretching away toward the horizon under a vast blue sky. The horizon was farther off than we had seen it for a year.

We paddled on for another twenty-four hours through the same monotonous surroundings, and gradually we felt ourselves becoming discouraged again. It hardly seemed as though we were making any progress at all.

The next day, toward evening, we saw our first sign of human civilization. It was a sign board standing in a clearing on the bank. Our two canoes converged toward it. The board was fastened to its post by two rusty nails and on it in faded blue letters was stenciled: *"Fazenda Porvenir."*

We read it out loud in chorus: "Settlement of the Future." It was in Portuguese. We were in Brazil.

In the clearing there were numerous hoof marks and our Indians stared at them in amazement. They had never seen such prints before and they could not imagine what sort of animals could have made them. We knew what they were and we told them. They were the hoof marks of the cows and bulls they had been talking about so much. They said nothing, but their silence was eloquent.

The track led away into the savanna and disappeared toward the horizon and on each side of it was something else that was strange to our Indians: the ruts left by the wheels of a cart. The track went through a sea of golden stems undulating in the breeze. Apart from the gigantic expanse all around, it was very much like the roads we had known in childhood.

We set off along it and soon we were strung out one behind the other. The savanna plants shook on either side in the wind and soon I began to tremble too. I was bringing up the rear and going forward only with difficulty. The bandage round my foot had come loose again and it hampered my progress. Soon there seemed too much air and my ears began to buzz. Then there was too much wind and too much light. Luis was not far ahead of me but the others were already little more than black specks in the distance.

We went on for about an hour without seeing anything but hoof marks and the ruts that guided us. We were following a new thread now and at the end of it we hoped to renew our contact with the civilized world of white men. But I was still doubtful. What did mere hoofprints mean? They were dry. They were old. I recalled the herds in the Colombian llano. They lived almost like wild animals, sometimes several days' journey from any human settlement.

But then Luis turned round to me and shouted:

"I can hear a dog barking."

I could hardly keep my feet and my toe was bleeding again and leaving a trail of blood behind me on the track, but I pressed on with determination. After a while I saw something that danced before my eyes amid the high growth. It was a long line of palings held together by three strands of thick wire. An enclosure! Now there could be no doubt.

Then I saw two thatched roofs with smoke rising from their chimneys. They were right ahead of me, nestling at the foot of a hill as though in the hollow of a hand. I followed Luis through a gateway and a pig ran up and rubbed itself against my legs. Then a man whose appearance I shall never forget came out of the house to welcome me. He was tall and thin and he wore a suit of blue pajamas of incredible cleanliness. On his head was a very broad-brimmed sombrero. Behind him was a young girl, and wordlessly she held out a small silver tray to me. On it was a cup of black coffee. Cup and saucer were of porcelain decorated with flower motifs and they rested on a small checked napkin.

I felt myself shaking hands, and then I was led in under an awning to where my comrades were already sitting comfortably in rattan rocking-chairs on the veranda. With a sigh of relief I also sat down. Our ordeal was over.

"What is the date?" I asked our host.

"July 2nd," he replied.

Within the past year my calendar had lost twenty-four hours somewhere. I brought it up to date.

Servants appeared carrying towels, soap, cotton wool, gauze, and basins of lukewarm water. Our host did not smoke but a peon brought us plug tobacco and *papel por cigarillo*.

Pancho leaned forward toward the man, stretching out his hand.

"Kawai néke," he said gently.

Give me tobacco.

Our adventure was now at an end. That of our Indians was about to begin.

ABOUT THE AUTHOR

ALAIN GHEERBRANT *was barely twenty-eight when he organized the expedition described in his book, and his colleagues were even younger than he.*

Educated in Paris (his professor of philosophy was the then unknown Jean-Paul Sartre), M. Gheerbrant entered the French Army before World War II, serving in North Africa. When the Nazis overran France, evading the gendarmes, he made his way home to Paris to join the Resistance and, in his own words, "entered the great prison created by the Nazi occupation." The man-hunt organized by the SS kept him confined to his room for months. Enforced solitude made him crystallize his ideas of life: spiritual values that had been unformed took shape for him.

In 1945, when France was liberated, Gheerbrant published his first poems. Then he founded a publishing house which he ran until he sailed for South America in 1948. He was also editor of a magazine that published contemporary poetry, philosophy, and art, and brought together a group of artists who, like himself, felt the urge to express a philosophy of hope and good-will. He took up his scientific studies again, concentrating on anthropology, ethnology, and medicine. Days and nights were spent in impassioned discussion. More and more, truth appeared to Gheerbrant to be synonymous with beauty. "There is nothing we need invent," he told his painter and writer friends, "but we have everything to discover."

This, then, was Gheerbrant's preparation for the expedition of discovery described in his book with scientific accuracy and lyric truth.

Paraguana
SIERRA NEVADA
DE SANTA MARTA
Lake
Maracaibo
CARA
Magdalena R.
Catatumbo R.
Guavico R.
CORDILLERA ORIENTAL
Guanare R.
Apure R.
Capanaparo R.
Arauca R.
Cinavuco R.
PUERTO
CAREÑO
COLOMBIA
Meta R.
PUERTO
AYACUCHO
Atures-
Maipur
Rapids
Metica R.
Tomo R.
PUERTO
NARIÑO
SANARIA
Muerto
Rapids
BOGOTÁ
SAN PEDRO
DE ARIMENA
CARIMAGUA
AWINI
TONINAS
Mario's Hut
Vichada R.
Caño Sama
Mataveni R.
Fruta R.
VILLAVICENCIO
SAN JOSÉ
DEL OCUNÉ
PIAROA
VILLAGE
Ventuari
SANTA BA
Guamal R.
SAN MARTÍN
CHAFURRAY
Uva R.
Guaviare R.
Ariavi R.
CONCORDIA
Inivida R.
Atabapo R.
SAN JOSÉ
DEL GUAVIARE
Guayabero R.
Rock Paintings
LINDOSA
Guainia R.
Vaupes R.
Icona R.
Rio